W9-BWQ-893

Practical Navigation for the Yachtsman

Practical Navigation for the Yachtsman

by Frederick L. Devereux, Jr.

illustrated by Richard Mikulski

W. W. NORTON & COMPANY, INC., NEW YORK

Copyright © 1972 by W. W. Norton & Company, Inc.
First Edition

Library of Congress Cataloging in Publication Data
Devereux, Frederick L., Jr.,   1914–
    Practical navigation for the yachtsman.
    Includes bibliographical references.
    1. Navigation. I. Title.
VK555.D46   623.89   73-155984
ISBN   0-393-03171-3

All Rights Reserved

Published simultaneously in Canada
by George J. McLeod Limited, Toronto

Printed in the United States of America

3 4 5 6 7 8 9 0

To a patient, understanding, loyal, and much beloved wife

RUTH FOSTER DEVEREUX

daughter and granddaughter of distinguished blue water sailors

and
to the memory of

Captain JAMES DEVEREUX of Salem

Master of the ship *Franklin*
Who voyaged from Boston to Japan in 1799

Contents

Acknowledgments

I NEEDED MUCH HELP with this work and was abundantly fortunate in having the cooperation and expertise—freely and cheerfully offered, and gratefully accepted—of several outstanding practitioners of navigational science and related subjects. Richard Mikulski, whose illustrations prove the ancient adage that "one picture is worth a thousand words," is an industrial designer whose hobby is navigation; his understanding of the principles, coupled with his talents as a draftsman, are a major contribution to clarity and understanding. Frederick A. Miller, who comprehends the theorems of celestial navigation as few men can hope to do, checked and criticized methods and techniques. John V. Von Sneidern, Jr., radio officer on *U.S.S. Northampton* when that cruiser was the Navy's "floating Pentagon," scrutinized the chapter on electronics and contributed significantly to its organization and comprehensibility. Joseph R. Toven, Jr., who once chased hurricanes for the Air Force, strengthened and clarified the sections on wind and weather; in addition, he read the chapters on piloting and made welcome suggestions to improve the scope and sequence of presentation. As a result of this combined wisdom, experience, and interest, I believe there are no errors in *Practical Navigation for the Yachtsman;* however, the final responsibility is mine, and I alone am accountable for any inadvertent error.

For assistance on specific topics other than the broad credits mentioned above I am indebted to Captain Ross E. Freeman of the Institute of Navigation; Dr. William Klepczynski of the Nautical Almanac Office, U.S. Naval Observatory; George N. Weston and Harry Ketts III of the Navigational Science Division, U.S. Naval Oceanographic Office; Anna C. Urband of the Navy's Office of Information; Lowell Fey of the National Bureau of Standards; Eugene A. Moore of the Federal Aviation Administration; and Vice Commander Elbert S. Maloney, Director of Education, U.S. Power Squadrons. Product information and photographs were provided through the courtesy of G. D. Dunlap of Weems and

Plath; Warren Lindsay of Danforth; and James F. Herslow of Sillcocks-Miller.

My horizons were widened by Griffith Jones, who introduced me in London to many of the extraordinarily comprehensive navigational reference sources of Great Britain. The interest and encouragement of Walter H. Jennings, veteran Bermuda race and transatlantic navigator who several years ago patiently and thoroughly drilled me in the fundamentals of navigation and their practical applications, has been of great help. I am also grateful to Rear Commander Allan E. Bayless, Chairman of the U.S. Power Squadron's Committee on Navigation, for his appreciation of the need for a work of this nature. And to John Tassos, master of the passage-making cutter *Gulvain,* my special thanks for the opportunity to serve as navigator, thus putting theory into blue water practice.

A nonprofessional writer badly needs an accomplished editor, and Eric Swenson—who by happy coincidence is an equally accomplished sailor—has been a benevolent taskmaster, knowledgeable critic, and invaluable partner. Finally, my lasting thanks go to Tran Mawicke, who started it all by bringing author and publisher together.

Frederick L. Devereux, Jr.

Bronxville, New York
August 1971

Introduction

MARINE NAVIGATION is the process of conducting a vessel from one point to another on earth's surface. The navigator's basic problem is that of knowing his *position* at all times, from whence he can establish a safe and accurate direction to his destination and solve the collateral problems of distance, speed, and time. Position in coastal waters (piloting) is found by reference to landmarks, man-made aids to navigation, and by soundings of the bottom; position offshore is determined by observation of celestial bodies. Deduction of approximate position (dead reckoning) is obtained by applying the quantities of time, speed, and direction from a previously determined or deduced position. Position by means of electronics is available in many waters but does not replace the need for visual observation and dead reckoning.

A sound knowledge of the fundamentals of piloting and offshore navigation can immeasurably enhance the coastwise sailor's range of activity and his ability to transit unfamiliar waters with confidence. However, the "mystique" of navigation—as perpetrated and perpetuated by mariners schooled in the complexities and obtuse formulas of spherical trigonometrics—has deterred many good sailors from attempting to learn much of the navigational skills that are the hallmark of a fully proficient yachtsman. Anyone who can perform eighth grade arithmetic can become fully proficient in all the modern methods of navigation the cruising yachtsman needs to know in order to make a confident passage on any of earth's navigable waters.

The purpose of this book is to present, succinctly, a comprehensive reference in a format suitable for daily on-board use, incorporating the full spectrum of piloting and navigational methods that will enable the yachtsman to go anywhere—from a day sail to a circumnavigation. All methods herein described may be solved by simple arithmetic in combination with graphics (plotting) and the extraction of precomputed data from convenient

11

and inexpensive reference tables. Topics are arranged to provide the beginning navigator with a logical study progression, and organized for the benefit of the self-taught navigator who needs to refresh his memory or to verify a method of which he may be uncertain.

The ability to navigate is predicated on a thorough understanding of navigation mathematics, mariner's charts, and the vagaries of the magnetic compass. Beginning navigators should first become completely familiar with chapters I, II, III, and Appendix A—which deal with these basics—before embarking on further study of piloting and offshore navigation.

Sooner or later most sailors wish to satisfy their curiosity about the "why" of the methods they have learned to practice. The theory of navigation is an exhaustive subject lying outside the scope of this book; those wishing to pursue the subject in depth should consult the standard reference, H. O. 9 *American Practical Navigator,* published by the U.S. Naval Oceanographic Office and popularly known as *Bowditch.*

Practical Navigation for the Yachtsman

chapter I

Earth and Its Coordinates

N AVIGATORS ASSUME earth to be a perfect sphere, as true and round as a billiard ball. Because much of the practice of navigation entails the determination and plotting of portions of earth's circles, this simplification, which does not affect practical accuracy, affords the important advantage of enabling any circle on earth's surface to be considered a perfect circle. Any position on earth may be located and identified at the intersection of two circles, hence an understanding of earth's basic geometry is the keystone upon which all other knowledge of navigation depends.

Earth rotates daily (eastward) around the *polar axis,* an imaginary line extending through the north and south geographic poles. The *equator,* a circumference of earth, is situated midway between the poles and at a right angle to the polar axis; because of this relationship distance east or west is measured *along* the equator and distance north or south is measured *from* the equator. Measurement is expressed in units (degrees, minutes, and tenths of minutes) of arc, the sum of the arcs in a circle being 360°. A *great circle* is one with a plane which passes through earth's center, thus dividing earth into two equal parts. The equator is a great circle; other great circles include those with planes passing through the polar axis which are termed *meridians.* A *small circle* is any circle not a great circle; those parallel to the equator are called *parallels.*

The nautical equivalents of "Broadway and 42nd Street" are *latitude*—a small circle parallel to the equator—and *longitude*— a great circle passing through the polar axis. They are always expressed in alphabetical order, "la" before "lo." Geographical direction is an integral part of the designation, as "north latitude," "east longitude."

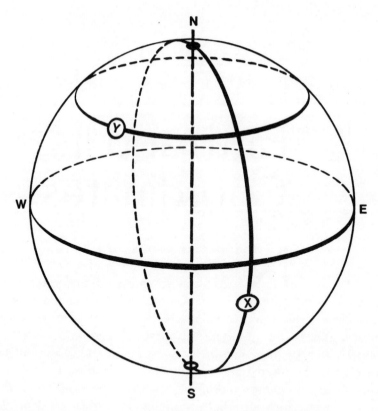

FIGURE 1. THE NAVIGATOR'S EARTH

    N: North Pole   S: South Pole
N–S: Polar axis
    x: Point on a plane of a great circle passing through the polar
       axis (a *meridian*).
W–E: Plane of the equator, a great circle perpendicular to the polar
       axis.
    y: Point on the plane of a small circle parallel to the equator
       (a *parallel*).

    Latitude (L or Lat.) is the distance north or south from the equator, from 0° at the equator to 90° at either geographic pole, and labeled N or S to indicate direction of measurement (e.g., Lat. 45° N). *Parallels of latitude* (they parallel the equator) are small circles of reference for distance from the equator, or from each other; distance between any two parallels is everywhere the same. One degree (1°) of latitude equals 60 nautical miles, one minute (1′) equals one nautical mile of 6076 feet or approximately 2000 yards when measured for short distances.

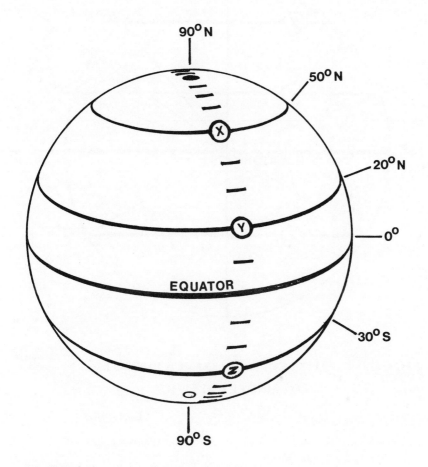

FIGURE 2.   LATITUDE

x, y, z: Parallels of latitude (small circles parallel to the equator).
The equator is Lat 0°, the poles are Lat 90°N and S. Distance
between any two parallels is everywhere the same.

Difference of latitude (*l*) between two positions on the same
side of the equator is the *difference* in their respective latitudes;
when the positions are on opposite sides of the equator (*l*) is the
sum of the two latitudes. Difference of latitude may be labeled N
or S to indicate direction. *Mid-latitude* (Lm) is the *mean* of two
latitudes on the same side of the equator. The expression is not
applicable to positions on opposite sides of the equator.

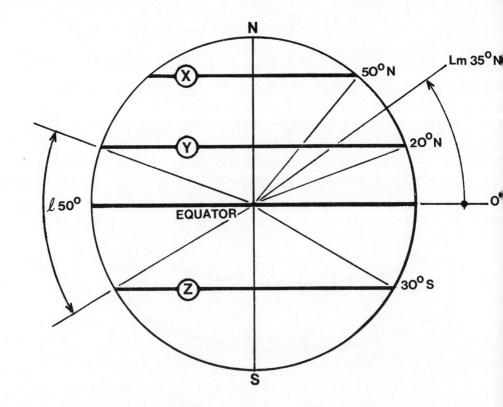

FIGURE 3. DIFFERENCE OF LATITUDE
AND MID-LATITUDE

Difference of latitude:

between x and y: 30°
   from x to y: 30°S
   from y to x: 30°N
between y and z: 50°
   from y to z: 50°S
   from z to y: 50°N

Mid-latitude:

between x and y: 35°

$$\left(\frac{50° + 20°}{2} = 35° \right)$$

Longitude (Lo, Long, or λ for lambda) is the distance east or west from Greenwich, England (Long 0°) to 180° at the international date line, and labeled E or W to indicate the direction of measurement from Greenwich. *Meridians* of longitude are great circles of reference for arc measurement from Greenwich (the *prime meridian*) or from each other; they intersect at the polar axis and are nowhere parallel to each other except momentarily at the equator. Longitude is derived from a knowledge of time at Greenwich (1 hour of time = 15° of longitude) and cannot be measured in terms of linear miles, except at the equator, because the distance between meridians is not constant at all points.

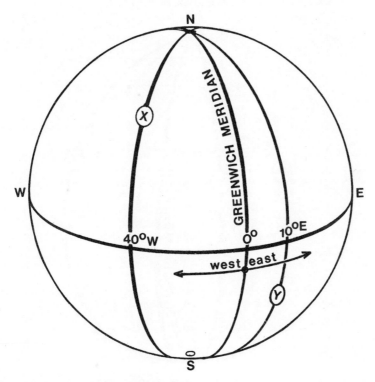

FIGURE 4. LONGITUDE

N–S: Polar axis   x: Point on meridian of Long 40°W
W-E: Plane of the equator   y: Point on meridian of Long 10°E

Difference of longitude (DLo) between two positions with the same longitude name (E or W) is the *difference* in their respective longitudes. When one position is in east longitude and the other in west, i.e., on opposite sides of Greenwich, DLo is the *sum* of the two longitudes. Should the sum exceed 180°, DLo is adjusted to equal 360° minus the sum (it is always the shorter arc between two points). DLo may be labeled E or W to indicate direction of measurement. Unlike mid-latitude, the quantity of mid-longitude is not employed in navigation.

Organization of earth's coordinates by N and S latitude and

E and W longitude divides earth's surface into quadrants according to the names of the coordinates (as Cape Hatteras Light: Lat 35° 15′ N, Long 75° 31′ W) as shown in Figure 6.

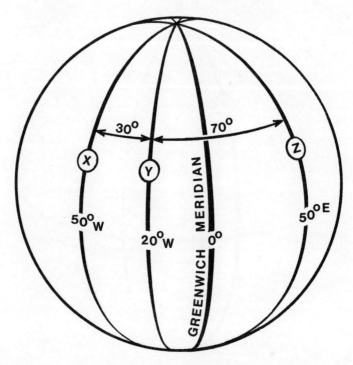

FIGURE 5. DIFFERENCE OF LONGITUDE

between x and y: 30°
 from x to y: 30°E
 from y to x: 30°W
between y and z: 70°
 from y to z: 70°E
 from z to y: 70°W

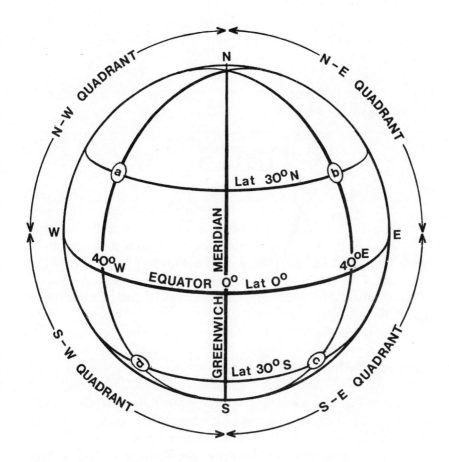

FIGURE 6. COORDINATE QUADRANTS

a, b, c, d: Points on earth
    a: Lat 30°N, Long 40°W
    b: Lat 30°N, Long 40°E
    c: Lat 30° S, Long 40°E
    d: Lat 30° S, Long 40°W

The working navigator obtains coordinates from a two dimensional chart rather than from a globe. This flattening out of earth's surface can take several forms, as discussed in Chapter II, Charts.

chapter II
Charts

A CHART is a flat representation of a portion of earth's curved surface, intended primarily for navigation purposes. Inasmuch as no portion of a sphere can be flattened without creating distortion (Fig. 7), a variety of projections has been developed of which two—*Mercator* and *gnomonic*—will suffice for surface navigation below the polar regions.

Mercator Projection

Charts constructed on the Mercator projection are universally employed by mariners because there are no curves thereon, a benefit which vastly simplifies plotting and measuring procedures. The global convergence of longitude meridians at the poles (Fig. 4) is eliminated so that parallels of latitude and meridians of longitude are both presented as straight lines at right angles to each other; they are respectively true east–west and north–south directional references. The one disadvantage of the Mercator system lies in the built-in defect of ever-increasing distortion as latitude increases north or south from the equator; on a Mercator projection Greenland appears to be the size of South America, whereas its actual area is only about one-tenth of that continent.

The great advantage of the Mercator projection, and the reason for its widespread use by marine navigators, is that it enables the plotting and sailing of a *rhumb line* (straight line) course which crosses all meridians at the same angle and does not require a change in ship's heading. A rhumb line on a Mercator chart is actually an arc of a circle, and therefore not the shortest distance between two points on the line (the shortest distance is along the

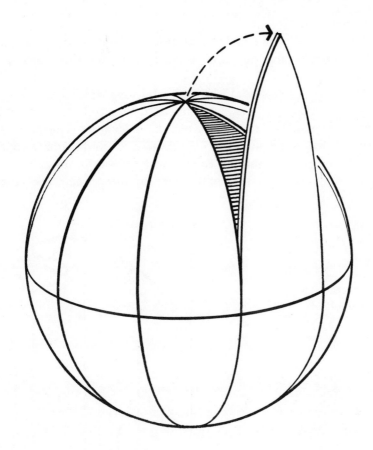

FIGURE 7. FLATTENING EARTH'S SURFACE
CREATES DISTORTION

When a segment of the globe is flattened it becomes distorted.

arc of a great circle), but rhumb line sailing is the most practicable for distances up to about 600 miles, or when traversing an approximately north–south course. For distances over 600 miles—particularly when the course is approximately east–west—the great circle course is transposed in a series of chords of its circumference to a Mercator chart; this modification allows the Mercator projection to be utilized for long-distance navigation by sailing the rhumb lines created by the chords. Figure 9 illustrates the significant difference in distance between rhumb line and great circle courses in east–west sailing, and their relative coincidence in north–south sailing.

Mercator charts contain latitude and longitude scales along the edge (latitude at each side of the chart, longitude at top and bottom) from which direct measurement is made to determine position, or to locate an object of known latitude and longitude coordinates. Any point on earth's surface may be located on the appropriate chart of its general area by intersecting the latitude

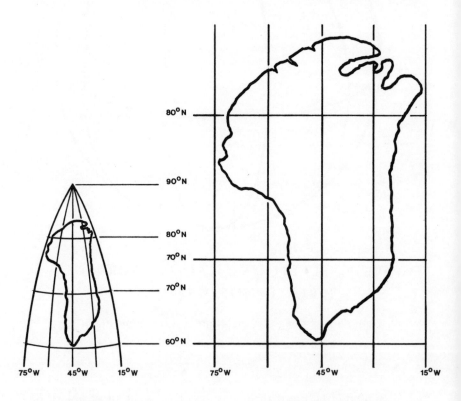

a. True scale   b. Mercator projection

FIGURE 8.   MERCATOR   DISTORTION
(Example: *Greenland*)

The linear separation of the longitudes of both projections is identical at the equator, but the latitude distortion on the Mercator projection increases significantly as it nears the pole.

and longitude scales. The usual need is to find the coordinates of the ship's position as plotted on the chart; the method is to construct perpendiculars horizontally (latitude) and vertically (longitude) from the plotted position to the respective latitude and longitude scales, and read the coordinate values at the points intersected on the scales. Dividers may be used as a shortcut method subject to less accuracy than constructing perpendiculars; span the dividers to the nearest parallel of latitude and transpose them to the latitude scale for reading, then repeat the process by spanning to the nearest longitude meridian and transpose to the longitude scale.

Distance between any two points on a Mercator chart is measured on the latitude scale (1' of latitude = 1 nautical mile). Because the latitude scale constantly increases in dimension as the distance from the equator increases, distance should be measured

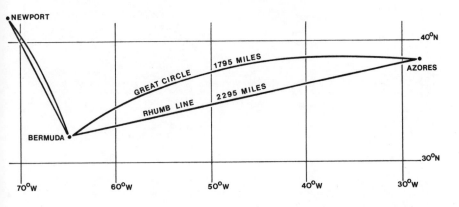

FIGURE 9. MERCATOR PROJECTION: RHUMB LINE AND GREAT CIRCLE DISTANCES

Bermuda lies 635 miles south southeast of Newport. Because of the relatively short distance (earth's curvature being navigationally unimportant up to about 600 miles) and the general north–south direction, the rhumb line and great circle courses and distances almost coincide. The east–west positioning and longer distance between Bermuda and the Azores create a different set of circumstances, the rhumb line distance being 500 miles (28%) longer than the great circle track.

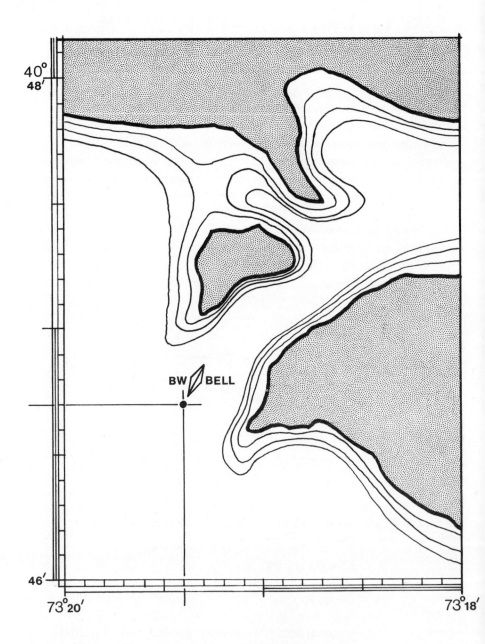

FIGURE 10. POSITION COORDINATES

Any point on earth's surface may be located at the intersection of
its latitude and longitude. The coordinates of this buoy are
Lat 40° 46.7'N, Long 73° 19.4'W.

at the approximate mid-latitude of the two points. Distance is most easily measured with the aid of dividers, as explained in Chapter V. The longitude scale cannot be employed for measuring distance.

Mercator charts contain a wealth of information, much of which is in the form of symbols and all of which the navigator must understand if he is to conduct his vessel in safety. The symbols are contained in the U.S. Navy Oceanographic Office's Chart 1: *Nautical Chart Symbols and Abbreviations,* a "must" in every sailor's library and deserving thorough study and understanding.

The detail contained on a Mercator chart varies according to the intensity with which the area has been surveyed and also according to the scale of the chart. Scale is a ratio indicating that one unit (inch, foot, etc.) on the chart equals the given number of equivalent units on the surface; a scale of 1:50,000, for example, means that one inch on the chart is equal to 50,000 inches on the surface of earth. The term "large scale" indicates a chart depicting a small area in a larger size and in more detail than on a small-scale chart. The higher the number of units in the ratio, the *smaller* the chart scale.

U.S. charts are loosely classified in five groups according to scale and intended use:

Sailing charts (1:600,000 and smaller)—intended for offshore approaches to coastal areas, with emphasis on soundings and principal lights, outer buoys, and landmarks visible at a distance.

General charts (1:100,000 to 1:600,000)—used for coastwise navigation outside of outlying reefs and shoals.

Coastal charts (1:50,000 to 1:100,000)—for inshore piloting, entering large harbors and bays, and for large inland waterways.

Harbor charts (1:50,000 and larger)—for harbors, anchorages, and narrower waterways.

Intracoastal Waterway charts (1:40,000)—special-purpose charts for the inside route from New Jersey to the Mexican Border via Key West.

Other special-purpose charts on the Mercator projection include those encompassing the various oceans (as Chart N. O. 15, North Atlantic Ocean, scale 1:9,189,000) and the *Pilot Charts* of the oceans which present indispensable information on wind, current, shipping lanes, fog, ice, location of ocean station vessels, and other essential data for blue water passage-making.

Before using a Mercator chart it should be inspected to determine the unit of depth measurement, which may be feet, meters, or fathoms (1 fathom = 6 feet). Most foreign language charts are in meters, English language charts are being converted upon reissue from fathoms or feet to meters to achieve international uniformity; the process is expected to be rather gradual. Other predeparture information to be ascertained by inspection includes assurance that the area covered in the chart (or charts) includes the total area of the passage, confirmation that the chart is up-to-date with all changes noted (from *Notice to Mariners*) since date of issue, and the water level from which charted depths are measured, which varies by countries and even within the U.S. The scale is observed to determine the unit of measurement—saltwater charts are usually scaled to the nautical mile (6076 feet) and freshwater charts to the statute mile (5280 feet).

Gnomonic Charts

Charts constructed on the gnomonic projection greatly distort land masses, and confusingly portray latitude parallels and longitude meridians as arcs of circles—a totally different format from that of the Mercator projection. The purpose of a gnomonic chart is to determine the great circle course between two points which, on this projection, is constructed as a straight line. (A rhumb line on a gnomonic chart appears as an arc of a circle.) A gnomonic chart is familiarly referred to as a "great circle" chart, which eliminates the need to know the correct pronunciation of "gn." Compare the great circle and rhumb line courses between Bermuda and the Azores as gnomonically plotted in Figure 11 with the Mercator projection of Figure 9.

The straight line representation of a great circle course constructed on a gnomonic chart must be transposed to a Mercator chart in order to be navigationally useful. The method is given in Chapter V. At times a combination of great circle and rhumb line sailing (termed composite sailing) is employed to avoid a hazard on the great circle track.

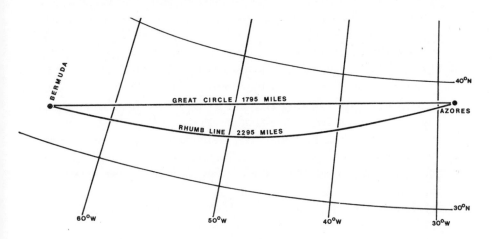

FIGURE 11. GNOMONIC PROJECTION: RHUMB LINE AND GREAT CIRCLE COURSE

On a gnomonic chart the great circle course is a straight line and the rhumb line becomes an arc of a great circle.

Plotting Sheets

A plotting sheet is actually a blank chart employed offshore because of the difficulty of plotting celestial observations and frequent dead reckoning (DR) positions on small-scale charts. A position found by celestial observation is plotted on the plotting chart and then transferred to the working Mercator chart, thus keeping the working chart uncluttered of extraneous construction lines not concerned with course direction. Plotting sheets in the 3000 series, issued by the U.S. Navy Oceanographic Office, are recommended for the cruising navigator. They contain a true compass rose with 4 inches between the longitude meridians (1° Long = 4 inches). The latitudes are numbered, hence the navigator must use the plotting sheet issued for the ship's latitude;

meridians of longitude are not numbered and the navigator merely inserts the appropriate longitude designations required for locali- zation of the plotting sheet. Latitude and longitude scales are printed to enable position determination, and the latitude scale is used for distance measurement, as on a conventional Mercator chart. When labeling the longitude it should be borne in mind that longitude increases in value as it increases in distance from Greenwich (Long 0°). A plotting sheet in the 3000 series, when properly labeled for longitude, becomes a small-scale Mercator chart suitable for plotting DR and fix positions, lines of position, current set and drift, course changes, and celestial observations.

The Universal Plotting Sheet (UPS) preferred by commercial and military navigators is applicable to any latitude where the Mercator projection is used but requires more construction on the part of the navigator. In a pinch, self-constructed plotting sheets may be made. *Bowditch* (H. O. 9) should be consulted for construction of UPS or self-made plotting sheets.

Chart Sources

The principal chart-issuing agencies in the United States are the National Ocean Survey (formerly the U.S. Coast and Geodetic Survey) of the National Oceanic and Atmosphere Administration (NOAA) and the U.S. Navy Oceanographic Office. The National Ocean Survey has charting responsibility for fresh and salt water areas within and adjacent to the United States and its territories and issues a free catalog (*Nautical Chart Catalog No. 1*) listing all of the agency's charts and chart agents for retail sales. The Ocean- ographic Office has charting responsibility for all areas of the world outside of United States waters, and lists its charts in H. O. publication 1-N, which is for sale. A listing of pertinent naviga- tional material available from governmental agencies of the United States, Canada, and Great Britain, will be found in Ap- pendix I.

Civilian sales agents are found wherever boating activity takes place and are normally the most convenient sources for charts of contiguous areas. The advantage of ordering charts direct from a governmental agency is the elimination of local sales taxes, as well as presumably receiving the latest chart issue with the latest corrections. As a precaution, regardless of where purchased, charts should be inspected before use for the date of latest correction (or date of issue if no corrections are given) and the *Notice to Mariners* then consulted for subsequent changes. Charts are available from many sources abroad, often at lower price than those produced by the Oceanographic Office. British Admiralty charts, for example, are superbly executed and quite low-priced. However, despite the price appeal, the American navigator will probably find himself more comfortable with the familiar methods of U.S. chartmaking, and is assured that the U.S. Navy has every nook and cranny of the maritime coasts of the world very well charted, regardless of where the navigator may choose to cruise.

Care of Charts

When possible, charts should be stored flat; failing this, because of limiting storage drawer dimensions, fold them once, map side out, on the shorter axis. Charts requiring to be folded more than once to fit a drawer are better kept rolled in a cylindrical carrying case. File or store charts in numerical order and mark the chart number and area description on a folded chart where it will be visible without being unfolded to consult the printed reference. A transparent plastic case protects a chart from spray or being blown about when being used topside.

chapter III

The Magnetic Compass

T HE PRIMARY PURPOSE of a compass is to provide a means of determining the direction of *true* north (the north geographic pole) from which any other true direction may be obtained. The modern magnetic compass suitable for marine use contains a floating card graduated in degrees on the circumference, from 0° at the north point through 360°. The *lubber's line,* a vertical marking on the inside of the compass bowl, is positioned parallel to the keel so that a reading of the compass card opposite the lubber's line is a reading of the ship's compass course—which seldom, if ever, is the true course and must be corrected to eliminate *compass error,* which is the difference between compass and true direction.

Compass Error

Two magnetic influences, *variation* and *deviation,* affect compass direction, their combined total effect being termed the compass error. *Variation changes with location* and is published on charts. *Deviation is caused by magnetic influences contained within the individual ship* and the location of the ship's compass in relation to these influences, and must be determined by observation and measurement.

Variation: The compass card is magnetized so that the 0° point (sometimes referred to as the "needle") constantly seeks *magnetic* north, which is not true north but rather follows an elliptical track several hundred miles northeast of Hudson's Bay. True north is a fixed point at the north geographic pole. The directions of magnetic north and true north can vary according to a ship's

FIGURE 12. COMPASS CARD   *Danforth*

location, therefore the difference in direction between the two norths has logically been termed *variation*. Variation is East (E) if the 0° points eastward of true north (as it will in the Gulf of Mexico) or West (W) if pointing westward of true north (as in Long Island Sound). *Variation is a significant component of compass error* and must be known for every area navigated. Mercator charts indicate the quantity of variation at the time of chart issue, plus an annual change factor to be applied for updating; the information is usually presented on the chart's compass rose.

The difference between a true direction and a magnetic direction caused by variation is neutralized by applying the arc measurement of the variation as a correction. The rule is:

Direction Conversion

From True to Magnetic	*From Magnetic to True*
Add West variation, subtract East	Add East variation, subtract West

The *compass rose* imprinted on most charts contains both true and magnetic directions. The outer circle is aligned with true north—parallel with the longitude meridian on a Mercator chart —and the inner circle coincides with the local magnetic variation, and is oriented to magnetic north. In the center of the rose the variation, and annual change from the base date when it was recorded, are given. Use of the compass rose is discussed in Chapter V.

Deviation is a component of compass error created by the ship's internal magnetism, and causes the magnetic compass to deflect from magnetic north (variation deflects the compass from true north). Unlike variation, which is a constant at a given location regardless of what course the ship is following, *deviation varies with the heading of the ship*. To oversimplify for clarity: If the only deviation factor affecting the compass were a backstay, then deviation would be negligible when the ship was heading southward because the deviation magnetism would be in line with the magnetic line of force. On the other hand, a course to the east or west would create a vector of magnetic forces, one north and one at the stern, and the compass error would be the result of both forces. Actually the magnetic forces creating deviation aboard ship are many and diverse, and exert different amounts of "pull" on the compass according to their location and the angle from magnetic north which the ship is following. The problem of deviation is most acute in a steel hull with high-powered engines and a topside load of sophisticated electronic gear, but no boat is immune to deviation error if it has any metal at all aboard.

Because deviation is a function of the ship's heading, its effect must be known for all directions through 360°. The method is to determine the deviation at selected intervals (usually each 15°) and prepare a *deviation card* indicating the corrections at those intervals. Intervening values are then interpolated as needed. Deviation determination is made by swinging the ship through 360°

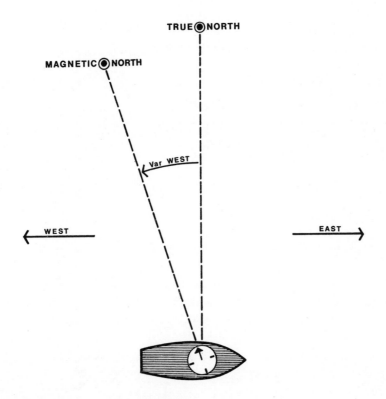

FIGURE 13. VARIATION

The compass is pointing to magnetic north and must be corrected for *west variation* to adjust for the westward deflection from true north.

while taking bearings on a known object; the operation is best left to professionals except in an emergency. The services of a compass adjuster are strongly advocated inasmuch as, by the judicious placement of compensating magnets, he can materially reduce deviation or even eliminate this tricky nuisance. The deviation card must always be kept aboard for quick reference, and its accuracy checked from time to time by bearings taken from observation of known landmarks while cruising in coastal or inland waters, as described in Chapter V. At sea very accurate correction can be made whenever a celestial body is observed; the method depends upon which of a number of available tables is used, and is discussed in Chapter XIV.

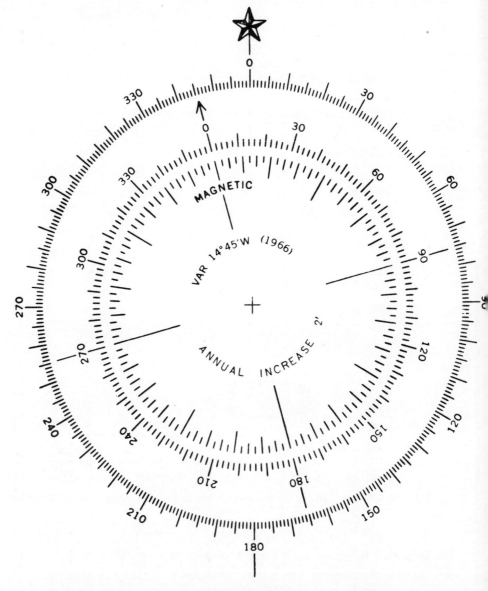

FIGURE 14. COMPASS ROSE

True direction shown on outer circle: A line through 0°–180° is true
N–S, a 90°–270° line is true E–W. *Magnetic* direction shown on inner
circle. *Variation* and *annual change* shown at center of rose.
Observe that the difference between true and magnetic direction
is the variation.

TRUE direction + West Variation = MAGNETIC Direction
MAGNETIC Direction − West Variation = TRUE Direction
(Reverse the sign when variation is east)

The correction for deviation is applied similarly to the correction for variation described above, i.e.:

From Magnetic to Compass   *From Compass to Magnetic*

Add West deviation,   Add East deviation,
subtract East   subtract West

The navigator should bear in mind that deviation influence on the ship's compass requires frequent checking, particularly if the vessel is not free to swing on a mooring when in harbor. Ships

---

STEERING COMPASS DEVIATION TABLE

YACHT: **GULVAIN**   COMPASS: **SESTREL**

MAGNETIC COURSE	DEVIATION	COMPASS COURSE	MAGNETIC COURSE	DEVIATION	COMPASS COURSE
015	2E	013	195	O	195
030	3E	027	210	O	210
045	3E	042	225	1W	226
060	3½E	056½	240	1W	241
075	4E	071	255	2W	257
090	3E	087	270	2½W	272½
105	3E	102	285	2W	287
120	3E	117	300	2W	302
135	2E	133	315	1W	316
150	2E	148	330	1W	331
165	1E	164	345	O	345
180	1E	179	360	1E	359

DATE: **15 JUNE 1971**   BY: **P. L. D.**

FIGURE 15. TYPICAL DEVIATION CARD

docked over periods of a week or more on an east–west axis, or moored fore and aft, often have their compasses affected by earth's north magnetic attraction to the point where marked deviation changes are noticeable in spite of a recent compass adjustment. Compasses adjusted for deviation in mid-latitudes often show changes when brought to the lower latitudes, as on a passage from Boston to Antigua.

Compass Correction

In the practice of navigation any one of three directions may be required: (1) *true direction* is always used when out of sight of land and is sometimes useful for coastal piloting, (2) *magnetic direction* is a time-saver when piloting on lakes and coastal waters (almost invariably employed there by racing sailors), and (3) *compass direction* is what the helmsman steers by. Therefore the navigator must know how to correct from any one of these three directions to any other; since interconversion is a matter of frequent occurrence he must do it quickly by memorization of a convenient method of applying variation and deviation in order to calculate the needed direction. There are a number of "catch" phrases to jog one's memory, of which the two most widely used are "Can Dead Men Vote Twice" and "True Virtue Makes Dull Company." Either will provide the necessary memory crutch and the selection becomes a matter of whether politics or morality is uppermost in one's mind. The key to either phrase is to remember the meaning indicated by the first letter of each word.

> T means *True* Direction
> V means *Variation*
> M means *Magnetic* Direction
> D means *Deviation*
> C means *Compass* Direction

TVMDC (or the reverse) indicates the sequence of correction from true to magnetic to compass (or vice versa). The sign (+ or −) for variation and deviation in the sequence must also be remembered; one method is to append *"add West down,"* thus making all other signs and directions obvious by deduction. A mnemonic popular in Great Britain for remembering the sequence of correction from compass to true is CADET, i.e., "Compass to True, Add East." A widely used form, with quantities added for illustration, is that shown below, which the U.S. Power Squadrons have successfully taught to more than one million embryonic sailors.

$$
\begin{array}{c c c c c c}
 & & \text{T} & 100° & \uparrow & \\
+ & \text{W} & \text{V} & 14°\text{W} & - & \text{W} \\
 & & \text{M} & 114° & & \\
- & \text{E} & \text{D} & 2°\text{E} & + & \text{E} \\
 & \downarrow & \text{C} & 112° & &
\end{array}
$$

An obvious shortcut when magnetic direction is not a factor is to combine the variation and deviation quantities into total compass error—feasible since the algebraic sum of these quantities is, in fact, the compass error—and thus make a rapid conversion between true and compass direction. In the example given above, the net compass error is 12°W, to be added when converting from true to compass direction or subtracted going the other way. On headings with 0° deviation (normally the result of skillful compass adjustment) the compass and magnetic directions will coincide, and variation will be the only factor necessary to correct.

chapter IV

Position

POSITION ANYWHERE on earth's surface is a point defined by the coordinates of latitude and longitude. *The whole purpose of the art of navigation is to know one's position at all times* so that distance and direction to the destination, and avoidance of hazards enroute, may be accurately determined. The navigator deals with several methods for finding position which vary in accuracy according to the amount and quality of the information available to him. Accurate plotting, as detailed in Chapter V, is an important ingredient in establishing accurate position.

Dead Reckoning

Dead reckoning (DR) position applies the factors of speed (S) and time (T) from a previous position to deduce the position along the course line at any given time (D = ST), and should be calculated at regular intervals (usually at each whole hour) as a matter of standard procedure. A new DR position is calculated and plotted whenever a change in course (C) or speed (S) is made. A DR position is only an approximation of true position, since the effects of wind, current, and steering error are not applied as correction factors.

Line of Position

A *line of position* (LOP) is a line on some point of which the ship is presumed to be located, the exact point being unknown. A LOP is obtained by observation of a range, circle of position, or bearing, as described below:

Range: When two fixed objects are in line with the ship, the ship is on the range of the objects and is positioned somewhere along the range.

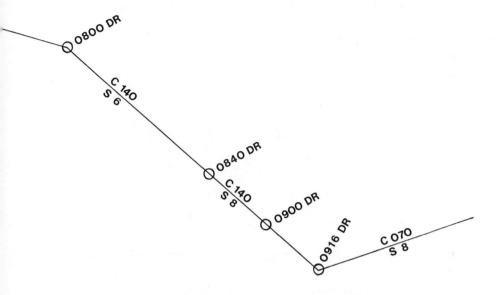

FIGURE 16. DEAD RECKONING POSITIONS

DR position should be calculated at every whole hour and must be calculated whenever a change of course (C) or speed (S) is made. Additionally, a DR position is plotted whenever a bearing is taken.

Circle of position: When the distance to a fixed object is known (as found by range finder, stadimeter, radar, sextant angle, or synchronized signals) the ship lies somewhere on the circumference of the circle formed by the object at the center and the known distance as the radius.

Bearing: A bearing is the direction of one point on earth's surface to another, measured from a reference direction clockwise through 360°, and is the most frequently employed means of finding a line of position. The bearing of an object as taken from the ship may be any of four types, all correctable as needed by the TVMDC method described in Chapter III.

True bearings use the reference point true north.

Magnetic bearings use the reference point magnetic north and must be corrected for variation (add East, subtract West variation) if conversion to a true bearing is wanted. A hand bearing compass provides magnetic bearings, as does a ship's compass with no deviation error.

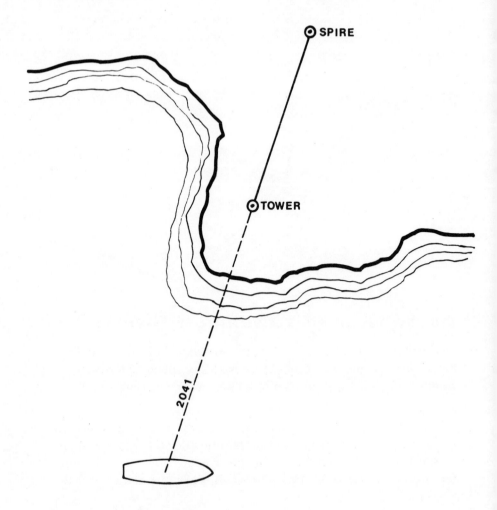

FIGURE 17. RANGE

The ship is in line with the spire and tower.

Compass bearings are read from the compass with the aid of a sighting vane positioned over the bowl; the method is not always feasible and depends on the height of the compass in relation to superstructure in line with the object of the bearing observation. A compass bearing must be corrected for deviation according to the ship's heading (which is not necessarily the ship's course) to convert it to a magnetic bearing.

A *relative bearing* is the angular direction relative to the ship's heading, i.e., the angle between the keel and the line of sight

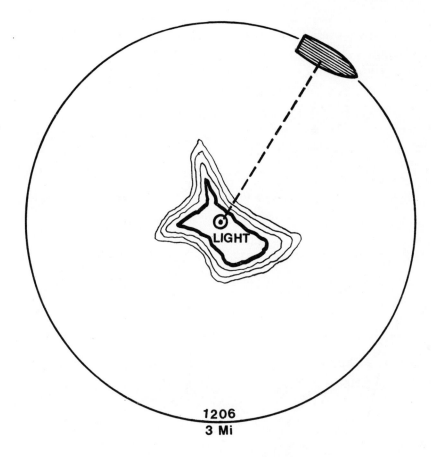

FIGURE 18.   CIRCLE OF POSITION

The ship is on the circumference of a circle at a known distance (radius) from the center.

to the object, measured clockwise from a reference point of 0° degrees at the bow. A pelorus, or "dumb compass," not subject to magnetic attraction, is used for this purpose. The shortcut of taking relative bearings counterclockwise through 180° can become confusing and therefore is not recommended.

A *radio bearing,* as received from a commercial broadcasting station or a radiobeacon, is a special case of relative bearing subject to several types of distortion. The navigator relying on radio direction finding (RDF) equipment for a line of position should familiarize himself with the vagaries of radio signals discussed in Chapter VIII. RDF is subject to *radio deviation,* the receiver must be calibrated and a table of deviation corrections prepared.

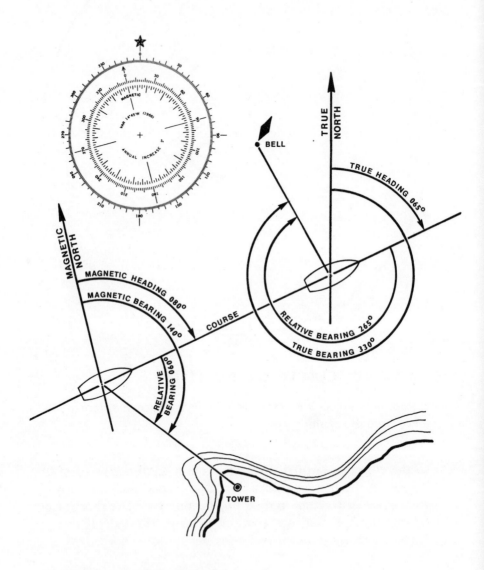

FIGURE 19. BEARINGS

Bearings are measured clockwise from a reference point: true bearings from true north, magnetic bearings from magnetic north, relative bearings from the ship's heading.

Consolan bearings require conversion tables (available in H. O. pub. 117 A and B, *Radio Navigational Aids)* before plotting on a Mercator chart. Loran, Decca, and Omega are hyperbolic systems which lie outside the purview of most small-craft sailors and are therefore not further discussed in this work.

The bearing quantity as measured is often not that required to establish a line of position on the chart, for example a compass or relative bearing is useless until converted to either a true or magnetic line of position bearing. The TVMDC (Chapter III) of compass correction is adaptable to the correction of bearings with the addition of two suffixes: B (bearing) and H (heading).

$$
\begin{array}{c|ccc|c}
+ & W & \text{TB} & 110° & \\
& W & \text{V} & 35°W & - & W \\
& & \text{MB} & 145° & \\
- & E & \text{D} & 20°E & + & E \\
& & \text{CB} & 125° & \\
\end{array}
$$

A relative bearing (RB) is measured from the ship's heading and is therefore applied by *adding* to the ship's true (TH), magnetic (MH), or compass (CH) heading in order to determine the required bearing (the distinction between course and heading must not be confused, course is the direction of movement, and heading is the direction in which the bow is pointed; a ship crabbing along a course of, say 090°, may only be headed 080° because of the actions of wind and current):

$$RB + TH = TB$$
$$RB + MH = MB$$
$$RB + CH = CB$$

Assuming in this example that the ship's heading is 090° true, then the line of position as determined by a relative bearing of 020° is calculated: RB + TH = TB, or:

$$
\begin{array}{ll}
\text{RB} & 020° \\
\text{TH} & +090° \\
\hline
\text{TB} & 110° \\
\end{array}
$$

Reciprocal bearings are those taken from the object to the ship, and differ by 180° (+ or −) from those taken from the ship to the object.

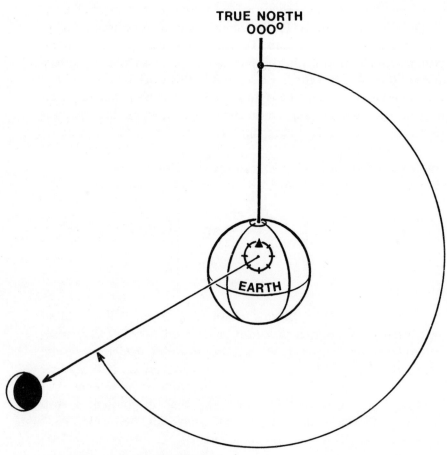

FIGURE 20. AZIMUTH

Azimuth quantity is extracted from any of a number of tables used in celestial navigation, and applied as a true bearing in position finding.

Azimuth: An azimuth is the horizontal direction of a celestial body from a point on earth, measured from 000° at true north (the north celestial pole, an extension of earth's polar axis) clockwise through 360°. An azimuth is a true direction, similar in all respects but nomenclature to a true bearing. The azimuth of a celestial body is a true line of position.

Soundings, or measurements of depth, are considered to provide a rough line of position if the readings can be oriented to charted depths adjusted for the state of the tide. The method—as widely taught in the classroom and largely ignored on the water —is to hold constant course and speed while plotting the depth recordings at stated intervals of time on a transparent paper. The depths are plotted along a course line on the paper at the same scale as if plotted on the chart. The paper is then used as an overlay and shuffled over the chart until it hopefully coincides with a charted depth pattern.

The Fix

A position may be "fixed" by proximity to a charted object, but is usually determined by the intersection of two or more lines of position. Intersection of three lines of position (a "three position fix") is a better assurance of accurate fixing, and is recommended whenever possible. Position from three lines often forms a small triangle instead of a common point of intersection; all three interior angles of such triangles are bisected—usually by "eyeball"—to find the center, which point is assumed to be the fix point. Examples of combinations of lines of position are shown in Figure 21, and are but a sample of the possibilities available.

The only truly accurate crossed lines of position composing a fix are those taken at anchor, or simultaneously when a vessel is underway; for example, when a range is abeam it is passed almost instantaneously. However, for practical small-craft navigation purposes, some tolerances are allowable: At sea a round of sights taken within fifteen minutes may be considered to have been taken simultaneously; in piloting waters bearings taken within two minutes of each other are acceptable for a fix under normal cruising conditions. There is no hard and fast rule, and the decision whether two observations can be considered to be simultaneous is a matter of judgment. As a guide, distance along the course line between observations (speed of the vessel multiplied by the time between observations) should be considered; if the scale of the chart is such that only a minute section of the course line is spanned between the observation there is no problem, but if the distance run is significant the fix will not be accurate.

The *bearing and distance off fix* is a special case of position finding. When the distance from a charted object is known, the

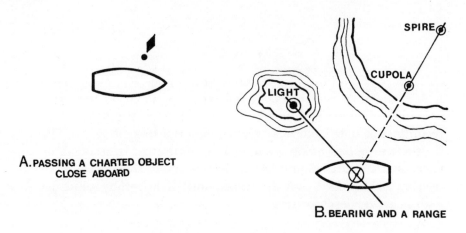

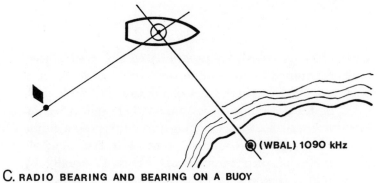

A. PASSING A CHARTED OBJECT
CLOSE ABOARD

B. BEARING AND A RANGE

C. RADIO BEARING AND BEARING ON A BUOY

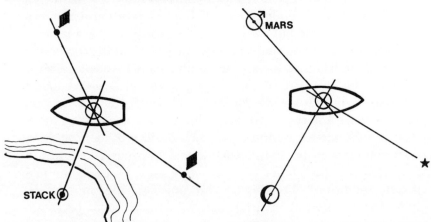

D. THREE CROSS BEARINGS

E. AZIMUTHS OF CELESTIAL BODIES

FIGURE 21. EXAMPLES OF FIX

   a. Passing a charted object close aboard.
   b. Bearing and a range.
   c. Radio bearing crosses with bearing on a buoy.
   d. Three cross bearings.
   e. Azimuths of celestial bodies.

ship is on a circle of position which is then convertible to a fix by taking a bearing on the object; the intersection of the bearing line and the circle is the position point of the fix. Three types of fixes are available by this technique:

1. *Radiobeacon* bearing is obtained by RDF and the distance off determined by observing the time lapse between the radio signal received on RDF and the synchronized audible (fog horn) signal heard by ear. Since radio waves and sound waves do not travel at the same rate of speed they are not received simultaneously and the ship's distance off is directly proportional to the time interval thus created. Distance from the radiobeacon in nautical miles and tenths is found by dividing the number of seconds elapsed between the signal receptions by 5.5 and should be correct within a tolerance of $\pm\ 10\%$.

2. *Visual* bearing on an object, such as a lighthouse or other tall structure, can be combined with a circle of position to fix position at the intersection of the bearing and circle. If a sextant is used to measure the angle subtended by the known height of the object, refer to *Bowditch* (Table 9) for the distance. Heights obtained from chart inspection must be corrected for the actual height of the tide above or below the datum level at the time of the observation.

3. A *radar fix* gives the bearing and distance of the object from the ship, i.e., the ship's position is the center of the circle and the observed object bears on the circle of position.

Running Fix

A *running fix* (R FIX) advances (or sometimes retards) an earlier bearing line of position to the time of a later bearing observation, the intersection of the two bearing lines forming an R FIX position. Because the distance of advance depends upon dead reckoning, a running fix is not as accurate as a true fix; nevertheless it is a valuable and much-used method of finding position inasmuch as the earlier bearing line may be carried forward for several hours between observations, as frequently happens at sea. The method is fully detailed in Chapter V.

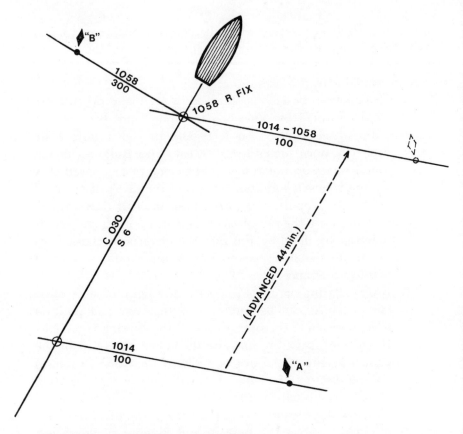

FIGURE 22. RUNNING FIX

The bearing taken on buoy A has been advanced to the time of the
bearing on buoy B, the intersection of the two bearing lines forming
a running fix.

Estimated Position

An *estimated position* (EP) is a correction of the DR position,
obtained by incorporating the effect of current. Although current,
technically, is the horizontal movement of water, the term is used
in navigation to include leeway (wind effect), steering error, and
all other factors which tend to take a ship off its ordered course.
Estimated position is the most probable position when a fix or
running fix is unobtainable. An EP may be either (1) the DR
position adjusted for current as stated above, or (2) the nearest

point on the bearing line to the DR position at the time the bearing was taken, which indicates the effect of current moving with, or against, the ship's course.

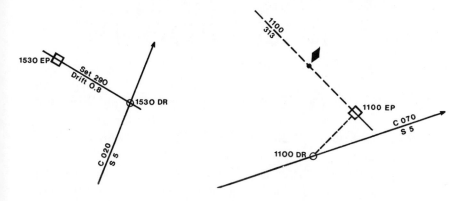

FIGURE 23.   ESTIMATED POSITION

a. The *set* (direction) and *drift* (speed) of the current result in an EP off the course line.
b. A bearing line of position gives an EP at the *nearest point on the bearing line* to the DR position at the time the bearing was taken.

Assumed Position

An assumed position (AP) is employed for convenience in using tables for celestial navigation, and is a point on the nearest parallel of latitude to the DR position, and at a longitude also assumed for convenience (see Chapter IX).

Position Coordinates

The location of a position obtained by dead reckoning or fixing, or of an estimated or assumed position, may be stated by expressing its coordinates of latitude and longitude as intersected from their respective scales on the chart.

chapter V

Plotting and Labeling

MODERN NAVIGATION relies heavily on *plotting*, the drawing of lines and points on a chart, for the graphic representation of position, direction, and distance. The hallmark of the good navigator is his ability to plot and label neatly and accurately; a sloppy plotter is a sloppy navigator. Good plotting habits can be acquired with practice, and good plotting equipment facilitates the acquisition.

Plotting Tools

A *pencil* (never ink) is used to draw on charts. Too soft a point will smudge and make blurry, imprecise lines, a hard point will crease the chart and be both difficult to read and difficult to erase. A number 2H lead will satisfy the requirement of most hands. The point must be kept sharp, which means that a pencil sharpener or knife are required accessories for a wooden-cased pencil. Many navigators prefer to use a draughtsman's metal-cased, retractable point pencil which may be sharpened with a swatch of sandpaper.

When constructing a line with the aid of a straightedge, consideration must be taken of the thickness of the lead and the angle at which the pencil is held, otherwise the line constructed will be offset from the line intended. One should avoid drawing a line over a printed chart symbol whenever possible; if two points are to be connected by plotting, the line should be drawn to—but not through—the points to avoid their becoming indistinct when erased, a precaution particularly to be observed when the chart is frequently used.

The *eraser* suitable for chart work must be a soft one. An art gum eraser will do the job very well on a plot made with a number 2H lead pencil, but is crumbly; a nondisintegrating type—the kneaded rubber eraser—does not crumble, does the job equally well, lasts indefinitely, and is well worth hunting for at an art supply store. Over-long lines and construction lines not needed for the final plot should be erased immediately, they are a confusing by-product of almost every instance of plotting if not eliminated. A typist's *erasing shield* is a helpful device for protecting adjoining work while removing unwanted lines.

A *plotting device* is used for drawing straight lines, moving lines parallel to themselves or extending them, and for measuring direction. *Parallel rules* are a popular tool for this purpose, the most convenient type being of transparent plastic construction. To measure the direction of a line, the parallel rules are set along the line and then "walked" to the center of the compass rose on the chart, where both the magnetic and true directions are read. Conversely, to plot a desired direction, the rules are oriented to the direction on the compass rose and walked to the point along which the direction is to be plotted on the chart. Parallel rules cannot be used in conjunction with plotting sheets not bearing a compass rose and are probably the least accurate (and most expensive) of the three plotting devices mentioned herein.

A *protractor-plotter* is a transparent elongated rectangular device with a protractor incorporated into the design. Courses and directions are measured from the nearest meridian of longitude and the device, once oriented correctly, does not require to be moved for purposes of constructing a plotting line. Because there are no moving parts to get out of adjustment, and no need to consult the compass rose for a true course or line of position direction, the protractor-plotter is preferred by many navigators.

The most accurate and versatile plotting device for small-craft navigation is a pair of large plastic right-angle *triangles*, preferably one with two 45° angles and the other with 30° and 60°; the hypotenuse can hardly be too long since it is the side along which most course lines are constructed and should be a minimum of fifteen inches on the 45° triangle. The method of use is more easily learned than described, and a minute or two of practice will implant it firmly and permanently in the user's mind: To measure a course line direction lay the hypotenuse (longest side)

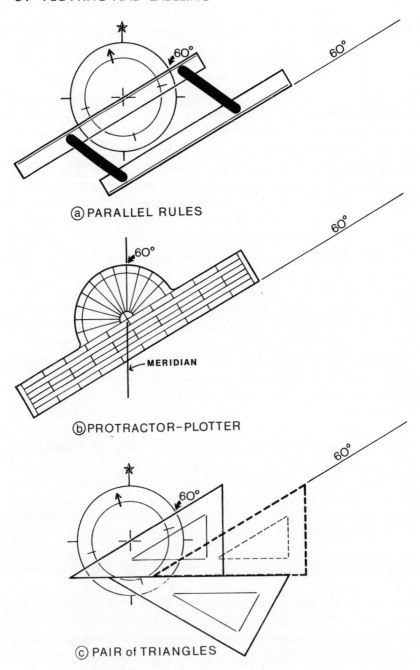

ⓐ PARALLEL RULES

ⓑ PROTRACTOR-PLOTTER

MERIDIAN

ⓒ PAIR of TRIANGLES

FIGURE 24. SMALL-CRAFT PLOTTING DEVICES

of the 45° triangle along the line and the hypotenuse of the other triangle along one of the short sides; this latter triangle is the guide, upon which slight pressure is maintained to prevent slippage. Slide the 45° triangle in the direction of the compass rose until the hypotenuse intersects the center mark of the rose. The true or magnetic direction of the course line is then read where the hypotenuse intersects their printed indication on the circumference of the rose. Reverse the process when making a directional plot based on transposition from the rose. The advantage of large triangles lies in the fact that only one movement is normally required, when small triangles are used it may be necessary to move the triangles both laterally and vertically to reach the center of the rose.

Dividers are used to measure distance and pinpoint a position by the latitude and longitude coordinates. A good pair is well worth the slight investment; they should be adjustable for tension, sharp-pointed, and long-legged. Seven-inch legs are ideal, hard to find, and worth seeking out. *Distance* is measured on the chart by placing the points of the dividers on the two points between which distance is wanted, and then transferring the dividers to the *latitude scale* at the side of the chart. The difference in minutes of latitude ($1' = 1$ mile) is the distance wanted, as spanned by the dividers and measured on the latitude scale. Interpolate for tenths of minutes (tenths of miles) between the marked minutes on the scale. The reverse procedure is used to find distance along a charted line, in which case the required distance is measured first along the latitude scale and transferred to the charted line. Should the distance be greater than capable of being spanned by the dividers they are "walked" at a known convenient distance and the remainder—an incomplete span—measured separately and its quantity combined with the product of the multiples walked. Because the latitude scale on a Mercator chart constantly expands toward either pole, the dividers should always be placed carefully on the scale, approximately opposite the midpoint of the latitude of the charted line being measured for distance.

Position with the aid of dividers involves both the latitude and longitude scales: For latitude determination the dividers are spanned from the position point vertically to the nearest charted parallel of latitude and then transferred to the latitude scale at the

nearest side of the chart where the latitude is read at the point
of the divider spanned from the parallel. Longitude determination
is a similar process—the dividers being spanned from the position
point horizontally to the nearest meridian of longitude and transferred to the nearest longitude scale (at top or bottom of chart).

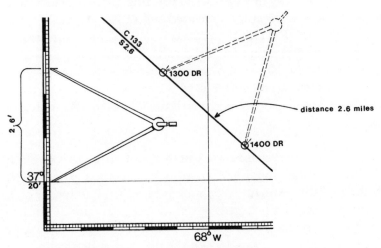

a. Measuring distance on the latitude scale.

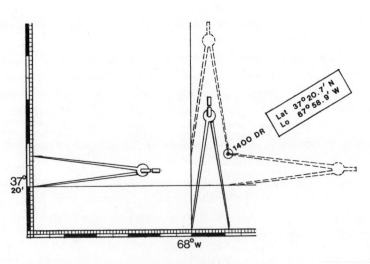

b. Locating position on a Mercator chart.

FIGURE 25. USE OF THE DIVIDERS

When it is desired to plot a position of known coordinates, the method is reversed, i.e., the appropriate quantities of latitude and longitude are spanned off with the dividers on their respective scales and transposed to the chart.

Other aids to plotting—helpful but not essential—include a *magnifying glass, protractor* (360° is best), pencil *compass,* draughtsman's *template, masking tape* to anchor the chart to a flat surface, and some cross-section (graph) paper.

Plotting and Labeling

The *plot* is composed of lines and points constructed on a chart. The *label* is the description of the plot. The label of a line is placed along the line, the label of a point on a line is placed at an angle to the line. Time is labeled with four digits, direction with three digits and the degree symbol (°) omitted. Direction labels are assumed to indicate true direction unless suffixed by "M" or "mag" to indicate a magnetic north reference point. All elements of a plot should be immediately labeled when constructed to avoid later chaos of interpretation; unnecessary lines should be erased. The techniques outlined below are understood by all navigators, and are recommended for adoption; it is important that others beside the navigator of the moment can understand his plotting and labeling.

Dead Reckoning

A DR plot is constantly maintained throughout a passage and starts at a fix, usually from proximity to a known aid to navigation, at departure outside the harbor. It is good practice to plot the intended track, in one or a series of rhumb lines, to the destination. A course line is continuously plotted, based on the actual track made good according to the compass readings as corrected to magnetic or true direction. DR position is calculated and plotted periodically (usually at every whole hour) and whenever a change in course or speed is made. DR position is the product of speed and time in transit since the last DR plot: If, for example, the speed is 6 knots and a DR position is to be calculated at fifteen minutes after the previous DR position, then the distance to be measured on the course line between the two DR positions will be 1.5 miles (D = ST, or D = 6 kts × .25 hrs). Whenever a position is plotted, the time and type are labeled (as 1100 DR, 1124 FIX, 1146 R FIX). Bearing lines of position are constructed from the course line toward the observed object and labeled for time and direction, the point of intersection with the course line being determined by D = ST from the previous DR position. The DR course line plot terminates when a new known position is obtained by fixing; a final DR position is plotted and labeled for the time of the new fix or running fix and a new DR course line constructed from the new fixed position. ▶

Plotting the Fix

A fix is the intersection of two or more lines of position, obtained simultaneously or nearly so. The time between observations is more critical in piloting waters than offshore where a round of

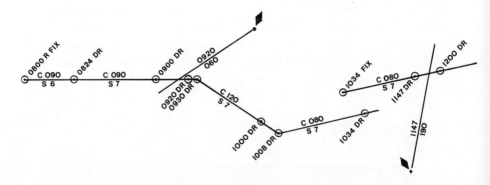

FIGURE 26. TYPICAL DEAD RECKONING COURSE PLOT

A DR course plot begins at a known location (fix or R FIX) and is continued without regard for current or leeway until another fixed position is obtained, the last DR plot being that at the time of the new fix. Observe that DR position has plotted each hour, whenever a change of course or speed has been made, and at the time of taking a bearing.

Labels of a DR Plot:

Course:

$$\frac{\text{C 090}}{\text{S 6}}$$

Label course (C) above the line and speed in knots (S) below.

DR Position:

0812 DR

Enclose the position point with a small circle, label the time (four digits) and DR tangential to the line.

Line of Position:
(Terrestrial)

0932
257

An LOP obtained by observation of a landmark or aid to navigation is labeled with time above the line and direction from the ship below. Three digits, with degree symbol omitted, are always used to indicate direction.

Line of Position:
(Celestial)

0932
Sun

Label time of observation above the line and name of the celestial object observed below.

Fix:

1156 FIX

Enclose the position point with a small circle, label time and FIX tangential to the line.

Running Fix:

1327 R Fix

Enclose the position point with a small circle, label time and R FIX tangential to the line.

sights, particularly when taken at sailing-craft speed, can be considered to be simultaneous when completed in fifteen minutes. The real criterion is the scale of the working chart (not the plotting sheet) used for the DR plot; if the time and speed between

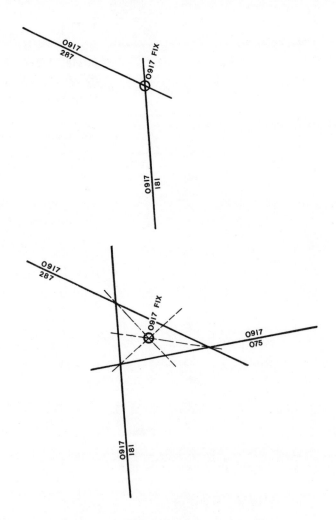

FIGURE 27. THE CENTER OF A FIX

a. The center of a fix obtained by two bearings is the point of intersection.
b. The center of a fix obtained by three bearings is the center of the triangle formed by their approximate intersection.

observations do not combine to create a significant distance measurement between observations, then the observations may be
plotted as a fix.

Where two lines of position intersect, the point of intersection
will be the fix position. A fix obtained from three LOP's is more
accurate, but the three lines will rarely intersect at a common
point, rather they will form a small triangle. The position point
is taken to be the center of the triangle as determined by bisecting
the interior angles.

When there is a choice of several LOPs to be plotted for a
fix, as with a round of sights on more than three celestial objects,
select the three LOPs which will give the best "cut"; an angle of

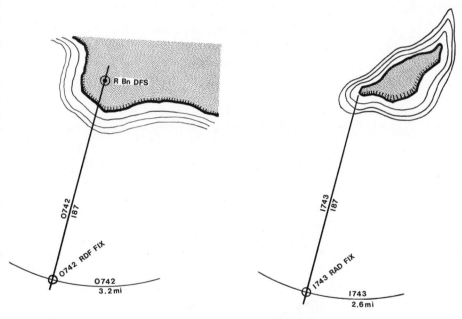

FIGURE 28. BEARING AND DISTANCE OFF
FIX PLOTS

a. A fix obtained by radio direction finding and distance
   measurement should be labeled RDF FIX to indicate probable
   less accuracy than if obtained by visual observation.
b. Radar Fix. Observe that the ship is plotted on a circle of position
   with the observed object at the center, although the reciprocal
   image is presented on the radar screen.

120° between each of three LOPs is ideal, angles of 30° or less should be discarded from any fix consideration if at all possible to do so.

Plotting a *bearing and distance off fix* is facilitated by the aid of a lead compass for inscribing an arc of the position circle to intersect the bearing line at the calculated distance from the object observed. The arc is labeled with time at the top (inside the circle) and the distance and unit of measurement underneath (outside). Bearing and fix labels are conventionally applied, except that a fix obtained by radar is labeled RAD FIX and a fix obtained by radio direction finding may optionally be labeled RDF FIX to indicate a probable less precise position than that of a visual fix.

Coordinates: The latitude and longitude of a fix should always be included in the label when offshore. Enclose the coordinates in a rectangle adjacent to the time and type of fix, as shown below:

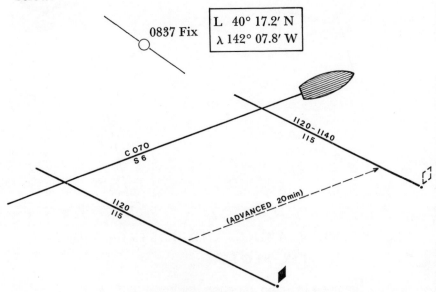

FIGURE 29. ADVANCING A BEARING LINE OF POSITION

The advanced line is labeled with two times, that of the original observation and that of the time to which it has been advanced.

The symbol for latitude (L, or Lat) and longitude (Lo, Long, or λ) should always be prefixed, and the direction suffixed, to each quantity; they are integral parts of the coordinate designation.

Running Fix

A running fix utilizes two lines of position (bearings) observed at different times; allowance for the time elapsed is accomplished by advancing the earlier LOP to the time of the second bearing. In effect the earlier line is moved parallel to itself, along the course line to the advanced position. The simplest method of plotting the advanced line: (1) determine the elapsed time between observations to the nearest whole minute, (2) multiply the elapsed time by the speed in knots to find the distance of advance, using $D = ST$ if time is more than one hour or $60D = ST$ if time is in minutes, (3) span with dividers the distance of advance, from the *original* intersection of the bearing and course line to the point of the advanced distance, and (4) reconstruct the bearing line from the advanced point on the course line in the original direction.

In the method shown in Figure 29:

(1) Elapsed time = 20 minutes

$$1140$$
$$-1120$$
$$\overline{20}$$

(2) Distance of advance = 2 miles

$$60D = 6S \times 20T$$
$$\text{and}$$
$$D = \frac{120}{60} = 2$$

The position point of the running fix is at the intersection of the later bearing line and the bearing line advanced to the later time, and is labeled with the later time and R FIX. The position will be found on the course line only by coincidence, since the

DR position for the time of the later observation is assumed to be the product of exact maintenance of course and speed, with no current influence. Nor should an R FIX position be considered to be as accurate as that of a true fix, since the distance of advance is subject to the same abberations of course, speed, and current. For these reasons it is inadvisable to carry a bearing forward for more than thirty minutes in piloting waters. The absence of landmarks offshore often requires that a celestial bearing be advanced by several hours; the practice is acceptable at sea because precision of position fixing is not as crucial there as it is close to shore.

A complete DR plot including an R FIX is shown in Figure 30.

Should a change in course or speed be made between the

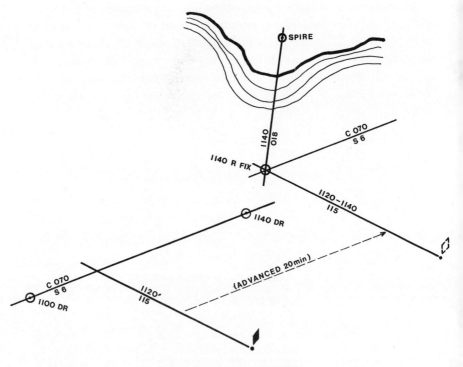

FIGURE 30. RUNNING FIX PLOT

(From two lines of position)
The first bearing is advanced to the time of the second, and their intersection is a running fix.

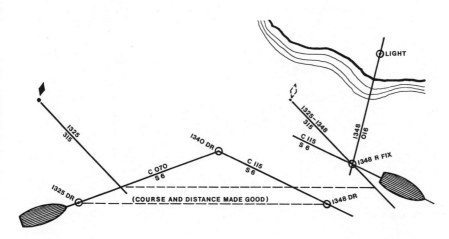

FIGURE 31. ADVANCING A LINE OF POSITION WITH CHANGE OF COURSE

The dashed construction lines are parallel to each other and of equal length. The line connecting the 1325 bearing and 1348 DR position represents course and distance made good during the elapsed time. The parallel dashed line of equal length advances the 1325 bearing from its intersection with the course line to its 1348 position.

times of taking two bearing lines of position, the earlier bearing may still be advanced to establish a running fix. The method is to advance the earlier line, parallel to itself, along the direction of the *course made good* in the time elapsed between the two observations for the amount of the *distance made good* in that period. DR positions must be plotted for both times; a line constructed from the first DR to the last DR is the source of both course and distance made good. A parallel construction line of the same length is then plotted from the intersection of the first bearing and the course line, its terminal is the point through which the advanced line is constructed, as diagramed in Figure 31. The method is applicable to any number of course changes between bearings.

A running fix does not necessarily depend on lines of position obtained by bearings on two different objects; *two bearings on the same object* at different times may be used, and are advantageous for finding the distance off at which a landmark will be passed: Plot the first bearing and the DR position for the time of the first

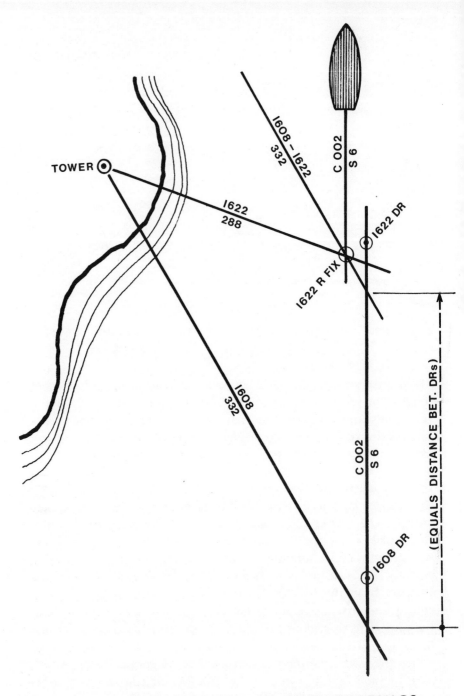

FIGURE 32. RUNNING FIX BY TWO BEARINGS
ON THE SAME OBJECT

The distance to advance the first bearing is equal to the distance between the DR positions plotted for the times of earlier and later bearings.

bearing and, similarly, plot the second bearing and DR position on the course line. Then advance the first bearing along the course line for the amount of the distance run between bearings (use dividers, don't bother with $D = ST$); the intersection of the advanced line and the second bearing gives an R FIX, as shown in Figure 32. The method may also be used with change of course and is useful for bearings such as on a lighthouse while rounding a headland.

Two special cases of a running fix by two bearings on the same object are well known to commercial pilots, the *bow and beam bearing* and the *7/10 rule*. Both are based on the geometrics of the plane triangle and require that constant course and speed be maintained. *All bearings are relative.*

The *bow and beam bearing* takes advantage of the known relationship of the component parts of a right isosceles triangle; a bearing is taken on a known object when it bears 45° and a second bearing is taken when the object bears 90°. The distance run between the first and second bearings is the distance off the object when abeam.

The *7/10 rule* also doubles the angle on the bow, the distance run between bearings equaling the object's distance off at the second bearing, and 7/10 of the distance run equaling the distance off the object when it is abeam. (Fig. 33.)

Other relationships will come to the minds of those geometrically astute: 30° and 60° bearings give a distance run between bearings equal to the object's distance off at the time of the second bearing, and 7/8 of that distance will equal the distance the object will be passed abeam. Bearing combinations of 22°–34°, 25°–41°, and 27°–46° all provide a distance when abeam equal to the distance run between bearings, as do several other combinations not involving whole degrees. *Bowditch* (Table 7) gives both distance off at a second bearing and predicted distance off when abeam for a run of one mile between relative bearings.

Estimated Position

An estimated position (EP) is the most probable position in the absence of a fix or running fix, and is obtained by adjusting the DR position for the effect of current and other influences on

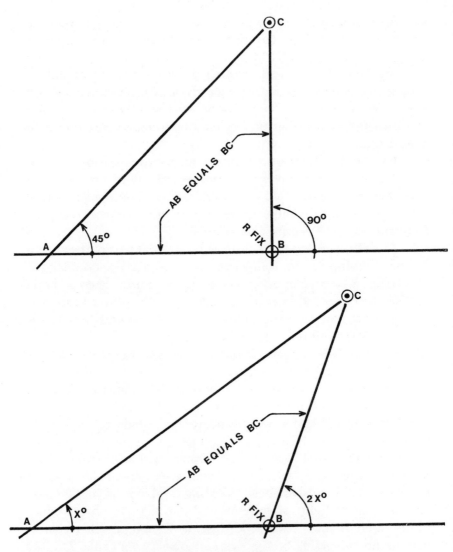

FIGURE 33. SPECIAL CASES OF THE RUNNING FIX

a. *Bow and beam bearing:* When the first bearing on object C is 45° the distance run from A to B (abeam, bearing 90°) equals the distance off C.

b. *Double the bearing:* When the bearing of C from B is double the bearing of C from A, the distance off C equals the distance run from A to B.

the DR course plot. Although a DR plot is always continuously maintained as the basic charted representation of position between fixes, an EP plot is desirable at times when it can contribute to the avoidance of sailing a hazardous course, as when approaching a headland or shoal. It is usually sufficient to plot an EP periodically, without constructing an auxiliary course line from it. The label of an estimated position is a small square enclosing the position point, with the time and EP entered alongside, as ⊡ 0847 EP.

An EP may be plotted whenever a bearing is taken—good practice when sailing along a shoreline to assure not being further inshore than the DR plot may indicate—by assuming that the ship is somewhere on the line of position (the bearing line) and that the EP is that point on the line closest to the DR position at the time of the bearing. The method of plotting an EP, therefore, is to plot a DR position for the time of the bearing and drop a perpendicular from the DR position to the bearing line. The point on the bearing line intersected by the perpendicular is the position point of the EP.

Estimated position, with current as a factor, is discussed below.

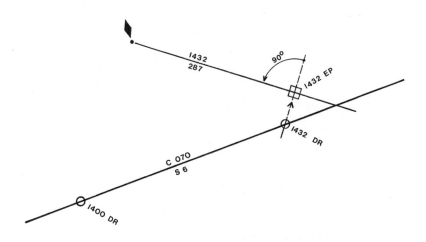

**FIGURE 34. ESTIMATED POSITION FROM A
BEARING LINE**

Current Plotting

Current is discussed in Chapter VII. To summarize its essential characteristics necessary to understand plotting: (1) current effect includes the horizontal movement of water, leeway, steering error, and other influences on the discrepancy between an EP and a DR position; (2) the *set* of a current is the true (never magnetic) direction toward which it flows; and (3) the *drift* of a current is its speed in knots and tenths of knots. Total drift is measured for the time it has been acting on the course since the time of the last fix (not the time elapsed from a previous DR or R FIX). Current charts are published for many popular waterways, pilot charts indicate the set and drift of ocean currents; in the absence of recorded data, or as a check on its local applicability, the navigator determines the actual current effect by plotting a fix in relation to a DR position.

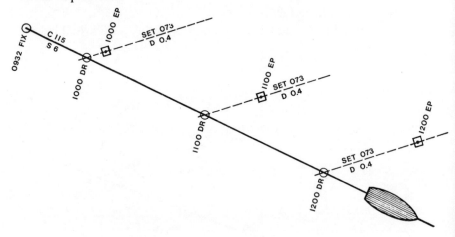

FIGURE 35. ESTIMATED POSITION WHEN CURRENT IS KNOWN

Observe that D (drift) is stated as speed and is not a measure of distance traveled by the current (which is the product of drift and the time elapsed from that of the last fix). A running fix cannot be used as a time base, however the advanced bearing line of a running fix may be adjusted for current.

Current labels: A dashed line is constructed to show direction of flow, with set and true direction (three digits, no symbol) labeled above the line and D (drift) in knots and tenths labeled below,

as $\dfrac{\text{Set } 043}{\text{D } 0.8}$.

More often than not the navigator is unsure of the current and seeks to determine its characteristics in order to establish position and the correct course to steer to compensate for its offset. Should the current parallel the course (a "fair" current) the EP will be on the course line in advance of a DR position calculated

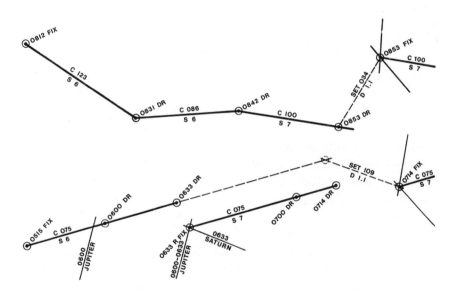

FIGURE 36. FINDING CURRENT SET AND DRIFT AT THE TIME OF A FIX

a. *With a continuous course line:* Set is measured from the DR to a fix of the same time; drift is the distance, expressed per hour, of the offset from the DR to the fix.

b. *With intervening running fix:* Any intervening R FIX is disregarded in finding current effect between the time of two fixes. The original course line is extended by the distance required for the time of the second fix, and the set and drift plotted and measured from that point to the point of the second fix.

for the same time. Should the current be foul the DR position will be in advance of the EP. Drift in these circumstances is easily found and is the difference between speed over the ground and speed in the water. Such simplification is rarely the case; current set is usually oblique to the course line and a fix (not running fix) is needed to determine the set and drift affecting the ship's progress. A DR position is plotted for the time of a fix; the set is indicated by a line constructed from the DR to the fix and the drift is then calculated by measurement of the distance between the DR and fix as divided by the time elapsed (in hours and tenths of hours) from the last fix. Changes of course or speed between fixes do not affect the solution.

The value of preplotting when the current characteristics are known, or have been determined as shown above, is of inestimable help in determining the course to steer in order to make good the intended course. Referring again to Figure 35, it is apparent that a steered course of 115° will not bring the ship to the 1200 DR position; it will be at the 1200 EP, or thereabouts. To arrive at the 1200 DR it will be necessary to compensate for the current effect. An approximate correction under sail is to measure the angle formed by the intended course line and a line constructed from the last fix (0932 FIX in the example) through the EPs, and apply the arc measurement so found as a correction to the charted course to find the course to steer in order to make good the DR track. A powered vessel can compensate more precisely with the aid of a simply constructed vector diagram (Fig. 37) which uses the known factors of speed, current set and drift, and intended track to solve for the course to steer and speed of advance. The method is as follows:

1. Plot the intended track, i.e., the DR course line, for an indefinite length.
2. From the origin point of the intended track (which label A for reference) plot a current line corresponding to the direction of the current set and equal in length to the drift, or current distance moved in one hour. Label the terminal point of the current line B.
3. Span, using dividers or a lead pencil compass, the distance to be run in one hour. Transpose this distance from B to its intersection with the intended track. Label this point C.
4. Measure the direction of line B–C. This is the course to steer.

5. Measure the distance from A to C on the intended track. This distance (since the vector was plotted for one hour's current effect) is the same as the speed of advance along the intended track (which will not be the ship's speed as registered by instrument).

As with all true courses, the course to steer must be corrected by TVMDC (Chapter III).

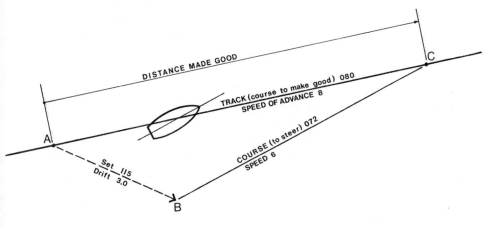

FIGURE 37. COURSE PLOTTING TO OFFSET CURRENT EFFECT

Plot of a one hour vector:

A–B: Set and drift of current.

B–C: Course to steer. Length of line B–C determined by predicted actual speed over the ground without current.

A–C: Course made good over the desired track. Distance from A to C equals actual speed of advance over the track.

Regardless of time and distance involved the course to steer remains unchanged until a change in current characteristics occurs, at which time a new vector is constructed.

Celestial Observations

When offshore the navigator finds position by observation of celestial bodies, and consolidates their lines of position into a fix or a running fix according to the time elapsed between observations. The time intervals at sea are much less stringent than those allowable inshore; a round of star sights may take fifteen minutes or more to complete but will be considered timely for a fix. The running sight is the mainstay of celestial position finding, a shot of the sun frequently being taken in the early morning and advanced to combine with another observation of the sun at noon. In general, celestial plotting is closely akin to the procedures employed in piloting waters; both depend on the DR course plot being continuously maintained for the basic graphical representations of the ship's travel pattern. Celestial plotting is essentially line of position (LOP) construction based on the azimuths (celestial bearings) of observed bodies. A body's geographic position (GP) having been determined, a terrestrial LOP is constructed on the chart or plotting sheet *at right angles to the bearing of the GP.* LOPs are plotted, according to the sight reduction method preferred (Chapter XIV), from the DR position or from an assumed position (AP). The difference between the altitude found by sextant and the computed altitude is termed the *intercept,* and positions the LOP either *toward* or *away* from the object observed in relation to the ship's assumed or DR position.

Plotting and labeling: With the few exceptions and special cases noted below, celestial plotting and labeling is synonymous with that for inshore waters previously described.

Line of position: Time labeled above the line (both times when advanced) and name of the object below, as

   1620   . Note that direction is not indicated.
Arcturus

Direction, other than course and current, is not labeled and is always *true,* whether labeled or implied.

Assumed position: Point enclosed with a small circle, with time (four digits) and AP entered alongside at an angle to the latitude line. Example: ☉ 1232 AP

Intercept: Not labeled on plot, being understood by inspection. Construct with a dashed line; some navigators prefer to extend the line in the direction of the body (as shown in Figure 38 for clarity) and label the symbol of the body at the terminus. It makes for a pretty chart but is fast fading into disuse as an unnecessary frill.

Coordinates: Always included in the label of a fix or running fix. Place in a rectangle, as

⊙ 1425 R FIX | L 14° 16.2′N |
               | λ 157° 39.2′W |

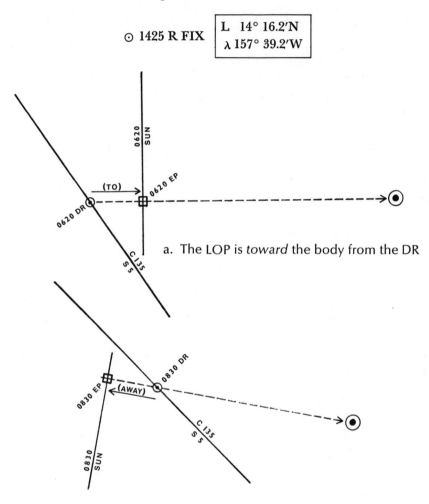

a. The LOP is *toward* the body from the DR

b. The LOP is *away* from the DR.

FIGURE 38. INTERCEPT AND ESTIMATED POSITION

The intercept is the distance from the DR to the EP along the azimuth line to the body, regardless of whether it is toward or away.

Estimated position with current: The strength of many ocean currents, and the availability of their characteristics from pilot charts and other reliable sources, makes it advisable to plot an *EP with current* on lines of position as obtained; the practice will reduce position error importantly in many instances: Plot total drift (calculated from the time of the last fix to the time of the LOP) from the DR in the direction of set. The EP with current is then located at the foot of a perpendicular constructed from the end of the current line to the LOP.

Fix: Two or more LOPs obtained in a round of sights con-

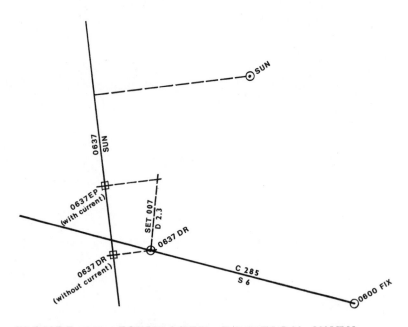

FIGURE 39. ESTIMATED POSITION WITH CURRENT

The importance of plotting for current effect is highlighted in the situation shown above; observe the more accurate location of the EP with current than the EP plotted at the nearest point on the LOP to the DR, which is customary when current effect is unknown. The modifier "current" need not be incorporated into the label because the angular construction lines make the type of EP obvious by inspection.

stitute a fix when adjusted for a common time, which may be any convenient minute during the observation period but usually is the time of the latest observation. The speed of the ship between observations determines the distance by which the LOPs are advanced or retarded. When the intercept is plotted from a DR, the LOPs are moved as if they were being applied to a running fix. When an AP intercept is involved, the AP is advanced or retired to parallel the movement of the ship during the interim and the LOP is then constructed.

Should a change in course be made between observations, the AP (or APs) established before the course change are advanced (or retarded) by the distance and direction made good by the ship between the time of observation and the time of the fix.

Running fix: In celestial navigation a line of position may be advanced several hours to combine with a later observation (fre-

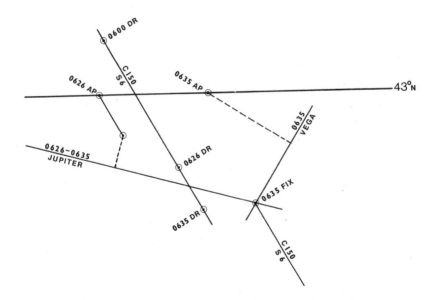

FIGURE 40. FIX FROM ASSUMED POSITIONS

The 0626 AP has been moved parallel to the course line for the equivalent distance the ship has moved from the time of the observation to the time of the fix. LOPs are then constructed for the time of the fix.

quently the same body observed twice) and form a running fix. The method of advancing an earlier celestial LOP is exactly that described previously for observations obtained in piloting waters of landmarks and aids to navigation (see pp. 63–65). When the set and drift are known, it is advisable to establish the *R FIX with current* which may be done, as shown in Figure 42, by following these steps:

1. From any point on the LOP to be advanced construct a dashed line parallel to the course line and equal in length to the distance transited from the time of the original observation to the

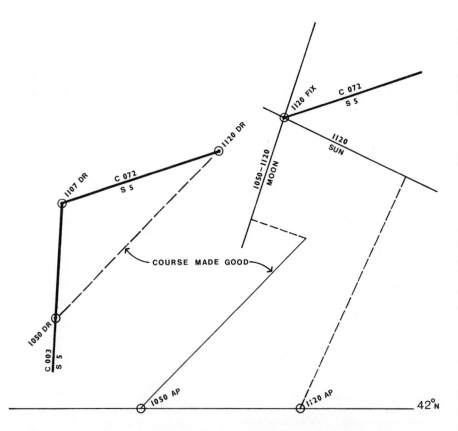

FIGURE 41. FIX WITH CHANGE OF COURSE

When an AP is established before a change in course, it is advanced by the amount of the direction and *course made good* from the time of the AP observation to the time of the fix.

time of the R FIX; the terminus of this line is the point where an LOP without current would intersect when advanced.

2. Knowing the set and drift, construct a current vector in the direction of the set and for a distance equal to the total drift between the times of observations; the origin of the current line is at the point where the LOP without current would intersect the parallel course line.

3. At the end of the current line construct the advanced LOP parallel to the original LOP. No correction for current is necessary for the LOP obtained for the time of the fix.

Set and drift are plotted from the point where an LOP without current would intersect the DR at the time of the second LOP observation.

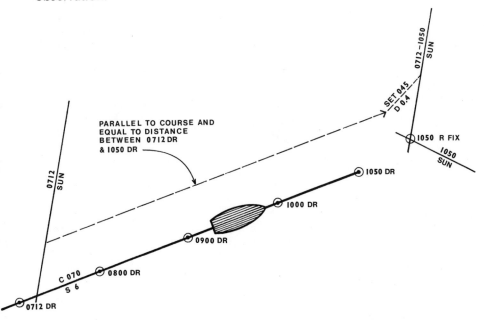

FIGURE 42. RUNNING FIX WITH CURRENT KNOWN

Time Zone Change

When crossing from one time zone to the next zone, the hour hand of the timepiece must be either advanced sixty minutes (crossing from west to east) or retarded (east to west). Practically, rather than changing time at the instant of traverse, the zone time should be changed at the first whole hour after crossing the zone boundary and so labeled on the hourly DR. On the chart, or plotting sheet, the zone boundary is indicated by a dashed vertical line labeled on each side with the proper zone description.

One hour of time has elapsed during the transit (eastward) from one time zone to another.

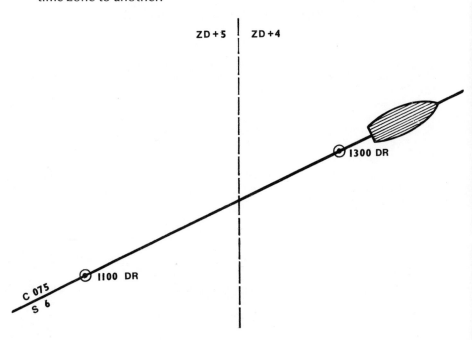

FIGURE 43. TIME ZONE PLOT

Great Circle Course

A great circle course provides the shortest distance between two points, but cannot be exactly followed because the course direction on the circumference of a circle is constantly changing; selected chords of the circle are therefore plotted as rhumb line courses to follow. Great circle and rhumb lines differ but little for distances up to 600 miles, or when constructed approximately

north–south. The significantly shorter distance of a great circle is
found east–west at distances of more than 600 miles.

A great circle course is obtained from a gnomonic, or "great
circle," chart (Chapter II) and transposed to a Mercator chart in
this way:

1. Construct a straight line on the gnomonic chart from departure
   to destination.

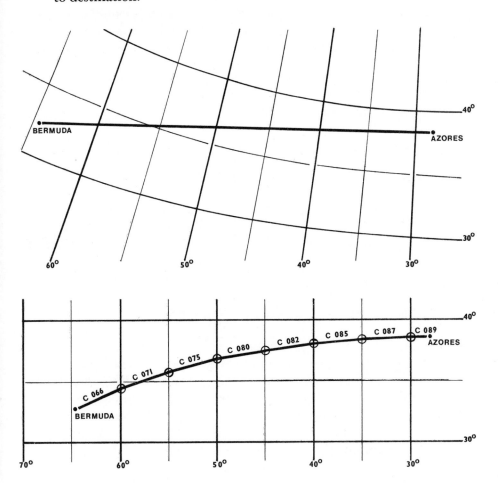

FIGURE 44. GREAT CIRCLE COURSE PLOT

a. Great circle course plotted on a gnomonic chart.
b. Great circle course in chord rhumb lines transferred to a Mercator
   chart.

2. At convenient equal distances along the line, label the coordinates of latitude and longitude (every 5° of longitude works well for most transoceanic passages).
3. Transfer to a Mercator chart, drawing rhumb lines between the coordinates selected along the line of the gnomonic chart. These rhumb lines become the chords of the great circle course to sail.
4. Measure the true direction of each rhumb line chord and label course for each. The cumulative distance of the course is obtained by combining the distances of the individual rhumb lines, none of which will exactly equal another.

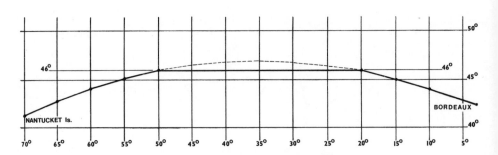

FIGURE 45. COMPOSITE COURSE

A *composite course* combines great circle and rhumb line courses to avoid hazards and is determined by plotting the course line on a gnomonic chart and then inspecting for danger areas crossed or adjacent to the line. A *limiting line* of latitude may be plotted to avoid prolonged exposure to ice (North Atlantic) or gale conditions (South Pacific below the "Roaring Forties"). For an obstacle hazarding a small sector, such as an island, two off-setting rhumb line courses from and returning to the great circle track may suffice. Should deviation from the great circle to avoid hazard be prolonged, it is usually advantageous to plot a new great circle track after passing the hazard. Figure 45 illustrates a composite course plotted to avoid passing north of latitude 46° N between Nantucket and Bordeaux.

Special Situation Plotting

Following are some assorted "wrinkles" for plotting in non-routine situations:

Making a landfall: When unsure of one's position in relation

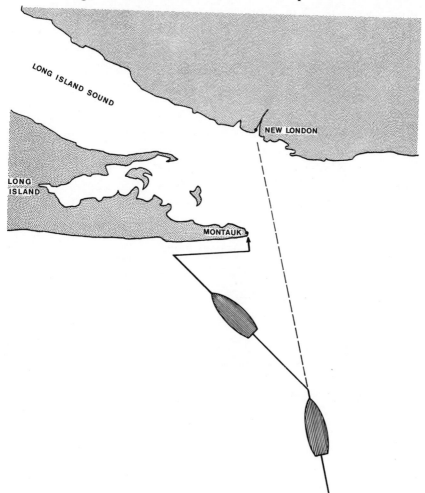

FIGURE 46. LANDFALL BY AN OFFSET COURSE

Approaching Montauk from seaward, and uncertain of the ship's position, an offset course to a landfall is sailed which will ensure not leaving Montauk abeam.

to the desired destination, chart a course from the DR position which will without question carry the ship to a known general direction from the destination when land is sighted, at which point sail along the coast toward the destination. The example of Figure 46, illustrates a situation where Montauk, at the tip of Long Island, is the wanted destination on an approach from seaward with uncertain DR position (perhaps caused by inability to obtain sights in fog and a distrust of RDF bearings). If the course is too high the ship will continue on toward New London on Long Island Sound, therefore a course is set for the Long Island shore sufficiently west of Montauk to ensure not passing it to the eastward.

Danger bearing: When a course must pass close to a danger, such as a shoal, a quicker method than fixing position several times in rapid succession is to construct a danger bearing from the aid to navigation marking the danger area which will indicate the limit of the hazard on the side being passed. The bearing is labeled *to* the aid on the chart.

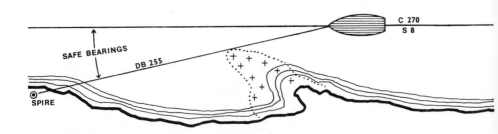

FIGURE 47. DANGER BEARING

In the example shown, the ship avoids the danger area as long as the bearings are less than the 255° danger bearing.

Position when a DR plot has not been kept: Many skippers out for a day sail do not bother with a DR plot in familiar waters, and sailing craft, when constantly tacking, present difficulty in plotting courses. When in need of a position, and only one known object is available for reference, a running fix can be made on the object without prior knowledge of DR course or speed: Take a bearing on the object and steer a steady course and speed toward an area from which another differing by at least 30° can be taken of the same object. Plot DR course and speed from a point anywhere on the bearing line, advance the first bearing according to the distance made good (same procedure as for an R FIX with known DR plot) and the running fix will give position, because the course line assumed for the plot is parallel to the actual course line traversed.

The three-minute rule is a useful rule of thumb for estimating distance along a course. Distance in yards in three minutes equals the speed multiplied by 100. The ratio is obviously applicable to multiples of three minutes, as $D = 100S$, $D = 200S$, etc.

The rule of sixty gives the course change mentally, without recourse to chart plotting, to sail a desired distance off a landmark directly on the course line. The situation occurs when a distant landmark has been utilized to home on, but must obviously be passed on one side eventually. Divide 60 by the known distance to the object, the answer obtained is the number of degrees to alter course to pass at the desired distance off when multiplied by the desired distance off. For example, the ship is 4 miles distant from a lighthouse and on a collision course with it. The navigator wants to pass the lighthouse abeam at .2 mile (roughly 350 yards) and mentally performs:

$$\frac{60}{4} = 15 \times .2 = 3°, \text{ the amount of the course change.}$$

Steering error: helmsmen tend to steer high of the ordered compass course. If a consistent discrepancy between DR and fix position is found after allowing for known current, a corrected course to steer may result in closer following of the intended track. The table below is figured for a 10-mile course, and may be liberally interpolated:

Steering Error
(in 10 miles)

Error	Distance
1°	1060 ft.
5°	0.9 mi.
10°	1.8 mi.

Distance abeam by tangent of one bearing angle: Trigonometrics are outside the scope of this work, however if a copy of
Bowditch is aboard (as it should be on every fully found ship),
Table 31 can be consulted, without being understood, to find the
distance abeam after a bearing has been taken on the object from
any angle prior to coming abeam. The practice is worthwhile because it gives a quick fix by one bearing and a known distance:
(1) record the time and bearing angle (relative bearing) and maintain course and speed, (2) record the time abeam (relative bearing
90°), (3) compute the distance run (60D = ST), and (4) multiply
the distance run by the tangent of the bearing angle found in
Table 31. The answer is the distance off.

Example: (relative bearing 35°)

0.700 (tangent value of 35° from *Bowditch,* page 1347, Table 31)
× 4.3 (distance run)
——
3.0   (distance off when abeam)

In using Table 31 for this purpose, round off the tangent value to
three decimal places (actual value is 0.70021, overly precise).

A simplified extract of Table 31, accurate within ± 1% is
given below for relative bearings in multiples of 5°:

Tangent Values

Relative Bearing	Tangent	Relative Bearing
0°	0.000	90°
5	0.087	85
10	0.176	80
15	0.268	75
20	0.364	70
25	0.466	65
30	0.577	60
35	0.700	55
40	0.839	50
45	1.000	45

Distance off by height of an object: Mercator charts list the
heights of many objects, but the information as given is seldom

accurate for the conditions under which the object is observed. One must usually apply a correction for tide, which may be unknown. Many objects, including all lighthouses, are shown for a visibility range when the observer's eye is 15 feet above sea level —seldom the exact case on a yacht. The table below gives visibility distances (top of the object assumed) for objects of various heights above sea level. Two distances must be added, both for the height of the object and the height of the observer's eye, to obtain the total range of visibility. The method is helpful when approaching land; a bearing on a lighthouse and its distance in this situation gives a rough fix, actually more of an educated estimated position.

Distances of Visibility of Objects from Sea Level

Height (ft.)	Distance (mi.)	Height (ft.)	Distance (mi.)
5	2.6	80	10.2
10	3.6	85	10.5
15	4.4	90	10.8
20	5.1	95	11.1
25	5.7	110	11.4
30	6.3	120	12.5
35	6.8	130	13.0
40	7.2	140	13.5
45	7.7	150	14.0
50	8.1	200	16.2
55	8.5	250	18.1
60	8.9	300	19.8
65	9.2	350	21.4
70	9.6	400	22.9
75	9.9	500	25.6

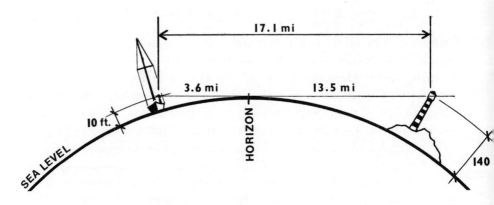

FIGURE 48. DISTANCE OFF BY VISIBILITY
OF AN OBJECT

	Height		Distance to Horizon
Observer:	10	=	3.6
Object:	140	=	13.5
			17.1

chapter VI

Time

TIME IS THE MEASUREMENT of earth's rotation, and the sun is its reference point. Since the apparent rotation of the sun around earth is not at a constant rate, several kinds of time have been devised to serve various requirements—for example, until the mid-1920s the nautical day began twelve hours earlier than the calendar day. Fortunately for today's navigator the exotic concepts are now relegated to the realm of pure astronomy; the simplification of time as used nowadays in navigation has been a major contribution in lifting the façade of mysticism which characterized the art for centuries. The importance of a thorough understanding of the applications of time can hardly be overemphasized; *more errors in navigation are attributable to time miscalculation than to any other cause.* It is suggested that the arithmetic of time (Appendix A) be reviewed until its methods become automatic. The neophyte navigator will find it helpful to concentrate on thinking in terms of the twenty-four-hour clock, rather than in the landsman's A.M. and P.M. equivalents.

Three kinds of time, interchangeable as circumstances dictate, are used in surface navigation:

1. *Apparent time:* The apparent rotation of the sun around earth is the basis of apparent time, its daily circuit seldom being exactly twenty-four hours. Modern navigation practice is to disregard apparent time except to find the time of apparent noon (Chapter XV), which enables an observation of the sun resulting in a latitude line of position.

2. *Mean time:* To compensate for the irregularity of apparent time the device of mean time is employed, based on a fictitious sun moving westward along the equator at a constant rate and thereby transiting every longitude meridian at a constant interval of time. The imaginary mean sun transits each 15° of longitude in exactly sixty minutes and completes its daily circuit of earth in exactly twenty-four hours. *Local mean time*

(LMT) is the time the mean sun transits the local meridian. *Greenwich mean time* (GMT), the standard almanac reference for celestial data, is the local mean time at the Greenwich meridian (longitude 0°). Mean time is impractical for the ordinary requirements of a time to regulate everyday activities because any two positions not on the same meridian will have different local mean times. For example, the LMT at Montauk Point at the eastern tip of Long Island differs (later) from LMT at New York Harbor by twelve and a half minutes.

Navigators have frequent need of reference to GMT, but LMT is rarely required; for this reason the ship's chronometer is habitually oriented to GMT.

Mean time may differ from apparent time by as much as fifteen minutes. The adjustment for interconversion is found on the daily pages of the *Nautical Almanac,* and termed the *Equation of Time* (Eq T).

3. *Zone time:* Because of the impracticability of attempting to regulate workaday activity by local mean time, an effective compromise is found in *zone time* (ZT) which takes the local mean time of a central meridian, all places within the boundaries of the zone keeping the same time; timepieces are reset by one whole hour whenever a zone boundary is crossed. At sea the central meridian of the zone is usually a longitude meridian which is an exact multiple of 15, with the boundaries extending east and west to 7½° from the central meridian. The zone system divides earth into 24 time zones, each encompassing 15° of longitude and individually numbered to indicate the hours by which the zone time differs from Greenwich mean time; the number, with its sign, is the *zone description* (ZD) and is applied to the zone time to obtain GMT. *Zone time is labeled on all chart plots* used in surface navigation.

Time zones are portrayed graphically on H. O. Chart 5192. The *Nautical* and *Air* almanacs list standard times kept by countries and principal islands, some of which do not adhere to the logical time of their longitude.

Daylight saving time (DST), ignored in navigation, adjusts the local time eastward by the amount of one time zone. Synonyms used outside the United States for DST are "summer time" or "fast time."

World Time Zones

West Longitude			East Longitude		
Descrip-tion	Central Meridian	Zone Boundaries	Descrip-tion	Central Meridian	Zone Boundaries
ZD 0	0°	0.0°– 7.5°	ZD 0	0°	0.0°– 7.5°
ZD + 1	15	7.5 – 22.5	ZD – 1	15	7.5 – 22.5
ZD + 2	30	22.5 – 37.5	ZD – 2	30	22.5 – 37.5
ZD + 3	45	37.5 – 52.5	ZD – 3	45	37.5 – 52.5
ZD + 4	60	52.5 – 67.5	ZD – 4	60	52.5 – 67.5
ZD + 5	75	67.5 – 82.5	ZD – 5	75	67.5 – 82.5
ZD + 6	90	82.5 – 97.5	ZD – 6	90	82.5 – 97.5
ZD + 7	105	97.5 –112.5	ZD – 7	105	97.5 –112.5
ZD + 8	120	112.5 –127.5	ZD – 8	120	112.5 –127.5
ZD + 9	135	127.5 –142.5	ZD – 9	135	127.5 –142.5
ZD +10	150	142.5 –157.5	ZD –10	150	142.5 –157.5
ZD +11	165	157.5 –172.5	ZD –11	165	157.5 –172.5
ZD +12	180	172.5 –180.0	ZD –12	180	172.5 –180.0

Observe that the Greenwich meridian (Long 0°) and the international date line (Long 180°) are centers of time zones with boundaries in both east and west longitude. The date changes when crossing the date line, but zone time does not.

Zone description: The correction applied to a time zone to obtain GMT is termed the zone description (ZD), which is composed of a sign (+ or —) and a number; the sign indicates whether the number is to be added or subtracted from zone time to find GMT ("follow the sign to Greenwich"). All signs in west longitude are *plus* because it is *later* to the eastward, the sun having passed Greenwich before passing any other point to the westward; the obvious converse is that the sign of ZD is *minus* in east longitude because time there is *earlier* than at Greenwich. The sign of ZD is never changed, regardless of how the number is applied. When ZD is used to find the zone time *from Greenwich* the sign is written as usual and suffixed (rev) indicating that the number has been applied in the reverse direction.

To determine the ZD number, select the nearest longitude meridian exactly divisible by 15 (it will be within $7\frac{1}{2}°$ of the position), the quotient, i.e., the number obtained from dividing by 15, becomes the ZD number as shown below for a DR in Long 71° 20.3′ W:

75°W　nearest central meridian within $7\frac{1}{2}°$

$$\frac{75}{15} = 5 = \text{ZD number}$$

sign $= +$　(west longitude, must *add* to go to later GMT)

ZD +5 (complete solution)

Zone time at another place: When the zone time at another place is in the *same* longitude (east or west) finding its ZT is a matter of simple addition or subtraction because both positions have the same ZD sign. When zone time at a position in *opposite* longitude is to be found it is safer to "go to Greenwich": Convert the first zone time to GMT and apply the time from Greenwich to the second position time zone. The methods for finding time at another place are shown in the examples below, which illustrate the difference in zone time at St. Thomas (ZD + 4) from New York (ZD + 5) in the same longitude, and from San Francisco (ZD + 8) and Sydney (ZD − 10) in opposite name longitudes:

			San Francisco	ZT 0900	
				ZD+ 8	
New York	ZT 0900			GMT 1700	(same day)
	ZD+ 5		Sydney	ZD−10	(rev)
	GMT 1400			2700	
	ZD+ 4	(rev.)		−24	
St. Thomas	1000			ZT 0300	(next day)

Observe above that the sign of the St. Thomas and Sydney ZDs is applied in *reverse* because time in this instance is being found *away* from Greenwich. When calculating time at another place it is essential to find whether a change in date takes place; if so, write both dates opposite their respective times.

International date line (Long 180° E and W): Zone time does not change when crossing the date line, but a named day is gained or lost with the date. One gains crossing eastward and loses westward. The slogan "Sunday Seattle, Monday Manila" is a useful reminder.

Time and Longitude

The relationship of time and longitude is frequently useful, particularly in celestial navigation. Prior to the development of the chronometer, which indicates accurate time at sea, it was impossible to find accurate longitude (which depends upon an accurate knowledge of time) and sailors such as Columbus had to "run down the latitude" of the destination and then sail due east or west until they made a landfall. The relationship is shown by the examples extracted below:

	Arc	*Time*	
(circle)	360° =	24 hours	(1 day)
	15° =	1 hour	
	1° =	4 minutes	
	15′ =	1 minute	
	1′ =	4 seconds	
(0.25′)	¼′ =	1 second	

Almanacs and most sight reduction tables contain inspection tables showing the interconversions of arc and time. Inspection is usually quicker (unless the conversion is obvious), and reduces the possibility of error, than working the problem mathematically. The conversion table published in the *Air Almanac* will be found in Appendix B.

Interconversion of zone time and local mean time: Aside from its uses in celestial navigation (Chapter IX) the arc-time relationship has important application in converting zone time to local mean time, since at any two places the local mean times differ by the difference of longitude (DLo) between the two places. Consider the method of finding LMT for a ship positioned in Long 55° 29.2′ W, at ZT 13h 26m 22s:

Central time meridian 60° 00.0′W
       (−) DR 55° 29.2′W

DLo 4° 30.8′E = 16m (1° = 4 min)
                    2m (15′ = 1 min)
                    03s (.25′ = 1 sec)

ZT 13h 26m 22s
(+) DLo 18m 03s   18m 03s

LMT 13h 44m 25s

Observe that the DLo arc converted to time is *added* to ZT in this example because the DR was east of the central meridian (where ZT and LMT are identical) and therefore the time is *later* than at the central meridian.

Timekeeping

Expressing time: In solving time problems, unless of a rudimentary nature, the navigator deals in time to the nearest second, as recorded on his work sheets. Time shown on chart plots, as time of a fix, bearing, etc., is recorded to the nearest whole minute even though seconds were calculated. Time is always given in the twenty-four-hour system, in four digits when seconds are omitted. Four-digit time is normally written without separation of hours and minutes, as 0853, but separated by dashes when seconds are to be included, as 08–53–20. When important for clarification, abbreviations are suffixed in place of the dashes, as 3d 16h 42m 08s. Unless otherwise indicated, a recorded time is assumed to be zone time.

The suffix "Z" (pronounced "Zulu" or "Zebra") is sometimes employed to designate GMT, and is part of a military communications system of substituting letters for zone description. The system has obvious disadvantages for the cruising civilian navigator and is only recorded here so that it may be recognized when encountered.

Beginning navigators betray their inexperience by mispronouncing four digit time: 1400 is "fourteen hundred," never "one four hundred"; zero is pronounced "oh" when used as a prefix, as "oh four hundred." The one area of poetic license is found in the first nine minutes after midnight, when every possible permutation and combination of "zero" and "oh" is emitted to enliven what otherwise is apt to be an uninspiring watch. Not even *Bowditch,* the bible of the black-shoe navy, has attempted to umpire this one.

Expressing date: Mentioned elsewhere and repeated here for emphasis, the importance of recording the proper date with time is obvious. *The date is an integral part of the time label on work sheets.* Error intrudes when a time at Greenwich is of a different date than that of the ship's zone time, and the almanac is then mistakenly consulted for a quantity twenty-four hours away from the true time and quantity; an observation on a celestial body so erroneously obtained can result in a position error of more than fifty miles. As a rule of thumb: Any time computation totaling more than twenty-four hours involves a date change, as does a calculation where twenty-four hours must first be added to achieve a positive result. Date changes are not necessarily limited to these two conditions.

Timepieces

The ideal minimum combination of timepieces carried aboard an offshore passage-maker includes: a chronometer (for GMT), a watch (ZT) and a stopwatch. This timekeeping triumvirate is far from essential, as proven rather conclusively by Joshua Slocum's solo circumnavigation aided only by an alarm clock for keeping track of time, but it is most desirable for convenience and safety. All of these timepieces are subject to cumulative inaccuracy:

Error is the difference between indicated and correct time, the amount being more nuisance than concern, provided it is a known quantity. To correct error subtract the amount fast or add the amount slow. Label error (f) or (s).

Rate is the amount gained or lost in twenty-four hours, a uniform rate being highly desirable. Rate is determined by dividing the net gain or loss (minutes and tenths) between two dates by the number of days (and tenths) intervening, and labeled *gaining* or *losing*.

Chronometer: A chronometer is a very accurate and expensive timepiece requiring and deserving tender loving care in order to preserve its uniform rate. It is invariably set to GMT, not only for convenience but also because it should never be reset at sea. As received from the retailer or repair shop a good chronometer should be running on GMT at a rate gaining or losing not more than one second per day, which should be so stated on the accompanying certificate. Such a chronometer need not be overhauled more than once in every three years (Navy practice) under normal conditions, hence the cumulative error can become substantial during the interim and should be computed and recorded at frequent intervals (multiply the known rate by the number of days since the last recording). Radio time signals are a convenient means of checking the rate and error.

Chronometer time (C) is the difference between *chronometer error* (CE) and Greenwich mean time:

$$\begin{array}{ll} \text{C} & \text{14h 06m 18s} \\ \text{CE} - & \quad\text{9m 43s (f)} \\ \hline \text{GMT} & \text{13h 56m 35s} \end{array}$$

Watch: Any reliable nonmagnetic, water-resistant watch with a sweep second hand may be used for zone timekeeping and should be reset at least daily unless the rate is minimal. The rate will be more stable, with consequent reduction of error, if the watch is positioned horizontally and kept as immobile as possible; wristwatches, when worn, fluctuate greatly in rate.

Watch time (WT) is the difference between *watch error* (WE) and zone time:

$$\begin{array}{ll} \text{WT} & \text{09h 55m 21s} \\ \text{WE} + & \quad\text{1m 14s (s)} \\ \hline \text{ZT} & \text{09h 56m 35s} \end{array}$$

Correcting watch error: By far the easiest method of correcting watch error is to find the correct time by radio signal, the difference between the watch setting and the time of the signal being the correction to make. One must know the zone time kept by the transmitting station and apply zone difference as needed. *Caution*: a time signal received from a commercial radio station may be for DST (one hour later than standard zone time), or may emanate from a locality not observing zone time according to its longitude. If in doubt, consult the *Nautical* or *Air* almanac listings of nonconforming areas.

A more laborious method of finding watch error, recommended only during periods of radio silence, is the ancient practice of simultaneously comparing the watch and chronometer: CE must be taken into account, "go to Greenwich," watch the dates, and reverse the application of the ZD sign, as shown here for a ship in Long 60° E:

$$
\begin{array}{lll}
\text{C} & \text{21h 15m 22s} & \\
\text{CE} + & \text{19m 13s} & \text{(s)} \\
\hline
\text{GMT} & \text{21h 34m 35s} & \text{same day} \\
\text{ZD} - \text{4h} & & \text{(rev)} \\
\hline
& \text{25h 34m 35s} & \\
& -24 & \\
\hline
\text{ZT} & \text{01h 34m 35s} & \text{next day} \\
\text{WT} & \text{01h 36m 17s} & \\
\hline
\text{WE} & \text{1m 32} & \text{(f)}
\end{array}
$$

Finding GMT by watch: Watch time, corrected for watch error, may be used to find GMT by applying the zone difference:

$$
\begin{array}{lll}
\text{WT} & \text{22h 15m 07s} & \\
\text{WE} + & \text{1m 21s} & \text{(s)} \\
\hline
\text{ZT} & \text{22h 16m 28s} & \\
\text{ZD} + 4 & & \text{(Long 65°W example)} \\
\hline
& \text{26h} & \\
& -24 & \\
\hline
\text{GMT} & \text{02h 16m 28s} & \text{next day}
\end{array}
$$

Many an amateur navigator has made a successful transoceanic voyage by using the above method of finding GMT with his watch, relying on radio time signals for correction of watch time without benefit of chronometer. In lieu of carrying a chronometer, the use of the battery powered "tuning fork" timepiece is finding increasing popularity with small-craft sailors who rely on the manufacturer's advertised rate when radio time correction is not obtainable.

Stopwatch: A stopwatch should be free of appreciable error for the period of its normal maximum use and is useful in checking the chronometer against radio time signals, finding the exact second of a celestial observation, and timing light periods and synchronized signals when in coastal waters. The method of using a stopwatch is usually an obvious one; as an aid in timing celestial observations it should first be started at a known correct time (ZT or GMT), then its reading at the time of each sight (do not *stop* the watch for a sight) is added to the base time at which the stopwatch was started to determine the precise time of the observation. Without a stopwatch one must take the sight and estimate the seconds intervening before consultation with the watch or chronometer; with practice, considerable accuracy can be obtained for short periods by saying aloud in cadence "one hippopotamus, two hippopotamus," etc., each "hippopotamus" representing one second of time, an old basketball referee's wrinkle that works surprisingly well. A herd of more than ten or twelve hippopotami is too many; keep the interval short between sight and time verification.

Radio Time Signals

Elsewhere (Chapter VIII), radio frequencies and the vagaries of electronic equipment in general are discussed in some detail. This section is devoted to information on the source and characteristics of American and Canadian time signals suitable for correcting time at sea. Complete information worldwide is contained in H. O. 117 A and B, *Radio Navigational Aids*.

Commercial radio stations issue times of varying accuracy on the hour and sometimes more frequently. Voice announcements are unsatisfactory since few announcers are concerned with split-second timing, they merely give approximations of the minute. A "bleep" signal not under control of the announcer may be regarded as approximately correct within 30 seconds. The time given is always the local time, which is not necessarily the standard zone time, nor the zone time of the receiver. A commercial signal is better than none at all, but should be given a low priority when accuracy is critical.

Time signal stations: The U.S. National Bureau of Standards and the Canadian government broadcast extremely precise time signals proceded by a voice announcement. The signals, or time "ticks," are broadcast continuously except for short periods of deliberate silence; one or more can be received (on good equipment attuned to a proper frequency) almost anywhere in the world.

WWV, Fort Collins, Colorado, makes a voice announcement of GMT just prior to every minute of the hour, as "the next tone begins at eleven hours, twenty-five minutes, Greenwich mean time." WWV signals are transmitted on 2.5, 5.0, 10.0, 15.0, 20.0, and 25.0 mHz.

WWVH, Maui, Hawaii makes a similar announcement, the voice preceding that on WWV but the tone signal synchronized with it. WWVH transmits on 2.5, 5.0, 10.0, 15.0 and 20.0 mHz.

CHU, Ottawa, Ontario, makes voice announcements in French and English just prior to each minute of the hour, giving the time of the next tone as "eastern standard time, eleven hours, twenty-five minutes." The station, which is powerful, is particularly well tuned in on by vessels on the Atlantic coast. The frequencies are 3.330, 7.335, and 14.670 mHz.

Telephone Time Signals

Affiliates of the American Telephone and Telegraph Company offer the revenue-producing service of exact time announcements every ten seconds. The time given is announced as local (standard) or daylight saving. This is not the same as dialing the operator and asking her what time it is; a specific number must be dialed as, in the New York area, ME 7–1212. Consult the local phone book for the number of the time service. WWV time signals may be heard by telephone; dial (303) 447–1192 to hear the broadcast as received by radio in Boulder, Colorado. Telephone time signals may be used to correct watch error, a helpful and expedient aid for one practicing with sextant ashore to improve familiarity and accuracy with that instrument.

Time Diagram

The time diagram is a cross section of the plane of the celestial equator as viewed from the celestial south pole. All westward movement along the equator is therefore counterclockwise. The diagram is helpful in visualizing a difference in dates between the observer's meridian and Greenwich, and the general correctness of GMT. Other constructions, not shown in Figure 49, can be plotted for celestial phenomena.

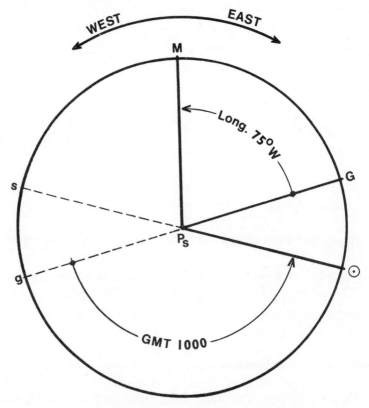

FIGURE 49. TIME DIAGRAM

The example is for GMT 1000 at Long 75°W. Position of the symbols will change according to other times and longitudes but the method remains constant. Observe that GMT in arc (1 hour = 15°) is constructed westward from g to position the sun.

Symbols:
M: Local (observer's) meridian.
G: Greenwich meridian (Long 0°).
g: International date line (Long 180°).
☉: Sun (1200 LMT).
s: Midnight (2400 LMT).
Ps: South celestial pole.

Basis of construction:

Aspect is from south celestial pole (ps).

15° arc = 1 hour time.

———— Upper branch of meridian, passing through a position zenith.

– – – – – Lower branch of meridian, passing through a position nadir.

Construction method:

1. Construct a circle on the plane of the celestial equator, with Ps at the center. Label Ps.
2. Construct upper branch of local meridian vertically from Ps. Label M.
3. Apply longitude (E or W) to locate Greenwich, which label G.
4. Construct Greenwich upper meridian from G to Ps. Extend lower branch to equator. Label g.
5. Find GMT for ZT of observer (apply zone difference; ZT ± ZD = GMT).
6. Plot sun position west from g by amount of GMT converted to arc (15° = 1 hour, use protractor). Label sun. Construct sun upper meridian to Ps, extend lower branch to equator and label s.

Interpretation: All measurements are made *westward* (counterclockwise). The diagram is useful to visualize celestial relationships (for moon, planet, and star location on diagram see Chapter XI) and is especially helpful when the date at the observer's meridian differs from that at Greenwich. To determine a difference in date extend the line M–Ps to the bottom of the diagram and label m (for lower branch of the observer's meridian). If the sun is then found to be *between* m and g, the meridian whose lower branch is westward of the sun will have an earlier date (one day) than Greenwich.

chapter VII

Tide, Current, Leeway, Wind

T IDE IS the vertical movement of water, current is its horizontal movement. Leeway is the effect of wind, and is generally considered to be a component of current since the end result of their combined force contributes to displacing the ship from the DR course.

Tide

Gravitational pull of the sun and moon is responsible for the changing levels of water, as most easily observed in tidewater areas. During any month the moon, due to its rapidly changing position with regard to earth, brings about correspondingly rapid changes in the heights of the tides. When the gravitational forces of moon and sun are in line, the tidal motion is exaggerated so that water rises and falls to extremes, termed *springs*. When the moon is in a first or last quarter these forces are at right angles, resulting in diminished high and low water levels known as *neap*. The high level of any tide is *high water* ("high tide" is a misnomer) and the low level is *low water*. Tide is motionless during the period of its *stand*. The difference in level between any two successive highs or lows is the *range*. One daily high and low is a *diurnal* tide, two highs and lows normally occurring in one day are a *semidiurnal* tide. In many parts of the United States the time interval between a high and low water is about six hours and fifteen minutes (semidiurnal). The average length of a tidal day is twenty-four hours and fifty minutes, hence tidal events tend to recur about fifty minutes later each day. Tide exists on the surface of oceans everywhere, not just inshore. The *height* of tide is measured from an arbitrarily established reference plane (*datum plane*) to the surface. Do not confuse height of tide with *depth* of water, which is the distance from the surface to the bottom and may at times be less than charted depth.

Datum levels: The water level from which charted depths are posted is an average of any one of several low waters, and not internationally standardized. References vary even on U.S. charts, the datum reference at one end of the Panama Canal not being that at the other end. Four principal references are:

> *Mean low water* (MLW): the average of all low tides, and the datum level on charts of the U.S. Atlantic and Gulf of Mexico Coasts.

> *Mean lower low water* (MLLW): the average of the lower of the two daily tides and datum level on charts of the U.S. Pacific Coast, Alaska, Hawaii, and the Philippines.

> *Lowest normal low water* (LNLW): Canadian charts.

> *Mean low water springs:* on many British Admiralty charts.

Other countries use other references, France perhaps playing it safest with *lowest low water* (than which there is nothing lower). References in most areas may be understood by derivation from the examples quoted here.

The datum plane is clearly printed on most charts issued today. When not, or if the reference is not understood, assume MLW for soundings, mean low water being the *highest* of the low water averages in use on modern charts.

Tide Tables: Predictions (not guarantees) of tidal height and time of occurrence are published annually in *Tide Tables* by the National Ocean Survey (formerly Coast and Geodetic Survey), and must be used only for the year of publication. Directions for use are clear and explicit, and not repeated here other than to state their general purpose and the cautions that should be observed in interpreting the data.

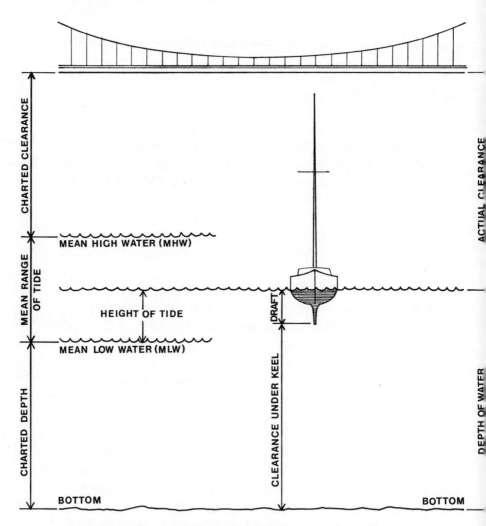

FIGURE 50. TIDE FACTORS

Table 1 lists the time and height of tide at each high and low water for each day of the year at selected reference stations, usually major ports. Because the tidal day's length does not coincide with a calendar day, three tides may at times be listed in twenty-four hours and only one tide on another day in areas of assumed semidiurnality.

Table 2 lists subordinate stations and their time difference from given reference stations as well as any other pertinent information needed to obtain the tidal data at the subordinate station. Apply the time difference, without change in sign, to the time of the phenomenon at the reference station. On occasion the result may be a *minus* correction to the datum plane at the subordinate station, which is not to be interpreted as a typographical error but rather to mean that the depth of the water is *less* than the charted depth by the amount of the negative quantity.

Interpolation for an area not listed may be made by selecting and computing the desired information for two subordinate stations (or the reference station and one subordinate station) on either side of the desired area. The results should be considered approximate, but the extreme limits will be known.

Table 3 is used to find height of the tide at any time other than those published in Table 1 or computed with Table 2.

Table 4 gives times of sunrise and sunset at LMT. See Chapter VI for method of converting local mean time to zone time.

Errors in working *Tide Tables* occur from failure to observe a different date at the subordinate station, applying the correction to the reference station instead of to the subordinate, reversing the correction sign, and carelessness with Table 3. The tables are intended for standard (zone) time; daylight saving time cannot be used, but must be adjusted to standard time by subtracting one hour from DST. A more serious error arises, even if the tables have been correctly worked, from misunderstanding their purpose and the meaning of the information derived from them: It must be remembered that *heights obtained from Tide Tables are heights above or below the datum level and not actual depths; they are corrections to charted depths.*

For semidiurnal tides, the height at any given time between high and low water can be roughly estimated by applying the cumulative percentage of hourly change, given below, to the range. The time of last high or low water must be known.

End of 1st hour	10% change in height
2nd	25%
3d	50%
4th	75%
5th	90%
6th	100%

Sources: *Tide Tables,* published annually by the National Ocean Survey in Washington, and available through authorized sales agents, are issued in four volumes: *Europe and West Coast of Africa* (including the Mediterranean Sea), *East Coast of North and South America* (including Greenland), *West Coast of North and South America* (including Hawaii), and the *Western Pacific and Indian Oceans.* In combination, the four volumes cover approximately 5000 stations worldwide. Many local area tables are published by private enterprise, based on the governmental data.

Current

Current may be any one of several types of horizontal water movement, and may be categorized under the two general headings of *tidal* or *ocean* current. The direction toward which current flows is its *set,* the speed is termed *drift.* The effect of current is to offset a vessel from its intended course if set and drift are not computed and a compensating heading adopted.

Tidal Current

Horizontal flow of water resulting from the rise and fall of tide is called tidal current, its phases being directly related to, but seldom coincident with, a tidal movement. A tidal current moving upstream or toward shore is a *flood* current, the reverse movement is an *ebb.* *Slack* current is comparable to the stand of a tide, the motionless period before reverse of direction.

Offshore the current experienced may be a combination of tidal and ocean currents. In a restricted area (such as a river, canal, or estuary) a tidal current flows alternately in opposite directions and is termed a *reversing* or *hydraulic* current. A tidal current in unrestricted waters is a *rotary* current, flowing through all points of the compass during the tidal period. *Counter currents* and *eddies* are found near straits and bights. *Tide rips* are formed by a rapid current moving over an irregular bottom.

Current Tables: The National Ocean Survey annually publishes *Current Tables* listing daily predictions of the times and strengths of currents and their intervening times of slack. Supplemental data enables prediction for places not specifically listed. As with the more extensive *Tide Tables,* directions for use are clear and explicit, and therefore not repeated here. However, the user should understand that predictions are for periods of normal circumstances and that tabulated drift is for maximum speed, which only occurs during the middle third of the period between slacks. It is normal for direction at a subordinate station to be different from that at the reference station—at times it may be reversed or nearly so.

Table 1 lists predicted data at reference stations, usually principal ports.

Table 2 lists subordinate stations with their reference stations indicated for the difference in the time of slack water and maximum current, and the direction and average velocities of flood and ebb currents. Differences should be applied according to their signs to obtain the time of phenomenon occurrence at the subordinate station. When direction of ebb is not listed, assume 180° from flood.

Table 3 enables the finding of current velocity at any specific time not otherwise listed.

Table 4 is used to find the duration of slack and the period surrounding slack when velocity does not exceed 1.0 knots.

Table 5 gives information on Atlantic rotary currents.

Sources: As with the companion *Tide Tables,* the National Ocean Survey and its sales agents distribute yearly *Current Tables.* There are two volumes: *Atlantic Coast of North America* and

Pacific Coast of North America and Asia. The appropriate volume for the year of issue must be used. Several nongovernmental tables, such as *Eldridge's* for Long Island Sound and contiguous waters, are regionally popular for the added detail and local knowledge they provide. The geographical scope of U.S. government tidal current data is not as extensive as for tides; one must consult the available tables published by the respective countries for areas not compiled by the National Ocean Survey. The *Sailing Directions* published by the U.S. Naval Hydrographic Office contain data on foreign harbors and their approaches.

Current Charts: Tidal current charts are published by the National Ocean Survey for Boston Harbor, Long Island Sound (including Block Island Sound), Naragansett Bay to Nantucket Sound, New York Harbor, Delaware Bay and River, San Francisco Bay, and Puget Sound. Unlike annual tables, the *Current Charts* are virtually perennial because they are concerned with direction and speed of tidal currents at hourly intervals before and after phenomena. The *Tide Tables* are consulted for the time of high, low, or slack water at the given reference station and the *Current Chart* visually reveals set (directional arrow) and drift at the selected hours from the reference station. The panoramic presentation of the state of tidal current in present and succeeding hours along the course simplifies the navigator's course planning.

Current diagram: Included in the *Current Tables* are diagrams of the principal U.S. tidal waterways, showing velocities at selected points and the time from current turning (reversal) at a reference station. From this information may be deduced the velocity of the current at any time for a given position, the average current along a section of the waterway, and the most advantageous time to take departure in terms of favorable current.

Ocean Current

Permanent currents: The oceans contain well-defined permanent current systems that change periodically, but predictably, with seasonal changes in the wind systems that are their generators. At sea, certain winds blow almost continuously in the same general direction over large areas (such as the well-known trade winds on either side of the equator) with the result that their forces mainly determine the set, drift, and permanence of the current created. North–south currents are affected by the Coriolis force (earth's rotation) as well, creating a circular deflection clockwise in the Northern Hemisphere, and counterclockwise below the equator. Contrary winds of temporary nature but long duration reduce the drift of a normal current substantially and, to a much lesser degree, alter the set; when the wind again becomes normal for the area the current returns to normal. Pilot charts (Chapter II) and surface current atlases delineate the known direction (indicated by arrow) and velocity of permanent ocean currents at selected and convenient points. The information given is for *average* current, area coverage is comprehensive.

Wind current: In addition to the known prevailing winds generating the permanent ocean currents, transient winds appear as a result of shifting pressure systems in the atmosphere (highs and lows). When exerting sufficient force, these winds cause the surface layer of water to move and form a temporary, or wind current; a build-up time of approximately twelve hours of steady wind usually precedes a detectable formation of current. The speed of the current (drift) depends on the speed and constancy of the wind and, on the average, should be about 2 percent of total wind velocity. Wind currents are greatly influenced by Coriolis force; in deep water the difference between the direction in which the wind is flowing and the wind current direction is frequently between 35° and 45°. In north latitude the deflection is clockwise, i.e., the current flows to the right of the wind flow; in south latitude current is deflected counterclockwise, or left. Deflection decreases as the shore line is approached and ultimately follows the fathom contours.

Although wind currents are not as predictable as the known permanent currents, the *wind rose* on the appropriate pilot chart for the area nearest the ship's position (in every 5° degree square on the monthly pilot chart of the North Atlantic Ocean) shows the character of the winds that have prevailed in the area. Wind percentages are concentrated upon eight points, or every 45°, with arrows indicating the direction of wind flow. Full detail of interpretation is clearly described on the chart, as well as for the prevailing direction and speed of the known permanent current.

Observe that wind is named for the general compass direction (NE, NW, etc.) *from* which it originates, and that wind arrows indicate the direction of movement; a NW wind moves SE. Unlike wind, current is named for the direction *toward* which it flows, either stated by a compass direction or, more precisely, in degrees (a westerly current sets more or less 270°). The methods

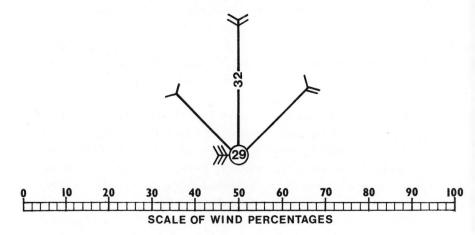

FIGURE 51. WIND ROSE

Direction (arrows fly with the wind):
Prevailing wind indicated by the longest arrow, broken when too long to be shown conventionally and percentage indicated (32% above).

Other winds indicated by arrows, percentage determined by measurement from scale (NE 20%, NW 18%).

Calms, light airs, and *variables* are encircled at the center (29%).

Force (indicated by number of feathers):
The Beaufort scale of wind force (Appendix F) is indicated on each arrow, the number of feathers corresponding to the force number. When the arrow shaft is too short (as for the westerly wind example) feathers are shown beyond the end. For the winds diagrammed in this example the forces are from N, 4; from NE, 3; from W, 6; from NW, 2.

of plotting current effect and of constructing a current vector diagram for compensating course to steer are detailed in Chapter IV.

Leeway

Leeway is the offsetting effect of wind and is named for the direction in which it tends to move a boat off course; *starboard leeway* offsets to the right, *port leeway* to the left. Wind abeam causes maximum leeway, wind from dead forward or aft creates none. In general, the deeper the draft (or keel) the less leeway, because of the increased resistance of the water; a planing hull is most affected by leeway.

Because leeway effect is hard to isolate it is generally assumed to be an unknown contributor to the total offset plotted for current effect. However, when leeway can be estimated, as from a comparison of the wake angle with the heading, it may be applied as a compass correction for the course: *Starboard leeway is an easterly correction* (steer less for starboard may be remembered by "Star of the East"), port leeway calls for a westerly conversion. The TVMDC sequence is helpful, with leeway (L) appended in the sequence (as TVMDCL) to find the course to steer.

Examples:

Starboard Leeway		Port Leeway
075°	Compass Course	075°
− 15° E	Leeway (15%)	+ 15° W
060°	Course to Steer	090°

Leeway and relative bearings: When current effect including leeway acts on a vessel, relative bearings must be converted according to the *heading* and not the course; a common error is to ignore the leeway angle in plotting, an easy habit to fall into since all other bearings are plotted from the course direction.

Wind

Although the study of wind is more properly a meteorological than a navigational pursuit, an understanding of certain as-

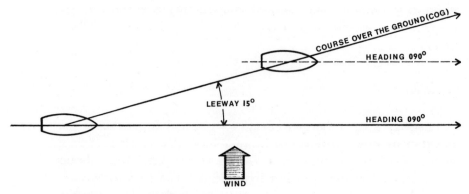

FIGURE 52. LEEWAY

In this situation a sailboat would be on the starboard tack (wind direction from starboard) but the wind effect is causing the boat to fall off to port and the leeway is called *port leeway*.

pects will be helpful in some navigation situations. Wind is the direction and speed of air motion, or horizontal air flow over the surface of earth. Like current, wind is deflected by the Coriolis force; clockwise in the Northern Hemisphere and counterclockwise below the equator. *Shifting* wind changes direction progressively, a *variable* wind is weak, puffy, and directionally unstable. A wind *veers* when its direction changes progressively clockwise, and *backs* counterclockwise. A backing wind is associated with low pressure, a veering wind with high pressure. The force of wind is directly proportional to the square of its velocity. The Beaufort scale (Appendix F) is a table for estimating the force of wind at sea visually.

True and apparent wind: The actual direction and velocity of air in motion defines *true* wind, whereas an *apparent* wind is the resultant of two forces, the motion of true wind and the motion of the ship. Pennants and telltales indicate the direction of apparent wind when the ship is in motion. The following relationships apply:

(a) True wind direction is further from the bow than apparent wind.
(b) When apparent wind is abaft the beam it is stronger than true wind.

(c) When apparent wind is forward of the beam, the true wind is stronger.

(d) When apparent wind is dead astern it coincides with true wind and the true wind is the stronger.

The direction and velocity of true wind may be found by constructing a simple vector diagram, proportionate to ship speed and velocity: (1) construct one side to represent the ship's heading at known speed, (2) from the origin point of the heading construct the apparent wind side for relative bearing and known velocity, and (3) connect the two open ends, scale off the length to find velocity of the true wind and measure for relative bearing. The method is shown in Figure 53.

Wind shifts: A veering wind (clockwise in the Northern Hemisphere) is an indicator of the approach or passing of a front, the boundary between air masses of different characteristics, and signifies a change in weather. Fronts are named *warm* or *cold* (also *occluded,* not further discussed) for the nature of the air mass. The importance of observing passage of a front is to anticipate the winds to follow.

		Warm Front	*Cold Front*
WIND:	Before Front	S or SE	SW, S or W
	At Front Passage	SE or SW	SE or SW
	Behind Front	S or SW	NW, W, or SW
BAROMETER:			
	Before Front	Falling	Falling
	At Front Passage	Steady (or falling slowly)	Slightly rising
	Behind Front	Steady	Abrupt and rapid rise
AIR TEMPERATURE:			
	Before Front	Steady, with gradual rise as front nears	Rising, then falling slowly
	At Front Passage	Rising	Abrupt change
	Behind Front	Steady at new higher level	Quick drop

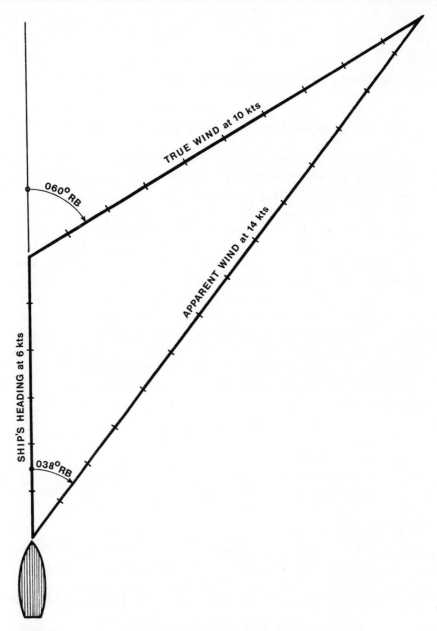

FIGURE 53. FINDING THE TRUE WIND

True wind (Relative bearing 060°, velocity 10 kts)

Apparent wind (Relative bearing 038°, velocity 14 kts)

Ship's speed (6 kts)

When any two forces are known, the third may be produced. Wind direction is the reciprocal of its relative bearing.

High and low-pressure areas: Because nature abhors a vacuum, wind tends to flow from high- to low-pressure areas, but is deflected by the Coriolis force (earth's rotation). The circulation pattern of highs and lows in the Northern Hemisphere (reversed below the equator) appears as diagrammed in Figure 54.

At the center of a high there is no wind, or at best a slightly variable wind of low velocity. Conversely, the center of a low receives high velocity wind from every point of the compass as nature attempts to equalize the pressure. As shown in figure 54, the direction of the wind depends on which quadrant of the low-pressure area the ship is positioned; Buys Ballot's Law aids the solution, stating: "If an observer in the Northern Hemisphere faces the wind, the center of low pressure is toward his right, somewhat behind him; and the center of high pressure is toward his left and somewhat in front of him. In the Southern Hemisphere the center of low pressure is toward his left and somewhat behind him; and the center of high pressure is toward his right and somewhat in front of him." Translated for finding the center of a low in the Northern Hemisphere, Buys Ballot's Law can be applied as in the table on page 116.

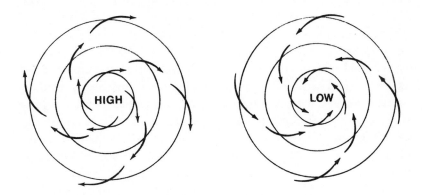

FIGURE 54. HIGH- AND LOW-PRESSURE AREAS

Arrows indicate the direction of wind flow, away from the center of a high and toward the center of a low. Diagram is for Northern Hemisphere; directions are reversed below the equator, i.e., wind there flows counterclockwise from a high and clockwise toward a low.

Wind from:	Direction of Low Center
NE	South
E	Southwest
SE	West
S	Northwest
SW	North
W	Northeast
NW	East
N	Southeast

Periodic observation with the Buys Ballot's method will reveal the low center's direction of movement in relation to ship's position, and the direction of winds to be encountered as the low moves through the area.

Hurricane navigation: Tropical cyclones (hurricanes, typhoons, or willy-willies, according to locality) are circular storms accompanied by high winds which create long-ranging waves (swells) of abnormal length and slow frequency, noticeable as much as 1500 miles from the source. The sea becomes a maelstrom in which small craft cannot survive, hence a course to avoid hurricane contact is essential to determine and take at the earliest realization of a hurricane alert. Buys Ballot's Law provides the direction of the hurricane center: Face the wind; the center will be from 90° to 112° (8 to 10 points) *to the right* of the direction from which the wind is coming (Northern Hemisphere, to the left in south latitude). North of the equator hurricane winds circulate counterclockwise and form two components, the *dangerous* and *navigable* semicircles (the navigable semicircle is also dangerous, but not as much so as the other) which it is important to identify quickly. The dangerous semicircle is that to the right of the hurricane's path, where the wind tends to draw in to the hurricane center; the navigable semicircle, *left* of the path, has winds of relatively lower velocity and a tendency to push off from the hurricane center.

The following rules for hurricane navigation, as developed by the U.S. Naval Oceanographic Office, apply to the Northern Hemisphere:

In the dangerous (right) semicircle: Sailing vessels keep close-hauled on the starboard tack, make as much way as possible. If absolutely necessary to heave to, do so on the starboard tack. Powered vessels bring wind on the starboard bow, make as much way as possible. If absolutely necessary to heave to, do so head to sea.

In the navigable (left) semicircle: Sail and power vessels both bring the wind on the starboard quarter, note the course and

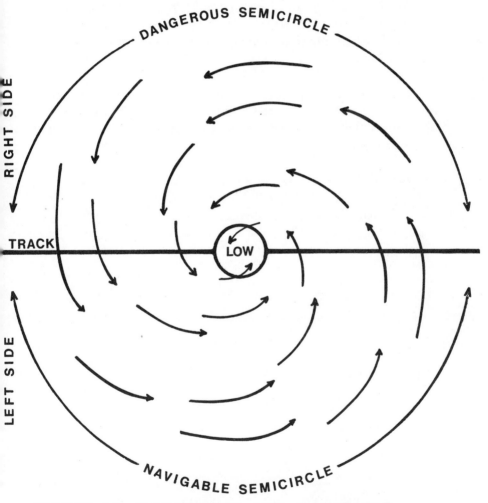

FIGURE 55. DANGEROUS AND NAVIGABLE SEMICIRCLES

hold it. If absolutely necessary to heave to, sailing vessels do so on port tack, powered vessels stern to sea.

On the track in front of hurricane center: Both sail and power vessels should bring the wind two points (about 22°) on the starboard quarter, note the course and hold it while running for the left semicircle; upon arrival in that (navigable) semi-circle maneuver as above.

On the track in rear of hurricane center: Avoid the center by the best practicable route, bearing in mind that Northern Hemisphere hurricanes tend to curve to the north and then eastward.

Inspection of Figure 55 will reveal the reasoning for these maneuvers, and the reversals that make them applicable to the Southern Hemisphere where all wind circulation is opposite from that north of the equator.

chapter VIII
Marine Electronics

MANY DESIRABLE ELECTRONIC aids provide the navigator with labor-saving convenience and extend the opportunities for safe passage-making. However, the millennium of completely automated, zero-defect navigation is still far in the future for the cruising yachtsman who, if prudent, will understand the inherent limitations of his electronic equipment and maintain his basic manual skills as back-up insurance against electronic malfunction. A non-technical discussion of the applications and capabilities of electronic aids suitable for coastal and offshore cruising purposes is summarized below.

Radio

Radio provides time signals, direction and distance finding, position fixing, weather and hazards to navigation advisories, and contact with ship and shore stations. Radio waves are classified according to their *frequency*, i.e., the number of waves per second expressed either in *kiloHertz* (kHz) of 1000 cycles or in *megaHertz* of 1,000,000 cycles (1,000 kHz). A radio *band* delineates a range of cycles. The radio frequencies for finding time, weather, and position are listed in Appendix D.

Radiotelephony

Radiotelephony (voice radio) is the usual means of communication between ships, and between ship and shore stations. Three frequency bands are available for transmitting and receiving on the crowded frequencies alloted for noncommercial marine use:

Citizens' Band Class D radio, in the high-frequency 27 mHz area, is a limited system for personal "walkie-talkie" conversation and does not satisfy the safety and operational requirements for coastal cruising.

The *Marine Band* of 2000–3000 kHz (2–3 mHz) contains the primary offshore safety and operating network, keystoned by the international calling and distress frequency of 2182 kHz. Two systems are contained in the Marine Band: *amplitude modulation* (AM) and *single-sideband modulation* (SSB). As of January 1, 1971, the Federal Communications Commission discontinued licensing new 2–3 mHz ship stations in the AM system and promulgated the requirement that all existing AM stations must be converted to SSB by January 1, 1977, from which date forward only SSB equipment will be approved for ship stations in the 2–3 mHz band. SSB radiotelephone, depending on power input, has great range.

The *VHF/FM* (very high frequency, frequency modulation) 156–162 mHz band is a line of sight system (up to forty miles depending on height of the transmitting antenna) utilizing the international calling and distress frequency of 156.800 mHz, and is intended by the FCC to replace the use of 2–3 mHz equipment in coastal waters and on inland waterways.

The small-craft sailor making a passage more than forty miles distant from a VHF/FM shore station should be equipped with both 2–3 mHz SSB and 156–162 mHz VHF/FM. The combination will reduce interference and provide more efficiency in both foreign and domestic waters. The FCC regulations in effect as of 1977 require VHF/FM to be used wherever possible, which for all practical purposes limits the legal use of SSB to areas not covered by VHF/FM shore stations.

Ship to ship calls are initiated on 2182 kHz or 156.8 mHz according to distance between stations (both frequencies are monitored by the Coast Cuard). Nonemergency traffic, after establishing initial contact, is then shifted to a mutually agreeable working frequency. The U.S. radiotelephone working frequencies for non-emergency traffic are:

mHz Band	Frequency	Purpose
2–3 mHz	2003 kHz	Great Lakes
	2142 kHz	Pacific Coast daytime, south of Lat 42°N.
	2638 kHz	All areas
	2670 kHz	Coast Guard, including ship to shore.
	2738 kHz	All areas except Great Lakes and Gulf of Mexico
	2830 kHz	Gulf of Mexico
156–162 mHz		

Channel		
6	156 300 mHz	Intership safety*
9	156.450 mHz	All areas, ship to ship contact between commercial and noncommercial vessels
68	156.425 mHz	All areas, noncommercial
70	156.525 mHz	All areas, noncommercial
12	156.600 mHz	Intership safety, including ship to shore*
72	156.625 mHz	All areas, noncommercial

* The Coast Guard monitors 156.800 mHz; shore stations will normally shift distress transmissions after initial contact to 156.300 mHz, a rescue vessel will shift to 156.600 mHz.

Radio telephone frequencies are assigned by international Treaty, with 2182 kHz and 156.800 mHz recognized world-wide for calling and distress transmissions. Other frequencies authorized in foreign areas should be determined before taking departure.

   Ship to shore communication is available in the United States through the telephone company, and in other areas through many government telephone monopolies. The shore station (technically the coast station) maintains continuous watch during its scheduled hours of operation. Unless the ship station is to be monitored continuously it is expedient to pre-arrange listening times, or else install a special alert device to signal when the ship station is being called. The simplex system of paired frequencies is used in many areas, the shore station transmitting on one assigned frequency and the ship station on the other. Conversation must flow in only one direction at a time, and not simultaneously—a limitation that often frustrates an uninitiated landlubber at the mainland end of a circuit. Transmissions emanating from ship or shore are completed by the marine operator at the coast station, who routes the ship radio signal into the land telephone network. Because of the FCC regulations phasing out 2–3 mHz AM radiotelephony and encouraging the widespread installations of VHF/FM equipment, a state of flux is expected, of long duration. Until equilibrium is attained—hopefully by the late 1970s—it will be incumbent on the ship station operator to obtain local knowledge of the latest shore station availabilities from time to time. Sources include the area telephone company, the nearest FCC field office, and the District Coast Guard headquarters.

Phonetic Alphabet

Much time is wasted, and many messages misunderstood, through careless voice enunciation over the radiotelephone. The internationally agreed upon phonetic alphabet is recommended for clarity in spelling out words or numerals that might otherwise be misunderstood. Certain key phrases listed below are employed by professional communicators as time-savers, and their use is advocated for all persons using voice radio.

Alphabet:

A	Alpha	J	Juliett	R	Romeo
B	Bravo	K	Kilo (Kee-lo)	S	Sierra
C	Charlie	L	Lima (Lee-mah)	T	Tango
D	Delta	M	Mike	U	Uniform
E	Echo	N	November	V	Victor
F	Foxtrot	O	Oscar	W	Whisky
G	Golf	P	Papa	X	X-ray
H	Hotel	Q	Quebec	Y	Yankee
I	India			Z	Zulu

Numerals:

1	Wun	5	Fiy-ev	8	Ait
2	Too	6	Six	9	Niner
3	Tree	7	Seven	0	Zay-roe
4	Foe-were				

Special words and phrases:

Affirmative:	Yes.
Charlie:	That is correct (used mainly by Coast Guard).
Negative:	No.
Over:	I am ending transmission and awaiting your reply.
Out:	I am terminating my transmission without asking you to reply. (*Over and out* is an amateurish contradiction.)
Roger:	I have received all of your last transmission without exception, and do not ask for any repetition.
Say again:	Repeat.
Wait:	Wait.
Wait one:	Wait a minute.
Wait out:	I will come back after a brief delay, do not acknowledge.
Wait over:	Same as *Wait out,* but *Roger* acknowledgment expected.
Wilco:	I have received your transmission, understand it, and will comply with its instruction. (*Roger Wilco* is redundant.)

Radiotelephone licenses: The Federal Communications Commission licenses both the ship station and the operator. An operator's permit, requiring absolutely no demonstration of intelligence or skill, is legally sufficient; as a matter of pride, and to gain familiarity with the proper techniques of using the radiotelephone, it is advocated that operators study the FCC regulations (Part 83) and take the not-difficult examination for a third-class operator's license.

Time Signals

Time signals are obtained by ship's radio in a variety of frequencies. Those received on the Standard Broadcast Band (535–1605 kHz) are not sufficiently accurate for navigational use. The U.S. National Bureau of Standards maintains two powerful long-range radio stations (WWV and WWVH) which continuously transmit precise Greenwich mean time (GMT) by voice announcement preceding a time signal. The Canadian government radio station (CHU) transmits eastern standard time (EST) by tone preceded by voice announcement in both English and French. Details of these operations are given in Chapter VI, the essentials are summarized below:

WWV, Fort Collins, Colorado (every minute) transmits GMT on 2.5, 5.0, 10.0, 15.0, 20.0, and 25.0 mHz.

WWVH, Maui, Hawaii (every minute) transmits GMT on 2.5, 5.0, 10.0, 15.0, and 20.0 mHz.

CHU, Ottawa, Ontario (every minute) transmits EST on 3.33, 7.335 and 14.670 mHz.

Frequencies useful in European waters for obtaining radio time signals are listed in Appendix D.

Position Finding

The *radio direction finder* (RDF) is a widely employed device for obtaining bearings, utilizing a directional antenna and a visual or audible signal-strength indicator to convert a signal transmitted from a signaling station of known location into an indicated line of position. The signalling, or transmitting, station may be either a commercial broadcasting station (must be plotted on the chart) or a radiobeacon. RDF sets are designed to cover one or more of three radio frequency bands, of which the low-frequency Beacon Band is the most essential and reliable. The reliability range of each band under normal circumstances is:

		Nautical Miles		
Radio Band	*Frequency Range*	*Day*	*Night*	*Sunrise and Sunset*
Beacon	190– 500 kHz	75	75	10
Standard Broadcast	535–1600 kHz	75	30	10
Marine	2000–3000 kHz	75	10	0

Dependability decreases as distance increases. The loudness of a signal is not related to its reliability. Fading or variable signals ("sky wave" or "night effect") are not reliable at any time and are most frequent at night, sunset, and sunrise. Fading effect is least at the lower frequencies; use Beacon Band whenever there is a choice.

Accuracy: The accuracy of any RDF bearing is less than that obtainable by careful visual observation, as with a pelorus or hand bearing compass. An inherent error of $\pm$ 2° is normal under ideal conditions, $\pm10°$ may be expected if the vessel is heeled, or yawing and pitching in confused seas. Errors up to $\pm$ 5° are found in signals which cross intervening land masses. A position determined by RDF bearings is best recorded as an estimated position (EP) and not as a true fix or running fix. When in the vicinity of shoals or other grounding hazards the area of uncertainty should be delineated by plotting the estimated angle of error from each RDF line of position forming the EP.

Certain station transmitters are capable of long-range emissions which may be received several hundred miles offshore. When more than 150 miles intervene between transmitter and receiver the earth's curvature must be considered and a conversion angle (*Bowditch*, Table I) applied as a correction to the bearing angle received. No correction is needed when transmitter and receiver are both on the same approximate longitude, i.e., in a north–south relationship. Offshore use of RDF is imprecise except with very sophisticated equipment and should not be regarded as a substitute for celestial observation.

Deviation: RDF is vulnerable to deviation caused by magnetism and metallic objects aboard. The problem is most acute on sailboats where rigging and masts can cause errors up to 30° on certain headings. Deviation for both powered and sailing craft is usually at a minimum over the stern. Unlike compass deviation, *RDF deviation is a function of the relative bearing,* which changes with a change in heading. It is absolutely essential that an RDF installation be carefully calibrated (a portable RDF should always be carefully set in the same position each time it is to be used) and that a radio deviation table be prepared and kept handy. Deviation on the several radio bands used for RDF is not necessarily common for an identical bearing, therefore calibration must be made for all frequencies and separate correction tables constructed as necessary. An uncalibrated RDF is like the "razor in the monkey's hand," a dangerous instrument.

Null ambiguity: In the newer, ferrite-antenna RDF, the weakest signal, or *null,* is obtained when the plane of the antenna is parallel to the direction of the signal, the strongest when it is at right angles. The opposite is true of the older, loop antennas. The null is utilized to find the direction to the transmitter since it is easier to detect little or no signal than to measure the strongest signal. Two nulls, more or less 180° apart depending on deviation influence, are inherent in such a directional antenna system; ambiguity will be present if the set is not equipped with a sensing device to indicate the correct bearing from its reciprocal. When uncertain of the correct bearing, the ambiguity may be resolved by continuing on course (altered only if the RDF bearings are bow or stern) and plotting both bearings from DR positions on the course line. The bearings will shortly converge in one direction and diverge in the other; the direction of convergence is the correct direction of the RDF bearing.

Radiobeacons: Some few prominent radiobeacons transmit their identifying signal (dot and dash combinations not signifying any Morse code letter except by coincidence) continuously. Marker radiobeacons of low power transmit continuous half-second dashes. The vast majority of radiobeacons transmit a characteristic signal for forty-eight seconds followed by two seconds of silence and then a ten-second dash, completing the cycle in one minute. Because of the limited availability of frequencies in comparison with the great number of radiobeacons emplaced, most radiobeacons share frequencies with other beacons and operate as *sequenced* radiobeacons, transmitting for one minute out of every six in sequence with the other beacons in the group. Sequence within a group is indicated on radiobeacon charts by a Roman numeral (I, II, III, etc.). Once sharp reception has been obtained, tuning need not be changed to receive any radiobeacon in the sequence; bearings are taken with the directional antenna on any of the received beacons, which are so positioned that there should be no confusion in identification provided one knows the general area of the ship's position.

Radiobeacons are listed in H.O. 117 and in the Coast Guard's

Light Lists which also contain chartlets of radiobeacon locations and frequencies in the several sub-areas of the *Light List's* coverage.

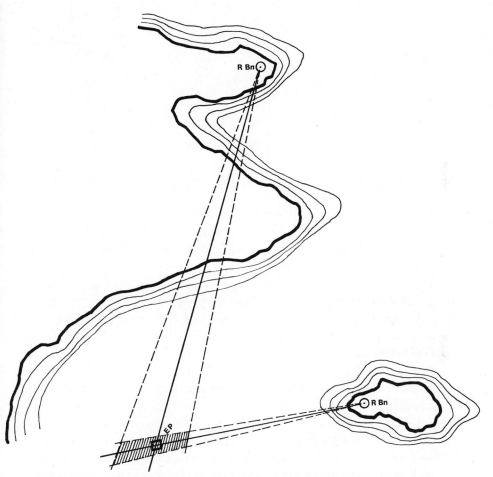

FIGURE 56. AREA OF UNCERTAINTY OF AN RDF POSITION

Signals transmitted over land mass are less accurate than those over water without land mass intervening.

Depth Finding

The modern *depth sounder* transmits high-frequency sound waves toward the bottom which are reflected back as an echo.

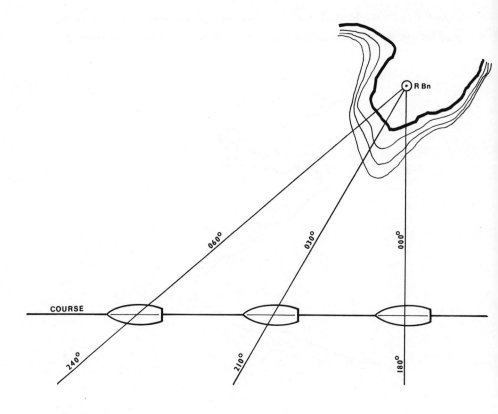

FIGURE 57. NULL AMBIGUITY

Radio bearings *converge* on the transmitter, reciprocal bearings diverge.

Depth is measured by the time required for sound to travel to the bottom and return at a rate of 4800 feet per second. The depth-finding equipment produces the sound, receives and amplifies the echo, and converts the interval into units of depth (feet or fathoms for present U.S. equipment, which will undoubtedly convert to meters when U.S. charts have been substantially converted to this international standard as begun in 1970). Essentially there are six types of depth indicators on the market:

Flashing light indicator is the usual type found aboard small craft and makes use of a small neon bulb on the end of a rotation arm. Although the light actually flashes from ten to thirty times per second, the appearance is that of a steady flow at the indicated depth.

A recorder has a small metal stylus instead of a bulb, burning an arc through the coating of a special paper which is steadily advanced to make a continuous line showing the bottom profile.

The *meter indicator* is a trouble-prone device with special circuitry for converting depth pulses to a reading on an electric meter.

A *cathode-ray* indicator is an elaborate device used almost exclusively by commercial fishermen and growing in popularity with pleasure-craft operators as mass production brings its cost to a more competitive position in comparison with other types.

A *digital indicator* provides read-out in numbers.

Dual beam indicators have an additional beam aimed forward to indicate underwater objects ahead. A number of factors combine to make most such readings unreliable with the type of equipment capable of being mounted on anything less than an antisubmarine naval vessel.

Uses in navigation: Knowledge of the depth of water beneath the keel is a comforting safety factor; it must be remembered that the depth finder registers the depth *from the position of the transducer* (the hull-fitted impulse sender) which is not located at the point of deepest draft. Both the vessel's draft and the height of the transducer above the lowest point of the keel must be known in order to interpret the recorded or indicated depth in terms of actual water under the hull (some models are adjustable to compensate for hull depth). Depth data may be combined with an estimated position or a running fix to verify accuracy of position, allowing for the state of the tide (Chapter VII) when comparing with charted depths. In extremis, a boat may be navigated from one known location to another by following a course of constant depth—"fathom-contour sailing."

Calibration: Some sounders are calibrated to read two scales on the dial, for example: A sounder with a full-scale dial of 100 feet will indicate 30 feet at depths of either 30 or 130 feet. Since it is difficult to detect the "second time around," caution and judgment must be exercised in interpreting the depth reading on such instruments. The dial reading of a flashing indicator varies in clarity according to the character of the bottom which reflects the impulse, and due to fish action under the keel (a fish's air bladder returns an echo). Proficiency in reading a flashing light indicator includes identification of the bottom as typified by the examples in Figure 58.

Automatic Steering

The "automatic pilot" is a convenience, especially when short-handed, in maintaining a predetermined course; a well-adjusted device will hold course as well or better than the average helmsman except in a following sea, where only very sophisticated equipment will act reliably. The usual installation includes a magnetic compass *sensor* which is subject to all the influences affecting any magnetic compass (Chapter III). The sensor is extremely sensitive and care must be taken to keep beer cans, keys, knives, and other casual metal away from its location. Serious accidents have occurred due to inadequate observation while running on automatic steering; its use is not advisable in crowded waterways or when an adequate watch cannot be posted. Automatic steering may be used to advantage on medium-size (35-ft. LWL and over) craft but the heavy current drain limits its acceptance for sailing vessels.

Consolan

Consolan (Consol in Europe), the "poor man's loran," is a

a. Hard sand or rock bottom.

d. Hardpan under mud.

Bottom at 49 feet, fish around 30 feet.

e. Sloping bottom.

Water weeds above bottom.

f. Soft bottom

FIGURE 58. FLASHING LIGHT DEPTH-SOUNDER INDICATIONS

© U.S. Power Squadrons, Inc.

long-range navigation aid, giving line of position up to 1200 miles from the transmitter (but not within 50 miles) on any RDF equipment (or other radio receiver) capable of receiving frequencies in the range of 194–200 kHz (U.S.) or 266–318 kHz (Europe). Accuracy under normal atmospheric conditions is ± 0.3° in daytime, ±0.7° nighttime. When the receiver is equipped with an internal beat frequency oscillator the signal is heard as a sharp *beep*, otherwise as a mushy *hiss;* since line of position is obtained by counting dots and dashes the beep is much preferred to the hiss. Dots and dashes may also be read from the null meter if the RDF is so equipped. The consolan station transmits a signal consisting of mixed dots and dashes, plus a three-letter call sign, the number of dots and dashes are counted and from these counts the bearing *from* the transmitter is determined by means of special tables found in H.O. 177-A, *Radio Navigational Aids,* or on special N.O. charts. The method and tables are fully explained in H.O. 117, both for Consolan and Consol, and therefore not duplicated here.

Radar

The availability of radar for use in medium-size pleasure craft is constantly increasing as design improvements and widened production combine to increase the feasibility of its use as an anticollision and position-finding device. Radar uses a highly directional antenna to "bounce" a signal from a target in pulses of some 2000 times per second, returning echos are displayed by a cathode-ray tube on a *plan position indicator* (PPI) which gives an aerial map appearance to the presentation, with the ship centered. The range of a target is proportionate to the distance of its echo signal (*blip*) from the radar scope's center; distance is measured by a series of concentric circles at known distances from the center, bearing is indicated by the direction of a blip from the scope center. When the presentation is with the ship heading upward, the top of the scope represents the ship's heading and the bearings are relative. When a movable compass rose is positioned concentric with the outer rim of the scope, true or magnetic bearings are obtained. Because radar provides both distance and bearing in simultaneous observation, a radar observation provides a fix; however since radar range is generally more accurate than radar bearing, a fix by two or more bearings is preferable.

Radar's effective distance is, by rule of thumb, restricted to line of sight of the horizon but actually depends on the height of the scanning antenna and the height of the target object, and may therefore be determined by the table of distances of visibility from sea level given in Chapter V. For the usual antenna height on a medium-size pleasure boat it may be assumed that the radar effective distance will be 115% of the horizon distance for the antenna height.

Radar beacons are shore-based installations similar in purpose to radiobeacons, providing a line of position appearing on the radar scope as a radial line—an important aid to piloting in crowded estuaries and harbors. Location of radar beacons is published in H.O. 117.

Loran

Loran, the acronym for *long range navigation*, utilizes synchronized pairs of radio transmitting stations which broadcast pulsed signals with a constant interval between them. Loran differs from RDF in that it measures differences in the time of arrival of the signals, rather than the direction of arrival. The time difference is employed to determine a loran line of position from special tables or charts. Two or more lines of position, from two or more paired stations, provide a loran fix which may normally be obtained in a matter of minutes. Indicator dials on the receiving set are manipulated into synchronization by the operator, who then reads the time difference identifying the line of position obtained at synchronization. The technique is simple and easily mastered.

Loran receiving equipment is compact and requires only a low power input, making it an ideal small-craft installation because of the low battery drain. Accuracy is equivalent to that expected from a celestial observation. Ground-wave coverage in daytime extends to 700 miles or more, the sky-wave range extends reception to 1200 miles during the day and 1400 miles at night, giving tranoceanic coverage in the Northern Hemisphere where loran installations are concentrated. Loran tables and installations are given in H.O. 117 A and B. Detailed information on the system is authoritatively presented in *Bowditch*.

chapter IX

Introduction to Celestial Navigation

C ELESTIAL NAVIGATION relies on the sun, moon, observable planets, and selected stars to find position on earth. The *navigational triangle* formed in the heavens by the positions of the celestial *body,* the nearest celestial *pole,* and the *zenith* (celestial point directly over the observer's head) are "brought down to earth" where their known terrestrial equivalents are measured for line of position. The method employs an inspection table containing precomputed solutions for the triangle and an almanac containing essential data about the body observed. In order to employ the tables and almanac, as described in subsequent chapters, the basic concepts and terminology of celestial navigation presented below must first be thoroughly understood.

A typical sequence of steps for finding position by observation of a celestial body includes:

1. Precomputation of the time and availability of the body for observation, including its approximate altitude above the horizon and azimuth (bearing).
2. Observation of the body by sextant to measure precise altitude, and notation of the precise zone time of the observation.
3. Conversion of the zone time (ZT) of the observation to Greenwich mean time (GMT).
4. Consultation of an almanac to determine the angle of the body from the Greenwich meridian at GMT.
5. Application of the observer's longitude to the Greenwich data to obtain the angle of the body at the local meridian.
6. "Bringing the body down to earth" with the aid of a table of

precomputed values, to determine a line of position for plotting on the chart.

The Celestial Sphere

In celestial navigation certain assumptions are made which, while astronomically incorrect, are practical because of the great distance involved and greatly simplify the arithmetic process. A *celestial* sphere is assumed, concentric with earth, upon which all celestial bodies are located; earth's center is the hub of the universe. The celestial sphere slowly rotates around immobile earth, causing heavenly bodies to rise in the east and set in the west. This, of course, was the universe as believed by the ancients, and is the *apparent* action upon which navigation tables are constructed. The components of the celestial sphere are extensions of earth's navigational components: The *polar axis* around which the sphere apparently revolves is an extension of earth's geographic axis; the *celestial equator* is an extension of the plane of earth's equator; celestial meridians are extensions of earth's meridians, of which both the Greenwich and local celestial meridians are important references for measurement.

Hour circles: Meridians of the celestial sphere, which rotate as the sphere rotates and thus go around earth once daily from east to west, are called hour circles to differentiate them from earth's immobile meridians. Every celestial body has its own hour circle, which passes through the celestial poles and the body, and rotates with the body. The sun, for example, is positioned on its own hour circle.

Aries (Υ): The hour circle of Aries is a special case of an arbitrary reference point in the sky. Aries, in navigation if not astronomy, is the point at which the sun on its annual trek northward (about 21 March) crosses the celestial equator. Some years before the advent of Christ, the constellation Aries was located at the sun's crossing point; this is no longer true (a factor conveniently overlooked by astrologers whose predictions of zodiacal influence on humanity are now several centuries out of synchronization with reality) but the name Aries has been retained as a point of reference in navigation despite its lack of present association with the constellation of the same name. Subconsciously the navigator tends to think of Aries as a true, if unseen, celestial body on its hour circle—a fiction which does no harm and can be helpful.

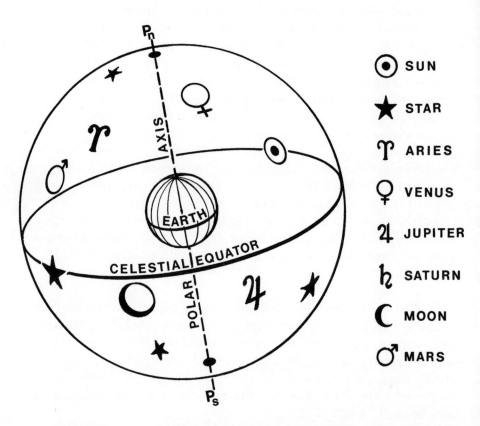

FIGURE 59. NAVIGATIONAL BODIES ON THE CELESTIAL SPHERE

Celestial bodies have been positioned schematically, not in any true relationship. Aries is a fictitious body, actually a reference point for measurement of a star's position. The zodiac (not shown) is a band parallel to the celestial equator and extending 31½° to either side of it; all bodies except stars are located within its confines. All points on the celestial sphere are considered to be equidistant from earth's center.

Hour Angles

The angular distance of a body *westward* from a designated hour circle of celestial meridian is the body's *hour angle,* measured through 360° (in degrees and tenths of degrees) from the point of reference. In practice, one of three hour angles is measured:

Grenwich hour angle (GHA) is the angular distance of a celestial body west from the Greenwich celestial meridian. GHA is tabulated in almanacs for the sun, moon, planets, and Aries.

Local hour angle (LHA) is the angular distance of a celestial body west from the local celestial meridian of the observer. LHA is derived by applying the observer's longitude (add east, subtract west) to GHA.

EXAMPLE: GHA Jupiter: 267° 14.3′
Long: − 46° 10.2′
LHA Jupiter: 221° 04.1′

Meridian angle (t) is a special case of local hour angle, and is equivalent to LHA except that it is measured *east or west* from the local celestial meridian of the observer from 0° to 180°. Meridian angle (t) is a factor in working most sight reduction tables where, to conserve space, the value of LHA is presented only to 180° rather than full circle. When LHA has been determined and the tables are to be entered, LHA is first converted to t(E) or t(W): t(W) = LHA; t(E) = 360° − LHA.

Sidereal hour angle (SHA) pertains only to stars and is the angular distance of a star west from the hour circle of Aries (♈). The SHA of major stars is listed in almanacs. The GHA of a star is obtained by adding the SHA of the star and the GHA of Aries.

EXAMPLE: SHA Arcturus: 146 12.3′
GHA ♈: + 91 37.2′
GHA Arcturus: 237° 49.5′

The relationships of hour angles and the angular distances

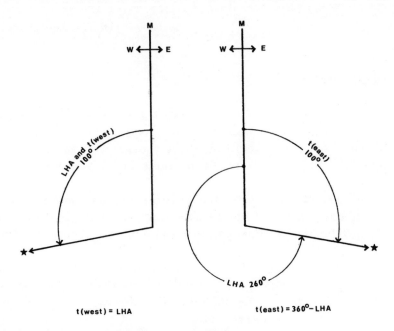

t(west) = LHA   t(east) = 360° − LHA

FIGURE 60. MERIDIAN ANGLE t

M represents the local celestial meridian, from which t (and local hour angle) are measured.

---

they measure are diagramed in Figure 61, in which G represents the Greenwich meridian, M the local meridian, ♈ Aries, and * any celestial body in the schematically positioned presentation. SHA is included in the diagram only for the purpose of showing its relationship to star measurement.

From Figure 61 the following relationships, frequently applied in celestial navigation solutions for position, are apparent:

All Bodies including Aries:

GHA Body = LHA Body + Long W (−Long E)
LHA Body = GHA Body − Long W (+Long E)

Stars Only:

GHA Star = GHA ♈ + SHA Star
LHA Star = LHA ♈ + SHA Star

Aries:

GHA ♈ = LHA ♈ + Long W (−Long E)
LHA ♈ = GHA ♈ − Long W (+Long E)

Celestial Coordinates

Declination (Dec, or d) is the celestial equivalent of earth's latitude, measured and stated in identical terms. Declination is measured through 90° (degrees and tenths of degrees) north or

(as shown for a star)

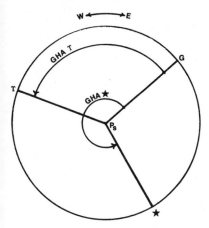

a. Greenwich hour angles

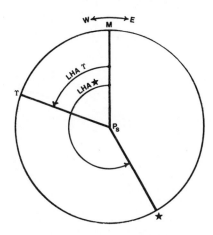

b. Local hour angles

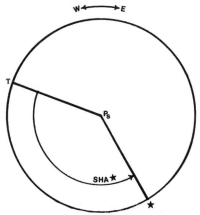

c. Sidereal hour angle (used only for a star)

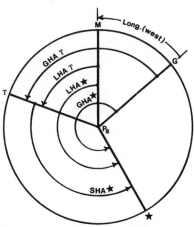

d. Combined hour angles

FIGURE 61. HOUR ANGLES

south from the celestial equator to the nearest celestial pole, and suffixed N or S to indicate the direction. Because of the great distances from earth to the heavens many bodies with south declination are visible from northern latitudes, and vice versa.

Greenwich hour angle (GHA) is the celestial equivalent of longitude, with the important difference that measurement from

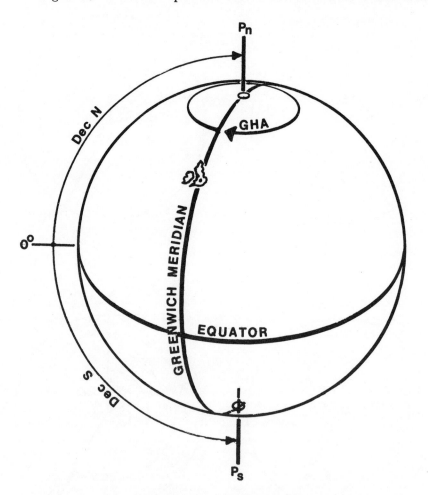

FIGURE 62. CELESTIAL COORDINATES

Declination is comparable to latitude, measured north or south from the equator through 90° to the poles. Greenwich hour angle is measured only westward from Greenwich through 360°.

the Greenwich celestial meridian is *westward through 360°* (degrees and tenths) and not east and west of the meridian as with longitude. Because direction west is understood, GHA is not suffixed. A body over Boston (Long 71°W) has a GHA of 71°; when it arrives over Rouen (Long 1°E) the GHA will be 359°.

Navigational Triangle

The sides of the navigational triangle in space intersect to form three position points on great circles, and are therefore transferable along their planes to equivalent positions on earth, where they may be located and the necessary angles measured to obtain line of position. Solution of the navigational triangle by spherical trigonometry was once the only available method; today's tables of precomputed values have eliminated the need for manual trigonometric calculation and with it the need to become familiar with the complex theory of the triangle. It is entirely possible to solve the triangle without knowledge of theory or much of the nomenclature, and no unnecessary theory or definition is contained in this chapter or elsewhere within these covers.

As brought down to earth, the triangle is located with points at (1) the *nearest geographical pole* (called the elevated pole) to the observer's position; (2) the *geographic position of the body,* the point on earth directly under the body's position in space; and (3) the *observer's position,* which is not necessarily in the same hemisphere as the geographic position of the body. A diagram of both the celestial and terrestrial navigational triangles may be found in Appendix A.

Altitude

Since the earthly coordinates of two points on the navigational triangle are known (nearest geographic pole and the observer's position), it remains only necessary to bring down the observed body to its equivalent geographic position (GP) on earth in order to complete a measurable triangle. To obtain the GP the navigator uses a sextant to measure the body's altitude (height) above the horizon.

Circle of equal altitude: If one were to walk around the Washington Monument on a circle of constant radius from the elevator shaft of that edifice, the angle from one's feet to the top of the structure would be the same at all points of the circle. The analogy is pertinent to the circle of equal altitude obtained with observation of a celestial body; the altitude is the same at any point of a circle on earth's surface. Observe from Figure 63 that the line of position found by observation of a celestial body is an arc of the circle of equal altitude.

Intercept: With minor correction, a *sextant altitude* (Ho) is obtained as a result of observation and compared with a table of precomputed values containing a *computed altitude* (Hc). The difference between Hc and Ho is termed *intercept* (a); its purpose is to position the lop (arc of the circle of equal altitude) which appears as a straight line in relation to the assumed position. The positioning rule is: Ho *greater* than Hc, position the bearing *toward* the GP from the observer; Ho *less* than Hc, position *away* from the observer. A popular mental crutch (the "Japanese" motto) is *Ho-Mo-To,* or Ho More, To.

EXAMPLES: Hc: 17° 13.2'   Hc: 17° 13.2'
              Ho: 17° 11.1'   Ho: 17° 15.3"
              _____   _____
        a: 2.1 miles Away   a: 2.1 miles Toward

Assumed Coordinates

Three of the modern precomputed tables for sight reduction (H.O. 214, 229 and 249) require assumed positions to be established (as opposed to the DR position which, of course, is also an assumption) for both latitude and longitude. The purpose is to make the arithmatic process as simple as possible, and does not affect accuracy of position determination.

Latitude: Assumed latitude (aL) is the nearest whole degree of latitude to the DR latitude.

EXAMPLES: DR Lat   47° 30.6'N   aL 48°N
              DR Lat   47° 29.4'N   aL 47°N

Longitude: An assumed longitude (aLong) is selected so that, when applied to the GHA of the body, no minutes of arc will remain. The aLong should be within 30.0′ of the DR longitude. The purpose is to establish meridian angle (t) as a whole degree for use when entering a table of precomputed values. In west longitude the minutes of aLong are the same as those of the GHA, in east

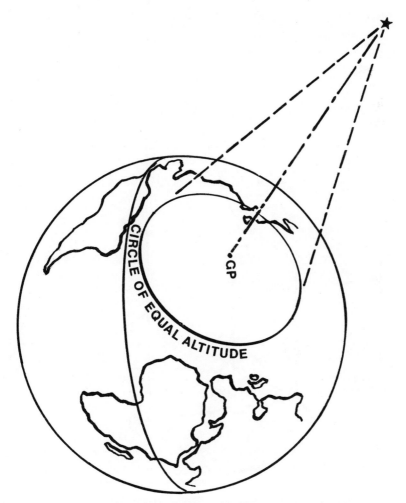

FIGURE 63. CIRCLE OF EQUAL ALTITUDE

The altitude of the observed body is the same from any point on the circle of which the geographic position (GP) of the body is the center.

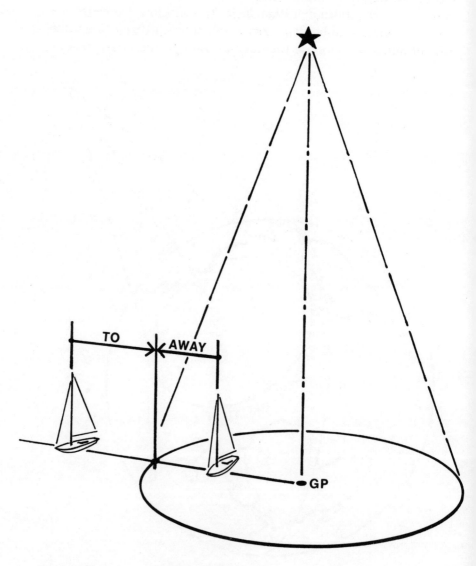

FIGURE 64. INTERCEPTS

An intercept is the distance from the DR or AP position to the circumference of the circle of equal altitude.

longitude they must equal 60.0' minus the minutes of GHA.

EXAMPLES:

DR Long 42° 35.4' W   GHA   162° 27.3'
                       aLong − 42° 27.3' W
                       LHA   120°
                       t   120° W   (tW = LHA)

DR Long 42° 35.4' E   GHA   162 27.3'
                       aLong + 42 32.7'
                       LHA   205°
                       t   155° E   (tE = 360° − LHA)

Declination: Some methods also require an assumed declination (aDec) to the nearest 30.0'. The exact declination is extracted from an almanac, and the tabulated declination in the H.O. table is found nearest to that of the exact value, the difference being the *declination difference* (d diff).

EXAMPLES:	*Declination*	*aDec*	*d Diff*
	14° 14.2' N	14° N	14.2'
	14° 16.1' S	14° 30' S	13.9'
	14° 43.4' N	14° 30' N	13.4'
	14° 48.2' N	14° N	11.8'

Azimuth Angle and Azimuth

All sight reduction tables tend to conserve space and avoid unnecessary bulk, an end result being that true azimuth (bearing) of objects is not listed therein through 360°. The computed value of the azimuth angle (Z) is tabulated, which must be converted to true azimuth (Zn) measured from true north. The conversion method is fully detailed in Appendix A; the relationships, which may be committed to memory, are:

$$Zn = Z \text{ NE}$$
$$Zn = 180° − Z \text{ SE}$$
$$Zn = 180° + Z \text{ SW}$$
$$Zn = 360° − Z \text{ NW}$$

In all cases N or S is determined by the observer's latitude and E or W according to whether the body is rising (E) or setting (W). The suffix of meridian angle (t) is a useful check, since it always agrees.

Plotting Celestial Lines of Position

The ingredients of a celestial plot for line of position have been dealt with in several preceding sections, and are recapitulated here for summary. The mechanics of plotting and labeling are as for any terrestrial plot (Chapter V). The arc of the circle of equal altitude is plotted as a straight line, the directional deviation being inconsequential for the short distance involved. It is necessary to remember the direction of the intercept. The steps of plotting the line of position in Figure 65 which assumes an observation of the moon bearing 206° at 1146, with intercept toward, are as follows:

1. From the DR select the aL at the nearest whole degree of latitude.
2. Having determined GHA (not shown) select the appropriate aLong.
3. Plot the assumed position (AP) at aL and aLong.
4. Construct a directional line through the AP toward the geographic position of the body (as obtained for Z converted to Zn).
5. Plot the intercept, to the body from the AP or away, according to the rule for the difference between Ho and Hc.
6. At the intercept distance from the AP construct a line perpendicular to the directional line indicating the GP. This is the line of position, which label.

Should a plot from the DR be made, omit steps 1 and 2 above, plot the DR position, and proceed as for the example described (substituting DR for AP).

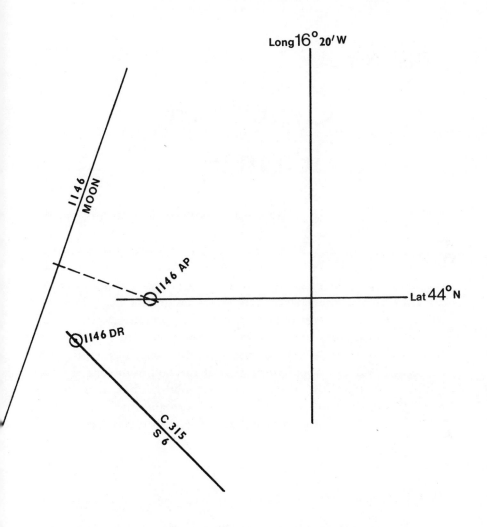

FIGURE 65. PLOT OF A CELESTIAL LINE OF
POSITION

chapter X
Celestial Bodies

ASTRONOMY CONSIDERS the heavenly bodies in their true spatial relationship, with earth an insignificant planet of an insignificant galaxy. On the other hand the navigator assumes that earth's center is the hub of the universe—perhaps a reason that so few eminent astronomers ever gain much recognition as navigators. In any event, the navigator's admittedly false premise works and is the simplest method yet devised for relating earth to the celestial bodies to which he looks for direction. In short, navigators are concerned with the apparent motion of the bodies in space in relation to earth, which is *apparently* immobile. Thus, because of earth's assumed fixed position, the heavens rotate slowly, from east to west, making an approximate complete circuit each twenty-four-hour day.

The Sun

The sun, an average-size star with a diameter of 864,400 miles and situated 93 million miles away from earth, provides the basis of our timekeeping and is the celestial body most frequently observed in navigation. The sun does not rise and set daily in the true east and west (except for two days in the year) because it does not follow the path of the celestial equator; rather its path (the ecliptic) is S-shaped, reaching northward to a maximum declination of 23.5° about 21 June and retreating to 23.5° S at about 22 December, crossing the equator at the approximate mid-dates of 23 September and 21 March, the latter time being the *vernal equinox,* or first point of Aries. *Sunrise* is the time when the sun's upper edge appears above the horizon; *sunset* takes place as the upper edge disappears.

Because the sun is, relatively, so close to earth, its diameter is prominent and a difference of altitude will be registered on the sextant depending upon whether the center, the *lower limb* (bottom), or *upper limb* (top) is measured from the horizon. The center is an impractical observation, most observations are made of the lower limb but at times the upper limb is more convenient. Correction tables are therefore given in the almanacs to find the semidiameter, or center, when a limb altitude has been observed. GHA and declination of the sun are tabulated in the almanacs.

Observations of the sun are customarily taken at the approximate times it is on the *prime vertical* (90° east or 270° west of the observer) to establish longitude or a line of position approximating longitude, and at or near the time of local apparent noon (LAN), which provides a latitude line of position since the sun is then either due north or south depending upon the observer's latitude. Observations at other times are taken to obtain bearings for a running fix, often by combination with a later sun observation. Sun observations provide accurate checks on compass accuracy; the Navy's custom is to check the compass with every sun bearing obtained. The *amplitude* method of checking the compass by observation of the sun on the horizon—rising or setting—does not require a sextant and is extremely accurate.

The Moon

Earth's satellite, the moon, is our closest celestial neighbor, at an average distance of 239,000 statute miles. This average, however, is seldom found, for the moon is constantly approaching or receding from earth, causing the navigator to make more corrections for the moon's semidiameter than is necessary for the sun; the apparently changing diameter (actually about 2,160 miles, or less than the width of the United States between Norfolk and San Francisco) is correctable by tables in the almanacs to obtain the altitude of the center when the upper or lower limb has been observed.

Observation of the moon returns a good LOP, its frequent availability in daylight offering an opportunity for a fix with the sun. At night, when the moon is low and bright, its shine often obscures the horizon, making an accurate measurement from the horizon difficult. Binoculars may be employed to discern whether the true horizon is visible in these circumstances. Upper limb observations are made as frequently as those on the lower limb, according to which limb offers the best target.

Moonrise and set occur about fifty minutes later each day, again an average figure because of the moon's erratic behavior in comparison with the sun's steady plod; the actual interval may range from fifteen to ninety minutes and is best anticipated by consulting the almanac. The belief that the moon "moves too fast" has deterred many navigators from attempting its observation, and it is an unpopular sight through long tradition. The fact is that the moon's change of position is no faster than the sun or stars, and it often presents excellent line of position opportunities that should not be ignored. Modern correction tables have greatly simplified the corrections which plagued the old-school navigator. GHA of the moon is tabulated in the almanacs, along with its declination at any time.

The Planets

Earth's fellow planets, all satellites of the sun and shining by its reflected light, follow a more erratic path through the heavens than do the stars they outshine but appear to resemble. To compensate for their nonroutine paths the almanacs contain special diagrams for their location, which at times change materially in a short period, and, at other times, may remain almost stationary in relation to the stars. Because of their brightness planets are usually the last objects observable at morning twilight and the first to appear in the evening. They may be observed, Venus in particular, during daylight at certain times and under favorable blue-sky conditions. A planet may be differentiated quickly from a star by its steady bright light, whereas a star twinkles.

Four planets are of interest in navigation:

Jupiter, the largest (86,000 miles in diameter)

Mars, smaller than Earth, easily identified by its reddish hue.

Saturn, the least brilliant, sometimes mistaken for a star.

Venus, the brightest, about Earth's size, and never more than 47° from the sun, which causes it to be called the "evening" or "morning" star at times. The "star bright" of the children's jingle.

The semidiameter of planets is not considered in altitude correction, the assumption being that their center is observed when altitude is measured from the horizon. The GHA and declination of Jupiter, Mars, Saturn, and Venus (the navigable planets of the solar system) are tabulated in the almanacs.

The Stars

Earth's galaxy, the Milky Way, contains about 100 billion stars, of which only about 6000 are visible—burning suns which appear to us as pinpoints of light. The magnitude of the heavens almost boggles the mind, the distances and dimensions of the stars being virtually incomprehensible in terms of the standards used on earth to describe dimension. Distance of a star is therefore measured in light years (the speed of light being 186,281 miles per second, a light year is the equivalent of 5.87 trillion miles). The nearest star, Rigel Kentaurus, is a mere 23 trillion miles away. With a suitable telescope and survival equipment, a man sitting on Deneb could now be observing Columbus landing on San Salvador and be woefully unaware of what is actually happening in the world he is observing. The largest star, Antares, is 428 times larger than the sun, which is considered to be more or less a run-of-the-mill star. The sun's navigational importance to us is its proximity.

Out of this vast conclave of stars, 57 have been selected as being easily identifiable and strategically located for fix observations. The SHA and declination of the select group are carried in both the *Nautical* and *Air* almanacs for ready reference. An additional group of 116 somewhat less convenient reference stars is also included in the *Nautical Almanac.* In actual practice most navigators become familiar with perhaps 15 to 20 stars which they recognize by their relationship to other stars or constellations. This familiarity, of course, takes practice but can be accomplished in surprisingly little time if some judgment and awareness are brought to bear. The landsman learns his stars by constellation or

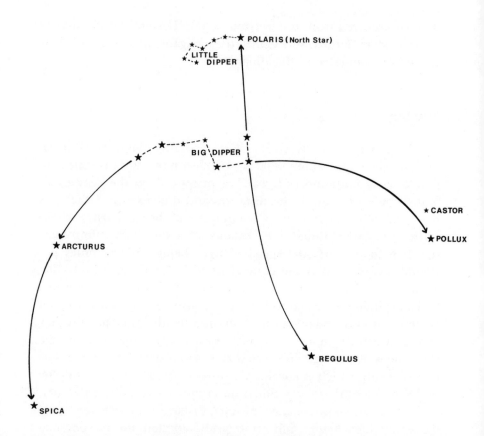

FIGURE 66. PROMINENT STARS AND CONSTELLATIONS

a. The pointers of the Big Dipper (or Plough) point to Polaris, the North Star. Cassiopeia, M- or W-shaped, is on the other side. Both constellations are circumpolar; one is always in sight in the Northern Hemisphere. Other Dipper pointers lead to Pollux and Regulus. "Follow the arc to Arcturus, and speed on to Spica."

by reference to a nearby constellation. While this method is practical during full darkness, the navigator must be able to identify stars quickly at twilight, before many evening constellations have formed or after morning constellations have dimmed. It is therefore advisable to learn a very few prominent constellations and some of the brighter (first-magnitude) stars for quick reference. Three constellations and the "summer triangle" are diagramed in Figure 66, with prominent stars associated.

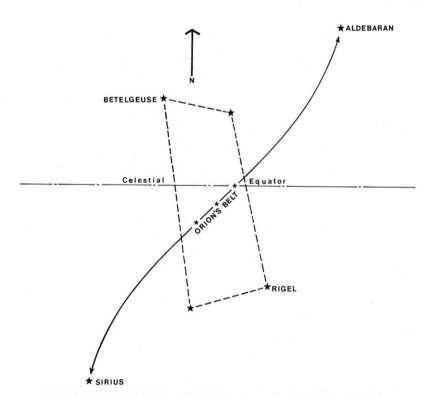

b. Orion once seen in the wintertime is not soon forgotten. The center star of the belt, Alnilam, is 1° south of the equator hence Orion is prominent in both latitudes. Betelgeuse ("Beetle Juice" to the World War II navy) is distinctively red, Rigel is blue white. Nearby Sirius, the "dog" star, is the brightest star in the heavens.

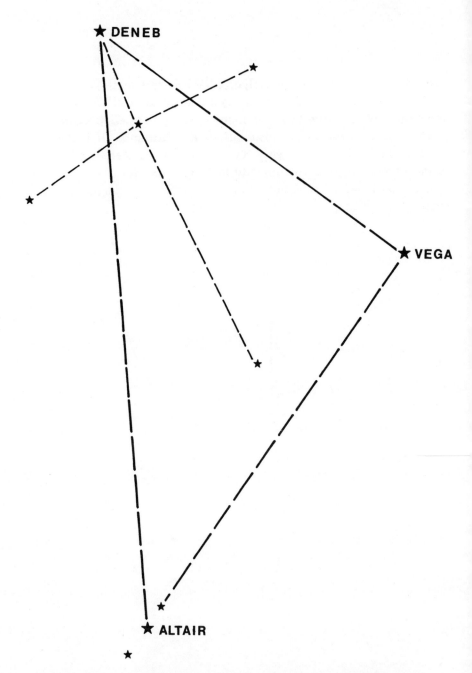

c. The Summer Triangle: Deneb is easily recognized at the apex of the Northern Cross constellation Cygnus. The right angle of the triangle is at Vega which, with Altair, is distinctively bright. Altair's declination is 9°N, making it visible throughout much of the Southern Hemisphere, as well as everywhere in the Northern Hemisphere.

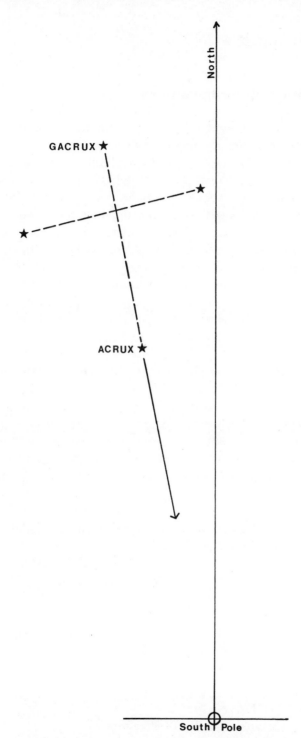

d. The Southern Cross: The Southern Hemisphere has no "south
   star" as Polaris serves near the North Pole. The Southern Cross is
   a visual indicator of approximate direction to the South Pole.

Identification of Celestial Bodies

Both the *Air* and *Nautical* almanacs contain star charts which aid in identifying the 57 major navigational stars. The H.O. Tables 211, 214, 229, and 249 (Chapter XII) all have well-described methods of star identification by use of the methods peculiar to the tables presented. By far the best device for identifying stars and planets (as well as the position of sun or moon at any given time) is the starfinder device constructed according to the Rude and Collins method. Formerly sold to civilians by the Oceanographic Office as H.O. 2102-D, this helpful aid is now restricted to official military use, but happily the same plates have been made available to private industry and the same starfinder, for all practical purposes, may be purchased at marine outlets under one or more trade names all of which include 2102-D somewhere in the description. The 2102-D *Star Finder and Identifier* consists of a star base with the 57 navigational stars distributed on the surface; there are two sides, one for north latitude, one for south. Nine transparent blue altitude-azimuth templates are included, one for each ten degrees of latitude from 5° to 85°. To locate stars for identification or pre-planning of observation, one selects the template nearest to his latitude and places it over the base plate, taking care to select the proper latitude side of the base plate and template. LHA of Aries is then computed as the setting to which the arrow on the template is oriented on the base plate; the closed curves then indicate the altitude of the body and the radial curves the azimuth. An elliptical curve indicates the horizon.

EXAMPLE: (for Lat 42° 14.6′ N, Long 68° 33.2′ W at ZT 0440, 20 April 1971)

1. Select template for Lat 45° N (nearest to DR Lat) and position over north side of star base.

2. Determine LHA ♈ for DR longitude at ZT 0400:

$$ZT \quad 0440 \ 20 \ Apr$$
$$ZD + 5$$
$$\overline{}$$
$$GMT \quad 0940 \ 20 \ Apr$$

9h GHA ♈   341° 48.8′ (almanac)

40 min   ♈ + 10° 01.6′ (almanac)

$$\overline{}$$

0940 GHA ♈   351° 50.4′

Long − 68° 33.2′ W

$$\overline{}$$

LHA ♈   283° 17.2′ (orient to 283.5°)

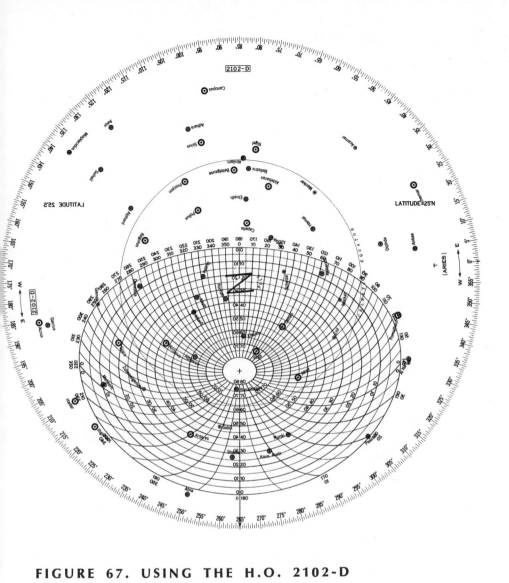

FIGURE 67. USING THE H.O. 2102-D
STARFINDER

Sillcocks-Miller Co.

In the example illustrated the navigator has determined that LHA of Aries will be 265° at the approximate time of star observation. He then has selected the blue template for the closest latitude (25°N) to that of his DR, and oriented the template on the starfinder base (for *north* latitude) with the arrow pointing to the LHA. He then determines that among the many stars available will be first-magnitude Antares (altitude 35°, azimuth 200°) and Altair (altitude 55°, azimuth 112°) which afford an excellent angle for a fix.

157

3. Read the altitude and azimuth of stars within the horizon ellipse, and select those most suitable for observation (or identify an unknown but observed star).

A magenta template included in the set has several uses, including a means for plotting planets, the sun, and the moon. The concentric magenta circles represent declination north or south of the celestial equator as represented on the base plate. To plot, one must first determine the *Right Ascension* of the body, as derived in the almanac (Right Ascension = GHA Aries — GHA Object). Set the magenta template, over the blue template already positioned, with the magenta O at the value of Right Ascension; at the declination value (from almanac) read the altitude and azimuth of the body through the slot on the magenta template.

Polaris

Polaris, the North Star, is not included in the list of 57 selected navigable stars because it is not employed for navigation in the same manner as the other stars. The use of Polaris to find latitude is described in Chapter XV, it is seldom if ever observed for any other purpose, being rather faint.

Altitude Correction of Celestial Bodies

Mention has been made in previous sections that correction of the altitude obtained by sextant observation must be made to find the correct altitude. The principal, or *main* correction, is concerned with the diameter of the body; several other corrections, according to circumstances of weather, low altitude, and other factors may also be needed. Rather than partially detail corrections for sun, moon, planets, and stars here, the entire correction method will be described in Chapter XI, which is concerned with the almanacs in which the corrections are found.

chapter XI

Almanacs

ALMANACS PROVIDE the data by which the coordinates of a celestial body may be found, plus other essential information of a related nature. Either of two almanacs jointly produced by the Nautical Almanac offices of the United States and United Kingdom is suitable for marine navigation: the *Nautical Almanac* is more comprehensive and precise, the *Air Almanac* provides adequate accuracy in a more facile format. Both contain data not required for the modern methods of navigation and they are not discussed below. One should become first familiar with the *Nautical Almanac,* from which the transition to an understanding of the *Air Almanac* is easily accomplished; the converse is more difficult.

Nautical Almanac

The *Nautical Almanac* contains celestial and related data for the entire calendar year, and is divided into three principal sections:

1. The daily pages (white section) tabulate essential data at each whole hour of GMT for the sun, moon, navigational planets, 57 selected stars, and Aries.
2. The yellow pages tabulate corrections for increments of time (minutes and seconds) between the whole hour values given on the daily pages.
3. Corrections for sextant altitude (Chapter XII) of sun, stars, and planets are tabulated proximate to the inside front cover; those for the moon are at the back of the almanac.

Supplementary information contained in the almanac includes a table for interconversion of arc and time, a table for finding latitude by observation of Polaris (Chapter XV), star charts, planet notes and diagram, and other data of navigational or astronomical interest. An explanatory section, which should be thoroughly digested, is inserted between the daily and yellow pages.

GHA and declination: The coordinates of a celestial body are its Greenwich hour angle (GHA) and declination (dec). The daily pages of the *Nautical Almanac* list the GHA of Aries and the GHA and declination of the sun, moon, and four navigational planets (Venus, Mars, Jupiter, and Saturn) at each whole hour of GMT. The sidereal hour angle (SHA) and declination of 57 selected stars are given once for every three-day period; although GHA of stars is not listed because of the problem of bulkiness which would result, it should be remembered that SHA of a star plus the GHA of Aries (both of which are listed on the daily pages) equals GHA of the star. Two minor values which must be corrected are also listed on the daily pages whenever applicable: v for GHA and d for declination. The sign of v is always assumed to be positive (+) unless otherwise indicated. There is no sign for d, the correction for which is added or subtracted according to whether declination is increasing or decreasing between the whole hours tabulated. Both v and d corrections are taken from the yellow page containing the required minutes and seconds increment of time correction. Observe that the left-hand daily page is concerned with bodies observed at twilight and that the right-hand page tabulates the sun and moon and related phenomena. Both daily pages contain three days of data broken down into hourly intervals for all bodies except the stars, whose SHA and declination may be considered to be constant for the period tabulated.

When GHA and declination are wanted only at a whole hour of GMT the data may be taken from the daily pages and the v and d factors, if any, ignored. Almost invariably, however, the coordinates are wanted for a time other than that of a whole hour, and the yellow-page corrections must be taken for minutes and seconds past the previous whole hour and for any v or d factors involved. For purposes of example assume that the GHA and declination of the sun, moon, planet Venus, and star Alphecca are wanted as of GMT 17 h 22m 43s on 20 April 1971, for which extracts from the *Nautical Almanac* are exhibited in Figure 68 a, b, and c:

Sun: The sun has no v factor correction. In this example the d correction was added (+) because the declination of the sun was increasing:

GMT 1700 GHA:	75° 15.2′	Dec:	11° 27.7′N (d 0.9′)
22m 43s:	+ 5° 40.8′	d corr: +	0.3′
GHA:	80° 56.0′	Dec:	11° 28.0′N

Moon: The moon carries both v and d factors to be corrected. Observe that the d correction was subtracted because the declination was decreasing:

GMT 1700 GHA:	133° 02.9′ (v 10.2′)	Dec:	11° 32.6′S (d 15.4′)
22m 43s:	5° 25.2′	d corr: −	5.8′
v corr:	3.8′	Dec:	11° 26.8′
GHA:	138° 31.9′		

Planet: As with the moon, planets require correction for v and d:

GMT 1700 GHA Venus:	105° 48.0′ (v 0.3′)	Dec:	2° 44.6′S (d 1.1′)
22m 43c:	5° 40.8′	d corr: −	0.4′
v corr:	0.1′	Dec:	2° 44.2′S
GHA:	111° 28.9′		

Star: Stars and Aries have no correction for v or d. GHA of a star is the sum of SHA Star plus GHA Aries, as shown for Alphecca:

SHA Alphecca:	126° 37.4′	Dec: 26° 48.3′ N
GMT 1700 GHA Aries:	103° 07.6′	
22m 43s:	5° 41.7′	
GHA:	235° 26.7′	

The use of GHA and declination varies somewhat according to the method of sight reduction employed (Chapter XIV) but both quantities are essential ingredients of position finding regardless of the method used. Error in obtaining correct GHA or declination is most usually the result of applying the v or d factor as a correction, rather than applying the yellow-page correction for v or d. Another source of error is the failure to apply the sign of d correctly because of failure to observe whether declination is increasing or decreasing.

Twilight, sunrise, sunset, moonrise, and moonset: The right-hand daily pages of the *Nautical Almanac* present the local mean time (LMT) of rising and setting phenomena at selected latitudes from 72° N to 60°S. Zone time of any phenomenon may be determined applying DLo (converted from arc to time using 1° = 4 minutes) from the time-zone center to the observer's longitude. For example, at Lat 40°N on 20 April 1971 (Fig. 68b) the LMT of sunrise is given as 0516 at any time-zone center. Assuming the observer is at Long 50°W (or 5° west of the time-zone center located at Long 45°W) the ZT of sunrise will be:

$$\begin{array}{ll} \text{LMT:} & \text{0516 at Long 45°W} \\ \text{DLo: } + & \text{20 (50° − 45° = 5° × 4 min)} \\ \hline \text{ZT} & \text{0536 at Long 50°W} \end{array}$$

The period between the almanac-listed times of nautical and civil twilight is used for observation of stars and planets as converted from LMT to ZT. For setting a starfinder the ZT of the nearest published latitude will suffice; should more precise time be required the correction tables on page xxxii of the almanac should be consulted according to the methodology detailed in the almanac's explanatory pages.

Altitude correction tables, the third major subdivision of the *Nautical Almanac,* are treated in Chapter XIII which discusses all corrections necessary for position finding.

Air Almanac

The *Air Almanac* presents celestial and related data over a period of four consecutive months and is published thrice yearly. Its methods are simpler than those of the *Nautical Almanac,* and thus attractive to many marine navigators who accept a lesser degree of accuracy (the *A.A.* is accurate only to ± 1.0′, the *N.A.* to ± 0.1′) in exchange for greater convenience. The daily pages begin immediately when the front cover is opened, with all data for one day contained on both sides of a single sheet; by removing the daily page at the end of the day current information is always on the first page. The daily page lists, at ten-minute intervals of GMT, the GHA of Aries, and the GHA of the sun, moon, and three navigational planets. Declination is given every ten minutes for the moon and every hour for the sun and planets. The inside front cover

G.M.T.	ARIES G.H.A.	VENUS −3·4 G.H.A.	Dec.	MARS +0·2 G.H.A.	Dec.	JUPITER −2·0 G.H.A.	Dec.	SATURN +0·4 G.H.A.	Dec.
00	206 26·6	211 01·2	S 3 30·9	272 31·0	S 22 37·1	322 47·3	S 20 12·1	156 01·4	N 16 29·1
01	221 29·1	226 00·9	29·8	287 32·0	36·9	337 50·0	12·1	171 03·5	29·2
02	236 31·5	241 00·5	28·6	302 32·9	36·8	352 52·6	12·0	186 05·7	29·3
03	251 34·0	256 00·2 ··	27·5	317 33·9 ··	36·6	7 55·3 ··	12·0	201 07·9 ··	29·4
04	266 36·4	270 59·9	26·4	332 34·9	36·5	22 58·0	12·0	216 10·0	29·5
05	281 38·9	285 59·6	25·3	347 35·8	36·3	38 00·6	11·9	231 12·2	29·6
06	296 41·4	300 59·3	S 3 24·1	2 36·8	S 22 36·2	53 03·3	S 20 11·9	246 14·3	N 16 29·6
07	311 43·8	315 58·9	23·0	17 37·7	36·0	68 06·0	11·9	261 16·5	29·7
08	326 46·3	330 58·6	21·9	32 38·7	35·9	83 08·7	11·8	276 18·6	29·8
09	341 48·8	345 58·3 ··	20·8	47 39·7 ··	35·7	98 11·3 ··	11·8	291 20·8 ··	29·9
10	356 51·2	0 58·0	19·6	62 40·6	35·6	113 14·0	11·7	306 23·0	30·0
11	11 53·7	15 57·6	18·5	77 41·6	35·5	128 16·7	11·7	321 25·1	30·1
12	26 56·2	30 57·3	S 3 17·4	92 42·6	S 22 35·3	143 19·3	S 20 11·7	336 27·3	N 16 30·1
13	41 58·6	45 57·0	16·3	107 43·5	35·2	158 22·0	11·6	351 29·4	30·2
14	57 01·1	60 56·7	15·1	122 44·5	35·0	173 24·7	11·6	6 31·6	30·3
15	72 03·6	75 56·3 ··	14·0	137 45·5 ··	34·9	188 27·4 ··	11·6	21 33·7 ··	30·4
16	87 06·0	90 56·0	12·9	152 46·4	34·7	203 30·0	11·5	36 35·9	30·5
17	102 08·5	105 55·7	11·7	167 47·4	34·6	218 32·7	11·5	51 38·1	30·5
18	117 10·9	120 55·4	S 3 10·6	182 48·4	S 22 34·4	233 35·4	S 20 11·4	66 40·2	N 16 30·6
19	132 13·4	135 55·1	09·5	197 49·3	34·3	248 38·1	11·4	81 42·4	30·7
20	147 15·9	150 54·7	08·4	212 50·3	34·1	263 40·7	11·4	96 44·5	30·8
21	162 18·3	165 54·4 ··	07·2	227 51·3 ··	34·0	278 43·4 ··	11·3	111 46·7 ··	30·9
22	177 20·8	180 54·1	06·1	242 52·3	33·8	293 46·1	11·3	126 48·8	31·0
23	192 23·3	195 53·8	05·0	257 53·2	33·7	308 48·8	11·3	141 51·0	31·0
00	207 25·7	210 53·4	S 3 03·8	272 54·2	S 22 33·5	323 51·4	S 20 11·2	156 53·2	N 16 31·1
01	222 28·2	225 53·1	02·7	287 55·2	33·4	338 54·1	11·2	171 55·3	31·2
02	237 30·7	240 52·8	01·6	302 56·1	33·2	353 56·8	11·2	186 57·5	31·3
03	252 33·1	255 52·5	3 00·5	317 57·1 ··	33·1	8 59·5 ··	11·1	201 59·6 ··	31·4
04	267 35·6	270 52·2 ··	2 59·3	332 58·1	32·9	24 02·1	11·1	217 01·8	31·5
05	282 38·1	285 51·8	58·2	347 59·0	32·8	39 04·8	11·0	232 03·9	31·5
06	297 40·5	300 51·5	S 2 57·1	3 00·0	S 22 32·6	54 07·5	S 20 11·0	247 06·1	N 16 31·6
07	312 43·0	315 51·2	55·9	18 01·0	32·5	69 10·2	11·0	262 08·3	31·7
08	327 45·4	330 50·9	54·8	33 02·0	32·3	84 12·9	10·9	277 10·4	31·8
09	342 47·9	345 50·5 ··	53·7	48 02·9 ··	32·2	99 15·5 ··	10·9	292 12·6 ··	31·9
10	357 50·4	0 50·2	52·5	63 03·9	32·0	114 18·2	10·9	307 14·7	31·9
11	12 52·8	15 49·9	51·4	78 04·9	31·9	129 20·9	10·8	322 16·9	32·0
12	27 55·3	30 49·6	S 2 50·3	93 05·8	S 22 31·7	144 23·6	S 20 10·8	337 19·0	N 16 32·1
13	42 57·8	45 49·3	49·1	108 06·8	31·6	159 26·2	10·7	352 21·2	32·2
14	58 00·2	60 48·9	48·0	123 07·8	31·4	174 28·9	10·7	7 23·3	32·3
15	73 02·7	75 48·6 ··	46·9	138 08·8 ··	31·3	189 31·6 ··	10·7	22 25·5 ··	32·4
16	88 05·2	90 48·3	45·7	153 09·7	31·1	204 34·3	10·6	37 27·7	32·4
17	103 07·6	105 48·0	44·6	168 10·7	31·0	219 37·0	10·6	52 29·8	32·5
18	118 10·1	120 47·7	S 2 43·5	183 11·7	S 22 30·8	234 39·6	S 20 10·5	67 32·0	N 16 32·6
19	133 12·5	135 47·3	42·3	198 12·7	30·6	249 42·3	10·5	82 34·1	32·7
20	148 15·0	150 47·0	41·2	213 13·6	30·5	264 45·0	10·5	97 36·3	32·8
21	163 17·5	165 46·7 ··	40·1	228 14·6 ··	30·3	279 47·7 ··	10·4	112 38·4 ··	32·9
22	178 19·9	180 46·4	38·9	243 15·6	30·2	294 50·4	10·4	127 40·6	32·9
23	193 22·4	195 46·1	37·8	258 16·6	30·0	309 53·1	10·4	142 42·7	33·0
00	208 24·9	210 45·7	S 2 36·7	273 17·5	S 22 29·9	324 55·7	S 20 10·3	157 44·9	N 16 33·1
01	223 27·3	225 45·4	35·5	288 18·5	29·7	339 58·4	10·3	172 47·0	33·2
02	238 29·8	240 45·1	34·4	303 19·5	29·6	355 01·1	10·2	187 49·2	33·3
03	253 32·3	255 44·8 ··	33·3	318 20·5 ··	29·4	10 03·8 ··	10·2	202 51·4 ··	33·4
04	268 34·7	270 44·5	32·1	333 21·5	29·3	25 06·5	10·2	217 53·5	33·4
05	283 37·2	285 44·1	31·0	348 22·4	29·1	40 09·2	10·1	232 55·7	33·5
06	298 39·7	300 43·8	S 2 29·9	3 23·4	S 22 28·9	55 11·8	S 20 10·1	247 57·8	N 16 33·6
07	313 42·1	315 43·5	28·7	18 24·4	28·8	70 14·5	10·1	263 00·0	33·7
08	328 44·6	330 43·2	27·6	33 25·4	28·7	85 17·2	10·0	278 02·1	33·8
09	343 47·0	345 42·9 ··	26·5	48 26·3 ··	28·5	100 19·9 ··	10·0	293 04·3 ··	33·8
10	358 49·5	0 42·5	25·3	63 27·3	28·4	115 22·6	09·9	308 06·4	33·9
11	13 52·0	15 42·2	24·2	78 28·3	28·2	130 25·3	09·9	323 08·6	34·0
12	28 54·4	30 41·9	S 2 23·0	93 29·3	S 22 28·0	145 27·9	S 20 09·9	338 10·8	N 16 34·1
13	43 56·9	45 41·6	21·9	108 30·3	27·9	160 30·6	09·8	353 12·9	34·2
14	58 59·4	60 41·3	20·8	123 31·2	27·7	175 33·3	09·8	8 15·1	34·3
15	74 01·8	75 40·9 ··	19·6	138 32·2 ··	27·6	190 36·0 ··	09·7	23 17·2 ··	34·3
16	89 04·3	90 40·6	18·5	153 33·2	27·4	205 38·7	09·7	38 19·4	34·4
17	104 06·8	105 40·3	17·4	168 34·2	27·3	220 41·4	09·7	53 21·5	34·5
18	119 09·2	120 40·0	S 2 16·2	183 35·2	S 22 27·1	235 44·1	S 20 09·6	68 23·7	N 16 34·6
19	134 11·7	135 39·7	15·1	198 36·2	27·0	250 46·8	09·6	83 25·8	34·7
20	149 14·2	150 39·3	13·9	213 37·1	26·8	265 49·4	09·5	98 28·0	34·8
21	164 16·6	165 39·0 ··	12·8	228 38·1	26·6	280 52·1 ··	09·5	113 30·1 ··	34·8
22	179 19·1	180 38·7	11·7	243 39·1	26·5	295 54·8	09·5	128 32·3	34·9
23	194 21·5	195 38·4	10·5	258 40·1	26·3	310 57·5	09·4	143 34·4	35·0
Mer. Pass. 10 08·6		v −0·3 d 1·1		v 1·0 d 0·2		v 2·7 d 0·0		v 2·2 d 0·1	

STARS

Name	S.H.A.	Dec.
Acamar	315 42·6	S 40 25·1
Achernar	335 50·6	S 57 22·8
Acrux	173 44·5	S 62 56·7
Adhara	255 37·6	S 28 56·1
Aldebaran	291 26·0	N 16 27·3
Alioth	166 47·6	N 56 06·8
Alkaid	153 23·1	N 49 27·2
Al Na'ir	28 23·5	S 47 05·9
Alnilam	276 18·7	S 1 13·1
Alphard	218 27·1	S 8 32·1
Alphecca	126 37·4	N 26 48·3
Alpheratz	358 16·7	N 28 55·8
Altair	62 39·1	N 8 47·2
Ankaa	353 47·1	S 42 27·6
Antares	113 04·9	S 26 22·3
Arcturus	146 24·2	N 19 19·6
Atria	108 34·9	S 68 58·6
Avior	234 31·1	S 59 25·3
Bellatrix	279 06·2	N 6 19·5
Betelgeuse	271 35·8	N 7 24·2
Canopus	264 10·5	S 52 40·9
Capella	281 21·6	N 45 58·5
Deneb	49 53·3	N 45 10·3
Denebola	183 05·6	N 14 43·8
Diphda	349 27·9	S 18 08·6
Dubhe	194 29·6	N 61 54·5
Elnath	278 52·9	N 28 35·2
Eltanin	91 00·6	N 51 29·1
Enif	34 18·4	N 9 44·4
Fomalhaut	15 59·0	S 29 46·4
Gacrux	172 36·0	S 56 57·4
Gienah	176 24·7	S 17 23·2
Hadar	149 32·6	S 60 14·3
Hamal	328 37·0	N 23 19·7
Kaus Aust.	84 25·6	S 34 24·0
Kochab	137 17·0	N 74 16·1
Markab	14 10·2	N 15 02·9
Menkar	314 48·5	N 3 58·7
Menkent	148 44·7	S 36 14·0
Miaplacidus	221 46·5	S 69 36·2
Mirfak	309 26·4	N 49 45·8
Nunki	76 37·4	S 26 20·1
Peacock	54 08·9	S 56 49·6
Pollux	244 06·4	N 28 05·9
Procyon	245 32·9	N 5 18·0
Rasalhague	96 35·6	N 12 34·5
Regulus	208 17·0	N 12 06·4
Rigel	281 42·7	S 8 14·0
Rigil Kent.	140 34·7	S 60 43·2
Sabik	102 48·7	S 15 41·6
Schedar	350 17·5	N 56 22·7
Shaula	97 04·7	S 37 05·1
Sirius	259 01·8	S 16 40·7
Spica	159 04·4	S 11 01·0
Suhail	223 15·8	S 43 19·2
Vega	81 00·3	N 38 45·0
Zuben'ubi	137 40·2	S 15 55·6

	S.H.A.	Mer. Pass.
Venus	3 27·7	9 57
Mars	65 28·5	5 48
Jupiter	116 25·7	2 24
Saturn	309 27·4	13 31

FIGURE 68. NAUTICAL ALMANAC EXTRACTS

a. Right-hand page

1971 APRIL 19, 20, 21 (MON., TUES., WED.)

SUN and MOON — G.M.T.

G.M.T. (d h)	SUN G.H.A.	SUN Dec.	MOON G.H.A.	v	MOON Dec.	d	H.P.
19 00	180 09.6	N10 52.2	259 36.5	8.6	S20 40.2	11.1	58.5
01	195 09.8	53.1	274 04.1	8.6	20 29.1	11.2	58.6
02	210 09.9	54.0	288 31.7	8.6	20 17.9	11.4	58.6
03	225 10.0	·· 54.9	302 59.3	8.8	20 06.5	11.5	58.6
04	240 10.2	55.7	317 27.1	8.7	19 55.0	11.6	58.7
05	255 10.3	56.6	331 54.8	8.8	19 43.4	11.7	58.7
06	270 10.5	N10 57.5	346 22.6	8.9	S19 31.7	11.8	58.7
07	285 10.6	58.3	0 50.5	8.8	19 19.9	12.0	58.7
08	300 10.7	10 59.2	15 18.3	9.0	19 07.9	12.1	58.8
M 09	315 10.9	11 00.1	29 46.3	9.0	18 55.8	12.2	58.8
O 10	330 11.0	00.9	44 14.3	9.0	18 43.6	12.3	58.8
N 11	345 11.2	01.8	58 42.3	9.1	18 31.3	12.5	58.9
D 12	0 11.3	N11 02.7	73 10.4	9.1	S18 18.8	12.5	58.9
A 13	15 11.4	03.5	87 38.5	9.2	18 06.3	12.7	58.9
Y 14	30 11.6	04.4	102 06.7	9.2	17 53.6	12.8	59.0
15	45 11.7	·· 05.3	116 34.9	9.3	17 40.8	12.9	59.0
16	60 11.8	06.1	131 03.2	9.3	17 27.9	13.0	59.0
17	75 12.0	07.0	145 31.5	9.3	17 14.9	13.1	59.1
18	90 12.1	N11 07.9	159 59.8	9.4	S17 01.8	13.3	59.1
19	105 12.3	08.7	174 28.2	9.5	16 48.5	13.3	59.1
20	120 12.4	09.6	188 56.7	9.4	16 35.2	13.5	59.1
21	135 12.5	·· 10.5	203 25.1	9.6	16 21.7	13.5	59.2
22	150 12.7	11.3	217 53.7	9.5	16 08.2	13.7	59.2
23	165 12.8	12.2	232 22.2	9.6	15 54.5	13.7	59.2
20 00	180 12.9	N11 13.1	246 50.8	9.7	S15 40.8	13.9	59.3
01	195 13.1	13.9	261 19.5	9.7	15 26.9	13.9	59.3
02	210 13.2	14.8	275 48.2	9.7	15 13.0	14.1	59.3
03	225 13.3	·· 15.7	290 16.9	9.8	14 58.9	14.1	59.4
04	240 13.5	16.5	304 45.7	9.8	14 44.8	14.3	59.4
05	255 13.6	17.4	319 14.5	9.8	14 30.5	14.3	59.4
06	270 13.8	N11 18.2	333 43.3	9.9	S14 16.2	14.5	59.4
07	285 13.9	19.1	348 12.2	9.9	14 01.7	14.5	59.5
T 08	300 14.0	20.0	2 41.1	9.9	13 47.2	14.6	59.5
U 09	315 14.2	·· 20.8	17 10.0	10.0	13 32.6	14.7	59.5
E 10	330 14.3	21.7	31 39.0	10.1	13 17.9	14.8	59.6
S 11	345 14.4	22.5	46 08.1	10.0	13 03.1	14.9	59.6
D 12	0 14.6	N11 23.4	60 37.1	10.1	S12 48.2	14.9	59.6
A 13	15 14.7	24.3	75 06.2	10.1	12 33.3	15.1	59.6
Y 14	30 14.8	25.1	89 35.3	10.2	12 18.2	15.1	59.7
15	45 15.0	·· 26.0	104 04.5	10.1	12 03.1	15.2	59.7
16	60 15.1	26.8	118 33.6	10.3	11 47.9	15.3	59.7
17	75 15.2	27.7	133 02.9	10.2	11 32.6	15.4	59.7
18	90 15.4	N11 28.6	147 32.1	10.3	S11 17.2	15.4	59.8
19	105 15.5	29.4	162 01.4	10.2	11 01.8	15.5	59.8
20	120 15.6	30.3	176 30.6	10.4	10 46.3	15.6	59.8
21	135 15.8	·· 31.1	191 00.0	10.3	10 30.7	15.7	59.8
22	150 15.9	32.0	205 29.3	10.4	10 15.0	15.7	59.9
23	165 16.0	32.8	219 58.7	10.4	9 59.3	15.8	59.9
21 00	180 16.1	N11 33.7	234 28.1	10.4	S 9 43.5	15.9	59.9
01	195 16.3	34.6	248 57.5	10.4	9 27.6	15.9	60.0
02	210 16.4	35.4	263 26.9	10.4	9 11.7	16.0	60.0
03	225 16.5	·· 36.3	277 56.3	10.5	8 55.7	16.1	60.0
04	240 16.7	37.1	292 25.8	10.5	8 39.6	16.1	60.0
05	255 16.8	38.0	306 55.3	10.5	8 23.5	16.2	60.1
06	270 16.9	N11 38.8	321 24.8	10.5	S 8 07.3	16.2	60.1
W 07	285 17.1	39.7	335 54.3	10.5	7 51.1	16.3	60.1
E 08	300 17.2	40.5	350 23.8	10.6	7 34.8	16.4	60.1
D 09	315 17.3	·· 41.4	4 54.4	10.6	7 18.4	16.4	60.2
N 10	330 17.4	42.3	19 23.0	10.6	7 02.0	16.5	60.2
E 11	345 17.6	43.1	33 52.5	10.6	6 45.5	16.5	60.2
S 12	0 17.7	N11 44.0	48 22.1	10.6	S 6 29.0	16.6	60.2
D 13	15 17.8	44.8	62 51.7	10.6	6 12.5	16.6	60.2
A 14	30 18.0	45.7	77 21.3	10.6	5 55.9	16.7	60.3
Y 15	45 18.1	·· 46.5	91 50.9	10.6	5 39.2	16.7	60.3
16	60 18.2	47.4	106 20.5	10.6	5 22.5	16.7	60.3
17	75 18.4	48.2	120 50.1	10.6	5 05.8	16.8	60.3
18	90 18.5	N11 49.1	135 19.7	10.6	S 4 49.0	16.8	60.4
19	105 18.6	49.9	149 49.3	10.7	4 32.2	16.8	60.4
20	120 18.7	50.8	164 19.0	10.6	4 15.4	16.9	60.4
21	135 18.9	·· 51.6	178 48.6	10.6	3 58.5	16.9	60.4
22	150 19.0	52.5	193 18.2	10.6	3 41.6	17.0	60.4
23	165 19.1	53.3	207 47.8	10.6	3 24.6	17.0	60.4
	S.D. 15.9	d 0.9	S.D. 16.0		16.2		16.4

Twilight, Sunrise, Moonrise

Lat.	Twilight Naut.	Twilight Civil	Sun-rise	Moonrise 19	20	21	22
N 72	////	01 08	03 14	■■	05 17	04 24	03 46
N 70	////	02 03	03 35	06 10	04 47	04 11	03 43
68	////	02 36	03 51	05 06	04 25	04 01	03 41
66	00 59	02 59	04 04	04 30	04 08	03 52	03 39
64	01 48	03 17	04 14	04 04	03 53	03 45	03 37
62	02 17	03 31	04 23	03 44	03 41	03 38	03 35
60	02 38	03 44	04 31	03 27	03 31	03 33	03 34
N 58	02 56	03 54	04 38	03 13	03 22	03 28	03 33
56	03 10	04 03	04 44	03 01	03 14	03 23	03 32
54	03 22	04 11	04 49	02 50	03 07	03 19	03 31
52	03 32	04 18	04 54	02 41	03 00	03 16	03 30
50	03 41	04 24	04 59	02 32	02 54	03 13	03 29
45	03 59	04 37	05 08	02 14	02 42	03 05	03 27
N 40	04 14	04 48	05 16	01 59	02 31	02 59	03 26
35	04 25	04 57	05 23	01 46	02 22	02 54	03 25
30	04 35	05 04	05 29	01 35	02 14	02 50	03 23
20	04 50	05 16	05 39	01 16	02 00	02 42	03 22
N 10	05 01	05 26	05 47	00 59	01 48	02 34	03 20
0	05 10	05 35	05 56	00 44	01 37	02 28	03 18
S 10	05 18	05 42	06 04	00 28	01 25	02 21	03 17
20	05 24	05 50	06 12	00 11	01 13	02 14	03 15
30	05 29	05 57	06 22	24 59	00 59	02 06	03 13
35	05 32	06 01	06 27	24 50	00 50	02 01	03 12
40	05 34	06 06	06 33	24 41	00 41	01 56	03 11
45	05 36	06 10	06 40	24 30	00 30	01 49	03 09
S 50	05 38	06 16	06 49	24 16	00 16	01 42	03 08
52	05 39	06 18	06 53	24 10	00 10	01 38	03 07
54	05 39	06 21	06 57	24 03	00 03	01 34	03 06
56	05 40	06 23	07 02	23 55	25 30	01 30	03 05
58	05 41	06 26	07 07	23 46	25 25	01 25	03 04
S 60	05 41	06 30	07 13	23 36	25 20	01 20	03 03

Sunset, Twilight, Moonset

Lat.	Sun-set	Twilight Civil	Twilight Naut.	Moonset 19	20	21	22
N 72	20 48	23 06	////	■■	10 49	13 31	15 59
N 70	20 27	22 02	////	08 04	11 16	13 41	15 57
68	20 11	21 27	////	09 06	11 36	13 48	15 55
66	19 57	21 03	23 13	09 41	11 52	13 54	15 54
64	19 46	20 44	22 17	10 05	12 05	14 00	15 53
62	19 37	20 29	21 45	10 25	12 16	14 04	15 52
60	19 29	20 17	21 23	10 40	12 25	14 08	15 51
N 58	19 22	20 06	21 05	10 54	12 33	14 12	15 51
56	19 16	19 57	20 51	11 05	12 40	14 15	15 50
54	19 10	19 49	20 39	11 15	12 46	14 18	15 50
52	19 05	19 42	20 28	11 24	12 52	14 20	15 49
50	19 00	19 35	20 19	11 32	12 57	14 22	15 49
45	18 50	19 22	20 00	11 48	13 08	14 27	15 48
N 40	18 43	19 11	19 45	12 02	13 16	14 31	15 47
35	18 36	19 02	19 34	12 14	13 24	14 35	15 46
30	18 30	18 55	19 24	12 24	13 31	14 38	15 45
20	18 20	18 42	19 09	12 41	13 42	14 43	15 44
N 10	18 11	18 32	18 57	12 55	13 52	14 47	15 43
0	18 02	18 23	18 48	13 09	14 01	14 52	15 42
S 10	17 54	18 16	18 40	13 23	14 10	14 56	15 41
20	17 46	18 08	18 34	13 37	14 20	15 00	15 40
30	17 36	18 00	18 28	13 54	14 31	15 05	15 39
35	17 31	17 56	18 26	14 03	14 37	15 08	15 38
40	17 24	17 52	18 24	14 14	14 44	15 11	15 37
45	17 17	17 47	18 21	14 26	14 52	15 15	15 36
S 50	17 09	17 42	18 19	14 42	15 02	15 19	15 35
52	17 05	17 39	18 18	14 49	15 06	15 21	15 35
54	17 00	17 37	18 18	14 57	15 11	15 23	15 34
56	16 56	17 34	18 17	15 05	15 16	15 25	15 33
58	16 50	17 31	18 16	15 15	15 22	15 28	15 33
S 60	16 44	17 27	18 16	15 26	15 29	15 31	15 32

SUN and MOON

Day	SUN Eqn. of Time 00h	12h	Mer. Pass.	MOON Mer. Pass. Upper	Lower	Age	Phase
19	00 38	00 45	11 59	06 57	19 23	24	
20	00 51	00 58	11 59	07 49	20 14	25	
21	01 04	01 11	11 59	08 40	21 05	26	

FIGURE 68. NAUTICAL ALMANAC EXTRACTS

b. Left-hand page

22ᵐ	SUN PLANETS	ARIES	MOON	v or d	Corrⁿ	v or d	Corrⁿ	v or d	Corrⁿ
s	° ′	° ′	° ′	′	′	′	′	′	′
00	5 30·0	5 30·9	5 15·0	0·0	0·0	6·0	2·3	12·0	4·5
01	5 30·3	5 31·2	5 15·2	0·1	0·0	6·1	2·3	12·1	4·5
02	5 30·5	5 31·4	5 15·4	0·2	0·1	6·2	2·3	12·2	4·6
03	5 30·8	5 31·7	5 15·7	0·3	0·1	6·3	2·4	12·3	4·6
04	5 31·0	5 31·9	5 15·9	0·4	0·2	6·4	2·4	12·4	4·7
05	5 31·3	5 32·2	5 16·2	0·5	0·2	6·5	2·4	12·5	4·7
06	5 31·5	5 32·4	5 16·4	0·6	0·2	6·6	2·5	12·6	4·7
07	5 31·8	5 32·7	5 16·6	0·7	0·3	6·7	2·5	12·7	4·8
08	5 32·0	5 32·9	5 16·9	0·8	0·3	6·8	2·6	12·8	4·8
09	5 32·3	5 33·2	5 17·1	0·9	0·3	6·9	2·6	12·9	4·8
10	5 32·5	5 33·4	5 17·4	1·0	0·4	7·0	2·6	13·0	4·9
11	5 32·8	5 33·7	5 17·6	1·1	0·4	7·1	2·7	13·1	4·9
12	5 33·0	5 33·9	5 17·8	1·2	0·5	7·2	2·7	13·2	5·0
13	5 33·3	5 34·2	5 18·1	1·3	0·5	7·3	2·7	13·3	5·0
14	5 33·5	5 34·4	5 18·3	1·4	0·5	7·4	2·8	13·4	5·0
15	5 33·8	5 34·7	5 18·5	1·5	0·6	7·5	2·8	13·5	5·1
16	5 34·0	5 34·9	5 18·8	1·6	0·6	7·6	2·9	13·6	5·1
17	5 34·3	5 35·2	5 19·0	1·7	0·6	7·7	2·9	13·7	5·1
18	5 34·5	5 35·4	5 19·3	1·8	0·7	7·8	2·9	13·8	5·2
19	5 34·8	5 35·7	5 19·5	1·9	0·7	7·9	3·0	13·9	5·2
20	5 35·0	5 35·9	5 19·7	2·0	0·8	8·0	3·0	14·0	5·3
21	5 35·3	5 36·2	5 20·0	2·1	0·8	8·1	3·0	14·1	5·3
22	5 35·5	5 36·4	5 20·2	2·2	0·8	8·2	3·1	14·2	5·3
23	5 35·8	5 36·7	5 20·5	2·3	0·9	8·3	3·1	14·3	5·4
24	5 36·0	5 36·9	5 20·7	2·4	0·9	8·4	3·2	14·4	5·4
25	5 36·3	5 37·2	5 20·9	2·5	0·9	8·5	3·2	14·5	5·4
26	5 36·5	5 37·4	5 21·2	2·6	1·0	8·6	3·2	14·6	5·5
27	5 36·8	5 37·7	5 21·4	2·7	1·0	8·7	3·3	14·7	5·5
28	5 37·0	5 37·9	5 21·6	2·8	1·1	8·8	3·3	14·8	5·6
29	5 37·3	5 38·2	5 21·9	2·9	1·1	8·9	3·3	14·9	5·6
30	5 37·5	5 38·4	5 22·1	3·0	1·1	9·0	3·4	15·0	5·6
31	5 37·8	5 38·7	5 22·4	3·1	1·2	9·1	3·4	15·1	5·7
32	5 38·0	5 38·9	5 22·6	3·2	1·2	9·2	3·5	15·2	5·7
33	5 38·3	5 39·2	5 22·8	3·3	1·2	9·3	3·5	15·3	5·7
34	5 38·5	5 39·4	5 23·1	3·4	1·3	9·4	3·5	15·4	5·8
35	5 38·8	5 39·7	5 23·3	3·5	1·3	9·5	3·6	15·5	5·8
36	5 39·0	5 39·9	5 23·6	3·6	1·4	9·6	3·6	15·6	5·9
37	5 39·3	5 40·2	5 23·8	3·7	1·4	9·7	3·6	15·7	5·9
38	5 39·5	5 40·4	5 24·0	3·8	1·4	9·8	3·7	15·8	5·9
39	5 39·8	5 40·7	5 24·3	3·9	1·5	9·9	3·7	15·9	6·0
40	5 40·0	5 40·9	5 24·5	4·0	1·5	10·0	3·8	16·0	6·0
41	5 40·3	5 41·2	5 24·7	4·1	1·5	10·1	3·8	16·1	6·0
42	5 40·5	5 41·4	5 25·0	4·2	1·6	10·2	3·8	16·2	6·1
43	5 40·8	5 41·7	5 25·2	4·3	1·6	10·3	3·9	16·3	6·1
44	5 41·0	5 41·9	5 25·5	4·4	1·7	10·4	3·9	16·4	6·2
45	5 41·3	5 42·2	5 25·7	4·5	1·7	10·5	3·9	16·5	6·2
46	5 41·5	5 42·4	5 25·9	4·6	1·7	10·6	4·0	16·6	6·2
47	5 41·8	5 42·7	5 26·2	4·7	1·8	10·7	4·0	16·7	6·3
48	5 42·0	5 42·9	5 26·4	4·8	1·8	10·8	4·1	16·8	6·3
49	5 42·3	5 43·2	5 26·7	4·9	1·8	10·9	4·1	16·9	6·3
50	5 42·5	5 43·4	5 26·9	5·0	1·9	11·0	4·1	17·0	6·4
51	5 42·8	5 43·7	5 27·1	5·1	1·9	11·1	4·2	17·1	6·4
52	5 43·0	5 43·9	5 27·4	5·2	2·0	11·2	4·2	17·2	6·5
53	5 43·3	5 44·2	5 27·6	5·3	2·0	11·3	4·3	17·3	6·5
54	5 43·5	5 44·4	5 27·9	5·4	2·0	11·4	4·3	17·4	6·5
55	5 43·8	5 44·7	5 28·1	5·5	2·1	11·5	4·3	17·5	6·6
56	5 44·0	5 44·9	5 28·3	5·6	2·1	11·6	4·4	17·6	6·6
57	5 44·3	5 45·2	5 28·6	5·7	2·1	11·7	4·4	17·7	6·6
58	5 44·5	5 45·4	5 28·8	5·8	2·2	11·8	4·4	17·8	6·7
59	5 44·8	5 45·7	5 29·0	5·9	2·2	11·9	4·5	17·9	6·7
60	5 45·0	5 45·9	5 29·3	6·0	2·3	12·0	4·5	18·0	6·8

FIGURE 68.
NAUTICAL
ALMANAC
EXTRACTS

c. Increments and corrections

GMT	SUN GHA	SUN Dec.	ARIES GHA γ	VENUS −3.4 GHA	VENUS Dec.	MARS 0.3 GHA	MARS Dec.	JUPITER −2.0 GHA	JUPITER Dec.	MOON GHA	MOON Dec.
h m	° '	° '	° '	° '	° '	° '	° '	° '	° '	° '	° '
12 00	0 14.5	N11 23.4	27 55.3	30 50	S 2 50	93 06	S22 32	144 24	S20 11	60 37	S12 47
10	2 44.5	23.6	30 25.7	33 20		95 36		146 54		63 02	44
20	5 14.5	23.7	32 56.1	35 50		98 06		149 24		65 27	42
30	7 44.6 ·	23.8	35 26.5	38 19 ·		100 36 ·		151 55 ·		67 52 ·	40
40	10 14.6	24.0	37 56.9	40 49		103 06		154 25		70 17	37
50	12 44.6	24.1	40 27.4	43 19		105 37		156 56		72 41	35
13 00	15 14.6	N11 24.3	42 57.8	45 49	S 2 49	108 07	S22 32	159 26	S20 11	75 06	S12 32
10	17 44.6	24.4	45 28.2	48 19		110 37		161 57		77 31	30
20	20 14.7	24.6	47 58.6	50 49		113 07		164 27		79 56	27
30	22 44.7 ·	24.7	50 29.0	53 19 ·		115 37 ·		166 58 ·		82 21 ·	25
40	25 14.7	24.8	52 59.4	55 49		118 07		169 28		84 46	22
50	27 44.7	25.0	55 29.8	58 19		120 38		171 58		87 10	19
14 00	30 14.8	N11 25.1	58 00.2	60 49	S 2 47	123 08	S22 31	174 29	S20 11	89 35	S12 17
10	32 44.8	25.3	60 30.6	63 19		125 38		176 59		92 00	14
20	35 14.8	25.4	63 01.0	65 49		128 08		179 30		94 25	12
30	37 44.8 ·	25.6	65 31.5	68 19 ·		130 38 ·		182 00 ·		96 50 ·	09
40	40 14.8	25.7	68 01.9	70 49		133 08		184 31		99 15	07
50	42 44.9	25.8	70 32.3	73 19		135 39		187 01		101 40	04
15 00	45 14.9	N11 26.0	73 02.7	75 49	S 2 46	138 09	S22 31	189 32	S20 11	104 05	S12 02
10	47 44.9	26.1	75 33.1	78 19		140 39		192 02		106 29	11 59
20	50 14.9	26.3	78 03.5	80 49		143 09		194 33		108 54	57
30	52 45.0 ·	26.4	80 33.9	83 18 ·		145 39 ·		197 03 ·		111 19 ·	54
40	55 15.0	26.6	83 04.3	85 48		148 09		199 33		113 44	52
50	57 45.0	26.7	85 34.7	88 18		150 40		202 04		116 09	49
16 00	60 15.0	N11 26.8	88 05.2	90 48	S 2 45	153 10	S22 31	204 34	S20 11	118 34	S11 47
10	62 45.0	27.0	90 35.6	93 18		155 40		207 05		120 59	44
20	65 15.1	27.1	93 06.0	95 48		158 10		209 35		123 23	42
30	67 45.1 ·	27.3	95 36.4	98 18 ·		160 40 ·		212 06 ·		125 48 ·	39
40	70 15.1	27.4	98 06.8	100 48		163 10		214 36		128 13	36
50	72 45.1	27.6	100 37.2	103 18		165 41		217 07		130 38	34
17 00	75 15.2	N11 27.7	103 07.6	105 48	S 2 44	168 11	S22 31	219 37	S20 11	133 03	S11 31
10	77 45.2	27.8	105 38.0	108 18		170 41		222 07		135 28	29
20	80 15.2	28.0	108 08.4	110 48		173 11		224 38		137 53	26
30	82 45.2 ·	28.1	110 38.9	113 18 ·		175 41 ·		227 08 ·		140 18 ·	24
40	85 15.2	28.3	113 09.3	115 48		178 11		229 39		142 42	21
50	87 45.3	28.4	115 39.7	118 18		180 42		232 09		145 07	18
18 00	90 15.3	N11 28.6	118 10.1	120 48	S 2 43	183 12	S22 31	234 40	S20 11	147 32	S11 16
10	92 45.3	28.7	120 40.5	123 18		185 42		237 10		149 57	13
20	95 15.3	28.9	123 10.9	125 48		188 12		239 41		152 22	11
30	97 45.4 ·	29.0	125 41.3	128 18 ·		190 42 ·		242 11 ·		154 47 ·	08
40	100 15.4	29.1	128 11.7	130 47		193 12		244 41		157 12	06
50	102 45.4	29.3	130 42.1	133 17		195 43		247 12		159 37	03
19 00	105 15.4	N11 29.4	133 12.5	135 47	S 2 42	198 13	S22 31	249 42	S20 11	162 01	S11 01
10	107 45.4	29.6	135 43.0	138 17		200 43		252 13		164 26	10 58
20	110 15.5	29.7	138 13.4	140 47		203 13		254 43		166 51	55
30	112 45.5 ·	29.9	140 43.8	143 17 ·		205 43 ·		257 14 ·		169 16 ·	53
40	115 15.5	30.0	143 14.2	145 47		208 13		259 44		171 41	50
50	117 45.5	30.1	145 44.6	148 17		210 43		262 15		174 06	48
20 00	120 15.6	N11 30.3	148 15.0	150 47	S 2 41	213 14	S22 30	264 45	S20 10	176 31	S10 45
10	122 45.6	30.4	150 45.4	153 17		215 44		267 15		178 56	42
20	125 15.6	30.6	153 15.8	155 47		218 14		269 46		181 21	40
30	127 45.6 ·	30.7	155 46.2	158 17 ·		220 44 ·		272 16 ·		183 45 ·	37
40	130 15.6	30.9	158 16.7	160 47		223 14		274 47		186 10	35
50	132 45.7	31.0	160 47.1	163 17		225 44		277 17		188 35	32
21 00	135 15.7	N11 31.1	163 17.5	165 47	S 2 40	228 15	S22 30	279 48	S20 10	191 00	S10 29
10	137 45.7	31.3	165 47.9	168 17		230 45		282 18		193 25	27
20	140 15.7	31.4	168 18.3	170 47		233 15		284 49		195 50	24
30	142 45.7 ·	31.6	170 48.7	173 17 ·		235 45 ·		287 19 ·		198 15 ·	22
40	145 15.8	31.7	173 19.1	175 47		238 15		289 50		200 40	19
50	147 45.8	31.9	175 49.5	178 16		240 45		292 20		203 04	16
22 00	150 15.8	N11 32.0	178 19.9	180 46	S 2 38	243 16	S22 30	294 50	S20 10	205 29	S10 14
10	152 45.8	32.1	180 50.4	183 16		245 46		297 21		207 54	11
20	155 15.9	32.3	183 20.8	185 46		248 16		299 51		210 19	08
30	157 45.9 ·	32.4	185 51.2	188 16 ·		250 46 ·		302 22 ·		212 44 ·	06
40	160 15.9	32.6	188 21.6	190 46		253 16		304 52		215 09	03
50	162 45.9	32.7	190 52.0	193 16		255 46		307 23		217 34	10 01
23 00	165 15.9	N11 32.9	193 22.4	195 46	S 2 37	258 17	S22 30	309 53	S20 10	219 59	S 9 58
10	167 46.0	33.0	195 52.8	198 16		260 47		312 24		222 24	55
20	170 16.0	33.1	198 23.2	200 46		263 17		314 54		224 49	53
30	172 46.0 ·	33.3	200 53.6	203 16 ·		265 47 ·		317 24 ·		227 13 ·	50
40	175 16.0	33.4	203 24.0	205 46		268 17		319 55		229 38	47
50	177 46.1	33.6	205 54.5	208 16		270 47		322 25		232 03	45

Sun SD 15.9
Moon SD 16'
Age 25d

Moonset

Lat.	Moonset	Diff.
N	h m	m
72	10 49	*
70	11 16	84
68	11 36	71
66	11 52	63
64	12 05	59
62	12 16	55
60	12 25	52
58	12 33	50
56	12 40	48
54	12 46	46
52	12 52	44
50	12 57	43
45	13 08	40
40	13 16	37
35	13 24	35
30	13 31	34
20	13 42	31
10	13 52	28
0	14 01	26
10	14 10	23
20	14 20	21
30	14 31	18
35	14 37	16
40	14 44	14
45	14 52	12
50	15 02	09
52	15 06	08
54	15 11	07
56	15 16	05
58	15 22	03
60	15 29	01
S		

Moon's P. in A.

Alt.	+Corr.	Alt.	+Corr.
°	'	°	'
0	60	53	35
5	60	54	35
11	59	55	34
15	58	57	33
19	57	58	32
21	56	59	31
24	54	60	30
26	53	61	28
28	53	62	28
30	52	63	27
32	51	64	26
34	50	65	25
35	49	66	24
37	48	67	23
38	47	68	22
40	46	69	21
41	45	70	20
43	44	71	19
44	43	72	18
46	42	73	17
47	41	74	16
48	40	75	15
49	39	76	14
51	38	77	13
52	37	78	12
53	36	79	11
54	35	80	10

| INTERPOLATION OF G.H.A.

Increment to be added for intervals of G.M.T. to G.H.A. of: Sun, Aries (γ) and planets; Moon

No.	Name		Mag.	S.H.A.	Dec.
				° ′	° ′
7*	Acamar		3·1	315 42	S.40 25
5*	Achernar		0·6	335 50	S.57 23
30*	Acrux		1·1	173 45	S.62 57
19	Adhara	†	1·6	255 38	S.28 56
10*	Aldebaran	†	1·1	291 26	N.16 27
32*	Alioth		1·7	166 48	N.56 07
34*	Alkaid		1·9	153 23	N.49 27
55	Al Na'ir		2·2	28 23	S.47 06
15	Alnilam		1·8	276 19	S. 1 13
25*	Alphard	†	2·2	218 27	S. 8 32
41*	Alphecca	†	2·3	126 37	N.26 49
1*	Alpheratz	†	2·2	358 16	N.28 56
51*	Altair	†	0·9	62 39	N. 8 47
2	Ankaa		2·4	353 47	S.42 27
42*	Antares	†	1·2	113 05	S.26 22
37*	Arcturus	†	0·2	146 24	N.19 20
43	Atria		1·9	108 35	S.68 59
22	Avior		1·7	234 32	S.59 25
13	Bellatrix	†	1·7	279 06	N. 6 20
16*	Betelgeuse	†	0·1–1·2	271 36	N. 7 24
17*	Canopus		−0·9	264 11	S.52 41
12*	Capella		0·2	281 21	N.45 58
53*	Deneb		1·3	49 53	N.45 11
28*	Denebola	†	2·2	183 06	N.14 44
4*	Diphda	†	2·2	349 27	S.18 08
27*	Dubhe		2·0	194 30	N.61 55
14	Elnath	†	1·8	278 53	N.28 35
47	Eltanin		2·4	91 00	N.51 29
54*	Enif	†	2·5	34 18	N. 9 45
56*	Fomalhaut	†	1·3	15 58	S.29 46
31	Gacrux		1·6	172 36	S.56 58
29*	Gienah	†	2·8	176 25	S.17 23
35	Hadar		0·9	149 33	S.60 15
6*	Hamal	†	2·2	328 37	N.23 20
48	Kaus Aust.		2·0	84 25	S.34 24
40*	Kochab		2·2	137 18	N.74 16
57	Markab	†	2·6	14 10	N.15 03
8*	Menkar	†	2·8	314 48	N. 3 59
36	Menkent		2·3	148 45	S.36 14
24*	Miaplacidus		1·8	221 47	S.69 36
9*	Mirfak		1·9	309 26	N.49 46
50*	Nunki	†	2·1	76 37	S.26 20
52*	Peacock		2·1	54 08	S.56 50
21*	Pollux	†	1·2	244 06	N.28 06
20*	Procyon	†	0·5	245 33	N. 5 18
46*	Rasalhague	†	2·1	96 35	N.12 35
26*	Regulus	†	1·3	208 17	N.12 07
11*	Rigel	†	0·3	281 43	S. 8 14
38*	Rigil Kent.		0·1	140 35	S.60 43
44	Sabik	†	2·6	102 48	S.15 42
3*	Schedar		2·5	350 17	N.56 23
45*	Shaula		1·7	97 04	S.37 05
18*	Sirius	†	−1·6	259 02	S.16 40
33*	Spica	†	1·2	159 04	S.11 01
23*	Suhail		2·2	223 16	S.43 19
49*	Vega		0·1	81 00	N.38 45
39	Zuben'ubi	†	2·9	137 40	S.15 56

SUN, etc.	MOON	SUN, etc.	MOON	SUN, etc.	MOON
m s	m s	m s	m s	m s	m s
00 00 ° 0 00	00 00	03 17 ° 0 50	03 25	06 37 ° 1 40	06 52
01 0 01	00 02	21 0 51	03 29	41 1 41	06 56
05 0 02	00 06	25 0 52	03 33	45 1 42	07 00
09 0 03	00 10	29 0 53	03 37	49 1 43	07 04
13 0 04	00 14	33 0 54	03 41	53 1 44	07 08
17 0 05	00 18	37 0 55	03 45	06 57 1 45	07 13
21 0 06	00 22	41 0 56	03 49	07 01 1 46	07 17
25 0 07	00 26	45 0 57	03 54	05 1 47	07 21
29 0 08	00 31	49 0 58	03 58	09 1 48	07 25
33 0 09	00 35	53 0 59	04 02	13 1 49	07 29
37 0 10	00 39	03 57 1 00	04 06	17 1 50	07 33
41 0 11	00 43	04 01 1 01	04 10	21 1 51	07 37
45 0 12	00 47	05 1 02	04 14	25 1 52	07 42
49 0 13	00 51	09 1 03	04 19	29 1 53	07 46
53 0 14	00 55	13 1 04	04 23	33 1 54	07 50
00 57 0 15	01 00	17 1 05	04 27	37 1 55	07 54
01 01 0 16	01 04	21 1 06	04 31	41 1 56	07 58
05 0 17	01 08	25 1 07	04 35	45 1 57	08 02
09 0 18	01 12	29 1 08	04 39	49 1 58	08 06
13 0 19	01 16	33 1 09	04 43	53 1 59	08 11
17 0 20	01 20	37 1 10	04 48	07 57 2 00	08 15
21 0 21	01 24	41 1 11	04 52	08 01 2 01	08 19
25 0 22	01 29	45 1 12	04 56	05 2 02	08 23
29 0 23	01 33	49 1 13	05 00	09 2 03	08 27
33 0 24	01 37	53 1 14	05 04	13 2 04	08 31
37 0 25	01 41	04 57 1 15	05 08	17 2 05	08 35
41 0 26	01 45	05 01 1 16	05 12	21 2 06	08 40
45 0 27	01 49	05 1 17	05 17	25 2 07	08 44
49 0 28	01 53	09 1 18	05 21	29 2 08	08 48
53 0 29	01 58	13 1 19	05 25	33 2 09	08 52
01 57 0 30	02 02	17 1 20	05 29	37 2 10	08 56
02 01 0 31	02 06	21 1 21	05 33	41 2 11	09 00
05 0 32	02 10	25 1 22	05 37	45 2 12	09 04
09 0 33	02 14	29 1 23	05 41	49 2 13	09 09
13 0 34	02 18	33 1 24	05 46	53 2 14	09 13
17 0 35	02 22	37 1 25	05 50	08 57 2 15	09 17
21 0 36	02 27	41 1 26	05 54	09 01 2 16	09 21
25 0 37	02 31	45 1 27	05 58	05 2 17	09 25
29 0 38	02 35	49 1 28	06 02	09 2 18	09 29
33 0 39	02 39	53 1 29	06 06	13 2 19	09 33
37 0 40	02 43	05 57 1 30	06 10	17 2 20	09 38
41 0 41	02 47	06 01 1 31	06 15	21 2 21	09 42
45 0 42	02 51	05 1 32	06 19	25 2 22	09 46
49 0 43	02 56	09 1 33	06 23	29 2 23	09 50
53 0 44	03 00	13 1 34	06 27	33 2 24	09 54
02 57 0 45	03 04	17 1 35	06 31	37 2 25	09 58
03 01 0 46	03 08	21 1 36	06 35	41 2 26	10 00
05 0 47	03 12	25 1 37	06 39	45 2 27	
09 0 48	03 16	29 1 38	06 44	49 2 28	
13 0 49	03 20	33 1 39	06 48	53 2 29	
17 0 50	03 25	37 1 40	06 52	06 41 2 30	
03 21	03 29	06 41	06 56	10 00	

* Stars used in H.O. 249 (A.P. 3270) Vol. 1.

† Stars that may be used with Vols. 2 and 3.

b. Inside front cover

FIGURE 69. AIR ALMANAC EXTRACTS

◄a. Daily page

supplies SHA and declination of the 57 selected navigational stars, the quantities being considered constant for the four-month period of the almanac's usefulness. Also on the inside front cover are given the incremental corrections to be added for minutes and seconds between the ten-minute intervals of GHA given on the daily page. The almanac also includes altitude corrections (discussed in Chapter XIII), sky diagrams, time of twilight tables, a table for inter-conversion of arc and time, and other data of interest. The explanatory section is succinct, clearly written, and comprehensive.

GHA and declination: The coordinates of a celestial body, which must be obtained as a preliminary step to finding position, are GHA and declination (Dec). The examples given below demonstrate the method of using the *Air Almanac* to find GHA and declination of any celestial body. For purposes of comparison, the same situation (sun, moon, Venus, and Alphecca at GMT 17h 22m 43s on 20 April 1971) illustrated in the preceding section (*Nautical Almanac* discussion) is repeated:

Sun:	GMT 1720 GHA:	80° 15.2′	Dec: 11° 28.0′ N
	2m 43s:	0° 41′	
	GHA:	80° 56.2′	
Moon:	GMT 1720 GHA:	137° 53′	Dec: 11° 26′ S
	2m 43s:	0° 39′	
	GHA:	138° 32′	
Planet:	GMT 1720 GHA Venus:	110° 48′	Dec: 2° 44′ S
	2m 43s:	0° 41′	
		111° 29′	
Star:	SHA Alphecca:	126° 37′	Dec: 26° 49′ N
	1720 GHA Aries:	108° 08.4′	
	2m 43s:	0° 41′	
	GHA:	235° 26.4′	

Sunrise, sunset, twilight, moonrise, and moonset: Curiously, in view of its obvious superiority of simplicity over the *Nautical Almanac* in all other areas, the *Air Almanac* presentation of sun and moon phenomena is somewhat more complicated. Separate tables must be consulted for the times of sunrise and sunset, and for the beginning and end of civil twilight. Times of moonrise and moonset are given on the daily page. For all practical purposes the times may considered to be LMT, and thus convertible to ZT of the observer by applying DLo converted from arc to time ($1° = 4$ minutes).

Altitude corrections contained in the *Air Almanac* are discussed in Chapter XIII.

Polaris (Pole Star) Tables

Both almanacs provide tables for determining latitude and azimuth by observation of Polaris; the tables and their methods of use are discussed in Chapter XV.

chapter XII

The Marine Sextant

THE MODERN MARINE SEXTANT is a precision optical instrument for measuring angles, primarily the vertical angle between a celestial body and the horizon. Its chief purpose is as a basic instrument in calculating a position on earth. The sextant can also be useful as a piloting instrument to measure the horizontal angle between two lateral aids to navigation (two buoys, a headland and a spire, etc.) or a vertical angle, such as that between the top and base of a lighthouse, in order to compute distance off. Operation of the device is simple and easily learned; "practice makes perfect" as with any operation requiring manual dexterity.

The best quality sextants are manufactured to fine tolerances and should be treated with great respect. A sextant should never be left where it may slide or fall; it is advisable to attach the instrument to a lanyard placed around one's neck when making observations, and to secure it in its case at all times when not in actual use.

The mechanical principle of the sextant's functioning may be understood by referring to Figure 70: Light from the observed celestial body is reflected from the index mirror to the horizon glass and then to the observer's eye at the telescope. The body is then brought down approximately to the horizon by moving the index arm. Final and precise adjustment is then accomplished by rotating the micrometer drum until the center of the body (if a star or planet) or the upper or lower limb (sun or moon) is tangent to the horizon. In order to view both the body and the horizon simultaneously, the horizon glass is vertically divided—half clear, half mirrored. The horizon appears through the clear glass, the body's image is reflected in the mirror. Once the body is observed through the horizon glass to be level with the horizon its exact altitude is found by reading the degrees of altitude on the arc, the minutes on the micrometer drum, and the tenths of minutes on the vernier (some very well made sextants, such as the model in Figure 70, do not provide vernier gradations, and the tenths must therefore be estimated).

A few vintage sextants still exist which do not incorporate a micrometer drum. The method of determining altitude by these instruments is not detailed here, but may be understood by consulting a 1962 or earlier edition of *Bowditch*.

Use of the sextant for celestial observations: The sextant is designed to be held with the right hand while the index arm is moved with the left hand. However, the telescope may be applied to either eye, and the master eye is recommended for best results. (To determine which is the master eye point a finger at a distant

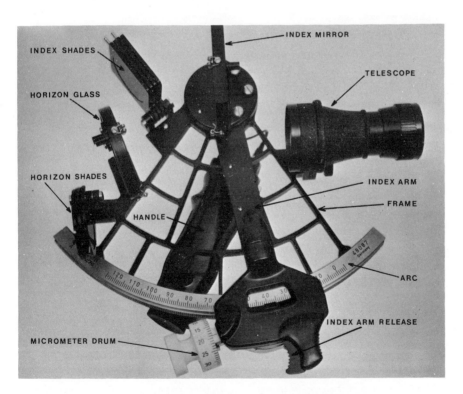

FIGURE 70. MICROMETER DRUM SEXTANT

Weems and Plath, Inc.

but sharply defined object, such as a telegraph pole, with both eyes open. Close each eye in turn; the master eye is that which remains zeroed in on the object sighted). With the index arm set at 0° on the arc, observe the celestial body through the telescope, utilizing the shades if the sun is being observed. Move the index arm slowly along the limb, keeping the body in view through the telescope, until the body is approximately tangent to the horizon as viewed through the clear glass of the horizon glass. Final adjustment to bring the body exactly to the horizon is then made by rotating the micrometer drum. While "bringing the body down" it is important to hold the sextant perpendicular to the horizon. If it is tilted, too great an angle will be registered. Tangency is obtained when the body is on the horizon, which appears only at one point, i.e.,

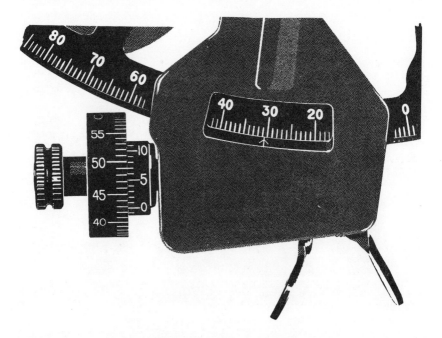

FIGURE 71. READING SEXTANT ALTITUDE

Whole degrees of altitude are read on the arc. Minutes are read on the large drum (opposite the 0 of the vernier). Tenths of minutes are read on the vernier where the gradation lines coincide. The body observed in this example has an altitude of 30° 42.7'.

when the sextant is held vertically. For stars and planets, tangency is considered to be that moment when the body is apparently resting on the horizon (the purists insist the *center* should be on the horizon, a degree of precision seldom if ever attained); tangency of the sun or moon can be obtained when either the upper or lower limb is touching the horizon. It is good practice to rock the sextant slightly from side to side after apparent tangency has been achieved. If the body rises from the horizon as the sextant is rocked, an accurate measurement has been obtained.

The method just described of "bringing down" the body to the horizon is basic and should be learned first. An alternative technique—but no substitute for complete familiarity with "bringing down"—depends on predetermination of approximate altitudes and azimuths, as with a starfinder, and enables the sextant to be pre-set to the approximate altitude of the body to be observed. The *horizon* is then searched at the known azimuth of the body until it is located, after which slight adjustment of the index arm and micrometer drum should bring the body to accurate tangency. The method is quick, and especially valuable for high-altitude observations and for locating bodies of lesser brilliance, such as Polaris, or Venus in daytime.

Regardless of method employed the end result as viewed through the horizon glass is the same; the body is split between the clear and mirrored sections as shown in Figure 72, illustrating the lower limb of the moon at the moment of tangency. Observe that the lowest part is precisely tangent to, or resting on, the horizon.

Timing the observation: An assistant with a timepiece is helpful, but not essential, to record the time (and altitude) of the observation. With an assistant, call "Mark" as tangency is observed; the assistant should then read the seconds first, then the minute, and finally the hour—otherwise the seconds may be in error and, if near the sixty second mark, an error of one minute may also ensue. Seconds are important in celestial observation, an error of four seconds can create an error of one mile in position. When no assistant is available, and one must perform single-handed, use the "hippopotamus" counting method described in Chapter VI until a timepiece can be observed, and deduct the seconds so counted from the time observed.

Developing skill: A survey of naval navigators revealed that their accuracy in taking sextant observations continued to increase until about 2000 sights had been made, after which the level of accuracy continued to improve but at a slower rate. This statistic is

FIGURE 72. CORRECT POSITION AT MOMENT OF OBSERVATION

The body is tangent to the horizon, the sextant having been "rocked" to assure being held vertically. Aspect is through the horizon glass, the left half affording a clear view of the horizon while the right half shows the body reflected by the index mirror after being "brought down" by manipulation of the index arm. Example is for lower limb (of the moon); depending upon configuration at the time of observation either limb may be observed.

quoted not to discourage, but rather to indicate that excellence with a sextant requires practice to obtain, and then maintain. Perhaps the beginner's first ten or fifteen sights will be in the unsatisfactory range, but soon thereafter, under calm sea conditions, he will find the majority of his observations to be within the normally acceptable limits of less than one mile in error. As proficiency increases his average (again under good conditions) should approach $\pm$ 0.2 of a mile, the range in which expertness is recognized. By the time this level is attained the navigator will be capable of "shooting the sun" at least three times per minute, and of making a round of star sights within five minutes.

Undoubtedly the best place for the neophyte to begin is on dry land, where terra firma offers a stable platform. Any beach with a five-mile or more stretch to the opposite shore will do; an east–west aspect is slightly to be preferred. If such an area is not available any river, bay, inlet, or lake will do but correction will have to be made with a Dip Short table (described later in this chapter) to compensate for the lack of a horizon. It is possible (and has been done) to practice on an arid desert using a frying pan filled with mercury as a substitute for water; the method is found in *Bowditch*. Hence, wherever his location, a navigator can practice sextant observations and develop his skill to whatever degree he may have set as a goal. When confident of results obtained on dry land the next progression ideally is in harbor where wave action is slight and the horizon still relatively steady. Finally, when manual dexterity is automatic, comes the acid test at sea where the swells can at times provide a most unstable platform. Sight-taking in turbulent blue water calls for quick reflexes and an intuitive knowledge based on experience as to whether the observation was on target or wide of the mark. Select that part of the ship where yawing and pitching are minimized (usually amidships) and learn to time each observation as the crest of a wave passes underneath, creating a momentary suspension of motion and affording the best view of the horizon.

Measurement of proficiency requires that the navigator be able to determine his accuracy, as indicated by the intercept. If the intercept is *toward* the geographic position of the body, he has "bought down" the body below the horizon; if *away*, the body was observed above the horizon. Keeping track of the intercepts is the navigator's method of determining progress in developing observational skill. One of the sight reduction methods explained in the following chapter provides a method of measuring intercept from a DR position; the tables for this method (H.O. 211, *Dead Reckoning Altitude and Azimuth Table*) will be found in Appendix G and their use is advocated to the beginning navigator for measuring his observational proficiency, as well as for several other reasons discussed in that chapter.

When conditions of limited visibility prevail the navigator must take his observations as opportunity permits; when conditions are favorable he usually is presented with several options. The following suggestions pertain to the latter, favorable, situation:

> Avoid extremely high- or low-altitude observations. High-altitude bodies (above 70°) are difficult to "bring down," they tend to "jump" off the mirror as the horizon is neared. Low-altitude bodies (below 5° altitude) must be corrected for refraction. The best range for non-problem planet and star observations, in particular, is between 20° and 60° altitude.

> Always observe the lower limb of the sun, when not obscured. The exception to this rule is when it is a low-altitude observation (below 5°) in which case observe the upper limb.

> Moon observations can be very helpful, and are frequently overlooked. Observe whichever limb is most distinct. A daylight fix, with moon and sun, should be taken at every opportunity.

> Venus is usefully available during daylight about 20 percent of the time, and provides a most welcome fix with the sun and/or moon. It is difficult to see with the naked eye, therefore precompute its position (with H.O. 2102-D, Starfinder device), pre-set the sextant to the computed altitude, and search the horizon in the direction of the computed azimuth with the sextant's telescope. Venus is always within 47° of the sun.

> Polaris, the North Star, provides a valuable line of position in the Northern Hemisphere. Because of its weak magnitude it is best observed near the dark edge of nautical twilight (early

in the morning and late at night). Pre-set the sextant at the approximate DR latitude and search the horizon to the north through the sextant's telescope.

The planets become visible earlier than stars at evening twilight and are last to fade at morning twilight. Therefore observe planets before stars at evening twilight and after stars in the morning.

Selection of a sextant: In acquiring a sextant certain desirable features should be considered: Weight is important and should be at least $4\frac{1}{2}$ pounds for steadiness; most metal sextants meet this standard, many plastic models do not. Illumination of the arc and micrometer drum eliminates the need of a flashlight; this is accomplished by means of a built-in battery compartment contained in the handle, with an exterior switch and bulb. A choice of telescopes is frequently offered, usually one of about $3\frac{1}{2}$ power and one of approximately 7 power. If affordable, having both is a convenience; if choosing one or the other bear in mind that the 7 power scope will bring in the fainter stars but present a shaky image (amplifying the hand's unsteadiness) of sun and moon (and planets too, when they are at maximum brilliance). For all but second- and third-magnitude stars the lower power is normally sufficient, and less expensive. The inverting telescope sometimes sold with sextants is generally considered to be a nuisance, and used infrequently if at all by most navigators. It is entirely possible to make observations without a telescope, using the tube sight, but for most navigators a telescope is practically a "must." The micrometer drum models with vernier are most convenient although, as noted, many well-made sextants do not contain the vernier feature. The better models have two sets of sun shades, one for the index mirror and one for the horizon clear glass; under conditions of bright sunlight both shades are practically indispensable. The case should be closable with the telescope in place. Finally, whether buying a brand-new or well-used sextant, it is essential to have it certificated for accuracy by a reputable sextant adjuster, who may very well be the maker or his sales agent. Never buy a sextant without an up-to-date certificate of accuracy; no sextant is mechanically perfect and all have built-in errors, what the user needs to know is the exact amount of error and the assurance that it is slight.

Plath sextants, made in Hamburg, Germany, have long set the standard by which all others are measured. Many excellent makes are found in Great Britain, most with the micrometer drum and vernier. Many lower-priced imports from Japan are available in the market, the quality is generally good but they do not appear to be as rugged and trouble-free as the European makes. A full-time professional navigator will usually prefer a European make whereas the part-time amateur sailor can often be fully satisfied with an Oriental model. Except for U.S. Navy sextants made under supervised contract there are few American brands to choose from.

Care of the sextant: A good sextant, properly cared for, will last a lifetime; in fact many navigators today are using their grandfather's instruments. Hold the sextant by the handle; secure it during use with a lanyard. Guard it against shock from falling, sliding or being dropped. When not in use keep the sextant in its wooden case, secured from uncontrolled movement. Except in dire emergency, refrain from making any adjustments—that is the province of the expert professional adjuster. Four adjustments are possible, if absolutely necessary to be made at sea: (1) for perpendicularity of the index mirror, (2) for perpendicularity of the horizon glass, (3) to make parallel the index mirror and horizon glass, and (4) to make the telescope parallel to the frame. The method of test and adjustment is detailed in *Bowditch*.

Aside from careless handling, the sextant's greatest enemies are dampness, excessive heat, and vibration; the greatest of these is dampness, particularly in its effect on the mirrors and arc, which should be wiped dry after each use. If sprayed with saltwater, first apply freshwater with a damp cloth to eliminate the salt. Wipe the mirrors dry with lens paper (linen, cotton, and chamois collect dust, which scratches) and dry the arc with a clean rag. Silica gel kept in the sextant case will help preserve the mirrors by absorbing moisture. Clean the arc with ammonia, never with a polishing compound. The tangent screw and limb teeth should be kept lightly oiled with the oil provided with the sextant, or one of light viscosity if the manufacturer's oil is not available. If the sextant is to be stowed ashore for any period of time, protect the arc with a light application of petroleum jelly. Never use pressure on the mirrors or arc when cleaning (or at any other time, for that matter). Eventually the mirrors will need to be resilvered; this is a task for which few amateurs are suited (although it can be done in an emergency as explained in *Bowditch*) and is normally a job for the professional instrument specialist.

chapter XIII

Sextant Altitude Corrections

Errors and Corrections

THE ALTITUDE of a celestial body as measured with a sextant is called *sextant altitude* (hs) and must undergo several corrections in the necessary process of being converted to *observed altitude* (Ho), which is the altitude used for finding position in celestial navigation. An intermediate altitude termed *apparent altitude* (ha), which reflects the subtotal of corrections for mechanical error (index correction) and height of eye above sea level (Dip), is utilized when solving with the *Nautical Almanac* but ignored when using the *Air Almanac*. In actual practice the apparent altitude (ha) subtotal can usually be ignored with most *Nautical Almanac* solutions but its application will be described below for the benefit of those yachtsmen interested in obtaining maximum precision in their sextant observations.

Index error is caused by non-alignment of the mirrors, and should be checked at the time of each observation. Determination is extremely simple: Set the index arm at 0° and sight a distant object (a celestial body, buoy, or the horizon), rotate the micrometer drum until the sharpest possible image is obtained and then read the altitude as shown on the arc, drum, and vernier. The difference between 0° and the new reading, which is usually a matter of a very few seconds and tenths, is the index error; its correction, termed *index correction* (IC), is applied to the sextant altitude (hs) and may be either plus or minus. If the reading is off the arc, the correction is additive (+), if on the arc it is subtractive (−). A helpful phrase in common usage as a reminder of the sign of the correction is, "if it's on, it's off."

Dip of the horizon (Dip, or D) refers to the height of the observer's eye above sea level. The correction is always *negative* (—) and is found on the inside front cover of the *Nautical Almanac* and on the back cover of the *Air Almanac*. The almanac Dip Tables are critical; when two possible values appear the upper one should be selected. In the extracted Dip correction tables from both almanacs shown below (Fig. 73) the correction for eye height of 21 feet is — 4.4' (*Nautical Almanac*) and — 4.0' (*Air Almanac*).

Apparent altitude (ha) represents the total of the corrections for index error and height of eye, as subtracted from sextant altitude (hs). Should the sextant certificate of accuracy contain an applicable instrument correction, this too should be included in determining ha. Apparent altitude is ignored when working with the *Air Almanac* and is optional for all practical purposes when the *Nautical Almanac* is used with bodies observed at 10° or higher altitude although, strictly speaking, it assures utmost possible accuracy. An example showing how ha is derived is given below, with an assumed sextant altitude and index error:

		Nautical Almanac
(*Assumed factors*)		
Sextant altitude	hs:	30° 47.4'
Index correction	IC: +	2.1'
Eye height 21 ft	D: —	4.4'
Apparent altitude	ha:	30° 45.1'

Low-temperature and pressure corrections are listed only in the *Nautical Almanac* (Table A4, facing title page). They apply equally to all celestial body observations when the weather conditions are found to be in the temperature and pressure brackets listed in the table. In actual practice the corrections need only to be applied when the altitude of the body is less than 10° regardless of the existing temperature or barometer reading. The *Air Almanac* ignores this correction for marine navigation.

DIP

Ht. of Eye (m)	Corrⁿ	Ht. of Eye (ft.)
2·4	−2·8	8·0
2·6	−2·9	8·6
2·8	−3·0	9·2
3·0	−3·1	9·8
3·2	−3·2	10·5
3·4	−3·3	11·2
3·6	−3·4	11·9
3·8	−3·5	12·6
4·0	−3·6	13·3
4·3	−3·7	14·1
4·5	−3·8	14·9
4·7	−3·9	15·7
5·0	−4·0	16·5
5·2	−4·1	17·4
5·5	−4·2	18·3
5·8	−4·3	19·1
6·1	−4·4	20·1
6·3	−4·5	21·0
6·6	−4·6	22·0
6·9	−4·7	22·9
7·2	−4·8	23·9
7·5	−4·9	24·9
7·9	−5·0	26·0
8·2	−5·1	27·1
8·5	−5·2	28·1
8·8	−5·3	29·2
9·2	−5·4	30·4
9·5	−5·5	31·5
9·9	−5·6	32·7
10·3	−5·7	33·9
10·6	−5·8	35·1
11·0	−5·9	36·3
11·4	−6·0	37·6
11·8	−6·1	38·9
12·2	−6·2	40·1
12·6	−6·3	41·5
13·0	−6·4	42·8
13·4	−6·5	44·2
13·8	−6·6	45·5
14·2	−6·7	46·9
14·7	−6·8	48·4
15·1	−6·9	49·8
15·5	−7·0	51·3
16·0	−7·1	52·8
16·5	−7·2	54·3
16·9	−7·3	55·8
17·4	−7·4	57·4
17·9	−7·5	58·9
18·4	−7·6	60·5
18·8	−7·7	62·1
19·3	−7·8	63·8
19·8	−7·9	65·4
20·4	−8·0	67·1
20·9	−8·1	68·8
21·4		70·5

Ht. of Eye	Corrⁿ
m	,
1·0 − 1·8	
1·5 − 2·2	
2·0 − 2·5	
2·5 − 2·8	
3·0 − 3·0	
See table ←	
m ,	
20 − 7·9	
22 − 8·3	
24 − 8·6	
26 − 9·0	
28 − 9·3	
30 − 9·6	
32 − 10·0	
34 − 10·3	
36 − 10·6	
38 − 10·8	
40 − 11·1	
42 − 11·4	
44 − 11·7	
46 − 11·9	
48 − 12·2	
ft. ,	
2 − 1·4	
4 − 1·9	
6 − 2·4	
8 − 2·7	
10 − 3·1	
See table ←	
ft. ,	
70 − 8·1	
75 − 8·4	
80 − 8·7	
85 − 8·9	
90 − 9·2	
95 − 9·5	
100 − 9·7	
105 − 9·9	
110 − 10·2	
115 − 10·4	
120 − 10·6	
125 − 10·8	
130 − 11·1	
135 − 11·3	
140 − 11·5	
145 − 11·7	
150 − 11·9	
155 − 12·1	

CORRECTION FOR DIP OF THE HORIZON
To be subtracted from sextant altitude

Ht. (Ft.)	Dip	Ht. (Ft.)	Dip	Ht. (Ft.)	Dip	Ht. (Ft.)	Dip	Ht. (Ft.)	D
0	1	114	11	437	21	968	31	1,707	
2	2	137	12	481	22	1,033	32	1,792	4
6	3	162	13	527	23	1,099	33	1,88c	4
12	4	189	14	575	24	1,168	34	1,970	4
21	5	218	15	625	25	1,239	35	2,061	4
31	6	250	16	677	26	1,311	36	2,155	4
43	7	283	17	731	27	1,386	37	2,251	4
58	8	318	18	787	28	1,463	38	2,349	4
75	9	356	19	845	29	1,543	39	2,449	4
93	10	395	20	906	30	1,624	40	2,551	4
114		437		968		1,707		2,655	5

FIGURE 73. CORRECTION FOR HEIGHT OF EYE (DIP)

a. Extract from *Nautical Almanac*
b. Extract from *Air Almanac*
Select the Dip correction (always minus) bracketed by the height range *except* when two values are possible (as at 21 feet) in which case select the upper correction.

The corrections discussed above apply to all celestial observations regardless of whether the body observed is sun, moon, star, or planet. Certain additional, and major, corrections apply individually, and are treated differently by the two almanacs. The *Nautical Almanac* lumps together, under the heading *main correction,* all of the compensations for: (1) refraction (bending light rays), (2) semi-diameter (angular adjustment from the circumference of a body to the center), and (3) parallax (difference in angle of the body as measured from the observer's eye and as measured from earth's center). The *Air Almanac* lists each correction separately, or not at all. For all corrections listed below it should be borne in mind that corrections are always added (+) for a lower limb observation and subtracted (−) for upper limb of sun or moon; the correction tables may be entered with apparent altitude (ha) but, optionally, may be entered with sextant altitude (hs) when that value is more than 10°. The *Air Almanac* is not intended to be used with ha, but the *Nautical Almanac* is designed to accommodate it. Extracts of tables illustrating application of these corrections will be found in Figure 74 (*Nautical Almanac*) and Figure 75 (*Air Almanac*), together with examples of their use.

Sun: The main altitude correction for the sun in the Nautical Almanac is contained in Table A2, located on the inside front cover and facing page. Observe that the table is divided into two seasons, October/March and April/September. The *Air Almanac* has two corrections: (1) semi-diameter (*Sun SD*) in the lower right-hand corner of each daily page, and (2) refraction (R or Ro) on the inside back cover and always subtracted (−).

Moon: Main altitude corrections for the moon are found on the inside back cover and facing page of the *Nautical Almanac;* they are much less formidable in execution than their description implies, and are readily understood with a little practice. The main correction is in two parts, the first taken from the upper part of the table and the second from the lower part. In order to make the second correction it is first necessary to ascertain the horizontal parallax (HP) of the moon from the daily page and use this factor to enter the

ALTITUDE CORRECTION TABLES 10°–90°—SUN, STARS, PLANETS

OCT.–MAR. SUN APR.–SEPT.							STARS AND PLANETS			
App. Alt.	Lower Limb	Upper Limb	App. Alt.	Lower Limb	Upper Limb		App. Alt.	Corrn	App. Alt.	Additional Corrn
9 34	+10.8	−21.5	9 39	+10.6	−21.2		9 56	−5.3		**1971**
9 45	+10.9	−21.4	9 51	+10.7	−21.1		10 08	−5.2		**VENUS**
9 56	+11.0	−21.3	10 03	+10.8	−21.0		10 20	−5.1		Jan. 1–Jan. 17
10 08	+11.1	−21.2	10 15	+10.9	−20.9		10 33	−5.0		46 +0.3
10 21	+11.2	−21.1	10 27	+11.0	−20.8		10 46	−4.9		
10 34	+11.3	−21.0	10 40	+11.1	−20.7		11 00	−4.8		Jan. 18–Mar. 5
10 47	+11.4	−20.9	10 54	+11.2	−20.6		11 14	−4.7		47 +0.2
11 01	+11.5	−20.8	11 08	+11.3	−20.5		11 29	−4.6		
11 15	+11.6	−20.7	11 23	+11.4	−20.4		11 45	−4.5		Mar. 6–Dec. 31
11 30	+11.7	−20.6	11 38	+11.5	−20.3		12 01	−4.4		42 +0.1
11 46	+11.8	−20.5	11 54	+11.6	−20.2		12 18	−4.3		
12 02	+11.9	−20.4	12 10	+11.7	−20.1		12 35	−4.2		
12 19	+12.0	−20.3	12 28	+11.8	−20.0		12 54	−4.1		**MARS**
12 37	+12.1	−20.2	12 46	+11.9	−19.9		13 13	−4.0		Jan. 1–Apr. 19
12 55	+12.2	−20.1	13 05	+12.0	−19.8		13 33	−3.9		60 +0.1
13 14	+12.3	−20.0	13 24	+12.1	−19.7		13 54	−3.8		
13 35	+12.4	−19.9	13 45	+12.2	−19.6		14 16	−3.7		Apr. 20–June 13
13 56	+12.5	−19.8	14 07	+12.3	−19.5		14 40	−3.6		41 +0.2
14 18	+12.6	−19.7	14 30	+12.4	−19.4		15 04	−3.5		75 +0.1
14 42	+12.7	−19.6	14 54	+12.5	−19.3		15 30	−3.4		
15 06	+12.8	−19.5	15 19	+12.6	−19.2		15 57	−3.3		June 14–Oct. 12
15 32	+12.9	−19.4	15 46	+12.7	−19.1		16 26	−3.2		34 +0.3
15 59	+13.0	−19.3	16 14	+12.8	−19.0		16 56	−3.1		60 +0.2
16 28	+13.1	−19.2	16 44	+12.9	−18.9		17 28	−3.0		80 +0.1
16 59	+13.2	−19.1	17 15	+13.0	−18.8		18 02	−2.9		
17 32	+13.3	−19.0	17 48	+13.1	−18.7		18 38	−2.8		Oct. 13–Dec. 8
18 06	+13.4	−18.9	18 24	+13.2	−18.6		19 17	−2.7		41 +0.2
18 42	+13.5	−18.8	19 01	+13.3	−18.5		19 58	−2.6		75 +0.1
19 21	+13.6	−18.7	19 42	+13.4	−18.4		20 42	−2.5		
20 03	+13.7	−18.6	20 25	+13.5	−18.3		21 28	−2.4		Dec. 9–Dec. 31
20 48	+13.8	−18.5	21 11	+13.6	−18.2		22 19	−2.3		60 +0.1
21 35	+13.9	−18.4	22 00	+13.7	−18.1		23 13	−2.2		
22 26	+14.0	−18.3	22 54	+13.8	−18.0		24 11	−2.1		
23 22	+14.1	−18.2	23 51	+13.9	−17.9		25 14	−2.0		
24 21	+14.2	−18.1	24 53	+14.0	−17.8		26 22	−1.9		
25 26	+14.3	−18.0	26 00	+14.1	−17.7		27 36	−1.8		
26 36	+14.4	−17.9	27 13	+14.2	−17.6		28 56	−1.7		
27 52	+14.5	−17.8	28 33	+14.3	−17.5		30 24	−1.6		
29 15	+14.6	−17.7	30 00	+14.4	−17.4		32 00	−1.5		
30 46	+14.7	−17.6	31 35	+14.5	−17.3		33 45	−1.4		
32 26	+14.8	−17.5	33 20	+14.6	−17.2		35 40	−1.3		
34 17	+14.9	−17.4	35 17	+14.7	−17.1		37 48	−1.2		
36 20	+15.0	−17.3	37 26	+14.8	−17.0		40 08	−1.1		
38 36	+15.1	−17.2	39 50	+14.9	−16.9		42 44	−1.0		
41 08	+15.2	−17.1	42 31	+15.0	−16.8		45 36	−0.9		
43 59	+15.3	−17.0	45 31	+15.1	−16.7		48 47	−0.8		
47 10	+15.4	−16.9	48 55	+15.2	−16.6		52 18	−0.7		
50 46	+15.5	−16.8	52 44	+15.3	−16.5		56 11	−0.6		
54 49	+15.6	−16.7	57 02	+15.4	−16.4		60 28	−0.5		
59 23	+15.7	−16.6	61 51	+15.5	−16.3		65 08	−0.4		
64 30	+15.8	−16.5	67 17	+15.6	−16.2		70 11	−0.3		
70 12	+15.9	−16.4	73 16	+15.7	−16.1		75 34	−0.2		
76 26	+16.0	−16.3	79 43	+15.8	−16.0		81 13	−0.1		
83 05	+16.1	−16.2	86 32	+15.9	−15.9		87 03	0.0		
90 00			90 00				90 00			

App. Alt. = Apparent altitude = Sextant altitude corrected for index error and dip.

◀ FIGURE 74a.
ALTITUDE CORRECTIONS

(Nautical Almanac)
For Sun, Stars, and Planets

App. Alt.	0°–4° Corrn	5°–9° Corrn	10°–14° Corrn	15°–19° Corrn	20°–24° Corrn	25°–29° Corrn	30°–34° Corrn	App Alt.
00	0 33·8	5 58·2	10 62·1	15 62·8	20 62·2	25 60·8	30 58·9	00
10	35·9	58·5	62·2	62·8	62·1	60·8	58·8	10
20	37·8	58·7	62·2	62·8	62·1	60·7	58·8	20
30	39·6	58·9	62·3	62·8	62·1	60·7	58·7	30
40	41·2	59·1	62·3	62·8	62·0	60·6	58·6	40
50	42·6	59·3	62·4	62·7	62·0	60·6	58·5	50
00	1 44·0	6 59·5	11 62·4	16 62·7	21 62·0	26 60·5	31 58·5	00
10	45·2	59·7	62·4	62·7	61·9	60·4	58·4	10
20	46·3	59·9	62·5	62·7	61·9	60·4	58·3	20
30	47·3	60·0	62·5	62·7	61·9	60·3	58·2	30
40	48·3	60·2	62·5	62·7	61·8	60·3	58·2	40
50	49·2	60·3	62·6	62·7	61·8	60·2	58·1	50
00	2 50·0	7 60·5	12 62·6	17 62·7	22 61·7	27 60·1	32 58·0	00
10	50·8	60·6	62·6	62·6	61·7	60·1	57·9	10
20	51·4	60·7	62·6	62·6	61·6	60·0	57·8	20
30	52·1	60·9	62·7	62·6	61·6	59·9	57·8	30
40	52·7	61·0	62·7	62·6	61·5	59·9	57·7	40
50	53·3	61·1	62·7	62·6	61·5	59·8	57·6	50
00	3 53·8	8 61·2	13 62·7	18 62·5	23 61·5	28 59·7	33 57·5	00
10	54·3	61·3	62·7	62·5	61·4	59·7	57·4	10
20	54·8	61·4	62·7	62·5	61·4	59·6	57·4	20
30	55·2	61·5	62·8	62·5	61·3	59·6	57·3	30
40	55·6	61·6	62·8	62·4	61·3	59·5	57·2	40
50	56·0	61·6	62·8	62·4	61·2	59·4	57·1	50
00	4 56·4	9 61·7	14 62·8	19 62·4	24 61·2	29 59·3	34 57·0	00
10	56·7	61·8	62·8	62·3	61·1	59·3	56·9	10
20	57·1	61·9	62·8	62·3	61·1	59·2	56·9	20
30	57·4	61·9	62·8	62·3	61·0	59·1	56·8	30
40	57·7	62·0	62·8	62·2	60·9	59·1	56·7	40
50	57·9	62·1	62·8	62·2	60·9	59·0	56·6	50

H.P.	L U	L U	L U	L U	L U	L U	L U	H.P.
54·0	0·3 0·9	0·3 0·9	0·4 1·0	0·5 1·1	0·6 1·2	0·7 1·3	0·9 1·5	54·0
54·3	0·7 1·1	0·7 1·2	0·7 1·2	0·8 1·3	0·9 1·4	1·1 1·5	1·2 1·7	54·3
54·6	1·1 1·4	1·1 1·4	1·1 1·4	1·2 1·5	1·3 1·6	1·4 1·7	1·5 1·8	54·6
54·9	1·4 1·6	1·5 1·6	1·5 1·6	1·6 1·7	1·6 1·8	1·8 1·9	1·9 2·0	54·9
55·2	1·8 1·8	1·8 1·8	1·9 1·9	1·9 1·9	2·0 2·0	2·1 2·1	2·2 2·2	55·2
55·5	2·2 2·0	2·2 2·0	2·3 2·1	2·3 2·1	2·4 2·2	2·4 2·3	2·5 2·4	55·5
55·8	2·6 2·2	2·6 2·2	2·6 2·3	2·7 2·3	2·7 2·4	2·8 2·4	2·9 2·5	55·8
56·1	3·0 2·4	3·0 2·5	3·0 2·5	3·0 2·5	3·1 2·6	3·1 2·6	3·2 2·7	56·1
56·4	3·4 2·7	3·4 2·7	3·4 2·7	3·4 2·7	3·4 2·8	3·5 2·8	3·5 2·9	56·4
56·7	3·7 2·9	3·7 2·9	3·8 2·9	3·8 2·9	3·8 3·0	3·8 3·0	3·9 3·0	56·7
57·0	4·1 3·1	4·1 3·1	4·1 3·1	4·1 3·1	4·2 3·1	4·2 3·2	4·2 3·2	57·0
57·3	4·5 3·3	4·5 3·3	4·5 3·3	4·5 3·3	4·5 3·3	4·5 3·4	4·6 3·4	57·3
57·6	4·9 3·5	4·9 3·5	4·9 3·5	4·9 3·5	4·9 3·5	4·9 3·5	4·9 3·6	57·6
57·9	5·3 3·8	5·3 3·8	5·2 3·8	5·2 3·7	5·2 3·7	5·2 3·7	5·2 3·7	57·9
58·2	5·6 4·0	5·6 4·0	5·6 4·0	5·6 4·0	5·6 3·9	5·6 3·9	5·6 3·9	58·2
58·5	6·0 4·2	6·0 4·2	6·0 4·2	6·0 4·2	6·0 4·1	5·9 4·1	5·9 4·1	58·5
58·8	6·4 4·4	6·4 4·4	6·4 4·4	6·3 4·4	6·3 4·3	6·3 4·3	6·2 4·2	58·8
59·1	6·8 4·6	6·8 4·6	6·7 4·6	6·7 4·6	6·7 4·5	6·6 4·5	6·6 4·4	59·1
59·4	7·2 4·8	7·1 4·8	7·1 4·8	7·1 4·8	7·0 4·7	7·0 4·7	6·9 4·6	59·4
59·7	7·5 5·1	7·5 5·0	7·5 5·0	7·5 5·0	7·4 4·9	7·3 4·8	7·2 4·7	59·7
60·0	7·9 5·3	7·9 5·3	7·9 5·2	7·8 5·2	7·8 5·1	7·7 5·0	7·6 4·9	60·0
60·3	8·3 5·5	8·3 5·5	8·2 5·4	8·2 5·4	8·1 5·3	8·0 5·2	7·9 5·1	60·3
60·6	8·7 5·7	8·7 5·7	8·6 5·7	8·6 5·6	8·5 5·5	8·4 5·4	8·2 5·3	60·6
60·9	9·1 5·9	9·0 5·9	9·0 5·9	8·9 5·8	8·8 5·7	8·7 5·6	8·6 5·4	60·9
61·2	9·5 6·2	9·4 6·1	9·4 6·1	9·3 6·0	9·2 5·9	9·1 5·8	8·9 5·6	61·2
61·5	9·8 6·4	9·8 6·3	9·7 6·3	9·7 6·2	9·5 6·1	9·4 5·9	9·2 5·8	61·5

FIGURE 74b.
ALTITUDE
CORRECTIONS
OF THE MOON

(Nautical Almanac)

ADDITIONAL REFRACTION CORRECTIONS FOR NON-STANDARD CONDITIONS

Temperature

App. Alt.	A	B	C	D	E	F	G	H	J	K	L	M	N	App. Alt.
0 00	−6·9	−5·7	−4·6	−3·4	−2·3	−1·1	0·0	+1·1	+2·3	+3·4	+4·6	+5·7	+6·9	0 00
0 30	5·2	4·4	3·5	2·6	1·7	0·9	0·0	0·9	1·7	2·6	3·5	4·4	5·2	0 30
1 00	4·3	3·5	2·8	2·1	1·4	0·7	0·0	0·7	1·4	2·1	2·8	3·5	4·3	1 00
1 30	3·5	2·9	2·4	1·8	1·2	0·6	0·0	0·6	1·2	1·8	2·4	2·9	3·5	1 30
2 00	3·0	2·5	2·0	1·5	1·0	0·5	0·0	0·5	1·0	1·5	2·0	2·5	3·0	2 00
2 30	−2·5	−2·1	−1·6	−1·2	−0·8	−0·4	0·0	+0·4	+0·8	+1·2	+1·6	+2·1	+2·5	2 30
3 00	2·2	1·8	1·5	1·1	0·7	0·4	0·0	0·4	0·7	1·1	1·5	1·8	2·2	3 00
3 30	2·0	1·6	1·3	1·0	0·7	0·3	0·0	0·3	0·7	1·0	1·3	1·6	2·0	3 30
4 00	1·8	1·5	1·2	0·9	0·6	0·3	0·0	0·3	0·6	0·9	1·2	1·5	1·8	4 00
4 30	1·6	1·4	1·1	0·8	0·5	0·3	0·0	0·3	0·5	0·8	1·1	1·4	1·6	4 30
5 00	−1·5	−1·3	−1·0	−0·8	−0·5	−0·2	0·0	+0·2	+0·5	+0·8	+1·0	+1·3	+1·5	5 00
6	1·3	1·1	0·9	0·6	0·4	0·2	0·0	0·2	0·4	0·6	0·9	1·1	1·3	6
7	1·1	0·9	0·7	0·6	0·4	0·2	0·0	0·2	0·4	0·6	0·7	0·9	1·1	7
8	1·0	0·8	0·7	0·5	0·3	0·2	0·0	0·2	0·3	0·5	0·7	0·8	1·0	8
9	0·9	0·7	0·6	0·4	0·3	0·1	0·0	0·1	0·3	0·4	0·6	0·7	0·9	9
10 00	−0·8	−0·7	−0·5	−0·4	−0·3	−0·1	0·0	+0·1	+0·3	+0·4	+0·5	+0·7	+0·8	10 00
12	0·7	0·6	0·5	0·3	0·2	0·1	0·0	0·1	0·2	0·3	0·5	0·6	0·7	12
14	0·6	0·5	0·4	0·3	0·2	0·1	0·0	0·1	0·2	0·3	0·4	0·5	0·6	14
16	0·5	0·4	0·3	0·3	0·2	0·1	0·0	0·1	0·2	0·3	0·3	0·4	0·5	16
18	0·4	0·4	0·3	0·2	0·2	0·1	0·0	0·1	0·2	0·2	0·3	0·4	0·4	18
20 00	−0·4	−0·3	−0·3	−0·2	−0·1	−0·1	0·0	+0·1	+0·1	+0·2	+0·3	+0·3	+0·4	20 00
25	0·3	0·3	0·2	0·2	0·1	−0·1	0·0	+0·1	0·1	0·2	0·2	0·3	0·3	25
30	0·3	0·2	0·2	0·1	0·1	0·0	0·0	0·0	0·1	0·1	0·2	0·2	0·3	30
35	0·2	0·2	0·1	0·1	0·1	0·0	0·0	0·0	0·1	0·1	0·1	0·2	0·2	35
40	0·2	0·1	0·1	0·1	−0·1	0·0	0·0	0·0	+0·1	0·1	0·1	0·1	0·2	40
50 00	−0·1	−0·1	−0·1	−0·1	0·0	0·0	0·0	0·0	0·0	+0·1	+0·1	+0·1	+0·1	50 00

The graph is entered with arguments temperature and pressure to find a zone letter; using as arguments this zone letter and apparent altitude (sextant altitude corrected for dip), a correction is taken from the table. This correction is to be applied to the sextant altitude in addition to the corrections for standard conditions (for the Sun, stars and planets from page A2 and for the Moon from pages xxxiv and xxxv).

◀FIGURE 74c. CORRECTION FOR TEMPERATURE AND PRESSURE   *(Nautical Almanac)*

---

lower table under the appropriate column heading, L (lower limb) or U (upper limb). An additional correction, always minus (—), is incorporated when the observation is of an *upper* limb.

The *Air Almanac*'s corrections are: Refraction, given on the inside back cover, Semi-diameter (Moon SD) in the lower right hand corner of each daily page, and parallax in altitude (P in A) in the right hand daily page column. P in A is always plus (+).

Star: The main altitude correction for a star is found in Table A of the *Nautical Almanac,* on the inside front cover and facing page. All corrections therein are minus (—). The *Air Almanac* requires only the correction for Refraction.

Planet: The main correction for planets is the same as for stars (above), however when using the *Nautical Almanac* an additional correction is applied to twilight observations of Venus and Mars as given in Table A2 on the inside front cover. This correction is always added (+).

The beginning navigator may find these corrections difficult to fix in his mind, and even experienced navigators find themselves having to refresh their memories at times. It is suggested that the work forms of Appendix G, which are arranged in a format intended to eliminate error and minimize the need for memorization of method, should be used in solving for observed altitude (Ho).

Polaris: Both the *Nautical* and *Air almanacs* provide sextant altitude correction tables for determining latitude and azimuth by observation of Polaris, the North Star. Use of these tables is discussed in Chapter XV.

Venus daylight correction: The *Nautical Almanac* contains a formula for an additional correction of Venus' altitude when observed in daylight, which may be safely ignored by the cruising navigator; the *Air Almanac* considers the correction too inconsequential for mention.

chapter XIV
Sight Reduction Methods

C OMPUTED TABLES of altitude and azimuth —the "new" methods of navigation—have greatly simplified finding position by observation of celestial bodies. Developed as a result of the Navy's impelling wartime need to make passable navigators out of "ninety-day wonder" wartime junior officers, the tables have superseded the old methods for solving the spherical triangle by mathematical formulae. Four tabular methods for sight reduction are discussed below, differing somewhat in format and extraction of data but all suitable to the purposes of the cruising yachtsman for obtaining line of position quickly, accurately, and with a minimum of computation.

H.O. 211, Dead Reckoning Altitude and Azimuth Table

Description: A convenient, small (49 pages in a pocket-size volume) table for sight reduction from the dead reckoning position, suitable for use with any declination and at any latitude. Requires more page turning and usually provides somewhat less accuracy than the other methods described below, hence publica- tion has been terminated by the Navy and H.O. 211 will soon become a collector's item. However the slight additional time re- quired is not considered to be as important to the cruising yachts- man as to the navigator of a destroyer on a flank speed mission. The size and single-volume presentation of all data are an impor- tant stowage factor in a small boat. H.O. 211 is the ideal lifeboat navigation table. The table is an invaluable aid to the beginning navigator wishing to practice sextant observation since it provides for a solution from the DR position (which is also the easiest solution to plot). For these reasons, the complete H.O. 211 table has been reproduced herein as Appendix H, with instructions and explanations revised to suit the more modern language of navigation developed since H.O. 211 was introduced.

Method: H. O. 211 presents a table of functions for each 0.5' of arc with main column headings for each whole and half degree (as 30°00' and 30°30'); intermediate values are positioned vertically. Functions between 0° and 89°59.5' are read downward; from 90° to 179°59.5' are read upward. Because functions beyond 180° are not listed it is necessary to convert azimuth angle (Chapter IX) to true azimuth in the final solution. A and B functions are listed for each 0.5' of arc and applied as discussed below. The steps in the method of solution are quickly mastered by reviewing them in conjunction with the appropriate pages of Appendix G, employed in working the complete solution of a typical problem shown below.

1. On the work form record all computations for time (Chapter VI), altitude (Chapter XIII), declination and Greenwich hour angle (Chapter IX), and the DR latitude and longitude. Observe that GHA, Dec, and Ho are recorded twice.

   Most of the procedures following involve extracting a function from the A and/or B column of a stated value of arc. The letters on the form indicate from which column the corresponding function is to be taken. When a function lies between two tabulated degrees of arc, take the function at nearest tabulated arc; if exactly midway take the function for the whole minute.

2. Determine local hour angle of Aries (LHA) and find the value of meridian angle (t) (Chapter IX). Record LHA and t on the form, and the A function of t.

3. Enter the A and B functions of declination on the form. Add the A function of t and the B function of Dec. Look up the corresponding B value and record the newly found A and B values on the form.

4. Subtract B from A in the second column to derive a new A. Find the arc value of K from its A function and enter on the form. K takes the name (N or S) of the declination.
5. Compute K ~ L: Add K and DR Latitude if different name, otherwise take their difference. Record the B function of K ~ L on the form.
6. Add the third column (of B functions) to derive the A and B functions of computed altitude (hc). Take hc from the table and record on the form.
7. Intercept (a) is the difference between hc and Ho. If Ho is greater than hc the intercept is *toward* the body; if less, the intercept is *away*.
8. Subtract the fourth column to find the A function of the azimuth angle. Convert azimuth angle (Chapter IX) to true azimuth (Zn).

> Note: Solutions when K lies between 87°30′ and 92°30′ are suspect, and best discarded. Interpolation is not normally required, but will slightly improve accuracy; see rules given in Appendix F.

Plotting lines of position obtained by H.O. 211 is demonstrated in Chapter V. An auxiliary use of H.O. 211 can be made for determining great circle course and distance, and is discussed in Chapter XV. (Fig 76.)

H.O. 214, Tables of Computed Altitude and Azimuth

Description: These tables, although the most popular currently in use, are scheduled to be replaced by H.O. 229 by the mid-1970s. Nevertheless they will undoubtedly remain in widespread use for several decades thereafter because of the ease with which they provide a line of celestial position. There appears to be no need for the navigator already experienced with H.O. 214 to switch to the newer tables, which do not appear to offer any significant advantage. H.O. 214 consists of nine volumes, each covering a 10° band of latitude; the British edition (H.D. 486) contains essentially the same data in six volumes of 15° latitude, and is therefore more convenient to stow and use. The number of volumes is a disadvantage in comparison with H.O. 211 (above); for example a passage from St. Thomas to Newport using H.O.

Moon's P. in A.

° Alt	+Corr '	° Alt	+Corr '
0	60	53	35
5	60	54	34
11	59	55	33
15	58	57	32
19	57	58	31
21	56	59	30
24	55	60	29
26	54	61	28
28	53	62	27
30	52	63	26
32	51	64	25
34	50	65	24
35	49	66	23
37	48	67	22
38	47	68	21
40	46	69	20
41	45	70	19
43	44	71	18
44	43	72	17
46	42	73	16
47	41	74	15
48	40	75	14
49	39	76	13
51	38	77	12
52	37	78	11
53	36	79	11
54	35	80	10

Sun SD 15'9
Moon SD 16'
Age 25d

◀ FIGURE 75a. ALTITUDE CORRECTIONS FOR SUN AND MOON   *(Air Almanac)*

FIGURE 75b. REFRACTION CORRECTION

(Air Almanac)
Marine navigation utilizes only the left-hand height column (0 feet above sea level).

CORRECTIONS TO BE APPLIED TO SEXTANT ALTITUDE

REFRACTION
To be subtracted from sextant altitude (referred to as observed altitude in A.P. 3270)

Height above sea level in units of 1 000 ft. — Sextant Altitude. $R = R_0 \times f$

R_0	0	5	10	15	20	25	30	35	40	45	50	55	R_0	0.9	1.0	1.1	1.2
0	90	90	90	90	90	90	90	90	90	90	90	90	0	0	0	0	0
1	63	59	55	51	46	41	36	31	26	20	17	13	1	1	1	1	1
2	33	29	26	22	19	16	14	11	9	7	6	4	2	2	2	2	2
3	21	19	16	14	12	10	8	7	5	4	2 40	1 40	3	3	3	3	4
4	16	14	12	10	8	7	6	5	3 10	2 20	1 30	0 40	4	4	4	4	5
5	12	11	9	8	7	5	4 00	3 10	2 10	1 30	0 39	+0 05	5	5	5	5	6
6	10	9	7	5 50	4 50	3 50	3 10	2 20	1 30	0 49	+0 11	−0 19	6	5	6	7	7
7	8 10	6 50	5 50	4 50	4 00	3 00	2 20	1 50	1 10	0 24	−0 11	−0 38	7	6	7	8	8
8	6 50	5 50	5 00	4 00	3 10	2 30	1 50	1 20	0 38	+0 04	−0 28	−0 54	8	7	8	9	10
9	6 00	5 10	4 10	3 20	2 40	2 00	1 30	1 00	0 19	−0 13	−0 42	−1 08	9	8	9	10	11
10	5 20	4 30	3 40	2 50	2 10	1 40	1 10	0 35	+0 03	−0 27	−0 53	−1 18	10	9	10	11	12
12	4 30	3 40	2 50	2 20	1 40	1 10	0 37	+0 11	−0 16	−0 43	−1 08	−1 31	12	11	12	13	14
14	3 30	2 50	2 10	1 40	1 10	0 34	+0 09	−0 14	−0 37	−1 00	−1 23	−1 44	14	13	14	15	17
16	2 50	2 10	1 40	1 10	0 37	+0 10	−0 13	−0 34	−0 53	−1 14	−1 35	−1 56	16	14	16	18	19
18	2 20	1 40	1 20	0 43	+0 15	−0 08	−0 31	−0 52	−1 08	−1 27	−1 46	−2 05	18	16	18	20	22
20	1 50	1 20	0 49	+0 23	−0 02	−0 26	−0 46	−1 06	−1 22	−1 39	−1 57	−2 14	20	18	20	22	24
25	1 12	0 44	+0 19	−0 06	−0 28	−0 48	−1 09	−1 27	−1 42	−1 58	−2 14	−2 30	25	22	25	28	30
30	0 34	+0 10	−0 13	−0 36	−0 55	−1 14	−1 32	−1 51	−2 06	−2 21	−2 34	−2 49	30	27	30	33	36
35	+0 06	−0 16	−0 37	−0 59	−1 17	−1 33	−1 51	−2 07	−2 23	−2 37	−2 51	−3 04	35	31	35	38	42
40	−0 18	−0 37	−0 58	−1 16	−1 34	−1 49	−2 06	−2 22	−2 35	−2 49	−3 03	−3 25	40	36	40	44	48
45			−0 53	−1 14	−1 31	−1 47	−2 03	−2 18	−2 33	−2 47	−2 59	−3 13	−3 25	45	40	45	50	54
50			−1 10	−1 28	−1 44	−1 59	−2 15	−2 28	−2 43	−2 56	−3 08	−3 22	−3 33	50	45	50	55	60
55				−1 40	−1 53	−2 09	−2 24	−2 38	−2 52	−3 04	−3 17	−3 29	−3 41	55	49	55	60	66
60				−2 03	−2 18	−2 33	−2 46	−3 01	−3 12	−3 25	−3 37	−3 48	60	54	60	66	72
							−2 53	−3 07	−3 19	−3 31	−3 42	−3 53					

f	0	5	10	15	20	25	30	35	40	45	50	55	f	0.9	1.0	1.1	1.2
0.9	+47	+36	+27	+18	+10	+ 3	− 5	−13					0.9				
1.0	+26	+16	+ 6	− 4	−13	−22	−31	−40					1.0				
1.1	+ 5	− 5	−15	−25	−36	−46	−57	−68					1.1				
1.2	−16	−25	−36	−46	−58	−71	−83	−95					1.2				
	−37	−45	−56	−67	−81	−95											

Temperature in °C.

For these heights no temperature correction is necessary, so use $R = R_0$

Where R_0 is less than 10' or the height greater than 35 000 ft. use $R = R_0$

Choose the column appropriate to height, in units of 1 000 ft., and find the range of altitude in which the sextant altitude lies; the corresponding value of R_0 is the refraction, to be subtracted from sextant altitude, unless conditions are extreme. In that case find f from the lower table, with critical argument temperature. Use the table on the right to form the refraction, $R = R_0 \times f$.

214 requires that four volumes (II, III, IV, and V) be carried aboard. (Volumes II and III of H.D. 486 would suffice for the same passage.) Despite the disadvantage of bulk (and cost) the popularity of H.O. 214 is soundly established because of the rapidity of

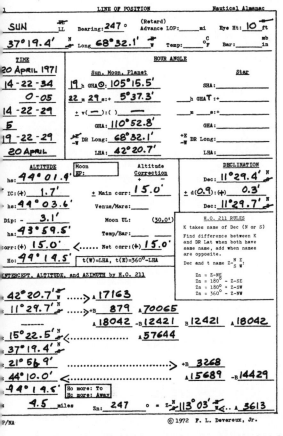

FIGURE 76. LINE OF POSITION BY H.O. 211 WITH NAUTICAL ALMANAC

solution, the simplicity of the method (all essential data on one page), and the accuracy of the position plotted.

The H.O. 214 method provides for entering its pages with a whole degree of meridian angle t (titled H.A. on each page) and either a whole or half degree of assumed declination. These assumed factors are those *nearest* to the actual components of the sight reduction.

Assumed latitude (aL) is the nearest whole degree to the DR latitude at the time of the observation.

Meridian angle t is presented as H.A. and assumed to be a whole degree (no minutes) when entering H.O. 214. This is accomplished by assuming a longitude which, when applied to the Greenwich hour angle (GHA) of the body, will result in a whole degree of arc. The assumed longitude (aLo) must be within 30' of the DR longitude at the time of the observation. The following examples clarify:

DR Longitude 57° 43.6'W: GHA: 172° 53.4'   GHA: 172° 03.4'
                                aLo: − 57° 53.4'W   aLo: − 58° 03.4'W

                                  LHA: 115°   LHA: 114°
                                      t: 115°W   t: 114°W

DR Longitude 57° 43.6'E :   GHA: 172° 53.4'   GHA: 172° 03.4'
                                  aLo: + 58° 06.6'E   aLo: + 57° 56.6'E

                                  LHA: 231°   LHA: 230°
                                      t: 129°E   t: 130°E

Assumed declination (aDec) is the nearest whole or half degree of declination, as tabulated in H.O. 214, to the actual declination of the body as obtained from an almanac. The difference between assumed and true declination is termed d diff, and has no sign (+ or −).

EXAMPLES:	*True Dec.*	*aDec*	*d diff*
	10° 40.2'N	10° 30'N	10.2'
	11° 13.9'S	11° S	13.9'
	30° 49.6'N	30° N	49.6'

Arrangement of pages: The tables are entered on the page containing the assumed latitude and the assumed declination. Column headings on each page are those of declination in ascending value; left-hand pages are for declination with the same name (N or S) as latitude, right-hand pages are for declination and latitude oppositely named, but sometimes with a bottom carry-over from the facing page. Meridian angle t (entitled H.A.) is tabulated vertically in whole degrees, by intersecting the declination column horizontally from the required meridian angle the user isolates the three factors required for solution of the celestial observation: altitude (Alt), azimuth angle (Z), and delta d (Δ d), which is the change in altitude for 1.0' of arc change in declination. The delta d values are in hundredths with the decimal point omitted, a Δ d of 86 should be written as .86 by the table user.

Method: A complete solution for sight reduction is given below by the delta d method. The steps in solution may be understood by examination of the accompanying extract (Fig. 77) of a page taken from H.O. 214.

11° 30′		
Alt.	Az.	H.A.
° ′ Δd Δt	°	°
64 30.0 1.0 02	180.0	00
64 29.0 1.0 05	177.7	1
64 26.2 1.0 08	175.5	2
64 21.5 1.0 11	173.2	3
64 14.8 99 14	170.9	4
64 06.4 99 17	168.7	05
63 56.1 98 20	166.5	6
63 44.1 98 23	164.3	7
63 30.3 97 26	162.2	8
63 14.8 96 29	160.1	9
62 57.6 95 31	158.0	10
62 38.9 94 34	156.0	1
62 18.7 93 36	154.0	2
61 56.9 92 39	152.0	3
61 33.8 91 41	150.1	4
61 09.2 90 43	148.3	15
60 43.4 89 45	146.5	6
60 16.3 88 47	144.7	7
59 48.0 87 49	143.0	8
59 18.6 86 51	141.3	9
58 48.2 85 53	139.7	20
58 16.7 84 54	138.1	1
57 44.2 83 56	136.6	2
57 10.8 82 57	135.1	3
56 36.5 81 58	133.6	4
56 01.4 80 60	132.2	25
55 25.5 79 61	130.8	6
54 48.8 78 62	129.5	7
54 11.5 77 63	128.2	8
53 33.5 76 64	126.9	9
52 54.9 75 65	125.7	30
52 15.6 74 66	124.5	1
51 35.9 73 67	123.3	2
50 55.5 72 68	122.1	3
50 14.7 72 69	121.0	4
49 33.4 71 70	120.0	35
48 51.7 70 70	118.9	6
48 09.5 69 71	117.9	7
47 27.0 69 72	116.9	8
46 44.0 68 72	115.9	9
46 00.7 67 73	114.9	40
45 17.1 67 73	114.0	1
44 33.2 66 74	113.1	2
43 48.9 66 74	112.2	3
43 04.4 65 75	111.3	4

DEC. DIFF. OR H. A. DIFF.						
Δ	0.1′	0.2′	0.3′	0.4′	0.5′	0.6′
01	0.0	0.0	0.0	0.0	0.0	0.0
2						
3						
4						
05	0.0	0.0	0.0	0.0	0.0	0.0
6						
7						
8						0.0
9					0.0	0.1
10	0.0	0.0	0.0	0.0	0.1	0.1
1						
2				0.0		
3				0.1		
4						
15	0.0	0.0	0.0	0.1	0.1	0.1
6			0.0			
7			0.1			
8						
9						
20	0.0	0.0	0.1	0.1	0.1	0.1
1						
2						
3						
4		0.0				0.1
25	0.0	0.1	0.1	0.1	0.1	0.2
6						
7						
8						
9					0.1	
30	0.0	0.1	0.1	0.1	0.2	0.2
1						
2						
3						
4						
35	0.0	0.1	0.1	0.1	0.2	0.2
6						
7				0.1		
8				0.2		
9						
40	0.0	0.1	0.1	0.2	0.2	0.2
1						0.2
2						0.3
3						
4						
45	0.0	0.1	0.1	0.2	0.2	0.3
6						
7						
8						
9	0.0		0.1		0.2	
50	0.1	0.1	0.2	0.2	0.3	0.3
1						
2						
3						
4						
55	0.1	0.1	0.2	0.2	0.3	0.3
6						
7						
8						0.3
9						0.4
60	0.1	0.1	0.2	0.2	0.3	0.4
1				0.2		
2				0.3		
3						
4						

FIGURE 77. H.O. 214 EXTRACT

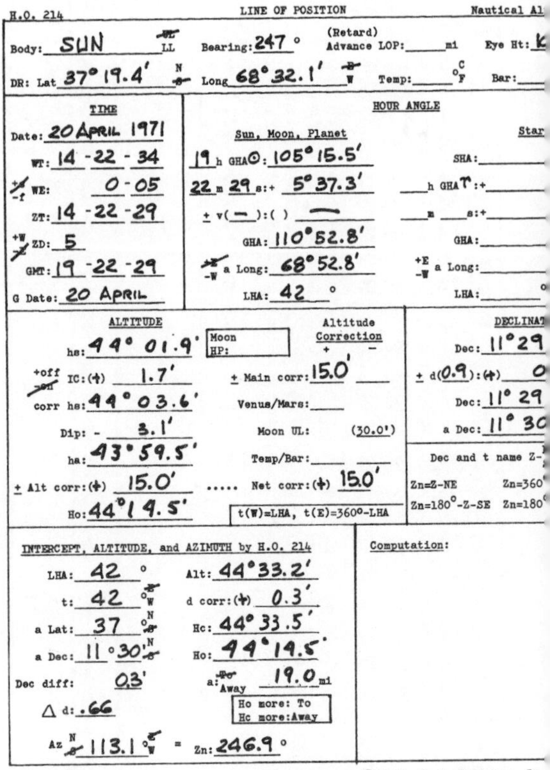

H.O. 214   LINE OF POSITION   Nautical Al

Body: **SUN** LL   Bearing: **247** °   (Retard) Advance LOP:_____mi   Eye Ht: **k**

DR: Lat **37° 19.4′** N   Long **68° 32.1′** W   Temp:____°F   Bar:____

TIME

Date: **20 APRIL 1971**

WT: **14 -22 -34**

WE: **0 -05**

ZT: **14 -22 -29**

+W ZD: **5**

GMT: **19 -22 -29**

G Date: **20 APRIL**

HOUR ANGLE

Sun, Moon, Planet   Star

19 h GHA☉: **105° 15.5′**   SHA:_____

22 m 29 s: + **5° 37.3′**   h GHA T: +_____

± v(—):( )   —   m s: +_____

GHA: **110° 52.8′**   GHA:_____

-W a Long: **68° 52.8′**   +E -W a Long:_____

LHA: **42** °   LHA:_____

ALTITUDE

hs: **44° 01.9′**   Moon HP:

+off IC: (+) **1.7′**

corr hs: **44° 03.6′**

Dip: - **3.1′**

ha: **43° 59.5′**

± Alt corr: (+) **15.0′**

Ho: **44° 14.5′**

Altitude Correction + / -

± Main corr: **15.0** ____

Venus/Mars:____

Moon UL: (30.0′)

Temp/Bar:____

..... Net corr: (+) **15.0**

t(W)=LHA, t(E)=360°-LHA

DECLINAT

Dec: **11° 29**

± d(0.9): (+)   0

Dec: **11° 29**

a Dec: **11° 30**

Dec and t name Z-

Zn=Z-NE   Zn=360

Zn=180°-Z-SE Zn=180

INTERCEPT, ALTITUDE, and AZIMUTH by H.O. 214   Computation:

LHA: **42** °   Alt: **44° 33.2′**

t: **42** °W   d corr: (+) **0.3′**

a Lat: **37** N   Hc: **44° 33.5′**

a Dec: **11° 30** N   Ho: **44° 14.5′**

Dec diff: **03′**   a: Away **19.0** mi

Δ d: **.66**   Ho more: To   Hc more: Away

Az **113.1** °W = Zn: **246.9** °

214 LOP/NA   © 1971 F. L. Devereux, Jr.

FIGURE 78. LINE OF POSITION BY H.O. 214 WITH NAUTICAL ALMANAC

1. On the work form record all computations for time (Chapter VI), altitude (Chapter XIII), declination and Greenwich hour angle (Chapter IX), and the DR latitude and longitude.
2. Compute: assumed longitude, LHA, meridian angle t, assumed latitude, assumed declination, and d diff. Record these values on the form.
3. Take altitude (Alt) from the table and record on the form; at the same time transcribe Δ d and azimuth angle (Z).
4. Convert angle to azimuth (Zn). (Chapter IX).
5. The delta correction (d corr) is the product of multiplying d diff by the value of Δ d. *Use the multiplication table* on the back cover or facing page in preference to manual calculation. The correction is applied to the tabulated altitude to obtain computed altitude (hc). The sign of the

correction is plus (+) if the tabulated altitude *increases* when moving from the tabulated declination toward the exact declination, and is minus (−) if the tabulated altitude *decreases*.

6. Intercept (a) is the difference between computed altitude (hc) and observed altitude (Ho); *toward* when Ho is greater, *away* when Ho is less than hc. Because the intercept is plotted from an assumed position (AP) based on assumed latitude and longitude, it will almost invariably be longer than if plotted from the DR position.

The Δ d method of sight reduction with H.O. 214 will satisfy the requirements of cruising navigators. Two other methods, employing Δ t and Δ Lat, are explained in the text, but not discussed here. The text also explains a method for identification of unknown stars and of finding great circle distance and initial course. Neither of these two latter techniques is believed preferable to the starfinder method of Chapter X or the great circle method with H.O. 211 discussed in Chapter XV, and therefore are not detailed herein.

Plotting lines of position obtained by H.O. 214 is described in Chapter V. It should be realized that, although the assumed latitude will normally remain constant during a round of sights, the assumed longitude will differ for each observation. H.O. 214 is not designed for reduction of altitudes under 5°.

H.O. 229, Sight Reduction Tables for Marine Navigation

Introduced in 1971, these inspection tables are intended eventually to obsolete all other tables for marine navigation, and are believed to offer the maximum degree of precision required by the navigator. H.O. 229 was jointly produced by the Nautical Almanac Office of the U.S. Naval Observatory and Her Majesty's Nautical Almanac Office (which issues them as H.D. 605) and are composed of six volumes, each covering a 15° band of latitude. The public relations efforts of the two services to obtain acceptance of the new tables may have resulted in some overstatement, since the advantages over H.O. 214 are not important and the type face may present some difficulty to middle-aged eyes in the uncertain light of twilight. There is no compelling reason for an experienced navigator to discard his library of another method and switch to H.O. 229. On the other hand, a beginning navigator is perhaps best advised to make H.O. 229 his basic method for study and future use since the tables are undoubtedly here to stay and will become the standard reference of the navy and merchant marine as time goes by.

Arrangement: Each volume covers a band of 15° latitude, with a 1° overlap between volumes. The latitude band is separated into two zones, or sub-bands, of 8° each (as 15°–22° and 23°–30°, etc.). As with H.O. 214 the tables are intended to be used with an assumed position (AP). Local hour angle (LHA), *not* meridian angle t, measured westward through 360°, is the basic page entry. Declination for each whole degree is presented vertically. Left-hand pages are used when latitude and declination have the same name (N or S), right-hand pages for latitude and declination of opposite names. A simple method for converting azimuth angle (Z) to azimuth (Zn) is contained on each page. Interpolation tables are presented on the front and back inside covers and their facing pages.

Method: The table is entered with an assumed latitude (abbreviated Tab Lat) nearest the DR latitude and the whole degree of local hour angle (LHA, obtained by applying DR longitude, − W or + E. LHA is abbreviated as Tab LHA. Declination is expressed as an integral degree (Tab Dec) and its minutes and decimal parts as the *declination increment* (Dec Inc). The whole number of the actual, not the nearest, declination is used. Pages are arranged for solution when latitude and declination are of the same name (N or S) or of different names. Rules for converting azimuth angle (Z) to azimuth (Zn) are given on each page. The method will become apparent if the following complete solution is inspected in conjunction with the accompanying table (Fig. 80) extracted from Volume III of H.O. 229.

EXAMPLE: Assume Arcturus observed April 20, 1971, at ZT 19ʰ22ᵐ15ˢ from DR Lat 42° 21.2′N, Long 63° 43.7′W.

H.O. 249, Sight Reduction Tables for Air Navigation

Description: These tables contain the "get-rich-quick" method advocated by the "navigation-is-simple" school, and it is quite true that Volume I (Selected Stars) is preferred by many marine navigators because it is more convenient to use than the H.O. tables described earlier. Volume I has two drawbacks, however, which should be considered carefully: (1) the method is the least accurate of any of the H.O. tables discussed above and is intended for use only with the *Air Almanac,* which further contributes to reduced accuracy; (2) only seven stars are tabulated—a limitation of little or no concern to the airman flying above cloud cover, but potentially a matter of great concern to the surface navigator passaging under a cumulus-patched sky. Volumes II and III, which complete the set, provide data for sun, moon, planets, and a wider selection of stars but these volumes are not considered to be as useful in marine navigation as are H.O. 211, 214, or 229 and their use is therefore not recommended to the yachtsman.

Arrangement: Volume I presents precomputed altitudes and azimuths of seven stars selected for their geometric distribution through 360°. Different stars are presented at different latitudes;

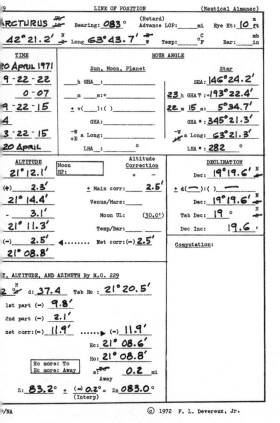

FIGURE 79. LINE OF POSITION BY H.O. 229

© 1972 F. L. Devereux, Jr.

INTERPOLATION TABLE

Dec. Inc.	10'	20'	30'	40'	50'	Dec.	0'	1'	2'	3'	4'	5'	6'	7'	8'	9'
	Tens					Decimals	Units									
24.0	4.0	8.0	12.0	16.0	20.0	.0	0.0	0.4	0.8	1.2	1.6	2.0	2.4	2.9	3.3	3.7
24.1	4.0	8.0	12.0	16.0	20.1	.1	0.0	0.4	0.9	1.3	1.7	2.1	2.5	2.9	3.3	3.7
24.2	4.0	8.0	12.1	16.1	20.1	.2	0.1	0.5	0.9	1.3	1.7	2.1	2.5	2.9	3.3	3.8
24.3	4.0	8.1	12.1	16.2	20.2	.3	0.1	0.5	0.9	1.3	1.8	2.2	2.6	3.0	3.4	3.8
24.4	4.1	8.1	12.2	16.3	20.3	.4	0.2	0.6	1.0	1.4	1.8	2.2	2.6	3.0	3.4	3.8
24.5	4.1	8.2	12.3	16.3	20.4	.5	0.2	0.6	1.0	1.4	1.8	2.2	2.7	3.1	3.5	3.9
24.6	4.1	8.2	12.3	16.4	20.5	.6	0.2	0.7	1.1	1.5	1.9	2.3	2.7	3.1	3.5	3.9
24.7	4.1	8.3	12.4	16.5	20.6	.7	0.3	0.7	1.1	1.5	1.9	2.3	2.7	3.1	3.6	4.0
24.8	4.2	8.3	12.4	16.6	20.7	.8	0.3	0.7	1.1	1.6	2.0	2.4	2.8	3.2	3.6	4.0
24.9	4.2	8.3	12.5	16.6	20.8	.9	0.4	0.8	1.2	1.6	2.0	2.4	2.8	3.2	3.6	4.0
25.0	4.1	8.3	12.5	16.6	20.8	.0	0.0	0.4	0.8	1.3	1.7	2.1	2.5	3.0	3.4	3.8
25.1	4.2	8.3	12.5	16.7	20.9	.1	0.0	0.5	0.9	1.3	1.7	2.2	2.6	3.0	3.4	3.9
25.2	4.2	8.4	12.6	16.8	21.0	.2	0.1	0.5	0.9	1.4	1.8	2.2	2.6	3.1	3.5	3.9
25.3	4.2	8.4	12.6	16.9	21.1	.3	0.1	0.6	1.0	1.4	1.8	2.3	2.7	3.1	3.5	4.0
25.4	4.2	8.5	12.7	16.9	21.2	.4	0.2	0.6	1.0	1.4	1.9	2.3	2.7	3.1	3.6	4.0
25.5	4.3	8.5	12.8	17.0	21.3	.5	0.2	0.6	1.1	1.5	1.9	2.3	2.8	3.2	3.6	4.0
25.6	4.3	8.5	12.8	17.1	21.3	.6	0.3	0.7	1.1	1.5	2.0	2.4	2.8	3.2	3.7	4.1
25.7	4.3	8.6	12.9	17.2	21.4	.7	0.3	0.7	1.1	1.6	2.0	2.4	2.8	3.3	3.7	4.1
25.8	4.3	8.6	12.9	17.2	21.5	.8	0.3	0.8	1.2	1.6	2.0	2.5	2.9	3.3	3.7	4.2
25.9	4.4	8.7	13.0	17.3	21.6	.9	0.4	0.8	1.2	1.7	2.1	2.5	2.9	3.4	3.8	4.2
26.0	4.3	8.6	13.0	17.3	21.6	.0	0.0	0.4	0.9	1.3	1.8	2.2	2.6	3.1	3.5	4.0
26.1	4.3	8.7	13.0	17.4	21.7	.1	0.0	0.5	0.9	1.4	1.8	2.3	2.7	3.1	3.6	4.0
26.2	4.3	8.7	13.1	17.4	21.8	.2	0.1	0.5	1.0	1.4	1.9	2.3	2.7	3.2	3.6	4.1
26.3	4.4	8.8	13.1	17.5	21.9	.3	0.1	0.6	1.0	1.5	1.9	2.3	2.8	3.2	3.7	4.1
26.4	4.4	8.8	13.2	17.6	22.0	.4	0.2	0.6	1.1	1.5	1.9	2.4	2.8	3.3	3.7	4.2
26.5	4.4	8.8	13.3	17.7	22.1	.5	0.2	0.7	1.1	1.5	2.0	2.4	2.9	3.3	3.8	4.2
26.6	4.4	8.9	13.3	17.7	22.2	.6	0.3	0.7	1.1	1.6	2.0	2.5	2.9	3.4	3.8	4.2
26.7	4.5	8.9	13.4	17.8	22.3	.7	0.3	0.8	1.2	1.6	2.1	2.5	3.0	3.4	3.8	4.3
26.8	4.5	9.0	13.4	17.9	22.4	.8	0.4	0.8	1.2	1.7	2.1	2.6	3.0	3.4	3.9	4.3
26.9	4.5	9.0	13.5	18.0	22.5	.9	0.4	0.8	1.3	1.7	2.2	2.6	3.0	3.5	3.9	4.4
27.0	4.5	9.0	13.5	18.0	22.5	.0	0.0	0.5	0.9	1.4	1.8	2.3	2.7	3.2	3.7	4.1
27.1	4.5	9.0	13.5	18.0	22.6	.1	0.0	0.5	1.0	1.4	1.9	2.3	2.8	3.3	3.7	4.2
27.2	4.5	9.0	13.6	18.1	22.6	.2	0.1	0.5	1.0	1.5	1.9	2.4	2.8	3.3	3.8	4.2
27.3	4.5	9.1	13.6	18.2	22.7	.3	0.1	0.6	1.1	1.5	2.0	2.4	2.9	3.3	3.8	4.3
27.4	4.6	9.1	13.7	18.3	22.8	.4	0.2	0.6	1.1	1.6	2.0	2.5	2.9	3.4	3.8	4.3
27.5	4.6	9.2	13.8	18.3	22.9	.5	0.2	0.7	1.1	1.6	2.1	2.5	3.0	3.4	3.9	4.4
27.6	4.6	9.2	13.8	18.4	23.0	.6	0.3	0.7	1.2	1.6	2.1	2.6	3.0	3.5	3.9	4.4
27.7	4.6	9.3	13.9	18.5	23.1	.7	0.3	0.8	1.2	1.7	2.2	2.6	3.1	3.5	4.0	4.4
27.8	4.7	9.3	13.9	18.6	23.2	.8	0.4	0.8	1.3	1.7	2.2	2.7	3.1	3.6	4.0	4.5
27.9	4.7	9.3	14.0	18.6	23.3	.9	0.4	0.9	1.3	1.8	2.2	2.7	3.2	3.6	4.1	4.5
28.0	4.6	9.3	14.0	18.6	23.3	.0	0.0	0.5	0.9	1.4	1.9	2.4	2.8	3.3	3.8	4.3
28.1	4.7	9.3	14.0	18.7	23.4	.1	0.0	0.5	1.0	1.5	1.9	2.4	2.9	3.4	3.8	4.3
28.2	4.7	9.4	14.1	18.8	23.5	.2	0.1	0.6	1.0	1.5	2.0	2.5	2.9	3.4	3.9	4.4
28.3	4.7	9.4	14.1	18.9	23.6	.3	0.1	0.6	1.1	1.6	2.0	2.5	3.0	3.5	3.9	4.4
28.4	4.7	9.5	14.2	18.9	23.7	.4	0.2	0.7	1.1	1.6	2.1	2.6	3.0	3.5	4.0	4.5
28.5	4.8	9.5	14.3	19.0	23.8	.5	0.2	0.7	1.2	1.7	2.1	2.6	3.1	3.6	4.0	4.5
28.6	4.8	9.5	14.3	19.1	23.8	.6	0.3	0.8	1.2	1.7	2.2	2.7	3.1	3.6	4.1	4.6
28.7	4.8	9.6	14.4	19.2	23.9	.7	0.3	0.8	1.3	1.8	2.2	2.7	3.2	3.7	4.1	4.6
28.8	4.8	9.6	14.4	19.2	24.0	.8	0.4	0.9	1.3	1.8	2.3	2.8	3.2	3.7	4.2	4.7
28.9	4.9	9.7	14.5	19.3	24.1	.9	0.4	0.9	1.4	1.9	2.3	2.8	3.3	3.8	4.2	4.7

Double Second Diff. and Corr.

Block (24.0–25.9):
0.8 (0.1), 2.5 (0.2), 4.1 (0.3), 5.8 (0.4), 7.4 (0.5), 9.1 (0.6), 10.7 (0.7), 12.3 (0.8), 14.0 (0.9), 15.6 (1.0), 17.3 (1.1), 18.9 (1.2), 20.6 (1.3), 22.2 (1.4), 23.9 (1.5), 25.5 (1.6), 27.2 (1.7), 28.8 (1.8), 30.4 (1.9), 32.1 (2.0), 33.7 (2.1), 35.4

Block (26.0–27.9):
0.8 (0.1), 2.4 (0.2), 4.0 (0.3), 5.7 (0.4), 7.3 (0.5), 8.9 (0.6), 10.5 (0.7), 12.1 (0.8), 13.7 (0.9), 15.4 (1.0), 17.0 (1.1), 18.6 (1.2), 20.2 (1.3), 21.8 (1.4), 23.4 (1.5), 25.1 (1.6), 26.7 (1.7), 28.3 (1.8), 29.9 (1.9), 31.5 (2.0), 33.1 (2.1), 34.7

Block (28.0–28.9):
0.8 (0.1), 2.4 (0.2), 4.0 (0.3), 5.6 (0.4), 7.2 (0.5), 8.8 (0.6), 10.4 (0.7), 12.0 (0.8), 13.6 (0.9), 15.2 (1.0), 16.8

the selection is excellent for obtaining a good fix "cut." Interpolation of data is unnecessary. Azimuth (Zn) is obtained directly, without the need to convert from azimuth angle (Z). All integral degrees of latitude are included, from 89° N through 89° S. Local hour angle of Aries (LHA ♈) is presented vertically on each page. Volume II includes data for latitudes 0° through 39°, Volume III covers 40° through 89°. Declination in both volumes is carried

LATITUDE
42° SAME NAME AS DECLINATION
L.H.A.

N. Lat. { L.H.A. greater than 180°......Zn=Z
{ L.H.A. less than 180°............Zn=360°−Z

Dec.	41° Hc	d	Z	42° Hc	d	Z	43° Hc	d	Z
°	° ′	′	°	° ′	′	°	° ′	′	°
0	9 01.7	+39.8	97.9	8 53.3	+40.6	98.1	8 44.8	+41.3	98.2
1	9 41.5	39.7	97.2	9 33.9	40.5	97.3	9 26.1	41.3	97.5
2	10 21.2	39.6	96.4	10 14.4	40.4	96.6	10 07.4	41.2	96.8
3	11 00.8	39.5	95.7	10 54.8	40.3	95.8	10 48.6	41.0	96.0
4	11 40.3	39.3	94.9	11 35.1	40.1	95.1	11 29.6	41.0	95.3
5	12 19.6	+39.3	94.1	12 15.2	+40.1	94.3	12 10.6	+40.8	94.5
6	12 58.9	39.1	93.3	12 55.3	39.9	93.6	12 51.4	40.7	93.8
7	13 38.0	38.9	92.6	13 35.2	39.7	92.8	13 32.1	40.6	93.0
8	14 16.9	38.8	91.8	14 14.9	39.6	92.0	14 12.7	40.4	92.3
9	14 55.7	38.6	91.0	14 54.5	39.5	91.3	14 53.1	40.2	91.5
10	15 34.3	+38.5	90.2	15 34.0	+39.3	90.5	15 33.3	+40.1	90.8
11	16 12.8	38.3	89.4	16 13.3	39.1	89.7	16 13.4	40.0	90.0
12	16 51.1	38.1	88.6	16 52.4	38.9	88.9	16 53.4	39.7	89.2
13	17 29.2	37.9	87.8	17 31.3	38.8	88.1	17 33.1	39.6	88.4
14	18 07.1	37.6	87.0	18 10.1	38.5	87.3	18 12.7	39.4	87.6
15	18 44.7	+37.5	86.2	18 48.6	+38.3	86.5	18 52.1	+39.2	86.8
16	19 22.2	37.2	85.3	19 26.9	38.1	85.7	19 31.3	38.9	86.0
17	19 59.4	37.1	84.5	20 05.0	37.9	84.9	20 10.2	38.7	85.2
18	20 36.5	36.7	83.7	20 42.9	37.6	84.0	20 48.9	38.5	84.4
19	21 13.2	36.5	82.8	21 20.5	37.4	83.2	21 27.4	38.3	83.6
20	21 49.7	+36.3	82.0	21 57.9	+37.2	82.4	22 05.7	+38.0	82.8
21	22 26.0	35.9	81.1	22 35.1	36.8	81.5	22 43.7	37.7	81.9
22	23 01.9	35.7	80.2	23 11.9	36.6	80.6	23 21.4	37.5	81.1
23	23 37.6	35.4	79.3	23 48.5	36.3	79.8	23 58.9	37.2	80.2
24	24 13.0	35.1	78.5	24 24.8	36.0	78.9	24 36.1	36.9	79.4
25	24 48.1	+34.7	77.6	25 00.8	+35.6	78.0	25 13.0	+36.5	78.5
26	25 22.8	34.5	76.7	25 36.4	35.4	77.1	25 49.5	36.3	77.6
27	25 57.3	34.0	75.8	26 11.8	35.0	76.2	26 25.8	35.9	76.7
28	26 31.3	33.8	74.8	26 46.8		75.3	27 01.7		75.8

FIGURE 80. H.O. 229 EXTRACTS

◄ a. Interpolation Table   b. Altitude and Azimuth Table ⬆

up to 29° only, which includes sun, moon, planets, and additional stars not contained in Volume I. No bodies are named, as in Volume I. Azimuth angle (Z) is given and must be converted to azimuth (Zn) according to the method given on each page. LHA (not LHA ♈) is presented vertically on each page.

Methods: Volume I is entered with LHA ♈ for the time of the observation, on the page containing the whole degree of latitude (assumed latitude) nearest the DR latitude. This page will have been previously consulted for its star listing, and one or more of the seven stars found on the page will then have been observed. Volumes II or III are entered with the local hour angle (LHA) of the observer's meridian, on the page containing the assumed latitude—either for same name and declination, or opposite. In the examples for complete solution given below the method of solution will be readily understood by consulting the accompanying extracts of volumes I and III (Figs. 82a and b).

Volume I (Selected Stars):

1. Record the sextant altitude (hs) of the observed star. Apply IC and Dip corrections and the correction for refraction (R)—found in Table 8 of Volume I or on inside back cover of the *Air Almanac*—to obtain observed altitude (Ho).
2. Determine GMT of the observation and record GHA Aries for the GMT. *(Air Almanac).*
3. Determine LHA ♈ by applying the DR longitude (+ E or − W) to GHA ♈.
4. Enter the table on the page of the assumed latitude. In the column thereon for the selected star record extract and record the computed altitude (Hc) and azimuth (Zn) for the nearest whole degree of LHA ♈.
5. Record azimuth (Zn) as extracted from the table, without interpolation.
6. Intercept (a) is the difference between Hc and Ho; *toward* if Ho is more, *away* if Ho is less than Hc.

EXAMPLE: Assume Arcturus observed April 20, 1971 at ZT 19^{h}22^{m}15^s from DR Lat 42° 21.2′N, Long 63° 43.7′W.

Volume II or III
(all bodies with declination not exceeding 29°)

1. Record the sextant altitude (hs) of the observed body. Apply IC and Dip corrections and the correction for refraction (R) found in Table 6 of volumes II and III or on inside cover of the *Air Almanac*. These corrections to hs provide observed altitude (Ho).
2. Determine GMT of the observation and record the GHA of the body at GMT (*Air Almanac*).
3. Apply the assumed longitude (aLo) nearest the DR longitude to GHA of the body, to derive LHA of the body.
4. Extract computed altitude (Hc) and azimuth angle (Z) as tabulated for the LHA.
5. The tabulated *d* is the difference between Hc and the Hc for the next larger value of declination. Interpolate, using

249 Vol I   STAR LINE OF POSITION   Air Almanac

Lat 42°21.2' N Long 63°43.7' W Temp:___ °F Bar:___ mb Eye Ht: 10 ft

	Body: ARCTURUS	Body:___	Body:___
	Bearing: 083°	Bearing:___°	Bearing:___°
	Date: 20 APRIL 1971	Date:___	Date:___
	WT: 19 - 22 - 22	WT:___ - ___ - ___	WT:___ - ___ - ___
	WE: 0 - 07	+s/-f WE:___ - ___	+s/-f WE:___ - ___
	ZT: 19 - 22 - 15	ZT:___ - ___	ZT:___ - ___ - ___
	+W/-E ZD: 4	+W/-E ZD:___	+W/-E ZD:___
	GMT: 23 - 22 - 15	GMT:___ - ___ - ___	GMT:___ - ___ - ___
	G Date: 20 APRIL	G Date:___	G Date:___
20M	h GHA: 198°23'	h GHA:___	h GHA:___
15 s:+	0°34'	m s:+___	m s:+___
	GHA: 198°57'	GHA:___	GHA:___
	+E/-W a Long: 63°57'	+E/-W a Long:___	+E/-W a Long:___
	LHA: 135°	LHA:___°	LHA:___°
	a Lat: 42° N	a Lat:___° N/S	a Lat:___° N/S
	hs: 21°12.1'	hs:___	hs:___
	+off IC:(+) 2.3'	+off/-on IC:( )___	+off/-on IC:( )___
	Dip: - 3'	Dip: -___	Dip: -___
	R: - 2'	R: -___	R: -___
	Ho: 21°09.4'	Ho:___	Ho:___
	Hc: 21°08'	Hc:___	Hc:___
	a: To 1.4 mi	a: To/Away ___ mi	a: To/Away ___ mi
	Zn: 083°	Zn:___°	Zn:___°
(Retard)	nce LOP:___ mi	(Retard) Advance LOP:___ mi	(Retard) Advance LOP:___ mi

I LOP/AA   © 1971 F. L. Devereux, Jr.

FIGURE 81. LINE OF POSITION BY H.O. 249 (Vol. I)

LHA ϒ	Hc Zn	Hc Zn	Hc Zn	Hc Zn	Hc Zn	Hc Zn	Hc Zn
	*Dubhe	REGULUS	PROCYON	*SIRIUS	RIGEL	ALDEBARAN	*Mirfak
90	42 42 038	29 01 100	47 21 143	30 28 168	38 38 195	58 31 222	61 49 300
91	43 09 038	29 44 101	47 48 144	30 37 169	38 26 196	58 01 224	61 10 300
92	43 37 039	30 28 102	48 14 145	30 45 170	38 13 197	57 30 225	60 31 300
93	44 05 039	31 12 102	48 39 147	30 52 171	37 59 199	56 58 227	59 53 300
94	44 33 039	31 55 103	49 03 148	30 59 172	37 45 200	56 25 228	59 14 300
95	45 01 039	32 39 104	49 26 149	31 04 173	37 29 201	55 51 230	58 35 300
96	45 29 039	33 22 105	49 48 151	31 09 174	37 13 202	55 17 231	57 57 300
97	45 57 039	34 05 106	50 10 152	31 13 176	36 55 203	54 42 232	57 18 300
98	46 25 039	34 48 106	50 30 154	31 16 177	36 37 205	54 06 234	56 39 300
99	46 53 039	35 30 107	50 49 155	31 18 178	36 18 206	53 30 235	56 01 300
100	47 21 039	36 13 108	51 07 157	31 19 179	35 58 207	52 54 236	55 22 300
101	47 50 039	36 55 109	51 24 158	31 20 180	35 38 208	52 16 237	54 44 300
102	48 18 039	37 37 110	51 40 160	31 19 181	35 16 209	51 39 238	54 05 301
103	48 46 039	38 19 111	51 55 161	31 18 182	34 54 210	51 00 240	53 27 301
104	49 14 039	39 01 111	52 09 163	31 16 183	34 31 211	50 22 241	52 48 301
	Dubhe	*Denebola	REGULUS	*SIRIUS	RIGEL	ALDEBARAN	*Mirfak
105	49 43 039	23 11 091	39 42 112	31 12 185	34 08 213	49 43 242	52 10 301
106	50 11 039	23 56 091	40 23 113	31 09 186	33 43 214	49 03 243	51 32 301
107	50 39 039	24 40 092	41 04 114	31 04 187	33 18 215	48 23 244	50 54 301
108	51 07 039	25 25 093	41 45 115	30 58 188	32 53 216	47 43 245	50 16 302
109	51 35 039	26 09 093	42 25 116	30 51 189	32 26 217	47 02 246	49 38 302
110	52 04 039	26 54 094	43 05 117	30 44 190	31 59 218	46 22 247	49 00 302
111	52 32 039	27 38 095	43 44 118	30 36 191	31 32 219	45 40 248	48 22 302
112	53 00 039	28 23 096	44 23 119	30 27 192	31 03 220	44 59 249	47 45 302
113	53 28 039	29 07 096	45 02 120	30 17 193	30 34 221	44 17 250	47 07 303
114	53 56 039	29 51 097	45 40 121	30 06 194	30 05 222	43 35 251	46 30 303
115	54 23 039	30 36 098	46 18 122	29 55 196	29 35 223	42 53 252	45 52 303
116	54 51 038	31 20 098	46 56 123	29 42 197	29 04 224	42 11 252	45 15 303
117	55 19 038	32 04 099	47 33 124	29 29 198	28 33 225	41 28 253	44 38 304
118	55 46 038	32 48 100	48 09 126	29 15 199	28 01 226	40 45 254	44 01 304
119	56 14 038	33 32 101	48 45 127	29 00 200	27 29 227	40 02 255	43 24 304
	*Kochab	Denebola	*REGULUS	SIRIUS	RIGEL	*ALDEBARAN	CAPELLA
120	36 52 019	34 15 101	49 21 128	28 45 201	26 56 228	39-19 256	60 18 292
121	37 06 019	34 59 102	49 56 129	28 29 202	26 23 229	38 36 257	59 37 292
122	37 21 020	35 43 103	50 30 130	28 12 203	25 50 229	37 52 257	58 55 292
123	37 36 020	36 26 104	51 04 132	27 54 204	25 16 230	37 09 258	58 14 293
124	37 51 020	37 09 105	51 37 133	27 35 205	24 41 231	36 25 259	57 33 293
125	38 06 020	37 52 105	52 09 134	27 16 206	24 06 232	35 41 260	56 52 293
126	38 22 020	38 35 106	52 40 136	26 56 207	23 31 233	34 57 261	56 11 293
127	38 37 020	39 18 107	53 11 137	26 35 208	22 55 234	34 13 261	55 30 293
128	38 52 020	40 00 108	53 41 138	26 14 209	22 19 235	33 29 262	54 49 294
129	39 08 020	40 43 109	54 10 140	25 52 210	21 42 236	32 45 263	54 08 294
130	39 24 021	41 25 110	54 39 141	25 30 211	21 05 236	32 01 263	53 28 294
131	39 39 021	42 07 111	55 06 143	25 06 212	20 28 237	31 16 264	52 47 294
132	39 55 021	42 48 112	55 32 144	24 42 213	19 50 238	30 32 265	52 06 295
133	40 11 021	43 30 112	55 58 146	24 18 214	19 12 239	29 48 266	51 26 295
134	40 27 021	44 11 113	56 22 148	23 53 215	18 34 240	29 03 266	50 46 295
	*Kochab	ARCTURUS	Denebola	*REGULUS	SIRIUS	BETELGEUSE	*CAPELLA
135	40 42 021	21 08 083	44 51 114	56 46 149	23 27 216	36 20 243	50 05 296
136	40 58 021	21 52 083	45 32 115	57 08 151	23 00 217	35 40 244	49 25 296
137	41 14 021	22 36 084	46 12 116	57 29 153	22 34 218	34 59 245	48 45 296
138	41 30 021	23 21 084	46 52 117	57 49 154	22 06 219	34 19 246	48 05 296
139	41 47 021	24 05 085	47 31 118	58 08 156	21 38 219	33 38 247	47 25 297
140	42 03 021	24 50 086	48 10 120	58 25 158	21 09 220	32 57 248	46 46 297
141	42 19 021	25 34 086	48 49 121	58 42 160	20 40 221	32 15 249	46 06 297
142	42 35 021	26 19 087	49 27 122	58 57 161	20 11 222	31 34 250	45 26 298
143	42 51 021	27 03 088	50 05 123	59 10 163	19 41 223	30 52 250	44 47 298
144	43 07 021	27 48 088	50 42 124	59 22 165	19 10 224	30 10 251	44 08 298
145	43 24 021	28 32 089	51 18 125	59 33 167	18 39 225	29 27 252	43 28 299
146	43 40 021	29 17 090	51 55 126	59 42 169	18 07 226	28 45 253	42 49 299
147	43 56 021	30 01 090	52 30 128	59 50 171	17 35 226	28 02 254	42 10 299
148	44 12 021	30 46 091	53 05 129	59 56 173	17 03 227	27 19 254	41 32 300
149	44 29 021	31 31 092	53 40 130	60 01 175	16 30 228	26 36 255	40 53 300

INTERPOLATION TABLE

Dec. Inc.	Tens 10'	20'	30'	40'	50'	Decimals	Units 0'	1'	2'	3'	4'	5'	6'	7'	8'	9'	Double Second Diff. and Corr.
16.0	2.6	5.3	8.0	10.6	13.3	.0	0.0 0.3	0.5 0.8	1.1 1.4	1.6 1.9	2.2 2.5						
16.1	2.7	5.3	8.0	10.7	13.4	.1	0.0 0.3	0.6 0.9	1.1 1.4	1.7 2.0	2.2 2.5						
16.2	2.7	5.4	8.1	10.8	13.5	.2	0.1 0.3	0.6 0.9	1.2 1.4	1.7 2.0	2.3 2.5						1.0 0.1
16.3	2.7	5.4	8.1	10.9	13.6	.3	0.1 0.4	0.6 0.9	1.2 1.5	1.7 2.0	2.3 2.6						3.0 0.1
16.4	2.7	5.5	8.2	10.9	13.7	.4	0.1 0.4	0.7 0.9	1.2 1.5	1.8 2.0	2.3 2.6						4.9 0.2
16.5	2.8	5.5	8.3	11.0	13.8	.5	0.1 0.4	0.7 1.0	1.2 1.5	1.8 2.1	2.3 2.6						6.9 0.3
16.6	2.8	5.5	8.3	11.1	13.8	.6	0.2 0.4	0.7 1.0	1.3 1.5	1.8 2.1	2.4 2.6						8.9 0.4
16.7	2.8	5.6	8.4	11.2	13.9	.7	0.2 0.5	0.7 1.0	1.3 1.6	1.8 2.1	2.4 2.7						10.8 0.5
16.8	2.8	5.6	8.4	11.2	14.0	.8	0.2 0.5	0.8 1.0	1.3 1.6	1.9 2.1	2.4 2.7						12.8 0.6
16.9	2.9	5.7	8.5	11.3	14.1	.9	0.2 0.5	0.8 1.1	1.3 1.6	1.9 2.2	2.4 2.7						14.8 0.7
																	16.7 0.8
17.0	2.8	5.6	8.5	11.3	14.1	.0	0.0 0.3	0.6 0.9	1.2 1.5	1.7 2.0	2.3 2.6						18.7 0.9
17.1	2.8	5.7	8.5	11.4	14.2	.1	0.0 0.3	0.6 0.9	1.2 1.5	1.8 2.1	2.4 2.7						20.7 1.0
17.2	2.8	5.7	8.6	11.4	14.3	.2	0.1 0.3	0.6 0.9	1.2 1.5	1.8 2.1	2.4 2.7						22.7 1.1
17.3	2.9	5.8	8.6	11.5	14.4	.3	0.1 0.4	0.7 1.0	1.3 1.5	1.8 2.1	2.4 2.7						24.6 1.2
17.4	2.9	5.8	8.7	11.6	14.5	.4	0.1 0.4	0.7 1.0	1.3 1.6	1.9 2.2	2.4 2.7						26.6 1.3
																	28.6 1.4
17.5	2.9	5.8	8.8	11.7	14.6	.5	0.1 0.4	0.7 1.0	1.3 1.6	1.9 2.2	2.5 2.8						30.5 1.5
17.6	2.9	5.9	8.8	11.7	14.7	.6	0.2 0.5	0.8 1.0	1.3 1.6	1.9 2.2	2.5 2.8						32.5 1.6
17.7	3.0	5.9	8.9	11.8	14.8	.7	0.2 0.5	0.8 1.1	1.4 1.7	2.0 2.2	2.5 2.8						34.5 1.7
17.8	3.0	6.0	8.9	11.9	14.9	.8	0.2 0.5	0.8 1.1	1.4 1.7	2.0 2.3	2.6 2.9						
17.9	3.0	6.0	9.0	12.0	15.0	.9	0.3 0.6	0.8 1.1	1.4 1.7	2.0 2.3	2.6 2.9						
18.0	3.0	6.0	9.0	12.0	15.0	.0	0.0 0.3	0.6 0.9	1.2 1.5	1.8 2.2	2.5 2.8						
18.1	3.0	6.0	9.0	12.0	15.1	.1	0.0 0.3	0.6 1.0	1.3 1.6	1.9 2.2	2.5 2.8						0.9 0.1
18.2	3.0	6.0	9.1	12.1	15.1	.2	0.1 0.4	0.7 1.0	1.3 1.6	1.9 2.2	2.5 2.8						2.8 0.1
18.3	3.0	6.1	9.1	12.2	15.2	.3	0.1 0.4	0.7 1.0	1.3 1.6	1.9 2.3	2.6 2.9						4.6 0.2
18.4	3.1	6.1	9.2	12.3	15.3	.4	0.1 0.4	0.7 1.0	1.4 1.7	2.0 2.3	2.6 2.9						6.5 0.3
18.5	3.1	6.2	9.3	12.3	15.4	.5	0.2 0.5	0.8 1.1	1.4 1.7	2.0 2.3	2.6 2.9						8.3 0.4
18.6	3.1	6.2	9.3	12.4	15.5	.6	0.2 0.5	0.8 1.1	1.4 1.7	2.0 2.3	2.7 3.0						10.2 0.5
18.7	3.1	6.3	9.4	12.5	15.6	.7	0.2 0.5	0.8 1.1	1.4 1.8	2.1 2.4	2.7 3.0						12.0 0.6
18.8	3.2	6.3	9.4	12.6	15.7	.8	0.2 0.6	0.9 1.2	1.5 1.8	2.1 2.4	2.7 3.0						13.9 0.7
18.9	3.2	6.3	9.5	12.6	15.8	.9	0.3 0.6	0.9 1.2	1.5 1.8	2.1 2.4	2.7 3.1						15.7 0.8
																	17.6 0.9
19.0	3.1	6.3	9.5	12.6	15.8	.0	0.0 0.3	0.6 1.0	1.3 1.6	1.9 2.3	2.6 2.9						19.4 1.0
19.1	3.2	6.3	9.5	12.7	15.9	.1	0.0 0.4	0.7 1.0	1.3 1.7	2.0 2.3	2.6 3.0						21.3 1.1
19.2	3.2	6.4	9.6	12.8	16.0	.2	0.1 0.4	0.7 1.0	1.4 1.7	2.0 2.3	2.7 3.0						23.1 1.2
19.3	3.2	6.4	9.6	12.9	16.1	.3	0.1 0.4	0.7 1.1	1.4 1.7	2.0 2.4	2.7 3.0						25.0 1.3
19.4	3.2	6.5	9.7	12.9	16.2	.4	0.1 0.5	0.8 1.1	1.4 1.8	2.1 2.4	2.7 3.1						26.8 1.4
																	28.7 1.5
19.5	3.3	6.5	9.8	13.0	16.3	.5	0.2 0.5	0.8 1.1	1.5 1.8	2.1 2.4	2.8 3.1						30.5 1.6
19.6	3.3	6.5	9.8	13.1	16.3	.6	0.2 0.5	0.8 1.2	1.5 1.8	2.1 2.5	2.8 3.1						32.3 1.7
19.7	3.3	6.6	9.9	13.2	16.4	.7	0.2 0.6	0.9 1.2	1.5 1.9	2.2 2.5	2.8 3.2						34.2 1.8
19.8	3.3	6.6	9.9	13.2	16.5	.8	0.3 0.6	0.9 1.2	1.6 1.9	2.2 2.5	2.9 3.2						
19.9	3.4	6.7	10.0	13.3	16.6	.9	0.3 0.6	0.9 1.3	1.6 1.9	2.2 2.6	2.9 3.2						

FIGURE 82. H.O. 229 (Vol. I) EXTRACTS

◀a. Altitude and Azimuth Table   b. Interpolation Table ↑

Table 5, for the minutes correction from actual declination (almanac) and tabulated declination.

6. Intercept (a) is the difference between computed altitude (Hc) and observed altitude (Ho); *toward* if Ho is greater, *away* if Ho is less than Hc.

7. Convert azimuth angle (Z) to azimuth (Zn) according to the rules printed on each page.

Evaluation of methods: Which method to select as one's basic choice depends on a number of factors; only the reader can weigh and decide. If price is a major consideration H.O. 211 is the logical choice since it may be purchased for 90¢ while the supply lasts, and is free (Appendix H) to owners of *Practical Navigation for the Yachtsman.* H.O. 211 is recommended for use by navigators wishing to practice their sextant observation techniques. It is the best back-up table to have aboard for lifeboat use or to replace a damaged or lost-overboard text. Its accuracy is adequate for cruising purposes and its small size a great convenience when space is limited.

H.O. 214 is the simplest and most rapid method of the three basic marine tables. Its accuracy is more than adequate. The nine volumes of the complete set represent quite an investment and take up a fair amount of bookshelf space. However, few navigators have occasion to use the complete set and, if one's cruising is not latitudinally extensive, the cost and stowage problems are correspondingly reduced.

H.O. 229 is unquestionably the method of the future, and therefore attractive to beginning navigators. The small type face may be disadvantageous and the problem of cost and bulk (six volumes) is similar to that expressed above for H.O. 214. If one is beginning the study of navigation, H.O. 229 is an obvious choice for the long run.

H.O. 249 is not recommended as a primary method, despite the quick solution for selected stars in Volume I. Volumes II and III require a more cumbersome method than either H.O. 214 or 229 and are not applicable to observation of bodies with a greater declination than 29°.

In summary, it is suggested that the "complete" navigator will first have mastered H.O. 211 and retained it for back-up while building his nautical library based on H.O. 214 or 229, either of which will serve his needs as standard methods of accurate sight reduction.

chapter XV
Special Techniques

T HREE TECHNIQUES of the old navigation for finding latitude or longitude still remain in the modern navigator's repertoire because of their simplicity of method and accuracy. They are discussed below, in conjunction with special procedures for taking altitude observations under abnormal conditions of high or low altitudes or when the horizon distance is inadequate; also presented is a method of finding the time of local apparent noon, finding compass deviation at sea, and determining great circle distance.

Longitude by Prime Vertical Observation

A body is on the *prime vertical* (PV) when its position is directly east (90°) or west (270°) of the observer, at this instant a line of position observation may be plotted as an accurate longitude determination. The observation is valid only when the observer's latitude and the declination of the body have the same name (N or S) and the latitude is greater than the declination. The observation may be made on any body but is usually employed with the sun, which offers two daily opportunities to find exact longitude. An observation made when the body is within 5° of the PV is sufficient for practical navigation purposes, and the time when the body will be in position need be calculated only to the nearest whole minute.

Two methods of finding the time of a body on the prime vertical are given below. The H.O. 214 method is advocated for navigators using those tables; *Bowditch* Table 25 is suggested as an alternate if H.O. 214 is not aboard; H.O. 249 (Vol. II and III) and H.O. 229 also can be used for the Prime Vertical observation. *By H.O. 214:* Using the nearest latitude and declination to enter the table, extract H.A. (meridian angle t) opposite the azimuth

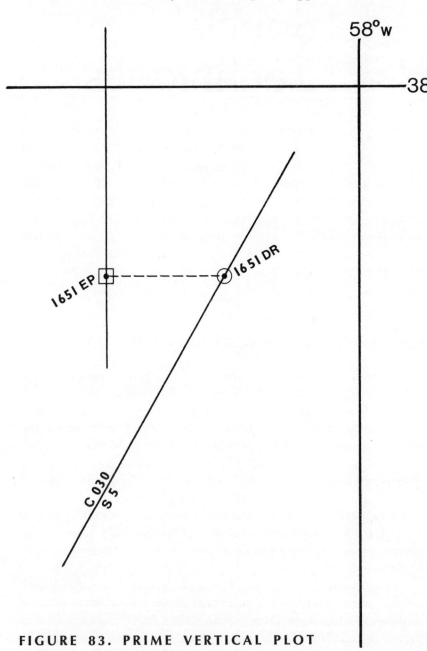

FIGURE 83. PRIME VERTICAL PLOT

angle nearest 90° for the approximate time the body will be on the prime vertical.

EXAMPLE: Afternoon observation of the sun on the PV 20 April 1971 at DR Lat 37° 54′N, Long 58° 12′W.

METHOD: Enter H.O. 214 at the tabulated latitude nearest the DR latitude (38°N). Enter the column of the estimated declination (11° 30′, same name) from *Nautical* or *Air Almanacs* and find meridian angle t for the tabulated azimuth angle nearest 90° (89.8° opposite a meridian angle t of 75°).

t:	75°E
LHA:	285°
DR Long:	+ 58.2°W
GHA:	343.2°

10h GHA:	330.2°	(*Nautical Almanac*)	
40m GHA:	10.0°	″	″
GMT:	1040		
ZD:	+ 4	(rev)	
ZT:	0640 sun on AM PV		

By *Bowditch* Table 25:

EXAMPLE: Same as given above for H.O. 214 method.

METHOD: Interpolate the value of t from Table 25 and then proceed as given above with H.O. 214. Interpolation for t is shown below as typical of the method for using Table 25.

	Dec 11	*Dec 11.4°*	*Dec 12°*
Lat 37°	75.1°		73.6°
Lat 37.9°		75.0°	
Lat 38°	75.6°		74.2°

Although prime vertical observations are normally made of the sun, they are equally valuable when made on the moon, stars, or planets. The trial-and-error method of determining time on the PV of stars (for which the almanacs do not list GHA) has miti-

POLARIS (POLE STAR) TABLES, 1971
FOR DETERMINING LATITUDE FROM SEXTANT ALTITUDE AND FOR AZIMUTH

L.H.A. ARIES	120°–129°	130°–139°	140°–149°	150°–159°	160°–169°	170°–179°	180°–189°	190°–199°	200°–209°	210°–219°	220°–229°	230°–239°
	a_0	a_0	a_0	a_0	a_0	a_0	a_0	a_0	a_0	a_0	a_0	a_0
0	0 58·3	1 07·3	1 16·0	1 24·2	1 31·6	1 38·0	1 43·3	1 47·2	1 49·7	1 50·6	1 50·0	1 47·9
1	0 59·2	08·2	16·9	25·0	32·3	38·6	43·7	47·5	49·8	50·6	49·8	47·6
2	1 00·1	09·1	17·7	25·8	33·0	39·2	44·2	47·8	50·0	50·6	49·7	47·2
3	01·0	09·9	18·5	26·5	33·7	39·7	44·6	48·1	50·1	50·6	49·5	46·9
4	01·9	10·8	19·4	27·3	34·3	40·3	45·0	48·4	50·2	50·5	49·3	46·6
5	1 02·8	1 11·7	1 20·2	1 28·0	1 35·0	1 40·8	1 45·4	1 48·6	1 50·3	1 50·5	1 49·1	1 46·2
6	03·7	12·6	21·0	28·8	35·6	41·3	45·8	48·8	50·4	50·4	48·9	45·9
7	04·6	13·4	21·8	29·5	36·2	41·8	46·2	49·1	50·5	50·3	48·6	45·5
8	05·5	14·3	22·6	30·2	36·8	42·3	46·5	49·3	50·5	50·2	48·4	45·1
9	06·4	15·2	23·4	30·9	37·5	42·8	46·9	49·5	50·6	50·1	48·1	44·7
10	1 07·3	1 16·0	1 24·2	1 31·6	1 38·0	1 43·3	1 47·2	1 49·7	1 50·6	1 50·0	1 47·9	1 44·7
Lat.	a_1	a_1	a_1	a_1	a_1	a_1	a_1	a_1	a_1	a_1	a_1	a_1
0	0·1	0·2	0·2	0·3	0·4	0·4	0·5	0·6	0·6	0·6	0·6	0·5
10	·2	·2	·3	·3	·4	·5	·5	·6	·6	·6	·6	·5
20	·3	·3	·3	·4	·4	·5	·5	·6	·6	·6	·6	·5
30	·4	·4	·4	·4	·5	·5	·6	·6	·6	·6	·6	·6
40	0·5	0·5	0·5	0·5	0·5	0·6	0·6	0·6	0·6	0·6	0·6	0·6
45	·5	·5	·5	·5	·6	·6	·6	·6	·6	·6	·6	·6
50	·6	·6	·6	·6	·6	·6	·6	·6	·6	·6	·6	·6
55	·7	·7	·7	·7	·6	·6	·6	·6	·6	·6	·6	·6
60	·8	·8	·8	·7	·7	·7	·6	·6	·6	·6	·6	·6
62	0·9	0·9	0·8	0·8	0·7	0·7	0·7	0·6	0·6	0·6	0·6	0·6
64	0·9	0·9	·9	·8	·8	·7	·7	·6	·6	·6	·6	·7
66	1·0	1·0	0·9	·9	·8	·7	·7	·6	·6	·6	·6	·7
68	1·1	1·1	1·0	0·9	0·9	0·8	0·7	0·6	0·6	0·6	0·6	0·7
Month	a_2	a_2	a_2	a_2	a_2	a_2	a_2	a_2	a_2	a_2	a_2	a_2
Jan.	0·7	0·6	0·6	0·6	0·6	0·5	0·5	0·5	0·5	0·5	0·5	0·5
Feb.	·8	·8	·8	·7	·7	·6	·6	·6	·5	·5	·4	·4
Mar.	0·9	0·9	0·9	0·9	0·8	·8	·7	·7	·6	·6	·5	·5
Apr.	1·0	1·0	1·0	1·0	1·0	0·9	0·9	0·8	0·8	0·7	0·6	0·6
May	0·9	1·0	1·0	1·0	1·0	1·0	1·0	0·9	0·9	·8	·8	·7
June	·8	0·9	0·9	1·0	1·0	1·0	1·0	1·0	1·0	0·9	0·9	·8
July	0·7	0·7	0·8	0·9	0·9	0·9	1·0	1·0	1·0	1·0	1·0	0·9
Aug.	·5	·6	·6	·7	·7	·8	0·8	0·9	0·9	0·9	0·9	1·0
Sept.	·3	·4	·4	·5	·5	·6	·7	·7	·8	·8	·9	0·9
Oct.	0·2	0·3	0·3	0·3	0·4	0·4	0·5	0·5	0·6	0·6	0·7	0·8
Nov.	·2	·2	·2	·2	·2	·3	·3	·3	·4	·5	·5	·6
Dec.	0·3	0·2	0·2	0·2	0·2	0·2	0·2	0·2	0·3	0·3	0·4	0·4
Lat.	AZIMUTH											
0	359·1	359·2	359·2	359·3	359·4	359·5	359·6	359·8	359·9	0·1	0·2	0·4
20	359·1	359·1	359·2	359·2	359·3	359·5	359·6	359·7	359·9	0·1	0·2	0·4
40	358·9	358·9	359·0	359·1	359·2	359·3	359·5	359·7	359·9	0·1	0·3	0·5
50	358·7	358·7	358·8	358·9	359·0	359·2	359·4	359·6	359·9	0·1	0·3	0·5
55	358·5	358·5	358·6	358·8	358·9	359·1	359·4	359·6	359·8	0·1	0·4	0·6-
60	358·3	358·3	358·4	358·6	358·8	359·0	359·3	359·5	359·8	0·1	0·4	0·7
65	358·0	358·0	358·2	358·3	358·6	358·8	359·1	359·5	359·8	0·1	0·5	0·8

A82

POLARIS (POLE STAR) TABLE, 1971

FOR DETERMINING THE LATITUDE FROM A SEXTANT ALTITUDE

L.H.A.♈	Q	L.H.A.♈	Q	L.H.A.♈	Q	L.H.A.♈	Q	L.H.A.♈	Q	L.H.A.♈	Q	L.H.A.♈	Q	L.H.A.♈	Q
358 24		80 25		113 24		143 58		187 22		266 40		298 42		329 39	
0 29	−44	81 50	−33	114 31	− 6	145 11	+21	190 20	+48	268 01	+29	299 48	+ 2	330 55	−25
2 42	−45	83 14	−32	115 37	− 5	146 24	+22	193 47	+49	269 20	+28	300 55	+ 1	332 11	−26
5 06	−46	84 37	−31	116 44	− 4	147 39	+23	198 06	+50	270 38	+27	302 02	0	333 29	−27
7 43	−47	85 58	−30	117 50	− 3	148 54	+24	204 50	+51	271 55	+26	303 08	− 1	334 47	−28
10 38	−48	87 18	−29	118 57	− 2	150 10	+25	217 15	+52	273 11	+25	304 15	− 2	336 07	−29
14 02	−49	88 36	−28	120 03	− 1	151 27	+26	223 59	+51	274 26	+24	305 21	− 3	337 28	−30
18 17	−50	89 54	−27	121 10	0	152 45	+27	228 18	+50	275 41	+23	306 28	− 4	338 51	−31
24 55	−51	91 10	−26	122 17	+ 1	154 04	+28	231 45	+49	276 54	+22	307 34	− 5	340 15	−32
37 10	−52	92 26	−25	123 23	+ 2	155 25	+29	234 43	+48	278 07	+21	308 41	− 6	341 40	−33
43 48	−51	93 40	−24	124 30	+ 3	156 46	+30	237 22	+47	279 19	+20	309 48	− 7	343 08	−34
48 03	−50	94 54	−23	125 36	+ 4	158 09	+31	239 48	+46	280 31	+19	310 55	− 8	344 37	−35
51 27	−49	96 07	−22	126 43	+ 5	159 34	+32	242 03	+45	281 42	+18	312 02	− 9	346 09	−36
54 22	−48	97 20	−21	127 50	+ 6	161 01	+33	244 09	+44	282 52	+17	313 10	−10	347 44	−37
56 59	−47	98 31	−20	128 57	+ 7	162 29	+34	246 09	+43	284 02	+16	314 18	−11	349 21	−38
59 23	−46	99 42	−19	130 04	+ 8	164 00	+35	248 03	+42	285 12	+15	315 26	−12	351 01	−39
61 36	−45	100 53	−18	131 12	+ 9	165 33	+36	249 52	+41	286 21	+14	316 34	−13	352 45	−40
63 41	−44	102 03	−17	132 19	+10	167 08	+37	251 37	+40	287 29	+13	317 43	−14	354 33	−41
65 39	−43	103 13	−16	133 27	+11	168 46	+38	253 19	+39	288 38	+12	318 52	−15	356 26	−42
67 32	−42	104 22	−15	134 36	+12	170 28	+39	254 57	+38	289 46	+11	320 02	−16	358 24	−43
69 20	−41	105 31	−14	135 44	+13	172 13	+40	256 32	+37	290 53	+10	321 12	−17	0 29	−44
71 04	−40	106 39	−13	136 53	+14	174 02	+41	258 05	+36	292 01	+ 9	322 23	−18	2 42	−45
72 44	−39	107 47	−12	138 03	+15	175 56	+42	259 36	+35	293 08	+ 8	323 34	−19	5 06	−46
74 21	−38	108 55	−11	139 13	+16	177 56	+43	261 04	+34	294 15	+ 7	324 45	−20	7 43	−47
75 56	−37	110 03	−10	140 23	+17	180 02	+44	262 31	+33	295 22	+ 6	325 58	−21	10 38	−48
77 28	−36	111 10	− 9	141 34	+18	182 17	+45	263 56	+32	296 29	+ 5	327 11	−22	14 02	−49
78 57	−35	112 17	− 8	142 46	+19	184 43	+46	265 19	+31	297 35	+ 4	328 25	−23	18 17	−50
80 25	−34	113 24	− 7	143 58	+20	187 22	+47	266 40	+30	298 42	+ 3	329 39	−24	24 55	−51

Q, which does *not* include refraction, is to be applied to the corrected sextant altitude of *Polaris*.
Polaris: Mag. 2·1, S.H.A. 328° 57′, Dec. N. 89° 08′·2

L.H.A.♈ 300°–120°	AZIMUTH OF *POLARIS*							L.H.A.♈ 120°–300°
	Latitude							
	0°	30°	50°	55°	60°	65°	70°	
300	0·9	1·0	1·3	1·5	1·7	2·0	2·5	300
310	0·8	1·0	1·3	1·5	1·7	2·0	2·5	290
320	0·8	0·9	1·3	1·4	1·6	1·9	2·4	280
330	0·7	0·9	1·2	1·3	1·5	1·8	2·2	270
340	0·7	0·7	1·0	1·1	1·3	1·5	1·9	260
350	0·5	0·6	0·8	0·9	1·1	1·3	1·6	250
0	0·4	0·5	0·7	0·7	0·8	1·0	1·2	240
10	0·3	0·3	0·4	0·5	0·6	0·7	0·8	230
20	0·1	0·2	0·2	0·2	0·3	0·3	0·4	220
30	0·0	0·0	0·0	0·0	0·0	0·0	0·0	210
40	359·9	359·8	359·8	359·8	359·7	359·7	359·6	200
50	359·7	359·7	359·6	359·5	359·4	359·3	359·2	190
60	359·6	359·5	359·3	359·3	359·2	359·0	358·8	180
70	359·5	359·4	359·2	359·1	358·9	358·7	358·4	170
80	359·3	359·3	359·0	358·9	358·7	358·5	358·1	160
90	359·3	359·1	358·8	358·7	358·5	358·2	357·8	150
100	359·2	359·1	358·7	358·6	358·4	358·1	357·6	140
110	359·2	359·0	358·7	358·5	358·3	358·0	357·5	130
120	359·1	359·0	358·7	358·5	358·3	358·0	357·5	120

When Cassiopeia is left (right), *Polaris* is west (east).

FIGURE 84.

POLARIS TABLES

◀ a. *Nautical Almanac*

b. *Air Almanac* ⟶

gated against their use in finding longitude. A short-cut method is suggested as a simple means of utilizing the many opportunities which stars present for finding longitude: When manipulating the starfinder device for pre-planning observations observe what stars are near the prime vertical (90° or 270° azimuth). If one is close, rotate the template on the base until exact LHA on the prime vertical is observed and convert the LHA to meridian angle t. Then proceed to determine time to the nearest minute according to either of the methods given above. As a rule of thumb, a star within 5° of the prime vertical as determined by the first inspection of the starfinder device will probably qualify for observation within the limitations of the twilight period.

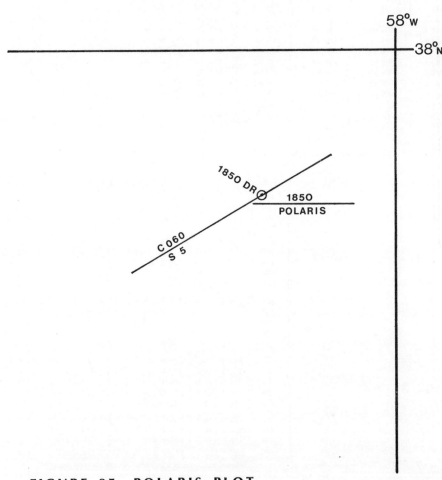

FIGURE 85. POLARIS PLOT

Latitude by Observation of Polaris

Polaris, the North Star, not only provides the sailor with a true direction by observation (always within 2° of true north) but is frequently employed to find latitude inasmuch as, with minor corrections, its altitude equals the latitude of the observer in the Northern Hemisphere. Both the *Nautical* and *Air* almanacs provide simple tables for solution, based on the LHA of Aries at the time of the observation. The *Air Almanac* correction is the simpler of the two. Both almanacs also provide the correct azimuth to be plotted; when 000° the LOP is plotted as a latitude line of position through the DR longitude, otherwise the LOP should be plotted perpendicular to the azimuth passing through the computed latitude and the DR longitude. This latter method is a fine distinction, for all practical purposes in middle latitudes or above, the LOP obtained can be considered to be the approximate, if not the precise, latitude.

Examples of finding latitude by Polaris observation, using either of the almanacs, are shown below. Examination of the Polaris tables extracted (Fig. 84) for the examples will reveal the method of applying correction.

EXAMPLES: for ZT 18–50–22 on 20 April 1971 at DR Lat 37° 54′ N, Long 58° 12′ W.

Nautical Almanac:

ZT:	18-50-22
ZD:	+ 4
GMT:	22-50-22
22h GHA ♈:	178° 19.9′
50m 22s:	+ 12° 37.8′
GHA ♈:	190° 57.7′
DR Long:	− 58° 12′W
LHA ♈:	132° 45.7′ (132.7°)
Ho:	37° 43.3′
a0:	+ 1° 09.7′
a1:	+ 0.5′
a2:	+ 1.0′
	− 1°
Lat:	37° 54.5′N
Zn:	358.9°

Air Almanac:

GMT:	22-50-22
22h 50m GHA ♈:	190° 52′
22s:	+ 0° 06′
GHA ♈:	190° 58′
DR Long:	− 58° 12′W
LHA ♈:	132° 46′ (132.8°)
Ho:	37° 43.3′
Q:	+ 11.0′
Lat:	37° 54.0′
Zn:	359.0°

Latitude by Meridian Transit Observation

An observation of a celestial body taken when it is due south (180°) or north (000°) of the observer can be used to determine latitude, and is customarily made of the sun as standard practice in the navy and merchant marine. The following discussion pertains only to the sun, which must be observed at local apparent noon (LAN) to obtain accurate latitude line of position. The method described is based on the fact that the GHA of the sun equals the longitude (when west) or 360° minus the longitude, if east. The GHA method, utilizing the *Nautical Almanac* is shown below; it requires extraction from the almanac of the GHA value of the sun next lower than the amount of the DR longitude. The difference between GHA and longitude is then used to extract

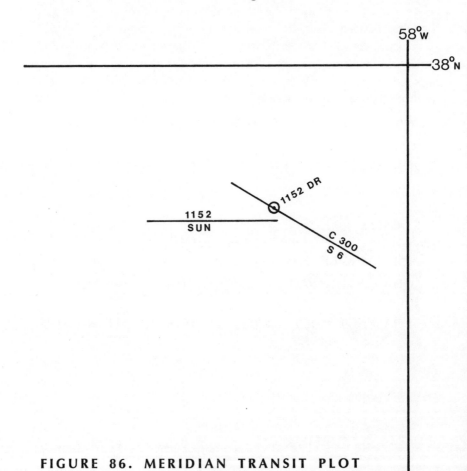

FIGURE 86. MERIDIAN TRANSIT PLOT

minutes and seconds from the appropriate yellow page of increments and corrections in the almanac's yellow pages.

EXAMPLE: On 20 April 1971, DR Lat 37° 54'N, Long 58° 12'W, the sun
will transit the meridian at 180°. An observation taken at
the exact time of transit can be used to determine exact latitude, therefore finding the time of transit (local apparent
noon) is the first step.

DR Long and GHA:	58° 12'W
15h GHA:	45° 15.0'
51m 48s:	12° 57.0'
GMT:	15-51-48
ZD:	+4 (rev)
LAN at ZT:	11-51-48

Having taken the meridian transit observation at the time of local
apparent noon, as described above, the latitude is found by subtracting the observed sextant altitude (Ho) from 90° to obtain
the *zenith* distance (z). If the sun is on the same side of the equator
as the observer, i.e., latitude and declination are both N or S, the
amount of the declination (from almanac) is added; if opposite
names the declination is subtracted. If the sun is closer to the
equator than the ship, z is subtracted from declination. To continue with the example cited above:

	90° 00.0'
Ho:	−63° 31.6'
z:	26° 28.4'
Dec:	+11° 26.8'N (at GMT)
Lat:	37° 55.2'N

A much simpler method of finding LAN, normally sufficiently
accurate for cruising purposes, is to convert the LMT of meridian
passage to ZT using either the *Nautical* or *Air Almanac*. LMT of
meridian passage is given at the bottom right hand corner of the
Nautical Almanac's daily pages, and is shown on page A71 of the
Air Almanac.

These methods of finding latitude at the exact moment of
local apparent noon are obviously dependent upon an accurate
knowledge of the longitude at that moment. On a powered vessel

maintaining constant course and speed the longitude at time of the observation can be readily anticipated; not so in a sailboat tacking or bucking headwinds. Therefore in situations where the longitude may be in doubt a better method is to take a number of observations, commencing at a positively recognized time *before* local apparent noon can occur. Record the altitudes obtained and continue the observations until the altitudes definitely decrease. The accompanying figure, "Hang of the Sun," demonstrates a typical parabola at noontime; the sun "hangs" longer at lower altitudes, and the curve is much steeper at higher altitudes. The highest altitude obtained should be considered to be the observation for latitude.

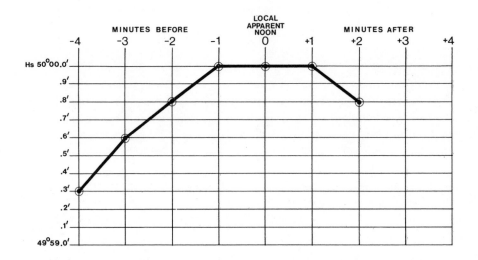

FIGURE 87. HANG OF THE SUN AT LOCAL APPARENT NOON

Run of Sights

When seas are running and the deck does not provide a stable platform a single celestial observation may be greatly in error, in which event a number of observations should be made and the best one selected. In fact it is good practice even under ideal conditions to take perhaps three sights on an object to make sure of obtaining the best possible accuracy—a single observation should

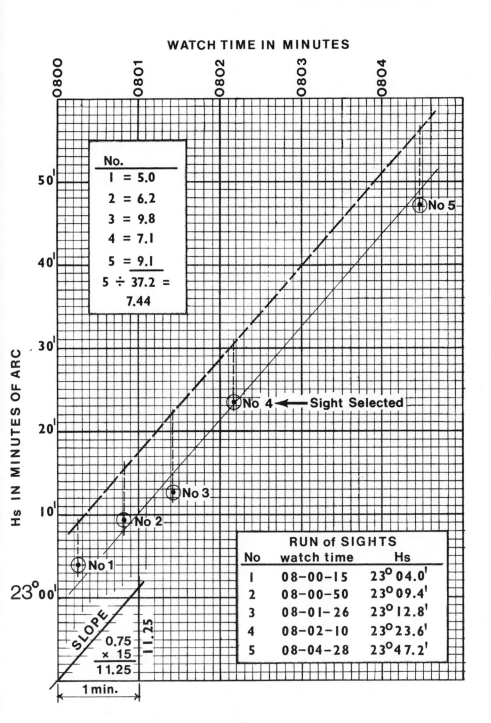

FIGURE 88. RUN OF SIGHTS

always be regarded as chancy. After throwing out any altitudes recorded which obviously are in error, one may average the altitudes and times of the observations retained and apply this finding as the observation to be plotted. An alternative graphic method, usually of greater accuracy than an average of sights, is shown in Figure 88, "Run of Sights," with sextant altitudes plotted against watch time on cross section, or graph, paper. A line is faired through the plotted points to select the most probably accurate observation. In the example, a slope line has been constructed using H.O. 214: The assumed meridian angle t, declination, and latitude for the approximate mid-time of the observations were used to determine Δ t, which is the change in altitude for every four seconds of time. When Δ t is multiplied by 15 the result is the change in altitude per minute of time. The slope line has been drawn to one side of the observations and the vertical distance from each observation to the slope line measured and averaged to draw a final slope line through the observations. The sight closest to the final slope line is the one selected for use.

Variations on the method, according to the situation and the tables of altitude and azimuth employed for sight reduction, are obvious. The graphic method of plotting is advantageous because of the immediate realization of sights that do not fit the pattern and should therefore be discarded.

Low-Altitude Observations

Whenever possible, observations of bodies at altitudes less than 10° should be avoided because of the corrections that must be made to compensate for their large and variable refraction factors. At times, obviously, no other choice may exist and a low-altitude observation will be preferable to none at all. Corrections for low-altitude refraction are discussed in Chapter XI.

All of the four H.O. tables of altitude and azimuth discussed in this book may be utilized for low-altitude observations, of these H.O. 211 is probably the easiest to use for altitudes under 5°. H.O. 214 does not tabulate factors for altitudes under 5°; to use H.O. 214 for this purpose an AP must be selected so that the resulting Hc is greater than 5°, which is then later subtracted in the final solution. The method is not recommended if any other means is available. It is described here so that it can be used in an emergency.

Observations of the upper limb of the sun or moon, when tangent to the horizon (0° altitude) may be made without the use of a sextant and are corrected as upper limb observations as explained in Chapter XII. When making horizon observations it is imperative to include all corrections for temperature and pressure.

High-Altitude Observations

Bodies observed at altitudes much in excess of 65° are frequently difficult to bring down to the horizon (they tend to

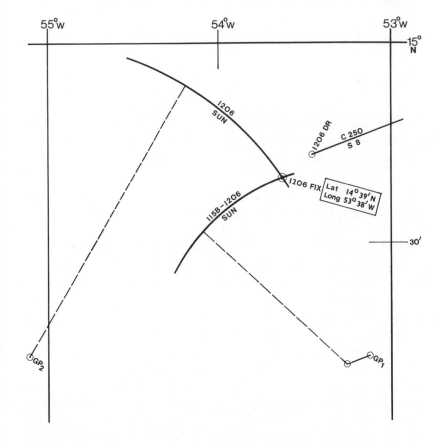

FIGURE 89. HIGH ALTITUDE FIX

"jump" sideways out of the telescope as they approach the horizon) and should be avoided whenever possible. Exception to this rule is necessary at times when observing the sun from low latitudes. When the sun is at 87° or higher altitude (as in the tropics) a special technique, plotting the circle of position or a large arc thereof is used. The geographic position (GP) of the body is used as the center of the circle and the zenith distance (z) as the radius. The entire solution is graphic and no tables of altitude or azimuth are employed. The method is particularly effective for obtaining a fix; because the position of the sun changes rapidly at high altitudes a period of one hour between observations will usually suffice. The method is illustrated in Figure 89; observe that a fix is obtained at the intersection of the two arcs of the circle of position. The GP of the sun is plotted by using the sun's declination as the GP latitude, and the sun's GHA as the GP longitude at the moment of observation.

Amplitudes

An amplitude is defined, for navigation purposes, as the arc of the horizon between the prime vertical (azimuth 90° or 270°) and a body at rising or setting. When the body is on the horizon its amplitude may be used to check compass accuracy by comparing the deviation card with the actual deviation observed. The method is a holdover from the days of the old navigation and is seldom used by military or merchant marine navigators today because of the development of accurate gyro compasses. However, for the cruising yachtsman far offshore with a magnetic compass, the opportunity of checking deviation by measurement of the sun's amplitude at sunrise and sunset still has considerable merit, particularly since the technique is a simple one.

Amplitudes are designated E or W according to whether the body is rising (E) or setting (W), and N or S according to the declination of the body. Two coordinates are required, as E × N, W × S, etc. The bearing is measured through the compass vane at the moment of rising or setting and *Bowditch* Table 28 consulted to obtain the correction to be applied to the compass observation. Comparison of this finding with the true amplitude contained in *Bowditch* Table 27 furnishes the correct deviation (after the variation has been applied). The *Bowditch* tables are not designed for the yachtsman's method of measuring on the *visible* horizon, and therefore the procedure to be followed for this method is to disregard the *Bowditch* footnote instructions and apply the correction taken from Table 28 with *reversed sign* to the value taken from Table 27, and then compare the result with the uncorrected value after including the variation.

Due to refraction, the sun should be observed when its *center* is on the visible horizon.

EXAMPLE: On 20 April 1971 at DR Lat 37° 54'N, Long 58° 12'W the variation is 16° W and the sun's declination is 11° 26.0'N. Compass bearing at sunrise is 118.5°. The problem is to determine the true azimuth of the sun and the amount of compass deviation.

METHOD: Enter Table 27 with the DR latitude and sun's declination and interpolate for amplitude (A).

	Dec 11°	*Dec 11.4°*	*Dec 11.5°*
Lat 36°	13.6°		14.3°
Lat 37.9°		14.6°	
Lat 38°	14.0°		14.7°

Amplitude (A) = E 14.6°N
Table 27: E 14.6°N   A on celestial horizon
Table 28: + 0.6°   Correction to visible horizon
           ─────────
           E 15.2°N   A on visible horizon

90° + 15.2° = 105.2°   (True sun's azimuth on horizon)

T	105.2°	
V	16 °W	
M	121.2°	
D	2.8°E	Variation is 2.8 (3.0°) E
C	118.4	

Dip Short of the Horizon

When the normal horizon is obscured, as when passing an island, the normal dip correction obtained from an almanac cannot be applied, and a "dip short" correction must be made to

GREAT CIRCLE DISTANCE by H.O. 211

From: **HAMILTON, BERMUDA**   To: **HORTA, AZORES**

Lat_1: **32° 18'** N⤢ Lat_2: **38° 32'** N⤢

$Long_1$: **64° 47'** ⤢W $Long_2$: **28° 38'** ⤢W

$Long_1$: **64° 47'** ⤢W

$Long_2$: **28° 38'** ⤢W

$(DLo)t$: **36° 09'**   ....> A **22922**

Lat_2: **38° 32'** N⤢ ....> +B **10666**   A **20553**

------   A **33588**   -B **5200**   B **5200**

K: **44° 36.5'** <.................. A **15353**

Lat_1: **32° 18** 'N⤢

$K \sim L_1$: **12° 18.5'** ....> +B **1010**

$D(arc)$: **29 ° 55 '** <............................ B **6210**
    x60

= **1740'**

+ **55'** ⤏

If t or $K \sim L_1$ exceeds 180° subtract 180° before entering H.O. 211 table

D: **1795** miles

- -

RULES:

Both Latitudes Same Name (N or S)	Latitudes Opposite Names (N and S)
K is taken from top of table except when t is greater than 90°.	K is taken from top of table except when t is greater than 90°.
$K \sim L_1$ is the difference between K and Lat_1. Subtract the smaller value.	$K \sim L_1$ is the sum of K and Lat_1. Add the two values.
D is taken from top of table except when t and $K \sim L_1$ are both greater than 90°.	D is taken from bottom of table except when t and $K \sim L_1$ are both less than 90°.

© 1971 F. L. Devereux, Jr.

FIGURE 90. GREAT CIRCLE DISTANCE BY

H.O. 211

compensate for the shortened distance. The correction is also of inestimable value to sextant practitioners in areas of limited water distance, such as lakes, rivers, and bays. The correction is always *subtracted* from sextant altitude (ha).

Three factors are applied to determine the correction:

> D is the dip correction in minutes of arc;
> d is the distance to the shore line in yards;
> h is the height of eye above water level in feet.

The correction for any known distance and height of eye may be found as follows:

$$D = 0.00021 \, d + \frac{1145.95 \, h}{d}$$

The dip value also may be found in *Bowditch*, Table 22.

Yards may be converted to miles by dividing the yards by 2025.37. Conversely miles are converted to yards by multiplying miles by 2025.37. The above figures are for *nautical* miles. To convert nautical miles to statute miles (as shown on inland charts) multiply nautical miles by 1.15.

Great Circle Distance

The simplest method of finding the approximate distance between any two points along a great circle course is to plot the two positions on a great circle (gnomonic) chart and measure the straight line distance between them, as discussed in Chapter II. The exact distance may be computed, using the H.O. 211 tables of Appendix H and solving as given in the example given below; observe that the form differs somewhat from that employed for finding line of position by H.O. 211.

EXAMPLE: Find the great circle distance between Hamilton, Bermuda (Lat 32° 18'N, Long 64° 47'W) and Horta, Azores (Lat 38° 32'N, Long 28° 38'W).

H.O. 211 method:

No measure of a great circle is practically accurate for navigation planning, since the actual arc cannot be sailed. The navigator must plot courses which are a series of chords of the circle, usually at intervals of 5° longitude. To find the actual distance which must be sailed, measure the length of *each* chord. Difference between great circle and chord distances is greatest on E–W courses and least when sailing generally N–S. There is no practical difference when distance total is less than 700 miles, and great circle computation is not necessary; rather measure and sail the rhumb line.

Both H.O. 214 and H.O. 229 can be used for great circle distance finding as explained in the introductory sections of each of their volumes. Their methods are more time-consuming, and no more accurate, than the H.O. 211 method described above.

Appendices

A • Navigation Mathematics

GEOMETRICS

Every navigation problem—directly or indirectly—involves measurement of an *angle,* defined as the intersection of two straight lines which meet at a point. The measurement may be obtained visually, by computation, or by consultation of prepared tables of values. Angles are measured in degrees of *arc,* or portions of the circumference of a circle formed by the intersection of the sides of a central angle (Fig. A1). The sum of the central angles of a circle totals 360°, as does the sum of the arcs of the circumference; therefore the number of degrees in a central angle equals the degrees of arc. For example, a 90° angle subtends 90° of arc.

Circles

For practical navigation purposes earth is considered to be a perfect sphere—absolutely round—with all surface points equidistant from the center and, because earth is perfectly round, all

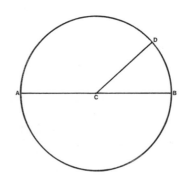

FIGURE A1. ELEMENTS OF A CIRCLE

C: Center   DB: Arc of angle DCB
AB: Diameter   AD: Arc of angle ACD
CD: Radius (also CA, CB)
(Diameter AB is a *straight* angle dividing the circumference into two equal parts, each with 180° of arc)

224

circles lying on earth's surface are also perfectly round. A cross section of earth is therefore in the form of a perfect circle, with central angles formed by the radii creating arcs at the circumference.

Great circles are those with planes bisecting earth into two equal parts. The equator is a great circle, as are all other circles passing through the polar axis. *Small circles* do not divide earth

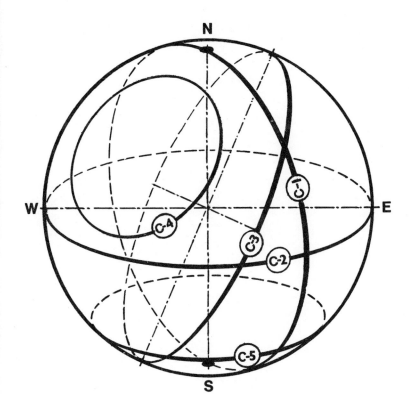

FIGURE A2. GREAT AND SMALL CIRCLES

NS and EW: Diameters (axes)
C-1: Circumference of great circle (bisecting NS)
C-2: Circumference of great circle (bisecting EW)
C-3: Circumference of great circle
C-4: Circumference of small circle
C-5: Circumference of small circle

equally because their planes do not pass through earth's center, e.g., any circle not a great circle is a small circle.

When two circles are *concentric* (having a common center) the arc measurement of a central angle is identical on either circumference. The astronomical distances from earth to the multitudinous bodies in space allow the workably practical assumption that the distances are infinite and that all celestial bodies are therefore equidistant from earth's center. Thus the arc formed by two bodies on the celestial sphere can be measured by the concentric arc on earth's (terrestrial) sphere formed by their common central angle. Observe in Figure A3 that all points lie in the plane of one great circle.

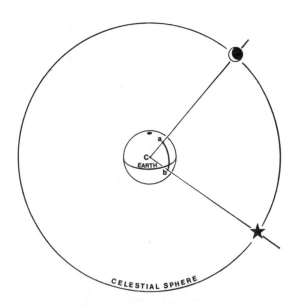

FIGURE A3. EARTH AND THE CELESTIAL SPHERE

(Cross Section)

      C: Center (concentric)
a and b: Points on earth
     ⊙ : Moon
     ★: Star

angle aCb = angle Moon/C/Star
arc ab = arc Moon/Star

Triangles

Triangles are closed figures formed by three sides; any two sides form an interior angle, measured in degrees of arc. Linear measurement of the sides is in direct proportion to the relative value of the angles formed by the sides. All triangles can be solved graphically or by simple computation with the methods of modern navigation.

A *plane triangle* is formed by three straight lines (sides), the sum of its interior angles being 180°. The plane right triangle (containing a right angle of 90°) is of particular value to navigators. Plane triangles are utilized to determine factors such as course and distance up to about 600 miles, after which earth's curvature over-distorts the plane.

The *navigational triangle* is spherical, formed by three arcs (sides) with the sum of all interior angles always more than 180°. Position on earth is found by bringing down the celestial navigational triangle to its concentrically equivalent, and measurable, terrestrial points. Modern techniques of simple arithmetic in combination with precomputed data enable the navigational triangle to be solved without any need to understand the component

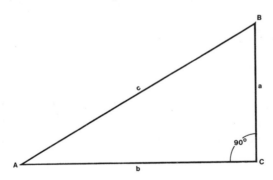

FIGURE A4. PLANE RIGHT TRIANGLE

A, B, C: Angles (total 180°)
   C: Right angle (90°)
a, b, c: Sides (labeled opposite their angles)
   c: Hypoteneuse (longest side)
A+B = 90°
   A = 90° − B
   B = 90° − A

parts and the intricacies of their relationships. The diagram of Figure A5, which need not be memorized, will aid in understanding the "why" of celestial navigation. Observe that all arcs are in the planes of great circles passing through earth's center.

ARITHMETIC

The Arc

Arc is measured in the *sexagesimal* system of degrees, minutes, and tenths of minutes (as 71°48.2'). *The base is sixty.*

One degree (1°) = Sixty minutes (60')

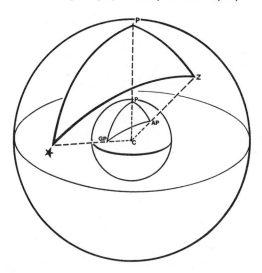

FIGURE A5. THE NAVIGATIONAL TRIANGLE

Celestial Triangle:

- Z: Zenith, point directly above observer's assumed position on earth.
- P: Nearest celestial pole (can be N or S).
- ★: Body observed (star in this instance).

Terrestrial (earth's) Triangle:

- AP: Observer's assumed position.
- P: Nearest pole (N or S).
- GP: Geographic position of the observed body.

All solutions are positive in navigation, with a maximum value of 360°. It is sometimes necessary to add or subtract 360° in order to obtain a positive solution in the range from 0° to 360°. Unlike the decimal system, one "borrows sixty" to perform an arithmetical function.

Addition: When the sum of minutes is more than sixty, subtract 60' and add 1°.

EXAMPLE:

$$
\begin{array}{r r}
71° & 48.2' \\
+\ \ 6° & 39.8' \\
\hline
77° & 88.0' \\
+\ \ 1° & -60\ \ ' \\
\hline
78° & 28.0' \\
\end{array}
$$

When the sum of degrees is more than 360°, subtract 360°.

EXAMPLE:

$$
\begin{array}{r r}
171° & 08.2' \\
+236° & 39.8' \\
\hline
407° & 48.0' \\
-360° & \\
\hline
47° & 48.0' \\
\end{array}
$$

Subtraction: When the minutes of the number to be subtracted (*subtrahend*) exceed minutes of the number from which the subtraction is to be made (*minuend*), add 60' and subtract 1° from the minuend.

EXAMPLE:

$$
\begin{array}{r r l}
71° & 48.2' & \text{(minuend)} \\
-\ \ 1° & +\ 60\ \ ' & \\
\hline
70° & 108.2' & \\
-\ 36° & 54.7' & \text{(subtrahend)} \\
\hline
34° & 53.5' & \\
\end{array}
$$

When degrees of minuend are less than degrees of subtrahend, add 360° to the minuend to avoid a negative solution.

EXAMPLE:　　　71°　48.2'　(minuend)
　　　　　　　+360°
　　　　　　　─────
　　　　　　　431°　48.2'
　　　　　　　−336°　19.7'　(subtrahend)
　　　　　　　─────
　　　　　　　 95°　28.5'

Multiplication: When total minutes exceed sixty, subtract 60 and add 1° (or 120 and 2°, etc.) Degrees and minutes are multiplied separately, and then combined.

EXAMPLE:　　71°　48.2'　　　　71°　48.2'
　　　　　　×2　 ×2　　　　 ×3　 ×3
　　　　　　────　────　　　────　────
　　　　　　142°　86.4'　　　213°　144.6'
　　　　　+　1° −60 '　　　+　2° −120 '
　　　　　　────　────　　　────　────
　　　　　　143°　30.4'　　　215°　24.6'

Division: When degrees of the number to be divided (*dividend*) contain a remainder, add the value of the remainder *in minutes* to the minutes of the dividend.

　　　　　　　　　　　　　　　8°　21.3'
EXAMPLE:　　3 /25°　03.9'　=　3 /24°　63.9'
　　　　　　　24°
　　　　　　　───
　　　　　　　1° = 60'
　　　　　　　63.9'
　　　　　　　────

Observe that the whole degrees of the dividend must first be converted to a number which the divisor can solve without a remainder; in effect the degrees and minutes of the dividend must be solved separately.

Conversion to decimal system: Degrees and tenths of degrees (as 71.8°) are sometimes required, and often chosen for simplicity when extreme precision is not a paramount consideration. To convert from the sexagesimal to the decimal system (to find the tenths of a degree): (1) divide minutes and tenths of minutes by 60, and (2) round off to the nearest tenth.

EXAMPLE: Convert 48.2′ to tenths of a degree

$$(1) \quad \frac{48.2'}{60} = .803°$$

(2)   .8°   (Round off)

Thus 71° 48.2′ = 71.8°

Rounding off is the process of reducing the number of decimal places, usually down to one tenth. 71.32° rounds off to 71.3°, 71.37° to 71.4°, etc. The nearest *even* value is selected when the number rounded off ends in 5.

EXAMPLES: 71° 45.0′ = 71.75° = 71.8°
and
71° 51.0′ = 71.85° = 71.8°

Observe that conversion to tenths of a degree, in combination with rounding off, can introduce an error of as much as 6.0′. To avoid compounding error, the rounding off should only be done for the final figure (product, sum, etc.) of a calculation, and not for the component parts of the problem.

Direction

Direction is the position of one point relative to that of another, without reference to the distance between them, and is measured in degrees of arc (sometimes to tenths of a degree) from a given reference point. The time-hallowed and cumbersome custom of boxing the compass has happily become obsolete and its only vestigal remains are to be found in the imprecise designations of wind and current direction and in the still-popular usages of east interchangably with 090°, south with 180°, west with 270°, and north with either 000° or 360°. Direction is stated with three digits: 007° is correct, never 7°.

BEARING

Direction on earth is termed a *bearing*. The arithmetic of bearings is a matter of simple addition or subtraction in the decimal system and requires no further explanation.

AZIMUTH AND AZIMUTH ANGLE

The direction of a celestial body from an observer's position on earth is termed *azimuth* (Az). True azimuth is measured clockwise from a true northerly direction (000°) and is the azimuth value required to establish a line of position in celestial navigation.

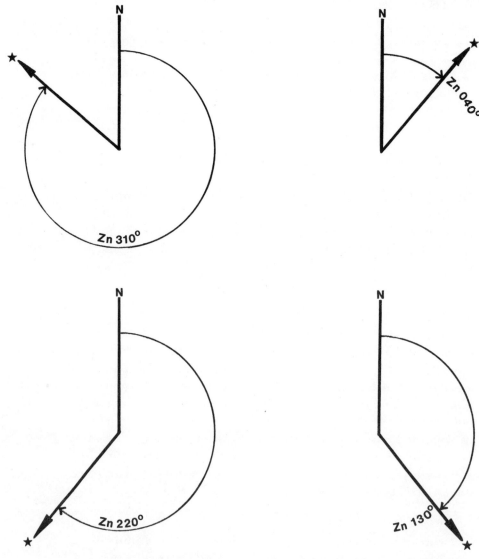

FIGURE A6. TRUE AZIMUTHS
(from True North 000°)

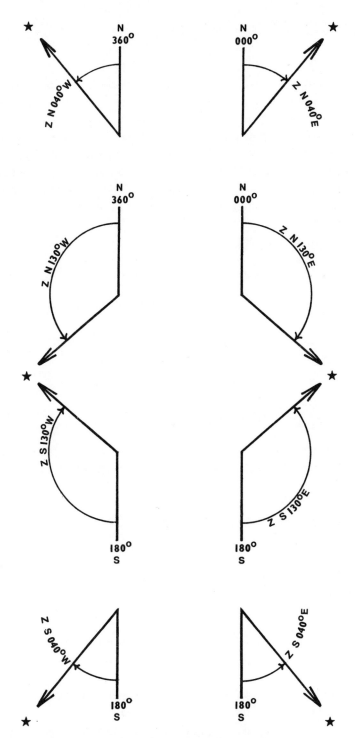

FIGURE A7. AZIMUTH ANGLES
(from 000° or 180°)

The azimuth of a celestial body is often obtained by reference to a table of computed values. These tables, to minimize bulkiness, record an *azimuth angle* (Z) which must be converted to true azimuth (Zn). *Azimuth angle (Z) is measured clockwise or counterclockwise* from a north or south reference point (000° or 180°) through 180°, prefixed N or S according to the observer's latitude and suffixed according to whether the body is rising (E) or has passed the observer's meridian and is setting (W).

The relationship of azimuth angle (Z) to true azimuth (Zn), which latter value is the one the navigator must employ as an element of position location, is diagramed in Figure A8. The basis of conversion, which should be memorized by celestial navigators, is:

$$Zn = Z \text{ NE}$$
$$Zn = 180° - Z \text{ SE}$$
$$Zn = 180° + Z \text{ SW}$$
$$Zn = 360° - Z \text{ NW}$$

COURSE AND COURSE ANGLE

A *course* is a horizontal direction of travel, usually measured from 000° at the reference direction clockwise through 360°. *Course angle* is a course measured from 000° at the reference direction clockwise or counterclockwise through 090° or 180°; it is a function of the "Sailings" (mathematical methods of navigation popular prior to World War II, and not presented in *Navigation Notebook*). Although the use of a Traverse Table is not a requirement of modern navigation technique, it should be mentioned that those familiar with their use can employ them to determine course and distance if desired. The solution for course (Cn) will be a course angle (C) which must be converted; the method is similar to that employed for conversion from azimuth angle to azimuth (see above) except that the E or W suffix is determined by the direction of the ship's heading. Substitution of C for Z wherever found in the preceeding section concerned with azimuth and azimuth angle will illustrate the principle. Use of a Traverse Table is not recommended for courses extending beyond 600 miles, nor is it essential for any of the techniques of modern navigation as practiced by civilian mariners.

RECIPROCALS

A *reciprocal* is "the other side of the compass rose" for the purposes of navigation, i.e., it is the complement of any given degree of arc and, in actual practice, is a matter of adding or subtracting 180° from the value of a bearing (sometimes from an azimuth value). Example: If a light bears 280° from a vessel, then the vessel bears 100° (280° − 180°) from the light or if the light bears 040° from another vessel, that vessel bears 220° (040° + 180°) from the light.

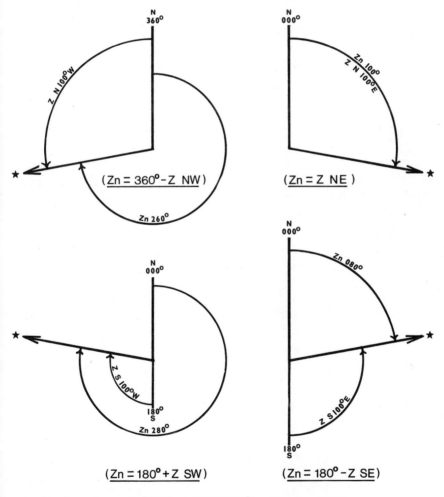

(Zn = 360°- Z NW)

(Zn = Z NE)

(Zn = 180° + Z SW)

(Zn = 180° - Z SE)

FIGURE A8. TRUE AZIMUTH (Zn) AND AZIMUTH ANGLE (Z)

Time

Time of day is expressed in the twenty-four-hour system, in four digits, to the nearest minute. Time prior to noon is identical with the system; time after noon is converted by adding twelve hours to watch time.

EXAMPLES: 0000 = Midnight at start of new day
0001 = One minute after midnight
0010 = Ten minutes after midnight
0100 = One o'clock AM
1000 = Ten o'clock AM
1200 = Noon
1300 = One o'clock PM
1800 = Six o'clock PM
2200 = Ten o'clock PM
2400 = Midnight at end of day

Time arithmetic frequently involves addition or subtraction of days, hours, minutes, and seconds. Each element should be separated to avoid confusion; the dash method is understood to identify hours, minutes, and seconds (as 4-16-32), labels are helpful when the computation becomes complex (as 3d 14h 16m 32s). Errors occur because of habits oriented to the decimal system; *minutes and seconds are in the sexagesimal system with a base of sixty,* thus sixty is borrowed as needed to perform as arithmetic function. The following conversions are frequently required:

24 hours to 1 day
60 minutes to 1 hour
60 seconds to 1 minute

Addition: When the sum of minutes or seconds exceeds 60, subtract 60 and carry the converted excess to the next (left) column.

EXAMPLES:

15h	20m	30s		15h	20m	30s		15h	20m	30s
+ 3h	10m	50s		+ 3h	50m	20s		+ 3h	50m	50s
18h	30m	80s		18h	70m	50s		18h	70m	80s
	+ 1	−60		+ 1	−60			+ 1	−60
18h	31m	20s		19h	10m	50s			71	20
								+ 1	−60	
								19h	11m	20s

When the sum of hours exceeds 24 (or multiples thereof), subtract 24 (or multiples) and add the equivalent number of days.

EXAMPLE:
$$
\begin{array}{lll}
\text{15h} & \text{20m} & \text{30s} \quad \text{(19 May)} \\
\text{+13h} & \text{30m} & \text{10s} \\
\hline
\text{28h} & \text{50m} & \text{40s} \\
\text{--24} \\
\hline
\text{4h} & \text{50m} & \text{40s} \quad \text{(20 May)}
\end{array}
$$

Subtraction: When minutes or seconds of the time to be subtracted (*subtrahend*) exceed those of the time from which the subtraction is to be made (*minuend*), add 60 to the minuend and carry the converted equivalent to the next (left) column.

EXAMPLES:

15h	20m	30s	← minuend →	15h	20m	30s
− 1	+60			− 1	+60	
15h	19m	90s		14h	80m	30s
− 3h	10m	50s	←subtrahend→	− 3h	50m	20s
12h	09m	40s		11h	30m	10s

When the hours of subtrahend exceed hours of minuend, add 24h (or multiples) to the minuend and subtract the equivalent number of days.

EXAMPLES
$$
\begin{array}{lll}
\text{4h} & \text{50m} & \text{40s} \quad \text{(20 May)} \\
\text{+24} \\
\hline
\text{28h} & \text{50m} & \text{40s} \\
\text{--13h} & \text{30m} & \text{10s} \\
\hline
\text{15h} & \text{20m} & \text{30s} \quad \text{(19 May)}
\end{array}
$$

Multiplication and *division* of time of day are rarely performed in navigation. The principles are obvious if the limits of the sexagesimal system are observed.

The date, *but not the time,* changes when crossing the international date line—increasing one day when making a westward passage, decreasing eastward (remember "Sunday Seattle, Monday Manila").

Elapsed time calculation is a matter of subtraction when both times occur on the same date.

EXAMPLE: 14h 52m 16s   (arrival 10 July)
          − 6h 37m 12s   (departure 10 July)
          ─────────────
            7h 15m 04s   (elapsed time)

Elapsed time between different dates, unless mentally obvious, is best found by subtracting time at the earlier date from 2400 and combining (add) that difference with the time after 0000 on the later date, adding 24 hours for each intervening day.

EXAMPLE: 24h 00m 00s
              −06h 37m 12s   (departure time 10 July)
              ─────────────
               17h 22m 48s   (time in transit 10 July)
              +24h   (11 July)
              ─────────────
              +14h 32m 16s   (arrival time 12 July)
              ─────────────
               55h 55m 04s   (total time in transit)
              −48h
              ─────────────
          2d   7h 55m 04s

Arc and Time

There being 360° in the circumference of a circle and twenty-four hours in a day, the following relationships are valid when measured along the equator or any circle parallel to it:

Arc	=	Time
360°		24 hours
15°		1 hour
1°		4 minutes
15′		1 minute
1′		4 seconds
¼′		1 second

Practicing navigators memorize one or more of these equivalents (usually 15° = 1 hour) because of the frequent need to convert arc to time. It is usually more expeditious to consult a conversion table such as those of the *Nautical* or *Air* almanac, however, solution can be made as shown below when a conversion table is not at hand.

EXAMPLE: $71°\ 48.2' = 4h\ 47m\ 13s$

$$
\begin{array}{rcl}
60° & = & 4h \\
11° & = & 44m \\
45' & = & 3m \\
3' & = & 12s \\
.2' & = & 1s\ (0.8s) \\
\hline
71°\ 48.2' & = & 4h\ 47m\ 13s
\end{array}
$$

Distance, Speed, Time

The quantities of distance, speed, and time are interrelated; when any two values are known the third is easily derived.

Distance (D) is the separation between two points, without regard to direction, and measured at sea on the surface in units of nautical miles. Distance equals speed (S) multiplied by time (T).

EXAMPLE: $(D = ST)$ 10 miles = 5 knots $\times$ 2 hours

Speed (S) is the rate of motion from one point to another, measured at sea in units of nautical miles per hour (knots). Speed equals distance divided by time.

EXAMPLE: $\left(S = \dfrac{D}{T} \right)$ 5 knots $= \dfrac{10\ \text{miles}}{2\ \text{hours}}$

Time (T) is an elapsed interval when applied to distance and speed. Time equals distance divided by speed.

EXAMPLE: $\left(T = \dfrac{D}{S} \right)$ 2 hours $= \dfrac{10\ \text{miles}}{5\ \text{knots}}$

Time in excess of a whole hour must first be converted to hours and tenths (divide minutes after the hour by 6) before employing any combination of $D = ST$. When total time is in minutes use the formula $60D = ST$ or its combinations. Tables are available for solution by inspection and interpolation; the above methods are often quicker and more convenient.

Interpolation

Solution of a navigation problem may require finding a proportionate (interpolated) value between two tabulated values, as in the extraction of intermediate quantities from the table below:

	Speed in Knots	
	6	8
Hours	Miles	Miles
10	60	80
12	72	96

Single interpolation is made either vertically or horizontally, depending on the format of the table and the interpolated value wanted. The method is to insert one desired factor between two tabulated values, establish the proportionate relationship thereto, and apply it to the other set of tabulated values to derive the other wanted interpolation, as exampled in the problem and solution given below:

Problem: Find distance in 10½ hours at 6-knot speed.

Solution:	Speed in Knots
	6
Hours	Miles
10	60
(10½)	(63)
12	72

Tabulated time difference is 2 hours (12 — 10); time wanted is 10½ hours or ¼ of the tabulated difference. Tabulated miles difference is 12 miles (72 — 60); ¼ × 12 = 3 miles which, added to the tabulated value of 60 miles, gives a solution of 63 miles in 10½ hours at 6 knots.

The method is the same for horizontal interpolation. From the exampled table, distance run in 12 hours at 7½ knots would be interpolated:

Speed in Knots

Hours	6 Miles	(7½) Miles	8 Miles
12	72	(90)	96

Double interpolation relies on the proportionate principle and is accomplished by solving first for both vertical interpolations and then solving horizontally between the derived vertical interpolated values (cross the "H"). In the exampled table, interpolation to find distance run in 11½ hours at 6½ knots would be solved:

Speed in Knots

Hours	6 Miles	(6½) Miles	8 Miles
10	60		80
(11½)	(69)	(74.8)*	(92)
12	72		96

* 74.75 rounded off to 74.8.

Interpolation is often solved mentally; caution should be observed when tabular values are not in whole numbers, or are declining. Critical tables (see below) are never interpolated.

CRITICAL TABLES

A critical table contains data which may not be interpolated. The arrangement of data reveals whether the table is a critical one—if a range of quantities is positioned against a specific quantity the table is critical, as shown in the following extract from the *Nautical Almanac*:

EXAMPLE: *Stars and Planets*

Apparent Altitude	Corr'n
11° 00′	−4.8′
11° 14′	−4.7′
11° 29′	

The correction (to sextant altitude) of a star with altitude observed to be within the range of 11° 15′ to 11° 29′ is extracted from the table without interpolation as − 4.7′. Note that the *upper* (not necessarily the numerically greater) of two possible values of a correction is taken whenever this situation occurs; an apparent altitude of 11° 14′ would be corrected with − 4.8′.

Noncritical tables are arranged with specific quantities opposed to each other on the same horizontal plane, and may be interpolated at will.

STANDARDS OF ACCURACY

The standards listed below are extracted from those prescribed at the U.S. Naval Academy. Express the following quantities to the indicated degree of accuracy in final computation:

Quantity	Degree of Accuracy
Altitude	0.1′
Azimuth	0.1°
Compass error	0.5°
Current:	
Drift	0.1 knot
Set	1.0°
Course	0.1°
Deviation	0.5°
Distance	0.1 mile
Height of tide	0.1 ft.
Latitude	0.1′
Longitude	0.1′
Speed	0.1 knot
Time	1 minute
Variation	0.5°
Visibility of a light	0.1 mile

Punctuation: For clarity and accuracy the following considerations should be borne in mind:

When expressing a quantity in tenths, the .0 should be shown if there are no tenths; 339° indicates a value to the nearest whole degree whereas 339.0° means that the value is to the nearest tenth of a degree.

Courses, bearings, and azimuths should be expressed in three digits, utilizing one or two 0's if necessary (as 002°, 022°, and 222°).

Express time of day in four digits, utilizing an 0 for the first digit if necessary (as 0543). When computing time, its components may be indicated by letters (d, h, m, s) or abbreviations (hrs, min, sec) if there is a possibility of confusion. The symbols ' and " are reserved for arc description and should never be employed to indicate minutes, seconds of time, or measures of feet and inches.

The sign (+ or −) of a referenced quantity should not be changed, even though its application is to be made in the reverse direction from that indicated by the sign. If, for example, a quantity is given as + 4 and circumstances require the quantity to be applied as a subtraction, write the quantity as + 4 (rev) which indicates the reverse application. This situation is sometimes encountered in problems involving time at another place.

Standard naval practice for the punctuation of components of arc includes the insertion of the minute symbol over the decimal point (as 36.2). In *Practical Navigation for the Yachtsman* the minute symbol is suffixed after the final numeral (as 36.2') in the belief that the latter method provides a clearer presentation of the quantity. Navigators of the "exclamation point" school will undoubtedly not want to change their familiar habits; beginning navigators are urged to experiment with both methods and select the one deemed most suitable.

B • Interconversion of Arc and Time

INTERCONVERSION OF ARC AND TIME

The table, extracted from the *Air Almanac,* is principally used for converting expressions in arc to their equivalent in time. The time equivalent for each of the 360° is given exactly, to which the time equivalent of all whole minutes of arc may be added by observation of the right-hand column. Interpolation for tenths of arc may be made by inspection, or calculated on the basis that .25' = 1 second of time. The table may also be used conversely for converting time into arc.

o	h m	o	h m	o	h m	o	h m	o	h m	o	h m	'	m s
0	0 00	60	4 00	120	8 00	180	12 00	240	16 00	300	20 00	0	0 00
1	0 04	61	4 04	121	8 04	181	12 04	241	16 04	301	20 04	1	0 04
2	0 08	62	4 08	122	8 08	182	12 08	242	16 08	302	20 08	2	0 08
3	0 12	63	4 12	123	8 12	183	12 12	243	16 12	303	20 12	3	0 12
4	0 16	64	4 16	124	8 16	184	12 16	244	16 16	304	20 16	4	0 16
5	0 20	65	4 20	125	8 20	185	12 20	245	16 20	305	20 20	5	0 20
6	0 24	66	4 24	126	8 24	186	12 24	246	16 24	306	20 24	6	0 24
7	0 28	67	4 28	127	8 28	187	12 28	247	16 28	307	20 28	7	0 28
8	0 32	68	4 32	128	8 32	188	12 32	248	16 32	308	20 32	8	0 32
9	0 36	69	4 36	129	8 36	189	12 36	249	16 36	309	20 36	9	0 36
10	0 40	70	4 40	130	8 40	190	12 40	250	16 40	310	20 40	10	0 40
11	0 44	71	4 44	131	8 44	191	12 44	251	16 44	311	20 44	11	0 44
12	0 48	72	4 48	132	8 48	192	12 48	252	16 48	312	20 48	12	0 48
13	0 52	73	4 52	133	8 52	193	12 52	253	16 52	313	20 52	13	0 52
14	0 56	74	4 56	134	8 56	194	12 56	254	16 56	314	20 56	14	0 56
15	1 00	75	5 00	135	9 00	195	13 00	255	17 00	315	21 00	15	1 00
16	1 04	76	5 04	136	9 04	196	13 04	256	17 04	316	21 04	16	1 04
17	1 08	77	5 08	137	9 08	197	13 08	257	17 08	317	21 08	17	1 08
18	1 12	78	5 12	138	9 12	198	13 12	258	17 12	318	21 12	18	1 12
19	1 16	79	5 16	139	9 16	199	13 16	259	17 16	319	21 16	19	1 16
20	1 20	80	5 20	140	9 20	200	13 20	260	17 20	320	21 20	20	1 20
21	1 24	81	5 24	141	9 24	201	13 24	261	17 24	321	21 24	21	1 24
22	1 28	82	5 28	142	9 28	202	13 28	262	17 28	322	21 28	22	1 28
23	1 32	83	5 32	143	9 32	203	13 32	263	17 32	323	21 32	23	1 32
24	1 36	84	5 36	144	9 36	204	13 36	264	17 36	324	21 36	24	1 36
25	1 40	85	5 40	145	9 40	205	13 40	265	17 40	325	21 40	25	1 40
26	1 44	86	5 44	146	9 44	206	13 44	266	17 44	326	21 44	26	1 44
27	1 48	87	5 48	147	9 48	207	13 48	267	17 48	327	21 48	27	1 48
28	1 52	88	5 52	148	9 52	208	13 52	268	17 52	328	21 52	28	1 52
29	1 56	89	5 56	149	9 56	209	13 56	269	17 56	329	21 56	29	1 56
30	2 00	90	6 00	150	10 00	210	14 00	270	18 00	330	22 00	30	2 00
31	2 04	91	6 04	151	10 04	211	14 04	271	18 04	331	22 04	31	2 04
32	2 08	92	6 08	152	10 08	212	14 08	272	18 08	332	22 08	32	2 08
33	2 12	93	6 12	153	10 12	213	14 12	273	18 12	333	22 12	33	2 12
34	2 16	94	6 16	154	10 16	214	14 16	274	18 16	334	22 16	34	2 16
35	2 20	95	6 20	155	10 20	215	14 20	275	18 20	335	22 20	35	2 20
36	2 24	96	6 24	156	10 24	216	14 24	276	18 24	336	22 24	36	2 24
37	2 28	97	6 28	157	10 28	217	14 28	277	18 28	337	22 28	37	2 28
38	2 32	98	6 32	158	10 32	218	14 32	278	18 32	338	22 32	38	2 32
39	2 36	99	6 36	159	10 36	219	14 36	279	18 36	339	22 36	39	2 36
40	2 40	100	6 40	160	10 40	220	14 40	280	18 40	340	22 40	40	2 40
41	2 44	101	6 44	161	10 44	221	14 44	281	18 44	341	22 44	41	2 44
42	2 48	102	6 48	162	10 48	222	14 48	282	18 48	342	22 48	42	2 48
43	2 52	103	6 52	163	10 52	223	14 52	283	18 52	343	22 52	43	2 52
44	2 56	104	6 56	164	10 56	224	14 56	284	18 56	344	22 56	44	2 56
45	3 00	105	7 00	165	11 00	225	15 00	285	19 00	345	23 00	45	3 00
46	3 04	106	7 04	166	11 04	226	15 04	286	19 04	346	23 04	46	3 04
47	3 08	107	7 08	167	11 08	227	15 08	287	19 08	347	23 08	47	3 08
48	3 12	108	7 12	168	11 12	228	15 12	288	19 12	348	23 12	48	3 12
49	3 16	109	7 16	169	11 16	229	15 16	289	19 16	349	23 16	49	3 16
50	3 20	110	7 20	170	11 20	230	15 20	290	19 20	350	23 20	50	3 20
51	3 24	111	7 24	171	11 24	231	15 24	291	19 24	351	23 24	51	3 24
52	3 28	112	7 28	172	11 28	232	15 28	292	19 28	352	23 28	52	3 28
53	3 32	113	7 32	173	11 32	233	15 32	293	19 32	353	23 32	53	3 32
54	3 36	114	7 36	174	11 36	234	15 36	294	19 36	354	23 36	54	3 36
55	3 40	115	7 40	175	11 40	235	15 40	295	19 40	355	23 40	55	3 40
56	3 44	116	7 44	176	11 44	236	15 44	296	19 44	356	23 44	56	3 44
57	3 48	117	7 48	177	11 48	237	15 48	297	19 48	357	23 48	57	3 48
58	3 52	118	7 52	178	11 52	238	15 52	298	19 52	358	23 52	58	3 52
59	3 56	119	7 56	179	11 56	239	15 56	299	19 56	359	23 56	59	3 56

C • *Abbreviations and Symbols*

A, amplitude; assumed; away (intercept)

a, assumed

A.A., *Air Almanac*

ᵃ0, first Polaris correction (*Nautical Almanac*)

ᵃ1, second Polaris correction (*Nautical Almanac*)

ᵃ2, third Polaris correction (*Nautical Almanac*)

aL, assumed latitude

aλ, assumed longitude

AM, amplitude modulation; ante meridian (before noon)

AP, assumed position

B, bearing; bearing angle

Bar, barometer (pressure reading)

C, centigrade (Celsius); chronometer time; compass (direction); course angle

c, correction (altitude)

C&GS, Coast and Geodetic Survey

CB, compass bearing

CC, compass course

CE, chronometer error; compass error

CH, compass heading

Cn, true course from north (to distinguish from course angle)

corr'n, correction

D, deviation; distance; drift

d, day(s); declination

d, declination change in one hour (Almanac)

dec, declination

Dev, deviation

diff, difference

DFS, distance finding station

DLo, difference of longitude (arc)

DR, dead (deduced) reckoning; position by dead reckoning

DSB, double-side-band

E, east

EP, estimated position

Eq T, equation of time

EST, eastern standard time

ETA, estimated time of arrival

F, Fahrenheit

f, fast

FAA, Federal Aviation Administration

FCC, Federal Communications Commission

FM, frequency modulation

ft, foot; feet

G, Greenwich; Greenwich meridian (upper branch)

g, Greenwich meridian (lower branch)

GHA, Greenwich hour angle

GMT, Greenwich mean time

GP, geographical position of a celestial body

h, altitude (astronomical); height above sea level; hour(s)

HA, hour angle

ha, approximate altitude

Hc, computed altitude

HF, high frequency

HHW, higher high water (tide)

HLW, higher low water (tide)

H.O., Hydrographic Office

Ho, observed altitude

hr, hour(s)

ht, tabulated altitude

HW, high water (tide)

IC, index correction

in, inch(es)

int, interval

kHz, kiloHertz

kt, knot (s)

L, latitude

Lat, latitude

l, difference of latitude

LAN, local apparent noon

LAT, local apparent time

LF, low frequency

LHA, local hour angle

LHW, lower high water (tide)

LL, lower limb (sun or moon)

LLW, lower low water (tide)

Lm, mid(dle) latitude

LMT, local mean time

Lo, longitude

Long, longitude

λ, longitude (Greek lambda)

LOP, line of position

LW, low water (tide)

M, meridian (upper branch); magnetic (direction)

m, meridian (lower branch); minute(s)

mag, magnetic

MB, magnetic bearing

MC, magnetic course

MF, medium frequency

MHHW, mean higher high water (tide)

MHW, mean high water (tide)

MHWN, mean high water neaps (tide)

MHWS, mean high water springs

mHz, megaHertz

mi, mile(s)

mid, middle

min, minute(s)

MLLW, mean lower low water (tide)

MLW, mean low water (tide)

MLWN, mean low water neaps (tide)

MLWS, mean low water springs (tide)

mph, miles per hour

MSL, mean sea level

MT, meridian transit

N, north

N.A., *Nautical Almanac*

NE, northeast

N.O., National Ocean Survey

NW, northwest

P, pressure; parallax; planet; pole

PM, post meridian (after noon); pulse modulation

Pn, North Pole; north celestial pole

PPP, plan position indicator
Ps, South Pole; south celestial pole
psc, per standard compass
p stg c, per steering compass
Pub, publication
PV, prime vertical
Q, Polaris correction (*Air Almanac*)
R, refraction; running (fix)
RA, right ascension
RAD, radar (line of position)
RB, relative bearing
RBn, radiobeacon
RDF, radio direction finder (ing)
rev, reverse(d)
RF, radio frequency
R FIX, running fix
S, south; speed
SD, semi-diameter
s, second(s)
SE, southeast
sec, second(s)
SH, ship's heading
SHA, sidereal hour angle
SHF, super high frequency
SOG, speed over ground (over bottom)
SSB, single-side-band
SW, southwest
T, temperature; time; true
t, meridian angle
tab, table; tabulated
TB, true bearing
TC, true course
Temp, temperature
TH, true heading
To, toward (intercept)
TR, track (ship's)
U, upper limb correction for moon (*Nautical Almanac*)
USN, United States Naval (or Navy)
V, variation
Var, variation

v, excess of GHA change from adopted value for one hour (Almanac)

VHF, very high frequency

VLF, very low frequency

W, watch time; west

Z, azimuth angle; zenith; zone

ZD, zone description

Zn, azimuth from true north (to distinguish from azimuth angle)

ZT, zone time

SYMBOLS

Position: ⊙ Dead reckoning position; fix; running fix.

  ☐ Estimated position.

  λ Longitude.

Mathematics: $+$ Plus (addition).

  $-$ Minus (subtraction).

  $\pm$ Plus or minus.

  $\sim$ Absolute difference.

  $\times$ Times (multiplication).

  $\div$ Divided by (division).

  $=$ Equals.

  ° Degrees (arc).

  ′ Minutes (arc).

  Δ Delta (the change in one quantity corresponding to the unit change in another).

  ⌐ or ⌙ Right angle(90°).

Celestial: ♈ Aries

  ⊙ Sun

  ☾ Moon

  ★ Star

  ♀ Venus

  ♂ Mars

♃ Jupiter
♄ Saturn
⊕ Earth
☉ Lower limb (sun)
☡ Upper limb (moon)

D • Radio Navigational Aids

Below—classified according to time, weather, and position—is a selected listing of radio navigational frequencies. Data sources for areas not covered herein are footnoted.

TIME

Frequency	Facility	Description
1214 kHz	BBC Radio 1, British Broadcasting Corp. Transmitters in England, Scotland, Wales, N. Ireland.*	GMT at 0600, 0900, 1100 daily and 1830 Monday through Saturday. Time signal consists of six dots (······) at one-second intervals; the final dot is the time of the signal.
2500 kHz 5000 kHz 10 mHz 15 mHz 20 mHz	WWV, Fort Collins, Colorado and WWVH, Maui, Hawaii. U. S. Bureau of Standards stations.	GMT every minute by tone, preceded by voice announcement (WWV, male; WWVH, female).
25 mHz	WWV additional frequency.	Same as for WWV above.
3300 kHz 7335 kHz 14.670 mHz	CHU, Ottawa, Ontario. Canadian government station.	Eastern standard time every minute (five hours earlier than Greenwich mean time) given by tone preceded by voice announcement in French and English.

* see H.O. 117 A, *Radio Navigational Aids* (Chapter III) for complete BBC time signal service directed to Africa, Europe, and North America.

Note: Time sources worldwide are listed in H.O. 117A (Atlantic and Mediterranean) and 117 B (Pacific and Indian Oceans), *Radio Navigational Aids* and in Volume V of the *Admiralty List of Radio Signals*.

WEATHER

Frequency	Facility	Description
1214 kHz	BBC Radio 1, British Broadcasting Corp. Transmitters in England, Scotland, Wales, N. Ireland.	At GMT 0532, 0602, 0731 daily; 0931 Saturday and Sunday; 1934 Saturday only; 1944 Monday through Friday. *Subject to change,* consult latest published reference.
2500 kHz 5000 kHz 10 mHz 15 mHz 20 mHz	WWV, Fort Collins, Colorado, and WWVH, Maui, Hawaii, U. S. Bureau of Standards stations.	Worldwide report by ten major areas given during first ten minutes of every fourth hour (GMT 0000–0010, 0400–0410, 0800–0810, 1200–1210, 1600–1610, 2000–2010).
25 mHz	WWV additional frequency.	Same as above for WWV.
2670 kHz	U. S. Coast Guard shore stations, various locations.	Storm warnings preceded by announcement on 2182 kHz.
2980 kHz 5519 kHz 8903 kHz 13.344 mHz	Federal Aviation Administration transmitters at Anchorage, Honolulu, Oakland.	Weather reports from which navigator can prepare local forecast.

Station	Minutes past each hour
Oakland	05–10, 35–40
Honolulu	20–25, 50–55
Anchorage	25–30, 55–60

Frequency	Facility	Description
2980 kHz 5519 kHz 8903 kHz 13.344 mHz	Japanese government.	Reports in Japanese and English for Japan and South Korea from which navigator can prepare local forecast. Broadcast at 10–15 and 40–45 minutes after each hour.

Frequency	Facility	Description
338 kHz 5519 kHz 8903 kHz 13.344 mHz	Crown Colony Government, Hong Kong.	Reports in English for Hong Kong, Formosa, Manila, Okinawa from which navigator can prepare local forecast. Broadcast at 15–20 and 45–50 minutes after each hour.
3001 kHz 5652 kHz 8868 kHz 13.272 mHz	Federal Aviation Administration, New York.	Weather reports from various stations east of the Mississippi from which navigator can prepare local forecast.

Area	Minutes past each hour
Bahamas, Bermuda, Florida	00–05
New York	05–10
Lake Erie	10–15
Lake Michigan, Boston	15–20
Bahamas, Bermuda, Florida, Gulf of Mexico	30–35
Chesapeake Bay	35–40
Lakes Erie and Michigan	40–45
Lake Michigan, Boston	45–50

Frequency	Facility	Description
156.300 mHz (Channel 6)	U. S. Coast Guard shore stations, various locations.	Storm warnings preceded by announcement on 156.800 mHz (Channel 16).
163.275 mHz	Environmental Science Services Administration (ESSA).	Continuous meteorological information.

POSITION

Frequency	Facility	Useful Range (miles)
84–135 kHz	Decca position	500
100 kHz	Loran C line of position	1200 day, 2400 night
190–550 kHz	Radiobeacon line of position and distance finding and aircraft beacon line of position	up to 100 depending on power output
200–400 kHz	Radiobeacon breakwater and marker line of position (low power)	up to 10
192–363 kHz	Consol(an) line of position: 192 kHz: San Francisco, U.S.A. 194 kHz: Nantucket, U.S.A. 257 kHz: Ploneis, France 266 kHz: Bushmills, Northern Ireland 285 kHz: Lugo, Spain 319 kHz: Stavanger, Norway	50 to 1500
530–1605 kHz	Commercial broadcasting stations, line of position*	25 to 100 depending on power output
1650–1950 kHz	Loran A line of position	900 day, 1500 night
2670 kHz	Coast Guard land station, line of position	25 or more depending on power output
108–118 mHz	Omni/VOR radiobeacon line of position*	Line of sight
9000–9400 mHz	Radar (small craft) position	Line of sight

* Coordinates of the *antenna* are not always contained on marine charts and must be known to plot line of position. Coastal Warning Facilities charts (ESSA) list geographic locations of broadcast station antennae. Airways charts locate broadcast station antennae, aircraft and omni/VOR beacons. Note: Consult the appropriate volume of H.O. 117, *Radio Navigational Aids* or the *Admiralty List of Radio Signals* for specific Decca, Loran, and radio-beacon frequencies worldwide. The Coast Guard's *Light Lists* give characteristics and location of radiobeacons in U.S. waters.

E•*Plotting and Labeling Constructions*

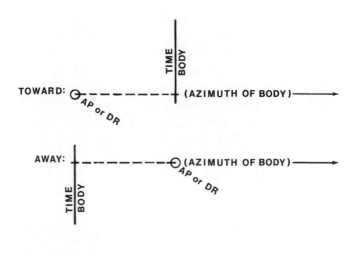

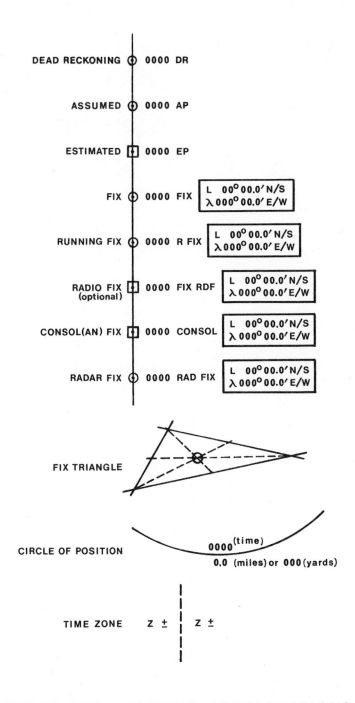

DEAD RECKONING   0000 DR

ASSUMED   0000 AP

ESTIMATED   0000 EP

FIX   0000 FIX

L 00° 00.0′ N/S
λ 000° 00.0′ E/W

RUNNING FIX   0000 R FIX

L 00° 00.0′ N/S
λ 000° 00.0′ E/W

RADIO FIX
(optional)   0000 FIX RDF

L 00° 00.0′ N/S
λ 000° 00.0′ E/W

CONSOL(AN) FIX   0000 CONSOL

L 00° 00.0′ N/S
λ 000° 00.0′ E/W

RADAR FIX   0000 RAD FIX

L 00° 00.0′ N/S
λ 000° 00.0′ E/W

FIX TRIANGLE

CIRCLE OF POSITION

0000 (time)
0.0 (miles) or 000 (yards)

TIME ZONE   Z ±   Z ±

PLOTTING AND LABELING CONSTRUCTIONS

F•Beaufort Scale
of Wind Velocity

Force	Velocity	Seaman's Description
0	1 kt	Calm
1	1–3	Light air
2	4–6	Light breeze
3	7–10	Gentle breeze
4	11–16	Moderate breeze
5	17–21	Fresh breeze
6	22–27	Strong breeze
7	28–33	Moderate gale
8	34–40	Fresh gale
9	41–47	Fresh gale
10	48–55	Whole gale
11	56–63	Whole gale
12–17	64–118	Hurricane

Weather Bureau Terminology	Wave Height	Appearance of Sea
Light	0 ft	Mirror-like
Light	½	Ripples, no foam crests
Light	1	Small wavelets not breaking
Gentle	1	Large wavelets, crests beginning to break, scattered whitecaps
Moderate	2½	Small waves growing larger, many whitecaps
Fresh	5	Moderate waves, many whitecaps, some spray
Strong	10	Larger waves, numerous whitecaps, increased spray
Strong	15	Sea tends to heap up, streaks of foam blown from breaking waves
Gale	20	Fairly high waves of greater length, well-marked foam streaks
Gale	25	Very rough sea, dense streaks of foam, high spray may reduce visibility
Whole gale	25–30	Waves have overhanging crests, sea white with foam, heavy rolling
Hurricane	30	Sea covered with foam visibility further reduced
Hurricane	35 or more	Sea completely covered with spray, air filled with foam, greatly reduced visibility

Note: H.O. 117 A (Atlantic and Mediterranean) and 117 B (Pacific and Indian Oceans), *Radio Navigational Aids* lists worldwide weather reporting stations, frequencies, and broadcast times. Much of the same information is available in H.O. 118, *Radio Weather Aids*. H.O. 119, *Weather Station Index,* completely lists international meteorological reporting stations. Volume III of the *Admiralty Lists of Radio Signals* contains all data normally required by cruising yachtsmen.

G • Work Forms

A systematic procedure for solving navigational problems encourages accuracy and familiarity with method. Forms for working line of position by each of the four tables of computed altitude and azimuth are contained herein, as well as a latitude by Polaris method and a simple procedure for finding great circle distance. The format is so constructed that any of the forms may be copied on a standard typewriter and then reproduced in quantity by photo reproduction.

LATITUDE BY POLARIS   (Nautical or Air Almanac)

DR: Lat_____ N / S Long_____ E / W   Eye_____ m / Ht:_____ft

TIME

Date:_____

+s / -f WT:_____ - _____ - _____

WE: _____ - _____

ZT:_____ - _____ - _____

+W / -E ZD:_____

GMT:_____ - _____ - _____

G Date:_____

ARIES

____h____m GHA Υ :_____

____m____s + _____

GHA Υ :_____

+E / -W DR Long:_____

LHA Υ :_____

NAUTICAL ALMANAC

+off / -on IC:( )_____

Dip: - _____   hs:_____

hs corr:( )_____ ·····▶ ( )_____

ha:_____

± Main corr * :( )_____

Ho:_____

± Polaris corr:( )_____ ◀····· _____

Lat:_____ N   Zn:_____ °

Corrn's from Polaris Table

a_0:_____

a_1:+ _____

a_2:+ _____

a_{tot}:_____

- $1°$

AIR ALMANAC

hs:_____

+off / -on IC:( )_____

Dip: - _____ (back cover)

R: - _____ (inside back cover)

Ho:_____

± Q:( )_____ (Table A82)

Lat:_____ N

Zn:_____ °

Computation:

P NA/AA   © 1972 F. L. Devereux, Jr.

GREAT CIRCLE DISTANCE By H.O. 211

From:_____   To:_____

  Lat₁:_____ N / S   Lat₂:_____ N / S

  Long₁:_____ E / W   Long₂:_____ E / W

Long₁:_____ E / W

Long₂:_____ E / W

(DLo)t:_____ ·······▶ A_____

  Lat₂:_____ N / S ·······▶ +B_____   A_____

        - - - - -   A_____ -B_____   B_____

   K:_____ ◀················· A_____

  Lat₁:_____ N / S

K ~ L₁:_____ ·······························▶ +B_____

D(arc):_____° _____' ◀······························ B_____
    x60

   = _____'

   + _____'

   D: _____ miles

> If t or K ~ L₁ exceed 180°, subtract 180° before entering H.O. 211 table.

- -

RULES:

Both Latitudes Same Name (N or S)	Latitudes Opposite Names (N and S)
K is taken from top of table except when t is greater than 90°.	K is taken from top of table except when t is greater than 90°.
K ~ L₁ is the difference between K and Lat₁. Subtract.	K ~ L₁ is the sum of K and Lat₁.
D is taken from top of table except when t and K ~ L₁ are both greater than 90°.	D is taken from bottom of table except when t and K ~ L₁ are both less than 90°.

211 GC   © 1972 F. L. Devereux, Jr.

H.O. 211   LINE OF POSITION   (Nautical Almanac)

Body:_____ UL   Bearing:_____°   (Retard)
                       LL   Advance:_____mi   Eye Ht:_____ft   m

DR: Lat_____ N   E   °C   mb
               S Long_____ W   Temp:_____ °F   Bar:_____in

TIME	HOUR ANGLE	

Date:_____

                          Sun, Moon, Planet   **Star**

WT:_____ - _____ - _____   ____h GHA___:_____   SHA:_____

WE:s _____ - _____   ____m ____s:+ _____   ____h GHA ♈ :+_____
   f

ZT:_____ - _____ - _____   ± v(____):( )_____   ____m ____s :+_____

ZD:_____ W   GHA:_____   GHA:_____
         E

GMT:_____ - _____ - _____   +E DR Long:_____   +E DR Long:_____
                            -W   -W

Date:_____   LHA:_____   LHA:_____

ALTITUDE		Altitude Correction	DECLINATION

                          Moon
                          HP:_____

hs:_____   +   −   Dec:_____ N
                                                                                       S

+off IC:( )_____   ± Main corr:_____ _____   ± d(____):( )_____
-on

corr hs:_____   Venus/Mars:_____   Dec:_____ N
                                                                             S

Dip: - _____   Moon UL: (30.0')

ha:_____   Temp/Bar:_____ _____

Alt corr:( )_____ ◄····· Net corr:( )_____

Ho:_____ | t(W)=LHA, t(E)= 360°-LHA |

K takes name of Dec (N or S)

Find difference between K and DR Lat when both have same name, add when names are opposite.

Dec and t name Z-N E:
                S W

Zn = Z-NE
Zn = 180° - Z-SE
Zn = 180° + Z-SW
Zn = 360° - Z-NW

INTERCEPT, ALTITUDE, AND AZIMUTH By H.O. 211

t:_____ E
              W   ·····► A_____
              N
Dec:_____ S ·····► +B_____   A_____

       -------   A_____ -B_____   B_____   A_____
              N
K:_____ S ◄·················· A_____
              N
DR Lat:_____ S

~ L:_____   ····························► +B_____

Hc:_____   ◄···························· A_____   -B_____

Ho:_____ | Ho more: To |
                      | Hc more: Away |

a:To _____ miles   Zn:_____° = Z-N _____ E
  Away   S   W = A_____

211 LOP/NA   © 1972 F. L. Devereux, Jr.

H.O. 214   LINE OF POSITION   (Nautical Almanac

	UL		(Retard)		m
Body:_____	LL	Bearing:_____ °	Advance LOP:_____ mi	Eye Ht:_____ ft	
DR: Lat_____	N S Long_____		E W Temp:_____ °F	C Bar:_____	mb in

TIME

Date:_____

WT:_____ ⁻_____ ⁻_____

+s
-f WE:_____ ⁻_____

ZT:_____ ⁻_____ ⁻_____

+W
-E ZD:_____

GMT:_____ _____ ⁻_____

G Date:_____

HOUR ANGLE

Sun, Moon, Planet

_____h GHA :_____

_____m _____s:+_____

± v(_____):( )_____

GHA:_____

+E
-W a Long:_____

LHA__:_____ °

Star

SHA:_____

_____h GHA ℑ :+_____

_____m _____s:+_____

GHA ✱ :_____

+E
-W a Long:_____

LHA ✱ :_____ °

ALTITUDE

hs:_____

+off
-on IC:( )_____

corr hs:_____

Dip: - _____

ha:_____

± Alt corr:( )_____ ◄········

Ho:_____

Moon	
HP:	

Altitude Correction

+	−
± Main corr:_____ _____	
Venus/Mars:_____	
Moon UL:	(30.0')
Temp/Bar:_____ _____	

Net corr:( )_____

t(W)=LHA, t(E)=360°-LHA

DECLINATION

Dec:_____

± d(_____):( )_____

Dec:_____

a Dec:_____

Dec and t name Z-$\frac{N\ E}{S\ W}$:

Zn=Z-NE   Zn=360°-Z-N

Zn=180°-Z-SE   Zn=180°+Z-S

INTERCEPT, ALTITUDE, AND AZIMUTH By H.O. 214

LHA:_____ °

t:_____ $\frac{°E}{°W}$

a Lat:_____ $\frac{N}{S}$ °

a Dec:_____ ° _____'$\frac{N}{S}$

Dec diff:_____ '

Δ d:_____

Az: $\frac{N}{S}$_____ $\frac{E}{W}$ = Zn:_____ °

Alt:_____

d corr:( )_____

Hc:_____

Ho:_____

a:To
Away _____ mi

Ho more: To
Hc more: Away

Computation:

214 LOP/NA

© 1972 F. L. Devereux, Jr.

O. 229   LINE OF POSITION   (Nautical Almanac)

	UL		(Retard)			m
dy:_____	LL Bearing:_____ °		Advance LOP:_____ mi	Eye Ht:_____ft		
	N		E	C		mb
: Lat_____	S Long_____		W Temp:_____ °F	Bar:_____in		

TIME

te:_____

WT:____ ⁻ ____ ⁻ _____

WE: ____ ⁻ _____

ZT:____ ⁻ ____ ⁻ _____

ZD:_____

GMT:____ ⁻ ____ ⁻ _____

Date:_____

HOUR ANGLE

Sun, Moon, Planet

___h GHA__:_____

___m ___s:+_____

± v(____):( )_____

GHA:_____

+E
−W a Long:_____

LHA:_____ °

Star

SHA:_____

___h GHA :+_____

___m ___s:+_____

GHA:_____

+E
−W a Long:_____

LHA:_____ °

ALTITUDE

hs:_____

roff IC:( )_____
on

corr hs:_____

Dip: − _____

ha:_____

t corr:( )_____ ◄········ Net corr:( )_____

Ho:_____

Moon		Altitude Correction
HP		+ −

± Main corr:_____ _____

Venus/Mars:_____

Moon UL: (30.0')

Temp/Bar:_____ _____

DECLINATION

Dec:_____ N
S

± d(___):( )_____

Dec:_____ N
S

Tab Dec:_____ °

Dec Inc: _____

Computation:

INTERCEPT, ALTITUDE, AND AZIMUTH By H.O. 229

Lat:_____ °N   d:_____   Tab Hc:_____
          S

t Tab: 1st part ( )_____

       2nd part ( )_____

       Net corr:( )_____ ············▶ ( )_____

                              Hc:_____

                              Ho:_____

Ho more: To
Hc more: Away

a: To
   Away _____mi

Z:_____ ° ± _____ ° = Zn_____ °
              (Interp)

© 1972 F. L. Devereux, Jr.

H.O 249 Vol I   STAR LINE OF POSITION   (Air Almanac

                    N   E   C   mb   Eye   m
DR: Lat_____ S Long_____ W   Temp:_____ °F   Bar:_____ in Ht:_____ ft

Body:_____	Body:_____	Body:_____
Date:_____	Date: _____	Date:_____
WT:____ ‾ ___ ‾ ___	WT:____ ‾ ___ ‾ ___	WT:____ ‾ ___ ‾ ___
WE: ___ ‾ ___	WE: ___ ‾ ___	WE: ___ ‾ ___
ZT:____ ‾ ___ ‾ ___	ZT:____ ‾ ___ ‾ ___	ZT:____ ‾ ___ ‾ ___
ZD:_____	ZD:_____	ZD:_____
GMT:____ ‾ ___ ‾ ___	GMT:____ ‾ ___ ‾ ___	GMT:____ ‾ ___ ‾ ___
G Date:_____	G Date:_____	G Date:_____
SHA ✳ :_____	SHA ✳ :_____	SHA ✳ :_____
___h___m♈ :+_____	___h___m♈ :+_____	___h___m♈ :+_____
___m___s :+_____	___m___s :+_____	___m___s :+_____
GHA ✳ :_____	GHA ✳ :_____	GHA ✳ :_____
+E a Long:_____ −W	+E a Long:_____ −W	+E a Long:_____ −W
LHA ✳ :_____	LHA ✳ :_____	LHA ✳ :_____
a Lat:_____ °N S	a Lat:_____ °N S	a Lat:_____ °N S
hs :_____	hs:_____	hs:_____
+off IC:( )_____ −on	+off IC:( )_____ −on	+off IC:( )_____ −on
Dip: − _____	Dip: − _____	Dip: − _____
R: − _____	R: − _____	R: − _____
Ho:_____	Ho:_____	Ho:_____
Hc:_____	Hc:_____	Hc:_____
a: To Away _____ mi	a: To Away _____ mi	a: To Away _____ mi
Zn:_____ °	Zn:_____ °	Zn:_____ °
(Retard) Advance LOP:_____ miles	(Retard) Advance LOP:_____ miles	(Retard) Advance LOP:_____ miles

249 I LOP/AA   © 1972 F. L. Devereux, Jr.

O. 249 Vols II & III   LINE OF POSITION   (Air Almanac)

	UL		N		C	(Retard)
dy:_____	LL	DR: Lat_____	S	Temp:_____	°F	Advance LOP:_____mi
			E		mb	m
aring:_____°		Long_____	W	Bar:_____in		Eye Height:_____ft

TIME | ### HOUR ANGLE

TIME

HOUR ANGLE

Sun, Moon, Planet   Star

ate:_____	
	SHA *:_____
WT:___-___-___	
WE:_____-_____	h___m GHA__:_____ h___m GHA ♈:+_____
ZT:___-___-___	___m___s :+___ ___m___s :+___
ZD:____	GHA__:_____ GHA *:_____
GMT:___-___-___	+E a Long:_____ +E a Long:_____
	-W -W
Date:_____	LHA__:_____° LHA *:_____°

ALTITUDE CORRECTIONS   ### INTERCEPT AND AZIMUTH

ALTITUDE CORRECTIONS

INTERCEPT AND AZIMUTH

```
                + -                                              N
+off  IC:____ ____                        Dec:_____ S
-on                                                      N
      Dip:    ____                        a Lat:_____°S
        R:    ____                        d:_____
) Sun/Moon UL: ____
                                          Tab Z:_____ = Zn_____°
) Sun/Moon LL:____
  Moon P in A:____        ALTITUDE        Tab Hc:_____
     total +:____ ____    hs:_____  ± d corr:( ) _____
net hs corr:( )____ ••••••▶ ( )_____  Hc:_____
                  Ho:_____ •••••▶ Ho:_____
```

Ho more: To
Hc more: Away

a: To
   Away _____mi

omputation:

49 II&III LOP/AA   © 1972 F.L. Devereux, Jr.

H • H.O. 211, Dead Reckoning Altitude and Azimuth Table

These tables provide solution of the navigational triangle in any latitude according to the method described in Chapter XIII and are reproduced here by permission of the Commander, U.S. Naval Oceanographic Office. The following precepts should be observed:

The tables were published before the practice of using meridian angle t became popular; wherever found, substitute t for LHA.

Observe the rules at the top of each page for taking K and Z from the top or bottom of the table.

When a figure lies exactly midway between two tabulated values take the value nearest the whole minute of arc.

Many navigators employ the tables without interpolation as advocated by Admiral Ageton, their developer, and taught by the U.S. Power Squadrons. The user should understand that non-interpolation can, at times, result in a position error. It is therefore recommended that solutions containing a K between 87°30′ and 92°30′ be discarded.

WHEN LHA (E OR) W IS <u>GREATER</u> THAN 90°, TAKE "K" FROM <u>BOTTOM</u> OF TABLE

′	0° 00′		0° 30′		1° 00′		1° 30′		2° 00′		′
	A	B	A	B	A	B	A	B	A	B	
0	-------	0. 0	205916	1. 7	175814	6. 6	158208	14. 9	145718	26. 5	30
	383730	0. 0	205198	1. 7	175454	6. 7	157967	15. 1	145538	26. 7	
1	353627	0. 0	204492	1. 8	175097	6. 8	157728	15. 2	145358	26. 9	29
	336018	0. 0	203797	1. 8	174742	7. 0	157490	15. 4	145179	27. 1	
2	323524	0. 0	203113	1. 9	174391	7. 1	157254	15. 6	145000	27. 3	28
	313833	0. 0	202440	1. 9	174042	7. 2	157019	15. 7	144823	27. 6	
3	305915	0. 0	201777	2. 0	173696	7. 3	156784	15. 9	144646	27. 8	27
	299221	0. 0	201124	2. 1	173352	7. 4	156552	16. 1	144470	28. 0	
4	293421	0. 0	200480	2. 1	173012	7. 5	156320	16. 2	144295	28. 3	26
	288306	0. 0	199846	2. 2	172674	7. 6	156090	16. 4	144120	28. 5	
5	283730	0. 0	199221	2. 3	172339	7. 8	155861	16. 6	143946	28. 7	25
	279591	0. 1	198605	2. 3	172006	7. 9	155633	16. 8	143773	28. 9	
6	275812	0. 1	197998	2. 4	171676	8. 0	155406	16. 9	143600	29. 2	24
	272336	0. 1	197399	2. 4	171348	8. 1	155180	17. 1	143428	29. 4	
7	269118	0. 1	196808	2. 5	171023	8. 2	154956	17. 3	143257	29. 6	23
	266121	0. 1	196225	2. 6	170700	8. 4	154733	17. 5	143086	29. 9	
8	263318	0. 1	195650	2. 7	170379	8. 5	154511	17. 6	142916	30. 1	22
	260685	0. 1	195082	2. 7	170061	8. 6	154290	17. 8	142747	30. 4	
9	258203	0. 1	194522	2. 8	169745	8. 7	154070	18. 0	142579	30. 6	21
	255855	0. 2	193969	2. 9	169432	8. 9	153851	18. 2	142411	30. 8	
10	253627	0. 2	193422	2. 9	169121	9. 0	153633	18. 4	142243	31. 1	20
	251508	0. 2	192883	3. 0	168811	9. 1	153417	18. 6	142077	31. 3	
11	249488	0. 2	192350	3. 1	168505	9. 3	153201	18. 7	141911	31. 5	19
	247558	0. 2	191824	3. 2	168200	9. 4	152987	18. 9	141745	31. 8	
12	245709	0. 3	191303	3. 2	167897	9. 5	152774	19. 1	141581	32. 0	18
	243936	0. 3	190790	3. 3	167597	9. 7	152561	19. 3	141417	32. 3	
13	242233	0. 3	190282	3. 4	167298	9. 8	152350	19. 5	141253	32. 5	17
	240594	0. 3	189780	3. 5	167002	9. 9	152140	19. 7	141090	32. 8	
14	239015	0. 4	189283	3. 6	166708	10. 1	151931	19. 9	140928	33. 0	16
	237491	0. 4	188793	3. 6	166415	10. 2	151722	20. 1	140766	33. 3	
15	236018	0. 4	188307	3. 7	166125	10. 3	151515	20. 3	140605	33. 5	15
	234594	0. 4	187827	3. 8	165836	10. 5	151309	20. 5	140445	33. 7	
16	233215	0. 5	187353	3. 9	165550	10. 6	151104	20. 6	140285	34. 0	14
	231879	0. 5	186883	4. 0	165265	10. 8	150899	20. 8	140125	34. 2	
17	230583	0. 5	186419	4. 1	164982	10. 9	150696	21. 0	139967	34. 5	13
	229324	0. 6	185959	4. 1	164701	11. 0	150494	21. 2	139809	34. 7	
18	228100	0. 6	185505	4. 2	164422	11. 2	150292	21. 4	139651	35. 0	12
	226910	0. 6	185055	4. 3	164144	11. 3	150092	21. 6	139494	35. 3	
19	225752	0. 7	184609	4. 4	163868	11. 5	149892	21. 8	139338	35. 5	11
	224624	0. 7	184168	4. 5	163594	11. 6	149693	22. 0	139182	35. 8	
20	223525	0. 7	183732	4. 6	163322	11. 8	149495	22. 2	139027	36. 0	10
	222452	0. 8	183300	4. 7	163052	11. 9	149299	22. 4	138872	36. 3	
21	221406	0. 8	182872	4. 8	162783	12. 1	149103	22. 6	138718	36. 5	9
	220384	0. 9	182448	4. 9	162516	12. 2	148907	22. 9	138564	36. 8	
22	219385	0. 9	182029	5. 0	162250	12. 4	148713	23. 1	138411	37. 1	8
	218409	0. 9	181613	5. 1	161986	12. 5	148520	23. 3	138258	37. 3	
23	217455	1. 0	181201	5. 2	161724	12. 7	148327	23. 5	138106	37. 6	7
	216521	1. 0	180794	5. 3	161463	12. 8	148135	23. 7	137955	37. 9	
24	215607	1. 1	180390	5. 4	161204	13. 0	147945	23. 9	137804	38. 1	6
	214711	1. 1	179990	5. 5	160946	13. 1	147755	24. 1	137653	38. 4	
25	213834	1. 1	179593	5. 6	160690	13. 3	147566	24. 3	137504	38. 6	5
	212974	1. 2	179200	5. 7	160435	13. 4	147377	24. 5	137354	38. 9	
26	212130	1. 2	178810	5. 8	160182	13. 6	147190	24. 7	137205	39. 2	4
	211303	1. 3	178424	5. 9	159930	13. 8	147003	24. 9	137057	39. 4	
27	210491	1. 3	178042	6. 0	159680	13. 9	146817	25. 2	136909	39. 7	3
	209695	1. 4	177663	6. 1	159431	14. 1	146632	25. 4	136761	40. 0	
28	208912	1. 4	177287	6. 2	159184	14. 2	146448	25. 6	136615	40. 3	2
	208143	1. 5	176914	6. 3	158938	14. 4	146264	25. 8	136468	40. 5	
29	207388	1. 5	176544	6. 4	158693	14. 6	146081	26. 0	136322	40. 8	1
	206646	1. 6	176178	6. 5	158450	14. 7	145899	26. 2	136177	41. 1	
30	205916	1. 7	175814	6. 6	158208	14. 9	145718	26. 5	136032	41. 4	0
′	A	B	A	B	A	B	A	B	A	B	′
	179° 30′		179° 00′		178° 30′		178° 00′		177° 30′		

′	2° 30′		3° 00′		3° 30′		4° 00′		4° 30′		′
	A	B	A	B	A	B	A	B	A	B	
0	136032	41. 4	128120	59. 6	121432	81. 1	115641	105. 9	110536	134. 1	30
	135888	41. 6	128000	59. 9	121329	81. 5	115551	106. 4	110455	134. 6	
1	135744	41. 9	127880	60. 2	121226	81. 9	115461	106. 8	110375	135. 1	29
	135600	42. 2	127760	60. 6	121124	82. 2	115371	107. 3	110296	135. 6	
2	135457	42. 5	127640	60. 9	121021	82. 6	115282	107. 7	110216	136. 1	28
	135315	42. 7	127521	61. 2	120919	83. 0	115192	108. 1	110136	136. 6	
3	135173	43. 0	127403	61. 6	120817	83. 4	115103	108. 6	110057	137. 1	27
	135031	43. 3	127284	61. 9	120715	83. 8	115014	109. 0	109977	137. 6	
4	134890	43. 6	127166	62. 2	120614	84. 2	114925	109. 5	109898	138. 1	26
	134749	43. 9	127049	62. 6	120513	84. 6	114836	109. 9	109819	138. 6	
5	134609	44. 2	126931	62. 9	120412	85. 0	114747	110. 4	109740	139. 1	25
	134469	44. 4	126814	63. 3	120311	85. 4	114659	110. 8	109662	139. 6	
6	134330	44. 7	126697	63. 6	120211	85. 8	114571	111. 3	109583	140. 1	24
	134191	45. 0	126581	63. 9	120110	86. 2	114483	111. 7	109505	140. 6	
7	134052	45. 3	126465	64. 3	120010	86. 6	114395	112. 2	109426	141. 1	23
	133914	45. 6	126349	64. 6	119910	87. 0	114307	112. 7	109348	141. 7	
8	133777	45. 9	126233	65. 0	119811	87. 4	114220	113. 1	109270	142. 2	22
	133640	46. 2	126118	65. 3	119711	87. 8	114133	113. 6	109192	142. 7	
9	133503	46. 5	126003	65. 7	119612	88. 2	114045	114. 0	109115	143. 2	21
	133367	46. 8	125888	66. 0	119513	88. 6	113958	114. 5	109037	143. 7	
10	133231	47. 1	125774	66. 4	119415	89. 0	113872	114. 9	108960	144. 2	20
	133096	47. 4	125660	66. 7	119316	89. 4	113785	115. 4	108882	144. 7	
11	132961	47. 6	125546	67. 1	119218	89. 8	113699	115. 9	108805	145. 2	19
	132826	47. 9	125433	67. 4	119120	90. 2	113612	116. 3	108728	145. 8	
12	132692	48. 2	125320	67. 8	119022	90. 6	113526	116. 8	108651	146. 3	18
	132558	48. 5	125207	68. 1	118925	91. 0	113440	117. 3	108574	146. 8	
13	132425	48. 8	125094	68. 5	118827	91. 4	113354	117. 7	108498	147. 3	17
	132292	49. 1	124982	68. 8	118730	91. 8	113269	118. 2	108421	147. 8	
14	132159	49. 4	124870	69. 2	118633	92. 3	113183	118. 7	108345	148. 4	16
	132027	49. 7	124759	69. 6	118537	92. 7	113098	119. 1	108269	148. 9	
15	131896	50. 0	124647	69. 9	118440	93. 1	113013	119. 6	108193	149. 4	15
	131764	50. 3	124536	70. 3	118344	93. 5	112928	120. 1	108117	149. 9	
16	131633	50. 7	124425	70. 6	118248	93. 9	112843	120. 5	108041	150. 5	14
	131503	51. 0	124315	71. 0	118152	94. 3	112759	121. 0	107965	151. 0	
17	131373	51. 3	124204	71. 3	118056	94. 7	112674	121. 5	107890	151. 5	13
	131243	51. 6	124095	71. 7	117961	95. 2	112590	121. 9	107814	152. 1	
18	131114	51. 9	123985	72. 1	117866	95. 6	112506	122. 4	107739	152. 6	12
	130985	52. 2	123875	72. 4	117771	96. 0	112422	122. 9	107664	153. 1	
19	130856	52. 5	123766	72. 8	117676	96. 4	112338	123. 4	107589	153. 6	11
	130728	52. 8	123657	73. 2	117581	96. 9	112255	123. 9	107514	154. 2	
20	130600	53. 1	123549	73. 5	117487	97. 3	112171	124. 3	107439	154. 7	10
	130473	53. 4	123441	73. 9	117393	97. 7	112088	124. 8	107364	155. 2	
21	130346	53. 7	123332	74. 3	117299	98. 1	112005	125. 3	107290	155. 8	9
	130219	54. 1	123225	74. 6	117205	98. 5	111922	125. 8	107216	156. 3	
22	130093	54. 4	123117	75. 0	117112	99. 0	111839	126. 2	107141	156. 9	8
	129967	54. 7	123010	75. 4	117018	99. 4	111757	126. 7	107067	157. 4	
23	129841	55. 0	122903	75. 8	116925	99. 8	111674	127. 2	106993	157. 9	7
	129716	55. 3	122796	76. 1	116832	100. 3	111592	127. 7	106919	158. 5	
24	129591	55. 7	122690	76. 5	116739	100. 7	111510	128. 2	106846	159. 0	6
	129466	56. 0	122584	76. 9	116647	101. 1	111428	128. 7	106772	159. 6	
25	129342	56. 3	122478	77. 3	116554	101. 6	111346	129. 2	106698	160. 1	5
	129218	56. 6	122372	77. 6	116462	102. 0	111264	129. 7	106625	160. 6	
26	129095	56. 9	122267	78. 0	116370	102. 4	111183	130. 1	106552	161. 2	4
	128972	57. 3	122161	78. 4	116278	102. 9	111101	130. 6	106479	161. 7	
27	128849	57. 6	122057	78. 8	116187	103. 3	111020	131. 1	106406	162. 3	3
	128727	57. 9	121952	79. 2	116096	103. 7	110939	131. 6	106333	162. 8	
28	128605	58. 2	121848	79. 5	116004	104. 2	110858	132. 1	106260	163. 4	2
	128483	58. 6	121743	79. 9	115913	104. 6	110777	132. 6	106187	163. 9	
29	128362	58. 9	121639	80. 3	115823	105. 0	110696	133. 1	106115	164. 5	1
	128240	59. 2	121536	80. 7	115732	105. 5	110616	133. 6	106043	165. 0	
30	128120	59. 6	121432	81. 1	115641	105. 9	110536	134. 1	105970	165. 6	0
	A	B	A	B	A	B	A	B	A	B	
′	177° 00′		176° 30′		176° 00′		175° 30′		175° 00′		′

WHEN LHA (E OR W) IS <u>GREATER</u> THAN 90°, TAKE "K" FROM <u>BOTTOM</u> OF TABLE

′	5° 00′ A	B	5° 30′ A	B	6° 00′ A	B	6° 30′ A	B	7° 00′ A	B	′
0	105970	165.6	101843	200.4	98076	239	94614	280	91411	325	30
	105898	166.1	101777	201.0	98017	239	94559	281	91359	326	
1	105826	166.7	101712	201.6	97957	240	94503	281	91308	326	29
	105754	167.2	101646	202.2	97897	241	94448	282	91257	327	
2	105683	167.8	101581	202.8	97837	241	94393	283	91205	328	28
	105611	168.4	101516	203.5	97777	242	94338	284	91154	329	
3	105539	168.9	101451	204.1	97717	243	94283	284	91103	330	27
	105468	169.4	101386	204.7	97658	243	94228	285	91052	330	
4	105397	170.0	101321	205.3	97598	244	94173	286	91001	331	26
	105325	170.6	101256	205.9	97539	245	94118	287	90950	332	
5	105254	171.1	101192	206.5	97480	245	94063	287	90899	333	25
	105183	171.7	101127	207.1	97420	246	94009	288	90848	333	
6	105113	172.3	101063	207.8	97361	247	93954	289	90798	334	24
	105042	172.8	100998	208.4	97302	247	93899	289	90747	335	
7	104971	173.4	100934	209.0	97243	248	93845	290	90696	336	23
	104901	174.0	100870	209.6	97184	249	93790	291	90646	337	
8	104830	174.5	100806	210.3	97126	249	93736	292	90595	337	22
	104760	175.1	100742	210.9	97067	250	93682	292	90545	338	
9	104690	175.7	100678	211.5	97008	251	93628	293	90494	339	21
	104620	176.2	100614	212.1	96950	251	93573	294	90444	340	
10	104550	176.8	100550	212.8	96891	252	93519	295	90394	341	20
	104480	177.4	100487	213.4	96833	253	93465	295	90344	341	
11	104411	178.0	100423	214.0	96774	253	93411	296	90293	342	19
	104341	178.5	100360	214.6	96716	254	93358	297	90243	343	
12	104272	179.1	100296	215.3	96658	255	93304	298	90193	344	18
	104202	179.7	100233	215.9	96600	255	93250	298	90143	345	
13	104133	180.3	100170	216.5	96542	256	93196	299	90093	345	17
	104064	180.8	100107	217.2	96484	257	93143	300	90044	346	
14	103995	181.4	100044	217.8	96426	257	93089	301	89994	347	16
	103926	182.0	99981	218.4	96368	258	93036	301	89944	348	
15	103857	182.6	99918	219.1	96310	259	92982	302	89894	349	15
	103788	183.2	99856	219.7	96253	260	92929	303	89845	349	
16	103720	183.7	99793	220.3	96195	260	92876	304	89795	350	14
	103651	184.3	99731	221.0	96138	261	92823	304	89746	351	
17	103583	184.9	99668	221.6	96080	262	92769	305	89696	352	13
	103515	185.5	99606	222.3	96023	262	92716	306	89647	353	
18	103447	186.1	99544	222.9	95966	263	92663	307	89597	353	12
	103379	186.7	99481	223.5	95909	264	92610	307	89548	354	
19	103311	187.2	99420	224.2	95851	264	92558	308	89499	355	11
	103243	187.8	99357	224.8	95795	265	92505	309	89450	356	
20	103175	188.4	99296	225.5	95737	266	92452	310	89401	357	10
	103107	189.0	99234	226.1	95681	267	92399	310	89352	357	
21	103040	189.6	99172	226.8	95624	267	92347	311	89303	358	9
	102973	190.2	99110	227.4	95567	268	92294	312	89254	359	
22	102905	190.8	99049	228.1	95510	269	92242	313	89205	360	8
	102838	191.4	98988	228.7	95454	269	92189	313	89156	361	
23	102771	192.0	98926	229.4	95397	270	92137	314	89107	362	7
	102704	192.6	98865	230.0	95341	271	92085	315	89059	362	
24	102637	193.2	98804	230.7	95285	271	92032	316	89010	363	6
	102570	193.8	98743	231.3	95228	272	91980	316	88961	364	
25	102504	194.4	98682	232.0	95172	273	91928	317	88913	365	5
	102437	195.0	98621	232.6	95116	274	91876	318	88864	366	
26	102371	195.6	98560	233.3	95060	274	91824	319	88816	366	4
	102304	196.2	98499	233.9	95004	275	91772	319	88767	367	
27	102238	196.8	98439	234.6	94948	276	91720	320	88719	368	3
	102172	197.4	98378	235.3	94892	276	91668	321	88671	369	
28	102106	198.0	98318	235.9	94836	277	91617	322	88623	370	2
	102040	198.6	98257	236.6	94781	278	91565	323	88574	371	
29	101974	199.2	98197	237.2	94725	279	91514	323	88526	371	1
	101908	199.8	98137	237.9	94670	279	91462	324	88478	372	
30	101843	200.4	98076	238.6	94614	280	91411	325	88430	373	0
′	A	B	A	B	A	B	A	B	A	B	′
	174° 30′		174° 00′		173° 30′		173° 00′		172° 30′		

′	7° 30′		8° 00′		8° 30′		9° 00′		9° 30′		′
	A	B	A	B	A	B	A	B	A	B	
0	88430	373	85644	425	83030	480	80567	538	78239	600	30
	88382	374	85599	426	82987	481	80527	539	78201	601	
1	88334	375	85555	426	82945	482	80487	540	78164	602	29
	88286	376	85510	427	82903	482	80447	541	78126	603	
2	88239	376	85465	428	82861	483	80407	542	78088	604	28
	88191	377	85420	429	82819	484	80368	543	78051	605	
3	88143	378	85376	430	82777	485	80328	544	78013	606	27
	88096	379	85331	431	82735	486	80288	545	77976	607	
4	88048	380	85286	432	82693	487	80249	546	77938	608	26
	88001	381	85242	433	82651	488	80209	547	77901	609	
5	87953	381	85197	434	82609	489	80170	548	77863	610	25
	87906	382	85153	434	82567	490	80130	549	77826	611	
6	87858	383	85108	435	82526	491	80091	550	77788	612	24
	87811	384	85064	436	82484	492	80051	551	77751	614	
7	87764	385	85020	437	82442	493	80012	552	77714	615	23
	87716	386	84976	438	82400	494	79973	553	77677	616	
8	87669	387	84931	439	82359	495	79933	554	77639	617	22
	87622	387	84887	440	82317	496	79894	555	77602	618	
9	87575	388	84843	441	82276	497	79855	556	77565	619	21
	87528	389	84799	442	82234	498	79816	557	77528	620	
10	87481	390	84755	443	82193	499	79777	558	77491	621	20
	87434	391	84711	444	82151	500	79737	559	77454	622	
11	87387	392	84667	444	82110	501	79698	560	77417	623	19
	87341	392	84623	445	82069	502	79659	561	77380	624	
12	87294	393	84579	446	82027	503	79620	562	77343	625	18
	87247	394	84535	447	81986	504	79581	563	77306	626	
13	87201	395	84492	448	81945	504	79542	564	77269	627	17
	87154	396	84448	449	81904	505	79503	565	77232	629	
14	87107	397	84404	450	81863	506	79465	566	77195	630	16
	87061	398	84361	451	81821	507	79426	567	77158	631	
15	87015	399	84317	452	81780	508	79387	568	77122	632	15
	86968	399	84273	453	81739	509	79348	569	77085	633	
16	86922	400	84230	454	81698	510	79309	570	77048	634	14
	86876	401	84186	454	81657	511	79271	571	77011	635	
17	86829	402	84143	455	81617	512	79232	573	76975	636	13
	86783	403	84100	456	81576	513	79193	574	76938	637	
18	86737	404	84056	457	81535	514	79155	575	76902	638	12
	86691	405	84013	458	81494	515	79116	576	76865	639	
19	86645	405	83970	459	81453	516	79078	577	76828	641	11
	86599	406	83927	460	81413	517	79039	578	76792	642	
20	86553	407	83884	461	81372	518	79001	579	76756	643	10
	86507	408	83840	462	81331	519	78962	580	76719	644	
21	86461	409	83797	463	81291	520	78924	581	76683	645	9
	86415	410	83754	464	81250	521	78886	582	76646	646	
22	86370	411	83711	465	81210	522	78847	583	76610	647	8
	86324	411	83668	466	81169	523	78809	584	76574	648	
23	86278	412	83626	467	81129	524	78771	585	76537	649	7
	86233	413	83583	467	81088	525	78733	586	76501	650	
24	86187	414	83540	468	81048	526	78694	587	76465	652	6
	86142	415	83497	469	81008	527	78656	588	76429	653	
25	86096	416	83455	470	80967	528	78618	589	76393	654	5
	86051	417	83412	471	80927	529	78580	590	76357	655	
26	86006	418	83369	472	80887	530	78542	591	76320	656	4
	85960	418	83327	473	80847	531	78504	592	76284	657	
27	85915	419	83284	474	80807	532	78466	593	76248	658	3
	85870	420	83242	475	80767	533	78428	594	76212	659	
28	85825	421	83199	476	80727	534	78390	595	76176	660	2
	85779	422	83157	477	80687	535	78352	597	76141	661	
29	85734	423	83114	478	80647	536	78315	598	76105	663	1
	85689	424	83072	479	80607	537	78277	599	76069	664	
30	85644	425	83030	480	80567	538	78239	600	76033	665	0
	A	B	A	B	A	B	A	B	A	B	
′	172° 00′		171° 30′		171° 00′		170° 30′		170° 00′		′

WHEN LHA (E OR W) IS GREATER THAN 90°, TAKE "K" FROM BOTTOM OF TABLE

′	10° 00′ A	10° 00′ B	10° 30′ A	10° 30′ B	11° 00′ A	11° 00′ B	11° 30′ A	11° 30′ B	12° 00′ A	12° 00′ B	′
0	76033	665	73937	733	71940	805	70034	881	68212	960	30
	75997	666	73903	735	71908	807	70003	882	68182	961	
1	75961	667	73869	736	71875	808	69972	883	68153	962	29
	75926	668	73835	737	71843	809	69941	885	68123	964	
2	75890	669	73801	738	71810	810	69910	886	68093	965	28
	75854	670	73767	739	71778	811	69879	887	68064	966	
3	75819	672	73733	740	71746	813	69849	888	68034	968	27
	75783	673	73699	742	71713	814	69818	890	68005	969	
4	75747	674	73665	743	71681	815	69787	891	67975	970	26
	75712	675	73631	744	71649	816	69756	892	67945	972	
5	75676	676	73597	745	71616	818	69725	894	67916	973	25
	75641	677	73563	746	71584	819	69694	895	67886	974	
6	75605	678	73530	747	71552	820	69664	896	67857	976	24
	75570	679	73496	749	71520	821	69633	897	67828	977	
7	75534	680	73462	750	71488	823	69602	899	67798	978	23
	75499	682	73429	751	71455	824	69571	900	67769	980	
8	75464	683	73395	752	71423	825	69541	901	67739	981	22
	75428	684	73361	753	71391	826	69510	903	67710	982	
9	75393	685	73328	755	71359	828	69479	904	67681	984	21
	75358	686	73294	756	71327	829	69449	905	67651	985	
10	75322	687	73260	757	71295	830	69418	907	67622	987	20
	75287	688	73227	758	71263	831	69387	908	67593	988	
11	75252	690	73193	759	71231	833	69357	909	67563	989	19
	75217	691	73160	761	71199	834	69326	910	67534	991	
12	75182	692	73127	762	71167	835	69296	912	67505	992	18
	75147	693	73093	763	71135	836	69265	913	67476	993	
13	75112	694	73060	764	71104	838	69235	914	67447	995	17
	75077	695	73026	765	71072	839	69204	916	67417	996	
14	75042	696	72993	766	71040	840	69174	917	67388	997	16
	75007	698	72960	768	71008	841	69144	918	67359	999	
15	74972	699	72926	769	70976	843	69113	920	67330	1000	15
	74937	700	72893	770	70945	844	69083	921	67301	1002	
16	74902	701	72860	771	70913	845	69053	922	67272	1003	14
	74867	702	72827	772	70881	846	69022	924	67243	1004	
17	74832	703	72794	774	70850	848	68992	925	67214	1006	13
	74797	704	72760	775	70818	849	68962	926	67185	1007	
18	74763	706	72727	776	70786	850	68931	928	67156	1008	12
	74728	707	72694	777	70755	851	68901	929	67127	1010	
19	74693	708	72661	779	70723	853	68871	930	67098	1011	11
	74659	709	72628	780	70692	854	68841	932	67069	1013	
20	74624	710	72595	781	70660	855	68811	933	67040	1014	10
	74589	711	72562	782	70629	856	68781	934	67011	1015	
21	74555	712	72529	783	70597	858	68750	935	66982	1017	9
	74520	714	72496	785	70566	859	68720	937	66953	1018	
22	74486	715	72463	786	70534	860	68690	938	66925	1020	8
	74451	716	72430	787	70503	862	68660	939	66896	1021	
23	74417	717	72397	788	70471	863	68630	941	66867	1022	7
	74382	718	72365	790	70440	864	68600	942	66838	1024	
24	74348	719	72332	791	70409	865	68570	943	66810	1025	6
	74313	721	72299	792	70377	867	68540	945	66781	1026	
25	74279	722	72266	793	70346	868	68510	946	66752	1028	5
	74245	723	72234	794	70315	869	68480	947	66724	1029	
26	74210	724	72201	796	70284	870	68450	949	66695	1031	4
	74176	725	72168	797	70252	872	68421	950	66666	1032	
27	74142	726	72135	798	70221	873	68391	951	66638	1033	3
	74107	728	72103	799	70190	874	68361	953	66609	1035	
28	74073	729	72070	800	70159	876	68331	954	66580	1036	2
	74039	730	72038	802	70128	877	68301	955	66552	1038	
29	74005	731	72005	803	70097	878	68272	957	66523	1039	1
	73971	732	71973	804	70065	879	68242	958	66495	1040	
30	73937	733	71940	805	70034	881	68212	960	66466	1042	0
	A	B	A	B	A	B	A	B	A	B	
	169° 30′		169° 00′		168° 30′		168° 00′		167° 30′		′

′	12° 30′ A	12° 30′ B	13° 00′ A	13° 00′ B	13° 30′ A	13° 30′ B	14° 00′ A	14° 00′ B	14° 30′ A	14° 30′ B	′
0	66466	1042	64791	1128	63181	1217	61632	1310	60140	1406	30
	66438	1043	64764	1129	63155	1218	61607	1311	60116	1407	
1	66409	1045	64736	1130	63129	1220	61582	1313	60091	1409	29
	66381	1046	64709	1132	63103	1221	61556	1314	60067	1411	
2	66352	1047	64682	1133	63076	1223	61531	1316	60042	1412	28
	66324	1049	64655	1135	63050	1224	61506	1317	60018	1414	
3	66296	1050	64627	1136	63024	1226	61481	1319	59994	1416	27
	66267	1052	64600	1138	62998	1227	61455	1321	59969	1417	
4	66239	1053	64573	1139	62971	1229	61430	1322	59945	1419	26
	66211	1054	64546	1141	62945	1230	61405	1324	59921	1421	
5	66182	1056	64518	1142	62919	1232	61380	1325	59896	1422	25
	66154	1057	64491	1144	62893	1234	61355	1327	59872	1424	
6	66126	1059	64464	1145	62867	1235	61330	1329	59848	1425	24
	66098	1060	64437	1147	62841	1237	61304	1330	59824	1427	
7	66069	1061	64410	1148	62815	1238	61279	1332	59800	1429	23
	66041	1063	64383	1150	62789	1240	61254	1333	59775	1430	
8	66013	1064	64356	1151	62763	1241	61229	1335	59751	1432	22
	65985	1066	64329	1152	62737	1243	61204	1336	59727	1434	
9	65957	1067	64302	1154	62711	1244	61179	1338	59703	1435	21
	65928	1069	64275	1155	62685	1246	61154	1340	59679	1437	
10	65900	1070	64248	1157	62659	1247	61129	1341	59654	1439	20
	65872	1071	64221	1158	62633	1249	61104	1343	59630	1440	
11	65844	1073	64194	1160	62607	1250	61079	1344	59606	1442	19
	65816	1074	64167	1161	62581	1252	61054	1346	59582	1444	
12	65788	1076	64140	1163	62555	1253	61029	1348	59558	1445	18
	65760	1077	64113	1164	62529	1255	61004	1349	59534	1447	
13	65732	1079	64086	1166	62503	1257	60979	1351	59510	1449	17
	65704	1080	64059	1167	62477	1258	60954	1352	59486	1450	
14	65676	1081	64032	1169	62451	1260	60929	1354	59462	1452	16
	65648	1083	64005	1170	62425	1261	60904	1356	59438	1454	
15	65620	1084	63978	1172	62400	1263	60879	1357	59414	1455	15
	65592	1086	63952	1173	62374	1264	60855	1359	59390	1457	
16	65564	1087	63925	1175	62348	1266	60830	1360	59366	1459	14
	65537	1089	63898	1176	62322	1267	60805	1362	59342	1460	
17	65509	1090	63871	1178	62296	1269	60780	1364	59318	1462	13
	65481	1091	63845	1179	62271	1270	60755	1365	59294	1464	
18	65453	1093	63818	1181	62245	1272	60730	1367	59270	1465	12
	65425	1094	63791	1182	62219	1274	60706	1368	59246	1467	
19	65398	1096	63764	1184	62194	1275	60681	1370	59222	1469	11
	65370	1097	63738	1185	62168	1277	60656	1372	59198	1470	
20	65342	1099	63711	1187	62142	1278	60631	1373	59175	1472	10
	65314	1100	63684	1188	62117	1280	60607	1375	59151	1474	
21	65287	1101	63658	1190	62091	1281	60582	1377	59127	1475	9
	65259	1103	63631	1191	62065	1283	60557	1378	59103	1477	
22	65231	1104	63605	1193	62040	1284	60533	1380	59079	1479	8
	65204	1106	63578	1194	62014	1286	60508	1381	59055	1480	
23	65176	1107	63551	1196	61989	1288	60483	1383	59032	1482	7
	65148	1109	63525	1197	61963	1289	60459	1385	59008	1484	
24	65121	1110	63498	1199	61938	1291	60434	1386	58984	1485	6
	65093	1112	63472	1200	61912	1292	60410	1388	58960	1487	
25	65066	1113	63445	1202	61887	1294	60385	1390	58937	1489	5
	65038	1114	63419	1203	61861	1295	60360	1391	58913	1490	
26	65011	1116	63392	1205	61836	1297	60336	1393	58889	1492	4
	64983	1117	63366	1206	61810	1299	60311	1394	58866	1494	
27	64956	1119	63340	1208	61785	1300	60287	1396	58842	1495	3
	64928	1120	63313	1209	61759	1301	60262	1398	58818	1497	
28	64901	1122	63287	1211	61734	1303	60238	1399	58795	1499	2
	64873	1123	63260	1212	61709	1305	60213	1401	58771	1500	
29	64846	1125	63234	1214	61683	1306	60189	1403	58748	1502	1
	64819	1126	63208	1215	61658	1308	60164	1404	58724	1504	
30	64791	1128	63181	1217	61632	1310	60140	1406	58700	1506	0
	A	B	A	B	A	B	A	B	A	B	′
	167° 00′		166° 30′		166° 00′		165° 30′		165° 00′		

WHEN LHA (E OR W) IS GREATER THAN 90°, TAKE "K" FROM BOTTOM OF TABLE

′	15° 00′ A	B	15° 30′ A	B	16° 00′ A	B	16° 30′ A	B	17° 00′ A	B	′
0	58700	1506	57310	1609	55966	1716	54666	1826	53406	1940	30
	58677	1507	57287	1611	55944	1718	54644	1828	53386	1942	
1	58653	1509	57265	1612	55922	1719	54623	1830	53365	1944	29
	58630	1511	57242	1614	55900	1721	54602	1832	53344	1946	
2	58606	1512	57219	1616	55878	1723	54581	1834	53324	1948	28
	58583	1514	57196	1618	55856	1725	54559	1836	53303	1950	
3	58559	1516	57174	1619	55834	1727	54538	1837	53283	1952	27
	58536	1517	57151	1621	55812	1728	54517	1839	53262	1954	
4	58512	1519	57128	1623	55790	1730	54496	1841	53241	1956	26
	58489	1521	57106	1625	55768	1732	54474	1843	53221	1958	
5	58465	1523	57083	1627	55746	1734	54453	1845	53200	1960	25
	58442	1524	57060	1628	55725	1736	54432	1847	53180	1962	
6	58418	1526	57038	1630	55703	1738	54411	1849	53159	1964	24
	58395	1528	57015	1632	55681	1739	54390	1851	53139	1966	
7	58372	1529	56992	1634	55659	1741	54368	1853	53118	1967	23
	58348	1531	56970	1635	55637	1743	54347	1854	53098	1969	
8	58325	1533	56947	1637	55615	1745	54326	1856	53077	1971	22
	58302	1534	56925	1639	55593	1747	54305	1858	53057	1973	
9	58278	1536	56902	1641	55572	1749	54284	1860	53036	1975	21
	58255	1538	56880	1642	55550	1750	54263	1862	53016	1977	
10	58232	1540	56857	1644	55528	1752	54242	1864	52995	1979	20
	58208	1541	56835	1646	55506	1754	54220	1866	52975	1981	
11	58185	1543	56812	1648	55484	1756	54199	1868	52954	1983	19
	58162	1545	56790	1649	55463	1758	54178	1870	52934	1985	
12	58138	1546	56767	1651	55441	1760	54157	1871	52914	1987	18
	58115	1548	56745	1653	55419	1761	54136	1873	52893	1989	
13	58092	1550	56722	1655	55397	1763	54115	1875	52873	1991	17
	58069	1552	56700	1657	55376	1765	54094	1877	52852	1993	
14	58046	1553	56677	1658	55354	1767	54073	1879	52832	1995	16
	58022	1555	56655	1660	55332	1769	54052	1881	52812	1997	
15	57999	1557	56632	1662	55311	1771	54031	1883	52791	1999	15
	57976	1559	56610	1664	55289	1772	54010	1885	52771	2001	
16	57953	1560	56588	1665	55267	1774	53989	1887	52751	2003	14
	57930	1562	56565	1667	55246	1776	53968	1889	52730	2005	
17	57907	1564	56543	1669	55224	1778	53947	1890	52710	2007	13
	57884	1565	56521	1671	55202	1780	53926	1892	52690	2009	
18	57860	1567	56498	1673	55181	1782	53905	1894	52670	2010	12
	57837	1569	56476	1674	55159	1783	53884	1896	52649	2012	
19	57814	1571	56454	1676	55138	1785	53864	1898	52629	2014	11
	57791	1572	56431	1678	55116	1787	53843	1900	52609	2016	
20	57768	1574	56409	1680	55095	1789	53822	1902	52588	2018	10
	57745	1576	56387	1682	55073	1791	53801	1904	52568	2020	
21	57722	1578	56365	1683	55051	1793	53780	1906	52548	2022	9
	57699	1579	56342	1685	55030	1795	53759	1908	52528	2024	
22	57676	1581	56320	1687	55008	1796	53738	1910	52508	2026	8
	57653	1583	56298	1689	54987	1798	53718	1911	52487	2028	
23	57630	1584	56276	1691	54965	1800	53697	1913	52467	2030	7
	57607	1586	56254	1692	54944	1802	53676	1915	52447	2032	
24	57584	1588	56231	1694	54922	1804	53655	1917	52427	2034	6
	57561	1590	56209	1696	54901	1806	53634	1919	52407	2036	
25	57538	1591	56187	1698	54880	1808	53614	1921	52387	2038	5
	57516	1593	56165	1700	54858	1809	53593	1923	52366	2040	
26	57493	1595	56143	1701	54837	1811	53572	1925	52346	2042	4
	57470	1597	56121	1703	54815	1813	53551	1927	52326	2044	
27	57447	1598	56099	1705	54794	1815	53531	1929	52306	2046	3
	57424	1600	56076	1707	54773	1817	53510	1931	52286	2048	
28	57401	1602	56054	1709	54751	1819	53489	1933	52266	2050	2
	57378	1604	56032	1710	54730	1821	53468	1935	52246	2052	
29	57356	1605	56010	1712	54708	1823	53448	1936	52226	2054	1
	57333	1607	55988	1714	54687	1824	53427	1938	52206	2056	
30	57310	1609	55966	1716	54666	1826	53406	1940	52186	2058	0
	A	B	A	B	A	B	A	B	A	B	
′	164° 30′		164° 00′		163° 30′		163° 00′		162° 30′		′

′	17° 30′ A	B	18° 00′ A	B	18° 30′ A	B	19° 00′ A	B	19° 30′ A	B	′
0	52186	2058	51002	2179	49852	2304	48736	2433	47650	2565	30
	52166	2060	50982	2181	49833	2306	48717	2435	47633	2568	
1	52146	2062	50963	2183	49815	2309	48699	2437	47615	2570	29
	52126	2064	50943	2185	49796	2311	48681	2439	47597	2572	
2	52106	2066	50924	2188	49777	2313	48662	2442	47579	2574	28
	52086	2068	50905	2190	49758	2315	48644	2444	47561	2576	
3	52066	2070	50885	2192	49739	2317	48626	2446	47544	2579	27
	52046	2072	50866	2194	49720	2319	48608	2448	47526	2581	
4	52026	2074	50846	2196	49702	2321	48589	2450	47508	2583	26
	52006	2076	50827	2198	49683	2323	48571	2453	47490	2585	
5	51986	2078	50808	2200	49664	2325	48553	2455	47472	2588	25
	51966	2080	50788	2202	49645	2328	48534	2457	47455	2590	
6	51946	2082	50769	2204	49626	2330	48516	2459	47437	2592	24
	51926	2084	50750	2206	49608	2332	48498	2461	47419	2594	
7	51906	2086	50730	2208	49589	2334	48480	2463	47402	2597	23
	51886	2088	50711	2210	49570	2336	48462	2466	47384	2599	
8	51867	2090	50692	2212	49551	2338	48443	2468	47366	2601	22
	51847	2092	50673	2214	49533	2340	48425	2470	47348	2603	
9	51827	2094	50653	2216	49514	2343	48407	2472	47331	2606	21
	51807	2096	50634	2218	49495	2345	48389	2474	47313	2608	
10	51787	2098	50615	2221	49477	2347	48371	2477	47295	2610	20
	51767	2100	50596	2223	49458	2349	48352	2479	47278	2613	
11	51747	2102	50576	2225	49439	2351	48334	2481	47260	2615	19
	51728	2104	50557	2227	49421	2353	48316	2483	47242	2617	
12	51708	2106	50538	2229	49402	2355	48298	2485	47225	2619	18
	51688	2108	50519	2231	49383	2357	48280	2488	47207	2622	
13	51668	2110	50499	2233	49365	2360	48262	2490	47189	2624	17
	51649	2112	50480	2235	49346	2362	48244	2492	47172	2626	
14	51629	2114	50461	2237	49327	2364	48225	2494	47154	2628	16
	51609	2116	50442	2239	49309	2366	48207	2496	47137	2631	
15	51589	2118	50423	2241	49290	2368	48189	2499	47119	2633	15
	51570	2120	50404	2243	49271	2370	48171	2501	47101	2635	
16	51550	2122	50385	2246	49253	2372	48153	2503	47084	2637	14
	51530	2124	50365	2248	49234	2375	48135	2505	47066	2640	
17	51510	2126	50346	2250	49216	2377	48117	2507	47049	2642	13
	51491	2128	50327	2252	49197	2379	48099	2510	47031	2644	
18	51471	2130	50308	2254	49179	2381	48081	2512	47014	2646	12
	51451	2132	50289	2256	49160	2383	48063	2514	46996	2649	
19	51432	2134	50270	2258	49141	2385	48045	2516	46978	2651	11
	51412	2136	50251	2260	49123	2387	48027	2519	46961	2653	
20	51392	2138	50232	2262	49104	2390	48009	2521	46943	2656	10
	51373	2141	50213	2264	49086	2392	47991	2523	46926	2658	
21	51353	2143	50194	2266	49067	2394	47973	2525	46908	2660	9
	51334	2145	50175	2269	49049	2396	47955	2527	46891	2662	
22	51314	2147	50156	2271	49030	2398	47937	2530	46873	2665	8
	51294	2149	50137	2273	49012	2400	47919	2532	46856	2667	
23	51275	2151	50117	2275	48993	2403	47901	2534	46839	2669	7
	51255	2153	50098	2277	48975	2405	47883	2536	46821	2672	
24	51236	2155	50080	2279	48957	2407	47865	2539	46804	2674	6
	51216	2157	50061	2281	48938	2409	47847	2541	46786	2676	
25	51197	2159	50042	2283	48920	2411	47829	2543	46769	2678	5
	51177	2161	50023	2285	48901	2413	47811	2545	46751	2681	
26	51158	2163	50004	2287	48883	2416	47793	2547	46734	2683	4
	51138	2165	49985	2290	48864	2418	47775	2550	46716	2685	
27	51119	2167	49966	2292	48846	2420	47758	2552	46699	2688	3
	51099	2169	49947	2294	48828	2422	47740	2554	46682	2690	
28	51080	2171	49928	2296	48809	2424	47722	2556	46664	2692	2
	51060	2173	49909	2298	48791	2426	47704	2559	46647	2694	
29	51041	2175	49890	2300	48772	2429	47686	2561	46630	2697	1
	51021	2177	49871	2302	48754	2431	47668	2563	46612	2699	
30	51002	2179	49852	2304	48736	2433	47650	2565	46595	2701	0
	A	B	A	B	A	B	A	B	A	B	
′	162° 00′		161° 30′		161° 00′		160° 30′		160° 00′		′

′	20° 00′ A	B	20° 30′ A	B	21° 00′ A	B	21° 30′ A	B	22° 00′ A	B	′
0	46595	2701	45567	2841	44567	2985	43592	3132	42642	3283	30
	46577	2704	45551	2844	44551	2988	43576	3135	42627	3286	
1	46560	2706	45534	2846	44534	2990	43560	3137	42611	3288	29
	46543	2708	45517	2848	44518	2992	43544	3140	42596	3291	
2	46525	2711	45500	2851	44501	2994	43528	3142	42580	3294	28
	46508	2713	45483	2853	44485	2997	43512	3145	42564	3296	
3	46491	2715	45466	2855	44468	2999	43496	3147	42549	3299	27
	46473	2717	45449	2858	44452	3002	43480	3150	42533	3301	
4	46456	2720	45433	2860	44436	3004	43464	3152	42518	3304	26
	46439	2722	45416	2862	44419	3007	43448	3155	42502	3306	
5	46422	2724	45399	2865	44403	3009	43432	3157	42486	3309	25
	46404	2727	45382	2867	44386	3012	43416	3160	42471	3312	
6	46387	2729	45365	2870	44370	3014	43400	3162	42455	3314	24
	46370	2731	45348	2872	44354	3016	43385	3165	42440	3317	
7	46353	2734	45332	2874	44337	3019	43369	3167	42424	3319	23
	46335	2736	45315	2877	44321	3021	43353	3170	42409	3322	
8	46318	2738	45298	2879	44305	3024	43337	3172	42393	3324	22
	46301	2741	45281	2881	44288	3026	43321	3175	42378	3327	
9	46284	2743	45265	2884	44272	3029	43305	3177	42362	3329	21
	46266	2745	45248	2886	44256	3031	43289	3180	42347	3332	
10	46249	2748	45231	2889	44239	3033	43273	3182	42331	3335	20
	46232	2750	45214	2891	44223	3036	43257	3185	42316	3337	
11	46215	2752	45198	2893	44207	3038	43241	3187	42300	3340	19
	46198	2755	45181	2896	44190	3041	43225	3190	42285	3342	
12	46181	2757	45164	2898	44174	3043	43210	3192	42269	3345	18
	46163	2759	45147	2901	44158	3046	43194	3195	42254	3347	
13	46146	2761	45131	2903	44142	3048	43178	3197	42238	3350	17
	46129	2764	45114	2905	44125	3051	43162	3200	42223	3353	
14	46112	2766	45097	2908	44109	3053	43146	3202	42207	3355	16
	46095	2768	45081	2910	44093	3056	43130	3205	42192	3358	
15	46078	2771	45064	2913	44077	3058	43114	3207	42176	3360	15
	46061	2773	45047	2915	44060	3060	43099	3210	42161	3363	
16	46043	2775	45031	2917	44044	3063	43083	3212	42145	3366	14
	46026	2778	45014	2920	44028	3065	43067	3215	42130	3368	
17	46009	2780	44997	2922	44012	3068	43051	3217	42115	3371	13
	45992	2782	44981	2924	43995	3070	43035	3220	42099	3373	
18	45975	2785	44964	2927	43979	3073	43020	3222	42084	3376	12
	45958	2787	44947	2929	43963	3075	43004	3225	42068	3379	
19	45941	2789	44931	2932	43947	3078	42988	3227	42053	3381	11
	45924	2792	44914	2934	43931	3080	42972	3230	42038	3384	
20	45907	2794	44898	2936	43914	3083	42956	3233	42022	3386	10
	45890	2797	44881	2939	43898	3085	42941	3235	42007	3389	
21	45873	2799	44864	2941	43882	3088	42925	3238	41991	3391	9
	45856	2801	44848	2944	43866	3090	42909	3240	41976	3394	
22	45839	2804	44831	2946	43850	3092	42893	3243	41961	3397	8
	45822	2806	44815	2949	43834	3095	42878	3245	41945	3399	
23	45805	2808	44798	2951	43818	3097	42862	3248	41930	3402	7
	45788	2811	44782	2953	43801	3100	42846	3250	41915	3404	
24	45771	2813	44765	2956	43785	3102	42830	3253	41899	3407	6
	45754	2815	44748	2958	43769	3105	42815	3255	41884	3410	
25	45737	2818	44732	2961	43753	3107	42799	3258	41869	3412	5
	45720	2820	44715	2963	43737	3110	42783	3260	41853	3415	
26	45703	2822	44699	2965	43721	3112	42768	3263	41838	3418	4
	45686	2825	44682	2968	43705	3115	42752	3266	41823	3420	
27	45669	2827	44666	2970	43689	3117	42736	3268	41808	3423	3
	45652	2829	44649	2973	43673	3120	42721	3271	41792	3425	
28	45635	2832	44633	2975	43657	3122	42705	3273	41777	3428	2
	45618	2834	44616	2978	43641	3125	42689	3276	41762	3431	
29	45601	2836	44600	2980	43624	3127	42674	3278	41746	3433	1
	45584	2839	44583	2982	43608	3130	42658	3281	41731	3436	
30	45567	2841	44567	2985	43592	3132	42642	3283	41716	3438	0
	A	B	A	B	A	B	A	B	A	B	
′	159° 30′		159° 00′		158° 30′		158° 00′		157° 30′		′

ALWAYS TAKE "Z" FROM BOTTOM OF TABLE, EXCEPT WHEN "K" IS SAME NAME AND GREATER THAN LATITUDE, IN WHICH CASE TAKE "Z" FROM TOP OF TABLE

′	22° 30′ A	B	23° 00′ A	B	23° 30′ A	B	24° 00′ A	B	24° 30′ A	B	′
0	41716	3438	40812	3597	39930	3760	39069	3927	38227	4098	30
	41701	3441	40797	3600	39915	3763	39054	3930	38213	4101	
1	41685	3444	40782	3603	39901	3766	39040	3932	38200	4103	29
	41670	3446	40768	3605	39886	3768	39026	3935	38186	4106	
2	41655	3449	40753	3608	39872	3771	39012	3938	38172	4109	28
	41640	3452	40738	3611	39857	3774	38998	3941	38158	4112	
3	41625	3454	40723	3613	39843	3777	38984	3944	38144	4115	27
	41609	3457	40708	3616	39828	3779	38969	3947	38130	4118	
4	41594	3459	40693	3619	39814	3782	38955	3949	38117	4121	26
	41579	3462	40678	3622	39799	3785	38941	3952	38103	4124	
5	41564	3465	40664	3624	39785	3788	38927	3955	38089	4127	25
	41549	3467	40649	3627	39771	3790	38913	3958	38075	4129	
6	41533	3470	40634	3630	39756	3793	38899	3961	38061	4132	24
	41518	3473	40619	3632	39742	3796	38885	3964	38048	4135	
7	41503	3475	40604	3635	39727	3799	38871	3966	38034	4138	23
	41488	3478	40590	3638	39713	3801	38856	3969	38020	4141	
8	41473	3480	40575	3640	39698	3804	38842	3972	38006	4144	22
	41458	3483	40560	3643	39684	3807	38828	3975	37992	4147	
9	41443	3486	40545	3646	39669	3810	38814	3978	37979	4150	21
	41427	3488	40530	3648	39655	3813	38800	3981	37965	4153	
10	41412	3491	40516	3651	39641	3815	38786	3983	37951	4155	20
	41397	3494	40501	3654	39626	3818	38772	3986	37937	4158	
11	41382	3496	40486	3657	39612	3821	38758	3989	37924	4161	19
	41367	3499	40471	3659	39597	3824	38744	3992	37910	4164	
12	41352	3502	40457	3662	39583	3826	38730	3995	37896	4167	18
	41337	3504	40442	3665	39569	3829	38716	3998	37882	4170	
13	41322	3507	40427	3667	39554	3832	38702	4000	37869	4173	17
	41307	3509	40413	3670	39540	3835	38688	4003	37855	4176	
14	41291	3512	40398	3673	39525	3838	38674	4006	37841	4179	16
	41276	3515	40383	3676	39511	3840	38660	4009	37828	4182	
15	41261	3517	40368	3678	39497	3843	38645	4012	37814	4185	15
	41246	3520	40354	3681	39482	3846	38631	4015	37800	4187	
16	41231	3523	40339	3684	39468	3849	38617	4017	37786	4190	14
	41216	3525	40324	3686	39454	3851	38603	4020	37773	4193	
17	41201	3528	40310	3689	39439	3854	38589	4023	37759	4196	13
	41186	3531	40295	3692	39425	3857	38575	4026	37745	4199	
18	41171	3533	40280	3695	39411	3860	38561	4029	37732	4202	12
	41156	3536	40266	3697	39396	3863	38547	4032	37718	4205	
19	41141	3538	40251	3700	39382	3865	38533	4035	37704	4208	11
	41126	3541	40236	3703	39368	3868	38520	4037	37691	4211	
20	41111	3544	40222	3705	39353	3871	38506	4040	37677	4214	10
	41096	3547	40207	3708	39339	3874	38492	4043	37663	4217	
21	41081	3549	40192	3711	39325	3876	38478	4046	37650	4220	9
	41066	3552	40178	3714	39311	3879	38464	4049	37636	4222	
22	41051	3555	40163	3716	39296	3882	38450	4052	37623	4225	8
	41036	3557	40149	3719	39282	3885	38436	4055	37609	4228	
23	41021	3560	40134	3722	39268	3888	38422	4057	37595	4231	7
	41006	3563	40119	3725	39254	3890	38408	4060	37582	4234	
24	40991	3565	40105	3727	39239	3893	38394	4063	37568	4237	6
	40976	3568	40090	3730	39225	3896	38380	4066	37554	4240	
25	40961	3571	40076	3733	39211	3899	38366	4069	37541	4243	5
	40946	3573	40061	3735	39197	3902	38352	4072	37527	4246	
26	40931	3576	40046	3738	39182	3904	38338	4075	37514	4249	4
	40916	3579	40032	3741	39168	3907	38324	4078	37500	4252	
27	40902	3581	40017	3744	39154	3910	38311	4080	37486	4255	3
	40887	3584	40003	3746	39140	3913	38297	4083	37473	4258	
28	40872	3587	39988	3749	39125	3916	38283	4086	37459	4261	2
	40857	3589	39974	3752	39111	3918	38269	4089	37446	4264	
29	40842	3592	39959	3755	39097	3921	38255	4092	37432	4266	1
	40827	3595	39945	3757	39083	3924	38241	4095	37419	4269	
30	40812	3597	39930	3760	39069	3927	38227	4098	37405	4272	0
′	A	B	A	B	A	B	A	B	A	B	′
	157° 00′		156° 30′		156° 00′		155° 30′		155° 00′		

WHEN LHA (E OR W) IS <u>GREATER</u> THAN 90°, TAKE "K" FROM <u>BOTTOM</u> OF TABLE

′	25° 00′ A	B	25° 30′ A	B	26° 00′ A	B	26° 30′ A	B	27° 00′ A	B	′
0	37405	4272	36602	4451	35816	4634	35047	4821	34295	5012	30
	37392	4275	36588	4454	35803	4637	35035	4824	34283	5015	
1	37378	4278	36575	4457	35790	4640	35022	4827	34270	5018	29
	37365	4281	36562	4460	35777	4643	35009	4830	34258	5022	
2	37351	4284	36549	4463	35764	4646	34997	4833	34246	5025	28
	37337	4287	36535	4466	35751	4649	34984	4837	34233	5028	
3	37324	4290	36522	4469	35738	4651	34971	4840	34221	5031	27
	37310	4293	36509	4472	35725	4656	34959	4843	34209	5034	
4	37297	4296	36496	4475	35712	4659	34946	4846	34196	5038	26
	37283	4299	36483	4478	35699	4662	34933	4849	34184	5041	
5	37270	4302	36469	4481	35686	4665	34921	4852	34172	5044	25
	37256	4305	36456	4484	35674	4668	34908	4856	34159	5047	
6	37243	4308	36443	4487	35661	4671	34896	4859	34147	5051	24
	37229	4311	36430	4490	35648	4674	34883	4862	34134	5054	
7	37216	4314	36417	4493	35635	4677	34870	4865	34122	5057	23
	37203	4317	36403	4496	35622	4680	34858	4868	34110	5060	
8	37189	4320	36390	4499	35609	4683	34845	4871	34097	5064	22
	37176	4323	36377	4503	35596	4686	34832	4875	34085	5067	
9	37162	4326	36364	4506	35583	4690	34820	4878	34073	5070	21
	37149	4329	36351	4509	35571	4693	34807	4881	34061	5073	
10	37135	4332	36338	4512	35558	4696	34795	4884	34048	5076	20
	37122	4334	36325	4515	35545	4699	34782	4887	34036	5080	
11	37108	4337	36311	4518	35532	4702	34770	4890	34024	5083	19
	37095	4340	36298	4521	35519	4705	34757	4894	34011	5086	
12	37081	4343	36285	4524	35506	4708	34744	4897	33999	5089	18
	37068	4346	36272	4527	35493	4711	34732	4900	33987	5093	
13	37055	4349	36259	4530	35481	4714	34719	4903	33974	5096	17
	37041	4352	36246	4533	35468	4718	34707	4906	33962	5099	
14	37028	4355	36233	4536	35455	4721	34694	4910	33950	5102	16
	37014	4358	36220	4539	35442	4724	34682	4913	33938	5106	
15	37001	4361	36206	4542	35429	4727	34669	4916	33925	5109	15
	36988	4364	36193	4545	35417	4730	34657	4919	33913	5112	
16	36974	4367	36180	4548	35404	4733	34644	4922	33901	5115	14
	36961	4370	36167	4551	35391	4736	34632	4925	33889	5119	
17	36948	4373	36154	4554	35378	4739	34619	4929	33876	5122	13
	36934	4376	36141	4557	35365	4742	34607	4932	33864	5125	
18	36921	4379	36128	4560	35353	4746	34594	4935	33852	5128	12
	36907	4382	36115	4563	35340	4749	34582	4938	33840	5132	
19	36894	4385	36102	4566	35327	4752	34569	4941	33827	5135	11
	36881	4388	36089	4569	35314	4755	34557	4945	33815	5138	
20	36867	4391	36076	4573	35302	4758	34544	4948	33803	5142	10
	36854	4394	36063	4576	35289	4761	34532	4951	33791	5145	
21	36841	4397	36050	4579	35276	4764	34519	4954	33779	5148	9
	36827	4400	36037	4582	35263	4769	34507	4957	33766	5151	
22	36814	4403	36024	4585	35251	4771	34494	4961	33754	5155	8
	36801	4406	36011	4588	35238	4774	34482	4964	33742	5158	
23	36787	4409	35998	4591	35225	4777	34469	4967	33730	5161	7
	36774	4412	35985	4594	35212	4780	34457	4970	33717	5164	
24	36761	4415	35972	4597	35200	4783	34445	4973	33705	5168	6
	36747	4418	35959	4600	35187	4786	34432	4977	33693	5171	
25	36734	4421	35946	4603	35174	4789	34420	4980	33681	5174	5
	36721	4424	35933	4606	35161	4793	34407	4983	33669	5178	
26	36708	4427	35920	4609	35149	4796	34395	4986	33657	5181	4
	36694	4430	35907	4612	35136	4799	34382	4989	33644	5184	
27	36681	4433	35894	4615	35123	4802	34370	4993	33632	5187	3
	36668	4436	35881	4619	35111	4805	34357	4996	33620	5191	
28	36655	4439	35868	4622	35098	4808	34345	4999	33608	5194	2
	36641	4442	35855	4625	35085	4811	34332	5002	33596	5197	
29	36628	4445	35842	4628	35073	4815	34320	5005	33584	5200	1
	36615	4448	35829	4631	35060	4818	34308	5009	33572	5204	
30	36602	4451	35816	4634	35047	4821	34295	5012	33559	5207	0
	A	B	A	B	A	B	A	B	A	B	
′	154° 30′		154° 00′		153° 30′		153° 00′		152° 30′		′

′	27° 30′ A	B	28° 00′ A	B	28° 30′ A	B	29° 00′ A	B	29° 30′ A	B	′
0	33559	5207	32839	5406	32134	5610	31443	5818	30766	6030	30
	33547	5210	32827	5410	32122	5614	31431	5822	30755	6034	
1	33535	5214	32815	5413	32110	5617	31420	5825	30744	6038	29
	33523	5217	32803	5417	32099	5620	31409	5829	30733	6041	
2	33511	5220	32792	5420	32087	5624	31397	5832	30721	6045	28
	33499	5224	32780	5423	32076	5627	31386	5836	30710	6048	
3	33487	5227	32768	5426	32064	5631	31375	5839	30699	6052	27
	33475	5230	32756	5430	32052	5634	31363	5843	30688	6055	
4	33462	5233	32744	5433	32041	5638	31352	5846	30677	6059	26
	33450	5237	32732	5437	32029	5641	31340	5850	30666	6062	
5	33438	5240	32720	5440	32018	5645	31329	5853	30655	6066	25
	33426	5243	32709	5443	32006	5648	31318	5857	30643	6070	
6	33414	5247	32697	5447	31994	5651	31306	5860	30632	6073	24
	33402	5250	32685	5450	31983	5655	31295	5864	30621	6077	
7	33390	5253	32673	5454	31971	5658	31284	5867	30610	6080	23
	33378	5257	32661	5457	31960	5662	31272	5871	30599	6084	
8	33366	5260	32649	5460	31948	5665	31261	5874	30588	6088	22
	33354	5263	32638	5464	31936	5669	31250	5878	30577	6091	
9	33342	5266	32625	5467	31925	5672	31238	5881	30566	6095	21
	33330	5270	32614	5470	31913	5675	31227	5885	30555	6098	
10	33318	5273	32602	5474	31902	5679	31216	5888	30544	6102	20
	33306	5277	32590	5477	31890	5682	31204	5892	30532	6106	
11	33293	5280	32579	5481	31879	5686	31193	5895	30521	6109	19
	33281	5283	32567	5484	31867	5689	31182	5899	30510	6113	
12	33269	5287	32555	5487	31856	5693	31170	5902	30499	6116	18
	33257	5290	32543	5491	31844	5696	31159	5906	30488	6120	
13	33245	5293	32532	5494	31833	5700	31148	5909	30477	6124	17
	33233	5296	32520	5498	31821	5703	31137	5913	30466	6127	
14	33221	5300	32508	5501	31809	5707	31125	5917	30455	6131	16
	33209	5303	32496	5504	31798	5710	31114	5920	30444	6134	
15	33197	5306	32484	5508	31786	5714	31103	5924	30433	6138	15
	33185	5310	32473	5511	31775	5717	31091	5927	30422	6142	
16	33173	5313	32461	5515	31763	5720	31080	5931	30411	6145	14
	33161	5316	32449	5518	31752	5724	31069	5934	30400	6149	
17	33149	5320	32438	5521	31740	5727	31058	5938	30389	6153	13
	33137	5323	32426	5525	31729	5731	31046	5941	30378	6156	
18	33125	5326	32414	5528	31717	5734	31035	5945	30367	6160	12
	33113	5330	32402	5532	31706	5738	31024	5948	30356	6163	
19	33101	5333	32391	5535	31694	5741	31013	5952	30345	6167	11
	33089	5336	32379	5538	31683	5745	31001	5955	30334	6171	
20	33077	5340	32367	5542	31672	5748	30990	5959	30322	6174	10
	33065	5343	32355	5545	31660	5752	30979	5963	30311	6178	
21	33054	5346	32344	5549	31648	5755	30968	5966	30300	6181	9
	33042	5350	32332	5552	31637	5759	30956	5970	30289	6185	
22	33030	5353	32320	5555	31626	5762	30945	5973	30278	6189	8
	33018	5356	32309	5559	31614	5766	30934	5977	30267	6192	
23	33006	5360	32297	5562	31603	5769	30923	5980	30256	6196	7
	32994	5363	32285	5566	31591	5773	30912	5984	30245	6200	
24	32982	5366	32274	5569	31580	5776	30900	5988	30235	6203	6
	32970	5370	32262	5572	31569	5780	30889	5991	30224	6207	
25	32958	5373	32250	5576	31557	5783	30878	5995	30213	6210	5
	32946	5376	32239	5579	31546	5787	30867	5998	30202	6214	
26	32934	5380	32227	5583	31534	5790	30856	6002	30191	6218	4
	32922	5383	32215	5586	31523	5794	30844	6005	30180	6221	
27	32910	5386	32204	5590	31511	5797	30833	6009	30169	6225	3
	32898	5390	32192	5593	31500	5801	30822	6012	30158	6229	
28	32887	5393	32180	5596	31488	5804	30811	6016	30147	6232	2
	32875	5396	32169	5600	31477	5808	30800	6020	30136	6236	
29	32863	5400	32157	5603	31466	5811	30788	6023	30125	6240	1
	32851	5403	32145	5607	31454	5815	30777	6027	30114	6243	
30	32839	5406	32134	5610	31443	5818	30766	6030	30103	6247	0
	A	B	A	B	A	B	A	B	A	B	
′	152° 00′		151° 30′		151° 00′		150° 30′		150° 00′		′

WHEN LHA (E OR W) IS <u>GREATER</u> THAN 90°, TAKE "K" FROM <u>BOTTOM</u> OF TABLE

′	30° 00′		30° 30′		31° 00′		31° 30′		32° 00′		′
	A	B	A	B	A	B	A	B	A	B	
0	30103	6247	29453	6468	28816	6693	28191	6923	27579	7158	30
	30092	6251	29442	6472	28806	6697	28181	6927	27569	7162	
1	30081	6254	29432	6475	28795	6701	28171	6931	27559	7166	29
	30070	6258	29421	6479	28785	6705	28161	6935	27549	7170	
2	30059	6262	29410	6483	28774	6709	28150	6939	27539	7174	28
	30048	6265	29399	6487	28763	6712	28140	6943	27528	7178	
3	30037	6269	29389	6490	28753	6716	28130	6947	27518	7182	27
	30026	6273	29378	6494	28743	6720	28119	6951	27508	7186	
4	30016	6276	29367	6498	28732	6724	28109	6954	27498	7190	26
	30005	6280	29357	6501	28722	6728	28099	6958	27488	7193	
5	29994	6284	29346	6505	28711	6731	28089	6962	27478	7197	25
	29983	6287	29335	6509	28701	6735	28078	6966	27468	7201	
6	29972	6291	29325	6513	28690	6739	28068	6970	27458	7205	24
	29961	6294	29314	6516	28680	6743	28058	6974	27448	7209	
7	29950	6298	29303	6520	28669	6747	28047	6978	27438	7213	23
	29939	6302	29293	6524	28659	6750	28037	6982	27428	7217	
8	29928	6305	29282	6528	28648	6754	28027	6985	27418	7221	22
	29917	6309	29271	6531	28638	6758	28017	6989	27408	7225	
9	29907	6313	29261	6535	28627	6762	28006	6993	27398	7229	21
	29896	6316	29250	6539	28617	6766	27996	6997	27387	7233	
10	29885	6320	29239	6543	28606	6770	27986	7001	27377	7237	20
	29874	6324	29229	6546	28596	6773	27976	7005	27367	7241	
11	29863	6328	29218	6550	28586	6777	27965	7009	27357	7245	19
	29852	6331	29207	6554	28575	6781	27955	7013	27347	7249	
12	29841	6335	29197	6558	28565	6785	27945	7017	27337	7253	18
	29831	6339	29186	6561	28554	6789	27935	7021	27327	7257	
13	29820	6342	29175	6565	28544	6793	27925	7024	27317	7261	17
	29809	6346	29165	6569	28533	6796	27914	7028	27307	7265	
14	29798	6350	29154	6573	28523	6800	27904	7032	27297	7269	16
	29787	6353	29144	6576	28513	6804	27894	7036	27287	7273	
15	29776	6357	29133	6580	28502	6808	27884	7040	27277	7277	15
	29766	6361	29122	6584	28492	6812	27874	7044	27267	7281	
16	29755	6364	29112	6588	28481	6815	27863	7048	27257	7285	14
	29744	6368	29101	6591	28471	6819	27853	7052	27247	7289	
17	29733	6372	29091	6595	28461	6823	27843	7056	27237	7293	13
	29722	6375	29080	6599	28450	6827	27833	7060	27227	7297	
18	29711	6379	29069	6603	28440	6831	27823	7064	27217	7301	12
	29701	6383	29059	6606	28429	6835	27812	7067	27207	7305	
19	29690	6386	29048	6610	28419	6839	27802	7071	27197	7309	11
	29679	6390	29038	6614	28409	6842	27792	7075	27187	7313	
20	29668	6394	29027	6618	28398	6846	27782	7079	27177	7317	10
	29657	6398	29016	6622	28388	6850	27772	7083	27167	7321	
21	29647	6401	29006	6625	28378	6854	27761	7087	27157	7325	9
	29636	6405	28995	6629	28367	6858	27751	7091	27147	7329	
22	29625	6409	28985	6633	28357	6862	27741	7095	27137	7333	8
	29614	6412	28974	6637	28346	6865	27731	7099	27127	7337	
23	29604	6416	28964	6640	28336	6869	27721	7103	27117	7341	7
	29593	6420	28953	6644	28326	6873	27711	7107	27107	7345	
24	29582	6423	28942	6648	28315	6877	27701	7111	27098	7349	6
	29571	6427	28932	6652	28305	6881	27690	7115	27088	7353	
25	29560	6431	28921	6655	28295	6885	27680	7118	27078	7357	5
	29550	6435	28911	6659	28284	6889	27670	7122	27068	7361	
26	29539	6438	28900	6663	28274	6893	27660	7126	27058	7365	4
	29528	6442	28890	6667	28264	6896	27650	7130	27048	7369	
27	29517	6446	28879	6671	28253	6900	27640	7134	27038	7373	3
	29507	6449	28869	6674	28243	6904	27630	7138	27028	7377	
28	29496	6453	28858	6678	28233	6908	27619	7142	27018	7381	2
	29485	6457	28848	6682	28222	6912	27609	7146	27008	7385	
29	29475	6461	28837	6686	28212	6916	27599	7150	26998	7389	1
	29464	6464	28827	6690	28202	6920	27589	7154	26988	7393	
30	29453	6468	28816	6693	28191	6923	27579	7158	26978	7397	0
	A	B	A	B	A	B	A	B	A	B	
′	149° 30′		149° 00′		148° 30′		148° 00′		147° 30′		′

′	32° 30′ A	32° 30′ B	33° 00′ A	33° 00′ B	33° 30′ A	33° 30′ B	34° 00′ A	34° 00′ B	34° 30′ A	34° 30′ B	′
0	26978	7397	26389	7641	25811	7889	25244	8143	24687	8401	30
	26968	7401	26379	7645	25801	7893	25235	8147	24678	8405	
1	26958	7405	26370	7649	25792	7898	25225	8151	24669	8409	29
	26949	7409	26360	7653	25782	7902	25216	8155	24660	8414	
2	26939	7413	26350	7657	25773	7906	25206	8160	24650	8418	28
	26929	7417	26340	7661	25763	7910	25197	8164	24641	8422	
3	26919	7421	26331	7665	25754	7914	25188	8168	24632	8427	27
	26909	7425	26321	7670	25744	7919	25178	8172	24623	8431	
4	26899	7429	26311	7674	25735	7923	25169	8177	24614	8435	26
	26889	7433	26302	7678	25725	7927	25160	8181	24605	8440	
5	26879	7437	26292	7682	25716	7931	25150	8185	24595	8444	25
	26869	7441	26282	7686	25706	7935	25141	8189	24586	8448	
6	26860	7445	26273	7690	25697	7940	25132	8194	24577	8453	24
	26850	7449	26263	7694	25687	7944	25122	8198	24568	8457	
7	26840	7453	26253	7698	25678	7948	25113	8202	24559	8461	23
	26830	7458	26244	7702	25668	7952	25104	8207	24550	8466	
8	26820	7462	26234	7707	25659	7956	25094	8211	24540	8470	22
	26810	7466	26224	7711	25649	7961	25085	8215	24531	8475	
9	26800	7470	26214	7715	25640	7965	25076	8219	24522	8479	21
	26790	7474	26205	7719	25630	7969	25066	8224	24513	8483	
10	26781	7478	26195	7723	25621	7973	25057	8228	24504	8488	20
	26771	7482	26185	7727	25611	7977	25048	8232	24495	8492	
11	26761	7486	26176	7731	25602	7982	25038	8237	24486	8496	19
	26751	7490	26166	7736	25592	7986	25029	8241	24477	8501	
12	26741	7494	26157	7740	25583	7990	25020	8245	24467	8505	18
	26731	7498	26147	7744	25573	7994	25011	8249	24458	8510	
13	26722	7502	26137	7748	25564	7998	25001	8254	24449	8514	17
	26712	7506	26128	7752	25554	8003	24992	8258	24440	8518	
14	26702	7510	26118	7756	25545	8007	24983	8262	24431	8523	16
	26692	7514	26108	7760	25536	8011	24973	8267	24422	8527	
15	26682	7518	26099	7764	25526	8015	24964	8271	24413	8531	15
	26672	7522	26089	7769	25517	8020	24955	8275	24404	8536	
16	26663	7526	26079	7773	25507	8024	24946	8280	24395	8540	14
	26653	7531	26070	7777	25498	8028	24936	8284	24385	8545	
17	26643	7535	26060	7781	25488	8032	24927	8288	24376	8549	13
	26633	7539	26051	7785	25479	8037	24918	8292	24367	8553	
18	26623	7543	26041	7789	25469	8041	24909	8297	24358	8558	12
	26614	7547	26031	7793	25460	8045	24899	8301	24349	8562	
19	26604	7551	26022	7798	25451	8049	24890	8305	24340	8567	11
	26594	7555	26012	7802	25441	8053	24881	8310	24331	8571	
20	26584	7559	26002	7806	25432	8058	24872	8314	24322	8575	10
	26574	7563	25993	7810	25422	8062	24862	8318	24313	8580	
21	26565	7567	25983	7814	25413	8066	24853	8323	24304	8584	9
	26555	7571	25974	7818	25403	8070	24844	8327	24295	8589	
22	26545	7575	25964	7823	25394	8075	24835	8331	24286	8593	8
	26535	7579	25954	7827	25385	8079	24825	8336	24276	8597	
23	26526	7584	25945	7831	25375	8083	24816	8340	24267	8602	7
	26516	7588	25935	7835	25366	8087	24807	8344	24258	8606	
24	26506	7592	25926	7839	25356	8091	24798	8349	24249	8611	6
	26496	7596	25916	7843	25347	8096	24788	8353	24240	8615	
25	26486	7600	25907	7848	25338	8100	24779	8357	24231	8619	5
	26477	7604	25897	7852	25328	8104	24770	8362	24222	8624	
26	26467	7608	25887	7856	25319	8108	24761	8366	24213	8628	4
	26457	7612	25878	7860	25309	8113	24752	8370	24204	8633	
27	26447	7616	25868	7864	25300	8117	24742	8375	24195	8637	3
	26438	7620	25859	7868	25291	8121	24733	8379	24186	8641	
28	26428	7625	25849	7873	25281	8125	24724	8383	24177	8646	2
	26418	7629	25840	7877	25272	8130	24715	8388	24168	8650	
29	26409	7633	25830	7881	25263	8134	24706	8392	24159	8655	1
	26399	7637	25821	7885	25253	8138	24696	8396	24150	8659	
30	26389	7641	25811	7889	25244	8143	24687	8401	24141	8663	0
′	A	B	A	B	A	B	A	B	A	B	′
	147° 00′		146° 30′		146° 00′		145° 30′		145° 00′		

283

WHEN LHA (E OR W) IS GREATER THAN 90°, TAKE "K" FROM BOTTOM OF TABLE

′	35° 00′ A	B	35° 30′ A	B	36° 00′ A	B	36° 30′ A	B	37° 00′ A	B	′
0	24141	8663	23605	8931	23078	9204	22561	9482	22054	9765	30
	24132	8668	23596	8936	23069	9209	22553	9487	22045	9770	
1	24123	8672	23587	8940	23061	9213	22544	9492	22037	9775	29
	24114	8677	23578	8945	23052	9218	22536	9496	22029	9779	
2	24105	8681	23569	8949	23043	9223	22527	9501	22020	9784	28
	24096	8686	23560	8954	23035	9227	22519	9505	22012	9789	
3	24087	8690	23551	8958	23026	9232	22510	9510	22003	9794	27
	24078	8694	23543	8963	23017	9236	22501	9515	21995	9798	
4	24069	8699	23534	8967	23009	9241	22493	9520	21987	9803	26
	24060	8703	23525	8972	23000	9246	22484	9524	21978	9808	
5	24051	8708	23516	8976	22991	9250	22476	9529	21970	9813	25
	24042	8712	23507	8981	22983	9255	22467	9534	21962	9818	
6	24033	8717	23498	8986	22974	9259	22459	9538	21953	9822	24
	24024	8721	23490	8990	22965	9264	22450	9543	21945	9827	
7	24015	8726	23481	8995	22957	9269	22442	9548	21937	9832	23
	24006	8730	23472	8999	22948	9273	22433	9552	21928	9837	
8	23997	8734	23463	9004	22939	9278	22425	9557	21920	9841	22
	23988	8739	23454	9008	22931	9282	22416	9562	21912	9846	
9	23979	8743	23446	9013	22922	9287	22408	9566	21903	9851	21
	23970	8748	23437	9017	22913	9292	22399	9571	21895	9856	
10	23961	8752	23428	9022	22905	9296	22391	9576	21887	9861	20
	23952	8757	23419	9026	22896	9301	22382	9581	21878	9865	
11	23943	8761	23410	9031	22887	9305	22374	9585	21870	9870	19
	23934	8766	23402	9035	22879	9310	22366	9590	21862	9875	
12	23925	8770	23393	9040	22870	9315	22357	9595	21853	9880	18
	23916	8775	23384	9044	22862	9319	22349	9599	21845	9885	
13	23907	8779	23375	9049	22853	9324	22340	9604	21837	9889	17
	23898	8783	23366	9054	22844	9329	22332	9609	21828	9894	
14	23889	8788	23358	9058	22836	9333	22323	9614	21820	9899	16
	23880	8792	23349	9063	22827	9338	22315	9618	21812	9904	
15	23871	8797	23340	9067	22818	9342	22306	9623	21803	9909	15
	23863	8801	23331	9072	22810	9347	22298	9628	21795	9913	
16	23854	8806	23323	9076	22801	9352	22289	9632	21787	9918	14
	23845	8810	23314	9081	22793	9356	22281	9637	21778	9923	
17	23836	8815	23305	9085	22784	9361	22272	9642	21770	9928	13
	23827	8819	23296	9090	22775	9366	22264	9647	21762	9933	
18	23818	8824	23288	9094	22767	9370	22256	9651	21754	9937	12
	23809	8828	23279	9099	22758	9375	22247	9656	21745	9942	
19	23800	8833	23270	9104	22750	9380	22239	9661	21737	9947	11
	23791	8837	23261	9108	22741	9384	22230	9665	21729	9952	
20	23782	8842	23252	9113	22732	9389	22222	9670	21720	9957	10
	23773	8846	23244	9117	22724	9394	22213	9675	21712	9962	
21	23764	8850	23235	9122	22715	9398	22205	9680	21704	9966	9
	23755	8855	23226	9126	22707	9403	22197	9684	21696	9971	
22	23747	8859	23218	9131	22698	9407	22188	9689	21687	9976	8
	23738	8864	23209	9136	22690	9412	22180	9694	21679	9981	
23	23729	8868	23200	9140	22681	9417	22171	9699	21671	9986	7
	23720	8873	23191	9145	22672	9421	22163	9703	21662	9990	
24	23711	8877	23183	9149	22664	9426	22154	9708	21654	9995	6
	23702	8882	23174	9154	22655	9431	22146	9713	21646	10000	
25	23693	8886	23165	9158	22647	9435	22138	9718	21638	10005	5
	23684	8891	23156	9163	22638	9440	22129	9722	21629	10010	
26	23675	8895	23148	9168	22630	9445	22121	9727	21621	10015	4
	23667	8900	23139	9172	22621	9449	22112	9732	21613	10019	
27	23658	8904	23130	9177	22612	9454	22104	9737	21605	10024	3
	23649	8909	23122	9181	22604	9459	22096	9741	21596	10029	
28	23640	8913	23113	9186	22595	9463	22087	9746	21588	10034	2
	23631	8918	23104	9190	22587	9468	22079	9751	21580	10039	
29	23622	8922	23095	9195	22578	9473	22070	9756	21572	10044	1
	23613	8927	23087	9200	22570	9477	22062	9760	21563	10049	
30	23605	8931	23078	9204	22561	9482	22054	9765	21555	10053	0
	A	B	A	B	A	B	A	B	A	B	
′	144° 30′		144° 00′		143° 30′		143° 00′		142° 30′		′

′	37° 30′		38° 00′		38° 30′		39° 00′		39° 30′		′
	A	B	A	B	A	B	A	B	A	B	
0	21555	10053	21066	10347	20585	10646	20113	10950	19649	11259	30
	21547	10058	21058	10352	20577	10651	20105	10955	19641	11265	
1	21539	10063	21050	10357	20569	10656	20097	10960	19634	11270	29
	21531	10068	21042	10362	20561	10661	20089	10965	19626	11275	
2	21522	10073	21033	10367	20553	10666	20082	10970	19618	11280	28
	21514	10078	21025	10372	20545	10671	20074	10975	19611	11285	
3	21506	10082	21017	10376	20537	10676	20066	10980	19603	11291	27
	21498	10087	21009	10381	20529	10681	20058	10986	19595	11296	
4	21489	10092	21001	10386	20522	10686	20050	10991	19588	11301	26
	21481	10097	20993	10391	20514	10691	20043	10996	19580	11306	
5	21473	10102	20985	10396	20506	10696	20035	11001	19572	11311	25
	21465	10107	20977	10401	20498	10701	20027	11006	19565	11317	
6	21457	10112	20969	10406	20490	10706	20019	11011	19557	11322	24
	21448	10116	20961	10411	20482	10711	20012	11016	19549	11327	
7	21440	10121	20953	10416	20474	10716	20004	11021	19541	11332	23
	21432	10126	20945	10421	20466	10721	19996	11027	19534	11338	
8	21424	10131	20937	10426	20458	10726	19988	11032	19527	11343	22
	21416	10136	20929	10431	20450	10731	19980	11037	19519	11348	
9	21407	10141	20921	10436	20442	10736	19973	11042	19511	11353	21
	21399	10146	20913	10441	20435	10741	19965	11047	19504	11359	
10	21391	10151	20905	10446	20427	10746	19957	11052	19496	11364	20
	21383	10155	20897	10451	20419	10751	19949	11057	19488	11369	
11	21375	10160	20888	10456	20411	10756	19942	11063	19481	11374	19
	21367	10165	20880	10461	20403	10761	19934	11068	19473	11380	
12	21358	10170	20872	10466	20395	10767	19926	11073	19466	11385	18
	21350	10175	20864	10471	20387	10772	19919	11078	19458	11390	
13	21342	10180	20856	10476	20379	10777	19911	11083	19450	11395	17
	21334	10185	20848	10481	20371	10782	19903	11088	19443	11400	
14	21326	10190	20840	10486	20364	10787	19895	11094	19435	11406	16
	21318	10195	20832	10491	20356	10792	19888	11099	19428	11411	
15	21309	10199	20824	10496	20348	10797	19880	11104	19420	11416	15
	21301	10204	20816	10500	20340	10802	19872	11109	19412	11422	
16	21293	10209	20808	10505	20332	10807	19864	11114	19405	11427	14
	21285	10214	20800	10510	20324	10812	19857	11119	19397	11432	
17	21277	10219	20792	10515	20316	10817	19849	11124	19390	11437	13
	21269	10224	20784	10520	20309	10822	19841	11130	19382	11443	
18	21260	10229	20776	10525	20301	10827	19834	11135	19375	11448	12
	21252	10234	20768	10530	20293	10832	19826	11140	19367	11453	
19	21244	10239	20760	10535	20285	10838	19818	11145	19359	11458	11
	21236	10243	20752	10540	20277	10843	19810	11150	19352	11464	
20	21228	10248	20744	10545	20269	10848	19803	11156	19344	11469	10
	21220	10253	20736	10550	20261	10853	19795	11161	19337	11474	
21	21212	10258	20728	10555	20254	10858	19787	11166	19329	11479	9
	21204	10263	20720	10560	20246	10863	19779	11171	19321	11485	
22	21195	10268	20712	10565	20238	10868	19772	11176	19314	11490	8
	21187	10273	20704	10570	20230	10873	19764	11181	19306	11495	
23	21179	10278	20696	10575	20222	10878	19756	11187	19299	11501	7
	21171	10283	20688	10580	20214	10883	19749	11192	19291	11506	
24	21163	10288	20680	10585	20207	10888	19741	11197	19284	11511	6
	21155	10293	20672	10590	20199	10894	19733	11202	19276	11516	
25	21147	10298	20665	10595	20191	10899	19726	11207	19269	11522	5
	21139	10302	20657	10600	20183	10904	19718	11213	19261	11527	
26	21131	10307	20649	10605	20175	10909	19710	11218	19253	11532	4
	21122	10312	20641	10610	20167	10914	19703	11223	19246	11537	
27	21114	10317	20633	10615	20160	10919	19695	11228	19238	11543	3
	21106	10322	20625	10620	20152	10924	19687	11233	19231	11548	
28	21098	10327	20617	10625	20144	10929	19680	11239	19223	11553	2
	21090	10332	20609	10630	20136	10934	19672	11244	19216	11559	
29	21082	10337	20601	10635	20128	10939	19664	11249	19208	11564	1
	21074	10342	20593	10640	20121	10945	19657	11254	19201	11569	
30	21066	10347	20585	10646	20113	10950	19649	11259	19193	11575	0
	A	B	A	B	A	B	A	B	A	B	
′	142° 00′		141° 30′		141° 00′		140° 30′		140° 00′		′

WHEN LHA (E OR W) IS GREATER THAN 90°, TAKE "K" FROM BOTTOM OF TABLE

′	40° 00′ A	B	40° 30′ A	B	41° 00′ A	B	41° 30′ A	B	42° 00′ A	B	′
0	19193	11575	18746	11895	18306	12222	17873	12554	17449	12893	30
	19186	11580	18738	11901	18298	12228	17866	12560	17442	12898	
1	19178	11585	18731	11906	18291	12233	17859	12566	17435	12904	29
	19171	11590	18723	11912	18284	12238	17852	12571	17428	12910	
2	19163	11596	18716	11917	18277	12244	17845	12577	17421	12915	28
	19156	11601	18709	11922	18269	12249	17838	12582	17414	12921	
3	19148	11606	18701	11928	18262	12255	17831	12588	17407	12927	27
	19141	11612	18694	11933	18255	12260	17824	12593	17400	12932	
4	19133	11617	18686	11939	18248	12266	17816	12599	17393	12938	26
	19126	11622	18679	11944	18240	12271	17809	12605	17386	12944	
5	19118	11628	18672	11949	18233	12277	17802	12610	17379	12950	25
	19111	11633	18664	11955	18226	12282	17795	12616	17372	12955	
6	19103	11638	18657	11960	18219	12288	17788	12622	17365	12961	24
	19096	11644	18650	11966	18211	12293	17781	12627	17358	12967	
7	19088	11649	18642	11971	18204	12299	17774	12633	17351	12972	23
	19081	11654	18635	11977	18197	12305	17767	12638	17344	12978	
8	19073	11660	18627	11982	18190	12310	17760	12644	17337	12984	22
	19066	11665	18620	11987	18182	12316	17752	12650	17330	12990	
9	19058	11670	18613	11993	18175	12321	17745	12655	17323	12995	21
	19051	11676	18605	11998	18168	12327	17738	12661	17316	13001	
10	19043	11681	18598	12004	18161	12332	17731	12667	17309	13007	20
	19036	11686	18591	12009	18154	12338	17724	12672	17302	13012	
11	19028	11692	18583	12014	18146	12343	17717	12678	17295	13018	19
	19021	11697	18576	12020	18139	12349	17710	12683	17288	13024	
12	19013	11702	18569	12025	18132	12354	17703	12689	17281	13030	18
	19006	11708	18561	12031	18125	12360	17696	12695	17274	13035	
13	18998	11713	18554	12036	18117	12365	17689	12700	17267	13041	17
	18991	11718	18547	12042	18110	12371	17681	12706	17260	13047	
14	18983	11724	18539	12047	18103	12376	17674	12711	17253	13053	16
	18976	11729	18532	12053	18096	12382	17667	12717	17246	13058	
15	18968	11734	18525	12058	18089	12387	17660	12723	17239	13064	15
	18961	11740	18517	12063	18081	12393	17653	12728	17232	13070	
16	18953	11745	18510	12069	18074	12398	17646	12734	17225	13075	14
	18946	11750	18503	12074	18067	12404	17639	12740	17218	13081	
17	18939	11756	18495	12080	18060	12410	17632	12745	17212	13087	13
	18931	11761	18488	12085	18053	12415	17625	12751	17205	13093	
18	18924	11766	18481	12091	18045	12421	17618	12757	17198	13098	12
	18916	11772	18473	12096	18038	12426	17611	12762	17191	13104	
19	18909	11777	18466	12102	18031	12432	17604	12768	17184	13110	11
	18901	11782	18459	12107	18024	12437	17597	12774	17177	13116	
20	18894	11788	18451	12112	18017	12443	17590	12779	17170	13121	10
	18886	11793	18444	12118	18010	12448	17583	12785	17163	13127	
21	18879	11799	18437	12123	18002	12454	17575	12790	17156	13133	9
	18872	11804	18429	12129	17995	12460	17568	12796	17149	13139	
22	18864	11809	18422	12134	17988	12465	17561	12802	17142	13144	8
	18857	11815	18415	12140	17981	12471	17554	12807	17135	13150	
23	18849	11820	18408	12145	17974	12476	17547	12813	17128	13156	7
	18842	11825	18400	12151	17966	12482	17540	12819	17121	13162	
24	18834	11831	18393	12156	17959	12487	17533	12824	17114	13168	6
	18827	11836	18386	12162	17952	12493	17526	12830	17108	13173	
25	18820	11842	18378	12167	17945	12499	17519	12836	17101	13179	5
	18812	11847	18371	12173	17938	12504	17512	12841	17094	13185	
26	18805	11852	18364	12178	17931	12510	17505	12847	17087	13191	4
	18797	11858	18357	12184	17924	12515	17498	12853	17080	13196	
27	18790	11863	18349	12189	17916	12521	17491	12859	17073	13202	3
	18783	11868	18342	12195	17909	12526	17484	12864	17066	13208	
28	18775	11874	18335	12200	17902	12532	17477	12870	17059	13214	2
	18768	11879	18327	12205	17895	12538	17470	12876	17052	13220	
29	18760	11885	18320	12211	17888	12543	17463	12881	17046	13225	1
	18753	11890	18313	12216	17881	12549	17456	12887	17039	13231	
30	18746	11895	18306	12222	17873	12554	17449	12893	17032	13237	0
	A	B	A	B	A	B	A	B	A	B	
	139° 30′		139° 00′		138° 30′		138° 00′		137° 30′		′

′	42° 30′ A	B	43° 00′ A	B	43° 30′ A	B	44° 00′ A	B	44° 30′ A	B	′
0	17032	13237	16622	13587	16219	13944	15823	14307	15434	14676	30
	17025	13243	16615	13593	16212	13950	15816	14313	15427	14682	
1	17018	13248	16608	13599	16205	13956	15810	14319	15421	14688	29
	17011	13254	16601	13605	16199	13962	15803	14325	15414	14694	
2	17004	13260	16595	13611	16192	13968	15797	14331	15408	14701	28
	16997	13266	16588	13617	16186	13974	15790	14337	15402	14707	
3	16990	13272	16581	13623	16179	13980	15784	14343	15395	14713	27
	16983	13277	16574	13628	16172	13986	15777	14349	15389	14719	
4	16977	13283	16567	13634	16166	13992	15771	14355	15382	14726	26
	16970	13289	16561	13640	16159	13998	15764	14362	15376	14732	
5	16963	13295	16554	13646	16152	14004	15758	14368	15370	14738	25
	16956	13301	16547	13652	16146	14010	15751	14374	15363	14744	
6	16949	13306	16540	13658	16139	14016	15744	14380	15357	14750	24
	16942	13312	16534	13664	16132	14022	15738	14386	15350	14757	
7	16935	13318	16527	13670	16126	14028	15731	14392	15344	14763	23
	16928	13324	16520	13676	16119	14034	15725	14398	15338	14769	
8	16922	13330	16513	13682	16112	14040	15718	14404	15331	14775	22
	16915	13336	16507	13688	16106	14046	15712	14411	15325	14782	
9	16908	13341	16500	13694	16099	14052	15705	14417	15318	14788	21
	16901	13347	16493	13700	16093	14058	15699	14423	15312	14794	
10	16894	13353	16487	13705	16086	14064	15692	14429	15306	14800	20
	16887	13359	16480	13711	16079	14070	15686	14435	15299	14807	
11	16880	13365	16473	13717	16073	14076	15679	14441	15293	14813	19
	16874	13370	16466	13723	16066	14082	15673	14447	15286	14819	
12	16867	13376	16460	13729	16060	14088	15666	14453	15280	14825	18
	16860	13382	16453	13735	16053	14094	15660	14460	15274	14831	
13	16853	13388	16446	13741	16046	14100	15653	14466	15267	14838	17
	16846	13394	16439	13747	16040	14106	15647	14472	15261	14844	
14	16839	13400	16433	13753	16033	14112	15640	14478	15255	14850	16
	16833	13405	16426	13759	16027	14118	15634	14484	15248	14857	
15	16826	13411	16419	13765	16020	14124	15627	14490	15242	14863	15
	16819	13417	16413	13771	16013	14130	15621	14496	15235	14869	
16	16812	13423	16406	13777	16007	14136	15614	14503	15229	14875	14
	16805	13429	16399	13783	16000	14142	15608	14509	15223	14882	
17	16798	13435	16392	13789	15994	14149	15602	14515	15216	14888	13
	16792	13440	16386	13794	15987	14155	15595	14521	15210	14894	
18	16785	13446	16379	13800	15980	14161	15589	14527	15204	14900	12
	16778	13452	16372	13806	15974	14167	15582	14533	15197	14907	
19	16771	13458	16366	13812	15967	14173	15576	14540	15191	14913	11
	16764	13464	16359	13818	15961	14179	15569	14546	15184	14919	
20	16757	13470	16352	13824	15954	14185	15563	14552	15178	14925	10
	16751	13476	16346	13830	15947	14191	15556	14558	15172	14932	
21	16744	13481	16339	13836	15941	14197	15550	14564	15165	14938	9
	16737	13487	16332	13842	15934	14203	15543	14570	15159	14944	
22	16730	13493	16325	13848	15928	14209	15537	14577	15153	14951	8
	16723	13499	16319	13854	15921	14215	15530	14583	15146	14957	
23	16717	13505	16312	13860	15915	14221	15524	14589	15140	14963	7
	16710	13511	16305	13866	15908	14227	15517	14595	15134	14969	
24	16703	13517	16299	13872	15901	14233	15511	14601	15127	14976	6
	16696	13523	16292	13878	15895	14240	15505	14608	15121	14982	
25	16689	13528	16285	13884	15888	14246	15498	14614	15115	14988	5
	16683	13534	16279	13890	15882	14252	15492	14620	15108	14995	
26	16676	13540	16272	13896	15875	14258	15485	14626	15102	15001	4
	16669	13546	16265	13902	15869	14264	15479	14632	15096	15007	
27	16662	13552	16259	13908	15862	14270	15472	14639	15089	15014	3
	16656	13558	16252	13914	15856	14276	15466	14645	15083	15020	
28	16649	13564	16245	13920	15849	14282	15459	14651	15077	15026	2
	16642	13570	16239	13926	15842	14288	15453	14657	15070	15033	
29	16635	13575	16232	13932	15836	14294	15447	14663	15064	15039	1
	16628	13581	16225	13938	15829	14300	15440	14670	15058	15045	
30	16622	13587	16219	13944	15823	14307	15434	14676	15051	15051	0
	A	B	A	B	A	B	A	B	A	B	
′	137° 00′		136° 30′		136° 00′		135° 30′		135° 00′		′

WHEN LHA (E OR W) IS GREATER THAN 90°, TAKE "K" FROM BOTTOM OF TABLE

′	45° 00′ A	45° 00′ B	45° 30′ A	45° 30′ B	46° 00′ A	46° 00′ B	46° 30′ A	46° 30′ B	47° 00′ A	47° 00′ B	′
0	15051	15051	14676	15434	14307	15823	13944	16219	13587	16622	30
	15045	15058	14670	15440	14300	15829	13938	16225	13581	16628	
1	15039	15064	14663	15447	14294	15836	13932	16232	13575	16635	29
	15033	15070	14657	15453	14288	15842	13926	16239	13570	16642	
2	15026	15077	14651	15459	14282	15849	13920	16245	13564	16649	28
	15020	15083	14645	15466	14276	15856	13914	16252	13558	16656	
3	15014	15089	14639	15472	14270	15862	13908	16259	13552	16662	27
	15007	15096	14632	15479	14264	15869	13902	16265	13546	16669	
4	15001	15102	14626	15485	14258	15875	13896	16272	13540	16676	26
	14995	15108	14620	15492	14252	15882	13890	16279	13534	16683	
5	14988	15115	14614	15498	14246	15888	13884	16285	13528	16689	25
	14982	15121	14608	15505	14240	15895	13878	16292	13523	16696	
6	14976	15127	14601	15511	14233	15901	13872	16299	13517	16703	24
	14969	15134	14595	15517	14227	15908	13866	16305	13511	16710	
7	14963	15140	14589	15524	14221	15915	13860	16312	13505	16717	23
	14957	15146	14583	15530	14215	15921	13854	16319	13499	16723	
8	14951	15153	14577	15537	14209	15928	13848	16325	13493	16730	22
	14944	15159	14570	15543	14203	15934	13842	16332	13487	16737	
9	14938	15165	14564	15550	14197	15941	13836	16339	13481	16744	21
	14932	15172	14558	15556	14191	15947	13830	16346	13476	16751	
10	14925	15178	14552	15563	14185	15954	13824	16352	13470	16757	20
	14919	15184	14546	15569	14179	15961	13818	16359	13464	16764	
11	14913	15191	14540	15576	14173	15967	13812	16366	13458	16771	19
	14907	15197	14533	15582	14167	15974	13806	16372	13452	16778	
12	14900	15204	14527	15589	14161	15980	13800	16379	13446	16785	18
	14894	15210	14521	15595	14155	15987	13794	16386	13440	16792	
13	14888	15216	14515	15602	14149	15994	13788	16392	13435	16798	17
	14882	15223	14509	15608	14142	16000	13783	16399	13429	16805	
14	14875	15229	14503	15614	14136	16007	13777	16406	13423	16812	16
	14869	15235	14496	15621	14130	16013	13771	16413	13417	16819	
15	14863	15242	14490	15627	14124	16020	13765	16419	13411	16826	15
	14857	15248	14484	15634	14118	16027	13759	16426	13405	16833	
16	14850	15255	14478	15640	14112	16033	13753	16433	13400	16839	14
	14844	15261	14472	15647	14106	16040	13747	16439	13394	16846	
17	14838	15267	14466	15653	14100	16046	13741	16446	13388	16853	13
	14831	15274	14460	15660	14094	16053	13735	16453	13382	16860	
18	14825	15280	14453	15666	14088	16060	13729	16460	13376	16867	12
	14819	15286	14447	15673	14082	16066	13723	16466	13370	16874	
19	14813	15293	14441	15679	14076	16073	13717	16473	13365	16880	11
	14807	15299	14435	15686	14070	16079	13711	16480	13359	16887	
20	14800	15306	14429	15692	14064	16086	13705	16487	13353	16894	10
	14794	15312	14423	15699	14058	16093	13699	16493	13347	16901	
21	14788	15318	14417	15705	14052	16099	13694	16500	13341	16908	9
	14782	15325	14411	15712	14046	16105	13688	16507	13336	16915	
22	14775	15331	14404	15718	14040	16112	13682	16513	13330	16922	8
	14769	15338	14398	15725	14034	16119	13676	16520	13324	16928	
23	14763	15344	14392	15731	14028	16126	13670	16527	13318	16935	7
	14757	15350	14386	15738	14022	16132	13664	16534	13312	16942	
24	14750	15357	14380	15744	14016	16139	13658	16540	13306	16949	6
	14744	15363	14374	15751	14010	16146	13652	16547	13301	16956	
25	14738	15370	14368	15758	14004	16152	13646	16554	13295	16963	5
	14732	15376	14362	15764	13998	16159	13640	16561	13289	16970	
26	14725	15382	14355	15771	13992	16166	13634	16567	13283	16977	4
	14719	15389	14349	15777	13986	16172	13628	16574	13277	16983	
27	14713	15395	14343	15784	13980	16179	13623	16581	13272	16990	3
	14707	15402	14337	15790	13974	16185	13617	16588	13266	16997	
28	14701	15408	14331	15797	13968	16192	13611	16595	13260	17004	2
	14694	15414	14325	15803	13962	16199	13605	16601	13254	17011	
29	14688	15421	14319	15810	13956	16205	13599	16608	13248	17018	1
	14682	15427	14313	15816	13950	16212	13593	16615	13243	17025	
30	14676	15434	14307	15823	13944	16219	13587	16622	13237	17032	0
′	A	B	A	B	A	B	A	B	A	B	′
	134° 30′		134° 00′		133° 30′		133° 00′		132° 30′		

′	47° 30′		48° 00′		48° 30′		49° 00′		49° 30′		′
	A	B	A	B	A	B	A	B	A	B	
0	13237	17032	12893	17449	12554	17873	12222	18306	11895	18746	30
	13231	17039	12887	17456	12549	17881	12216	18313	11890	18753	
1	13225	17045	12881	17463	12543	17888	12211	18320	11885	18760	29
	13220	17052	12876	17470	12538	17895	12205	18327	11879	18768	
2	13214	17059	12870	17477	12532	17902	12200	18335	11874	18775	28
	13208	17066	12864	17484	12526	17909	12195	18342	11868	18783	
3	13202	17073	12859	17491	12521	17916	12189	18349	11863	18790	27
	13196	17080	12853	17498	12515	17924	12184	18357	11858	18797	
4	13191	17087	12847	17505	12510	17931	12178	18364	11852	18805	26
	13185	17094	12841	17512	12504	17938	12173	18371	11847	18812	
5	13179	17101	12836	17519	12499	17945	12167	18378	11842	18820	25
	13173	17108	12830	17526	12493	17952	12162	18386	11836	18827	
6	13168	17114	12824	17533	12487	17959	12156	18393	11831	18834	24
	13162	17121	12819	17540	12482	17966	12151	18400	11825	18842	
7	13156	17128	12813	17547	12476	17974	12145	18408	11820	18849	23
	13150	17135	12807	17554	12471	17981	12140	18415	11815	18857	
8	13144	17142	12802	17561	12465	17988	12134	18422	11809	18864	22
	13139	17149	12796	17568	12460	17995	12129	18429	11804	18872	
9	13133	17156	12790	17576	12454	18002	12123	18437	11799	18879	21
	13127	17163	12785	17583	12448	18010	12118	18444	11793	18886	
10	13121	17170	12779	17590	12443	18017	12112	18451	11788	18894	20
	13116	17177	12774	17597	12437	18024	12107	18459	11782	18901	
11	13110	17184	12768	17604	12432	18031	12102	18466	11777	18909	19
	13104	17191	12762	17611	12426	18038	12096	18473	11772	18916	
12	13098	17198	12757	17618	12421	18045	12091	18481	11766	18924	18
	13093	17205	12751	17625	12415	18053	12085	18488	11761	18931	
13	13087	17212	12745	17632	12410	18060	12080	18495	11756	18939	17
	13081	17218	12740	17639	12404	18067	12074	18503	11750	18946	
14	13075	17225	12734	17646	12398	18074	12069	18510	11745	18953	16
	13070	17232	12728	17653	12393	18081	12063	18517	11740	18961	
15	13064	17239	12723	17660	12387	18089	12058	18525	11734	18968	15
	13058	17246	12717	17667	12382	18096	12053	18532	11729	18976	
16	13053	17253	12711	17674	12376	18103	12047	18539	11724	18983	14
	13047	17260	12706	17681	12371	18110	12042	18547	11718	18991	
17	13041	17267	12700	17689	12365	18117	12036	18554	11713	18998	13
	13035	17274	12695	17696	12360	18125	12031	18561	11708	19006	
18	13030	17281	12689	17703	12354	18132	12025	18569	11702	19013	12
	13024	17288	12683	17710	12349	18139	12020	18576	11697	19021	
19	13018	17295	12678	17717	12343	18146	12014	18583	11692	19028	11
	13012	17302	12672	17724	12338	18154	12009	18591	11686	19036	
20	13007	17309	12666	17731	12332	18161	12004	18598	11681	19043	10
	13001	17316	12661	17738	12327	18168	11998	18605	11676	19051	
21	12995	17323	12655	17745	12321	18175	11993	18613	11670	19058	9
	12990	17330	12650	17752	12316	18182	11987	18620	11665	19066	
22	12984	17337	12644	17760	12310	18190	11982	18627	11660	19073	8
	12978	17344	12638	17767	12305	18197	11976	18635	11654	19081	
23	12972	17351	12633	17774	12299	18204	11971	18642	11649	19088	7
	12967	17358	12627	17781	12293	18211	11966	18650	11644	19096	
24	12961	17365	12622	17788	12288	18219	11960	18657	11638	19103	6
	12955	17372	12616	17795	12282	18226	11955	18664	11633	19111	
25	12950	17379	12610	17802	12277	18233	11949	18672	11628	19118	5
	12944	17386	12605	17809	12271	18240	11944	18679	11622	19126	
26	12938	17393	12599	17816	12266	18248	11939	18686	11617	19133	4
	12932	17400	12593	17824	12260	18255	11933	18694	11612	19141	
27	12927	17407	12588	17831	12255	18262	11928	18701	11606	19148	3
	12921	17414	12582	17838	12249	18269	11922	18709	11601	19156	
28	12915	17421	12577	17845	12244	18277	11917	18716	11596	19163	2
	12910	17428	12571	17852	12238	18284	11912	18723	11590	19171	
29	12904	17435	12566	17859	12233	18291	11906	18731	11585	19178	1
	12898	17442	12560	17866	12227	18298	11901	18738	11580	19186	
30	12893	17449	12554	17873	12222	18306	11895	18746	11575	19193	0
	A	B	A	B	A	B	A	B	A	B	
′	132° 00′		131° 30′		131° 00′		130° 30′		130° 00′		′

WHEN LHA (E OR W) IS GREATER THAN 90°, TAKE "K" FROM BOTTOM OF TABLE

′	50° 00′ A	50° 00′ B	50° 30′ A	50° 30′ B	51° 00′ A	51° 00′ B	51° 30′ A	51° 30′ B	52° 00′ A	52° 00′ B	′
0	11575	19193	11259	19649	10950	20113	10646	20585	10347	21066	30
	11569	19201	11254	19657	10945	20121	10640	20593	10342	21074	
1	11564	19208	11249	19664	10939	20128	10635	20601	10337	21082	29
	11559	19216	11244	19672	10934	20136	10630	20609	10332	21090	
2	11553	19223	11239	19680	10929	20144	10625	20617	10327	21098	28
	11548	19231	11233	19687	10924	20152	10620	20625	10322	21106	
3	11543	19238	11228	19695	10919	20160	10615	20633	10317	21114	27
	11537	19246	11223	19703	10914	20167	10610	20641	10312	21122	
4	11532	19253	11218	19710	10909	20175	10605	20649	10307	21131	26
	11527	19261	11213	19718	10904	20183	10600	20657	10302	21139	
5	11522	19269	11207	19726	10899	20191	10595	20665	10298	21147	25
	11516	19276	11202	19733	10894	20199	10590	20672	10293	21155	
6	11511	19284	11197	19741	10888	20207	10585	20680	10288	21163	24
	11506	19291	11192	19749	10883	20214	10580	20688	10283	21171	
7	11501	19299	11187	19756	10878	20222	10575	20696	10278	21179	23
	11495	19306	11181	19764	10873	20230	10570	20704	10273	21187	
8	11490	19314	11176	19772	10868	20238	10565	20712	10268	21195	22
	11485	19321	11171	19779	10863	20246	10560	20720	10263	21204	
9	11479	19329	11166	19787	10858	20254	10555	20728	10258	21212	21
	11474	19337	11161	19795	10853	20261	10550	20736	10253	21220	
10	11469	19344	11156	19803	10848	20269	10545	20744	10248	21228	20
	11464	19352	11150	19810	10843	20277	10540	20752	10243	21236	
11	11458	19359	11145	19818	10838	20285	10535	20760	10239	21244	19
	11453	19367	11140	19826	10832	20293	10530	20768	10234	21252	
12	11448	19375	11135	19834	10827	20301	10525	20776	10229	21260	18
	11443	19382	11130	19841	10822	20308	10520	20784	10224	21269	
13	11437	19390	11124	19849	10817	20316	10515	20792	10219	21277	17
	11432	19397	11119	19857	10812	20324	10510	20800	10214	21285	
14	11427	19405	11114	19864	10807	20332	10505	20808	10209	21293	16
	11421	19412	11109	19872	10802	20340	10500	20816	10204	21301	
15	11416	19420	11104	19880	10797	20348	10496	20824	10199	21309	15
	11411	19428	11099	19888	10792	20356	10491	20832	10195	21318	
16	11406	19435	11094	19895	10787	20364	10486	20840	10190	21326	14
	11400	19443	11088	19903	10782	20371	10481	20848	10185	21334	
17	11395	19450	11083	19911	10777	20379	10476	20856	10180	21342	13
	11390	19458	11078	19918	10772	20387	10471	20864	10175	21350	
18	11385	19466	11073	19926	10767	20395	10466	20872	10170	21358	12
	11380	19473	11068	19934	10761	20403	10461	20880	10165	21367	
19	11374	19481	11063	19942	10756	20411	10456	20888	10160	21375	11
	11369	19488	11057	19949	10751	20419	10451	20897	10155	21383	
20	11364	19496	11052	19957	10746	20427	10446	20905	10151	21391	10
	11359	19504	11047	19965	10741	20435	10441	20913	10146	21399	
21	11353	19511	11042	19973	10736	20442	10436	20921	10141	21407	9
	11348	19519	11037	19980	10731	20450	10431	20929	10136	21416	
22	11343	19527	11032	19988	10726	20458	10426	20937	10131	21424	8
	11338	19534	11027	19996	10721	20466	10421	20945	10126	21432	
23	11332	19542	11021	20004	10716	20474	10416	20953	10121	21440	7
	11327	19549	11016	20012	10711	20482	10411	20961	10116	21448	
24	11322	19557	11011	20019	10706	20490	10406	20969	10112	21457	6
	11317	19565	11006	20027	10701	20498	10401	20977	10107	21465	
25	11311	19572	11001	20035	10696	20506	10396	20985	10102	21473	5
	11306	19580	10996	20043	10691	20514	10391	20993	10097	21481	
26	11301	19588	10991	20050	10686	20522	10386	21001	10092	21489	4
	11296	19595	10986	20058	10681	20529	10381	21009	10087	21498	
27	11291	19603	10980	20066	10676	20537	10376	21017	10082	21506	3
	11285	19611	10975	20074	10671	20545	10372	21025	10078	21514	
28	11280	19618	10970	20082	10666	20553	10367	21033	10073	21522	2
	11275	19626	10965	20089	10661	20561	10362	21042	10068	21531	
29	11270	19634	10960	20097	10656	20569	10357	21050	10063	21539	1
	11265	19641	10955	20105	10651	20577	10352	21058	10058	21547	
30	11259	19649	10950	20113	10646	20585	10347	21066	10053	21555	0
	A	B	A	B	A	B	A	B	A	B	
′	129° 30′		129° 00′		128° 30′		128° 00′		127° 30′		′

′	52° 30′ A	52° 30′ B	53° 00′ A	53° 00′ B	53° 30′ A	53° 30′ B	54° 00′ A	54° 00′ B	54° 30′ A	54° 30′ B	′
0	10053	21555	9765	22054	9482	22561	9204	23078	8931	23605	30
	10049	21563	9760	22062	9477	22570	9200	23087	8927	23613	
1	10044	21572	9756	22070	9473	22578	9195	23095	8922	23622	29
	10039	21580	9751	22079	9468	22587	9190	23104	8918	23631	
2	10034	21588	9746	22087	9463	22595	9186	23113	8913	23640	28
	10029	21596	9741	22096	9459	22604	9181	23122	8909	23649	
3	10024	21605	9737	22104	9454	22612	9177	23130	8904	23658	27
	10019	21613	9732	22112	9449	22621	9172	23139	8900	23667	
4	10015	21621	9727	22121	9445	22630	9168	23148	8895	23675	26
	10010	21629	9722	22129	9440	22638	9163	23156	8891	23684	
5	10005	21638	9718	22138	9435	22647	9158	23165	8886	23693	25
	10000	21646	9713	22146	9431	22655	9154	23174	8882	23702	
6	9995	21654	9708	22154	9426	22664	9149	23183	8877	23711	24
	9990	21662	9703	22163	9421	22672	9145	23191	8873	23720	
7	9986	21671	9699	22171	9417	22681	9140	23200	8868	23729	23
	9981	21679	9694	22180	9412	22690	9136	23209	8864	23738	
8	9976	21687	9689	22188	9407	22698	9131	23218	8859	23747	22
	9971	21696	9684	22197	9403	22707	9126	23226	8855	23755	
9	9966	21704	9680	22205	9398	22715	9122	23235	8850	23764	21
	9962	21712	9675	22213	9394	22724	9117	23244	8846	23773	
10	9957	21720	9670	22222	9389	22732	9113	23252	8842	23782	20
	9952	21729	9665	22230	9384	22741	9108	23261	8837	23791	
11	9947	21737	9661	22239	9380	22750	9104	23270	8833	23800	19
	9942	21745	9656	22247	9375	22758	9099	23279	8828	23809	
12	9937	21754	9651	22256	9370	22767	9094	23288	8824	23818	18
	9933	21762	9647	22264	9366	22775	9090	23296	8819	23827	
13	9928	21770	9642	22272	9361	22784	9085	23305	8815	23836	17
	9923	21778	9637	22281	9356	22793	9081	23314	8810	23845	
14	9918	21787	9632	22289	9352	22801	9076	23323	8806	23854	16
	9913	21795	9628	22298	9347	22810	9072	23331	8801	23863	
15	9909	21803	9623	22306	9342	22818	9067	23340	8797	23871	15
	9904	21812	9618	22315	9338	22827	9063	23349	8792	23880	
16	9899	21820	9614	22323	9333	22836	9058	23358	8788	23889	14
	9894	21828	9609	22332	9329	22844	9054	23366	8783	23898	
17	9889	21837	9604	22340	9324	22853	9049	23375	8779	23907	13
	9885	21845	9599	22349	9319	22862	9044	23384	8775	23916	
18	9880	21853	9595	22357	9315	22870	9040	23393	8770	23925	12
	9875	21862	9590	22366	9310	22879	9035	23402	8766	23934	
19	9870	21870	9585	22374	9305	22887	9031	23410	8761	23943	11
	9865	21878	9581	22382	9301	22896	9026	23419	8757	23952	
20	9861	21887	9576	22391	9296	22905	9022	23428	8752	23961	10
	9856	21895	9571	22399	9292	22913	9017	23437	8748	23970	
21	9851	21903	9566	22408	9287	22922	9013	23446	8743	23979	9
	9846	21912	9562	22416	9282	22931	9008	23454	8739	23988	
22	9841	21920	9557	22425	9278	22939	9004	23463	8734	23997	8
	9837	21928	9552	22433	9273	22948	8999	23472	8730	24006	
23	9832	21937	9548	22442	9269	22957	8995	23481	8726	24015	7
	9827	21945	9543	22450	9264	22965	8990	23490	8721	24024	
24	9822	21953	9538	22459	9259	22974	8985	23498	8717	24033	6
	9818	21962	9534	22467	9255	22983	8981	23507	8712	24042	
25	9813	21970	9529	22476	9250	22991	8976	23516	8708	24051	5
	9808	21978	9524	22484	9246	23000	8972	23525	8703	24060	
26	9803	21987	9520	22493	9241	23009	8967	23534	8699	24069	4
	9798	21995	9515	22501	9236	23017	8963	23543	8694	24078	
27	9794	22003	9510	22510	9232	23026	8958	23551	8690	24087	3
	9789	22012	9505	22519	9227	23035	8954	23560	8686	24096	
28	9784	22020	9501	22527	9223	23043	8949	23569	8681	24105	2
	9779	22029	9496	22536	9218	23052	8945	23578	8677	24114	
29	9775	22037	9491	22544	9213	23061	8940	23587	8672	24123	1
	9770	22045	9487	22553	9209	23069	8936	23596	8668	24132	
30	9765	22054	9482	22561	9204	23078	8931	23605	8663	24141	0
	A	B	A	B	A	B	A	B	A	B	
′	127° 00′		126° 30′		126° 00′		125° 30′		125° 00′		′

WHEN LHA (E OR W) IS <u>GREATER</u> THAN 90°, TAKE "K" FROM <u>BOTTOM</u> OF TABLE

′	55° 00′ A	B	55° 30′ A	B	56° 00′ A	B	56° 30′ A	B	57° 00′ A	B	′
0	8663	24141	8401	24687	8143	25244	7889	25811	7641	26389	30
	8659	24150	8396	24696	8138	25253	7885	25821	7637	26399	
1	8655	24159	8392	24706	8134	25263	7881	25830	7633	26409	29
	8650	24168	8388	24715	8130	25272	7877	25840	7629	26418	
2	8646	24177	8383	24724	8125	25281	7873	25849	7624	26428	28
	8641	24186	8379	24733	8121	25291	7868	25859	7620	26438	
3	8637	24195	8375	24742	8117	25300	7864	25868	7616	26447	27
	8633	24204	8370	24752	8113	25309	7860	25878	7612	26457	
4	8628	24213	8366	24761	8108	25319	7856	25887	7608	26467	26
	8624	24222	8362	24770	8104	25328	7852	25897	7604	26477	
5	8619	24231	8357	24779	8100	25338	7848	25907	7600	26486	25
	8615	24240	8353	24788	8096	25347	7843	25916	7596	26496	
6	8611	24249	8349	24798	8092	25356	7839	25926	7592	26506	24
	8606	24258	8344	24807	8087	25366	7835	25935	7588	26516	
7	8602	24267	8340	24816	8083	25375	7831	25945	7584	26526	23
	8597	24276	8336	24825	8079	25385	7827	25954	7579	26535	
8	8593	24286	8331	24835	8075	25394	7823	25964	7575	26545	22
	8589	24295	8327	24844	8070	25403	7818	25974	7571	26555	
9	8584	24304	8323	24853	8066	25413	7814	25983	7567	26565	21
	8580	24313	8318	24862	8062	25422	7810	25993	7563	26574	
10	8575	24322	8314	24872	8058	25432	7806	26002	7559	26584	20
	8571	24331	8310	24881	8053	25441	7802	26012	7555	26594	
11	8567	24340	8305	24890	8049	25451	7798	26022	7551	26604	19
	8562	24349	8301	24899	8045	25460	7793	26031	7547	26614	
12	8558	24358	8297	24909	8041	25469	7789	26041	7543	26623	18
	8553	24367	8292	24918	8036	25479	7785	26051	7539	26633	
13	8549	24376	8288	24927	8032	25488	7781	26060	7535	26643	17
	8545	24385	8284	24936	8028	25498	7777	26070	7531	26653	
14	8540	24395	8280	24946	8024	25507	7773	26079	7526	26663	16
	8536	24404	8275	24955	8020	25517	7769	26089	7522	26672	
15	8531	24413	8271	24964	8015	25526	7764	26099	7518	26682	15
	8527	24422	8267	24973	8011	25536	7760	26108	7514	26692	
16	8523	24431	8262	24983	8007	25545	7756	26118	7510	26702	14
	8518	24440	8258	24992	8003	25554	7752	26128	7506	26712	
17	8514	24449	8254	25001	7998	25564	7748	26137	7502	26722	13
	8510	24458	8249	25011	7994	25573	7744	26147	7498	26731	
18	8505	24467	8245	25020	7990	25583	7740	26157	7494	26741	12
	8501	24477	8241	25029	7986	25592	7736	26166	7490	26751	
19	8496	24486	8237	25038	7982	25602	7731	26176	7486	26761	11
	8492	24495	8232	25048	7977	25611	7727	26185	7482	26771	
20	8488	24504	8228	25057	7973	25621	7723	26195	7478	26781	10
	8483	24513	8224	25066	7969	25630	7719	26205	7474	26790	
21	8479	24522	8219	25076	7965	25640	7715	26214	7470	26800	9
	8475	24531	8215	25085	7961	25649	7711	26224	7466	26810	
22	8470	24540	8211	25094	7956	25659	7707	26234	7462	26820	8
	8466	24550	8207	25104	7952	25668	7702	26244	7458	26830	
23	8461	24559	8202	25113	7948	25678	7698	26253	7453	26840	7
	8457	24568	8198	25122	7944	25687	7694	26263	7449	26850	
24	8453	24577	8194	25132	7940	25697	7690	26273	7445	26860	6
	8448	24586	8189	25141	7935	25706	7686	26282	7441	26869	
25	8444	24595	8185	25150	7931	25716	7682	26292	7437	26879	5
	8440	24605	8181	25160	7927	25725	7678	26302	7433	26889	
26	8435	24614	8177	25169	7923	25735	7674	26311	7429	26899	4
	8431	24623	8172	25178	7919	25744	7670	26321	7425	26909	
27	8427	24632	8168	25188	7914	25754	7665	26331	7421	26919	3
	8422	24641	8164	25197	7910	25763	7661	26340	7417	26929	
28	8418	24650	8160	25206	7906	25773	7657	26350	7413	26939	2
	8414	24660	8155	25216	7902	25782	7653	26360	7409	26949	
29	8409	24669	8151	25225	7898	25792	7649	26370	7405	26958	1
	8405	24678	8147	25234	7893	25801	7645	26379	7401	26968	
30	8401	24687	8143	25244	7889	25811	7641	26389	7397	26978	0
	A	B	A	B	A	B	A	B	A	B	′
′	124° 30′		124° 00′		123° 30′		123° 00′		122° 30′		

′	57° 30′		58° 00′		58° 30′		59° 00′		59° 30′		′
	A	B	A	B	A	B	A	B	A	B	
0	7397	26978	7158	27579	6923	28191	6693	28816	6468	29453	30
	7393	26988	7154	27589	6920	28202	6690	28827	6464	29464	
1	7389	26998	7150	27599	6916	28212	6686	28837	6460	29475	29
	7385	27008	7146	27609	6912	28222	6682	28848	6457	29485	
2	7381	27018	7142	27619	6908	28233	6678	28858	6453	29496	28
	7377	27028	7138	27630	6904	28243	6674	28869	6449	29507	
3	7373	27038	7134	27640	6900	28253	6671	28879	6446	29517	27
	7369	27048	7130	27650	6896	28264	6667	28890	6442	29528	
4	7365	27058	7126	27660	6892	28274	6663	28900	6438	29539	26
	7361	27068	7122	27670	6889	28284	6659	28911	6434	29550	
5	7357	27078	7118	27680	6885	28295	6655	28921	6431	29560	25
	7353	27088	7115	27690	6881	28305	6652	28932	6427	29571	
6	7349	27098	7111	27701	6877	28315	6648	28942	6423	29582	24
	7345	27107	7107	27711	6873	28326	6644	28953	6420	29593	
7	7341	27117	7103	27721	6869	28336	6640	28964	6416	29604	23
	7337	27127	7099	27731	6865	28346	6637	28974	6412	29614	
8	7333	27137	7095	27741	6862	28357	6633	28985	6409	29625	22
	7329	27147	7091	27751	6858	28367	6629	28995	6405	29636	
9	7325	27157	7087	27761	6854	28378	6625	29006	6401	29647	21
	7321	27167	7083	27772	6850	28388	6622	29016	6397	29657	
10	7317	27177	7079	27782	6846	28398	6618	29027	6394	29668	20
	7313	27187	7075	27792	6842	28409	6614	29038	6390	29679	
11	7309	27197	7071	27802	6839	28419	6610	29048	6386	29690	19
	7305	27207	7068	27812	6835	28429	6607	29059	6383	29701	
12	7301	27217	7064	27823	6831	28440	6603	29069	6379	29711	18
	7297	27227	7060	27833	6827	28450	6599	29080	6375	29722	
13	7293	27237	7056	27843	6823	28461	6595	29091	6372	29733	17
	7289	27247	7052	27853	6819	28471	6591	29101	6368	29744	
14	7285	27257	7048	27863	6815	28481	6588	29112	6364	29755	16
	7281	27267	7044	27874	6812	28492	6584	29122	6361	29766	
15	7277	27277	7040	27884	6808	28502	6580	29133	6357	29776	15
	7273	27287	7036	27894	6804	28513	6576	29144	6353	29787	
16	7269	27297	7032	27904	6800	28523	6573	29154	6349	29798	14
	7265	27307	7028	27914	6796	28533	6569	29165	6346	29809	
17	7261	27317	7024	27925	6792	28544	6565	29175	6342	29820	13
	7257	27327	7021	27935	6789	28554	6561	29186	6338	29831	
18	7253	27337	7017	27945	6785	28565	6558	29197	6335	29841	12
	7249	27347	7013	27955	6781	28575	6554	29207	6331	29852	
19	7245	27357	7009	27965	6777	28586	6550	29218	6327	29863	11
	7241	27367	7005	27976	6773	28596	6546	29229	6324	29874	
20	7237	27377	7001	27986	6770	28607	6543	29239	6320	29885	10
	7233	27387	6997	27996	6766	28617	6539	29250	6316	29896	
21	7229	27398	6993	28006	6762	28627	6535	29261	6313	29907	9
	7225	27408	6989	28017	6758	28638	6531	29271	6309	29917	
22	7221	27418	6985	28027	6754	28648	6528	29282	6305	29929	8
	7217	27428	6982	28037	6750	28659	6524	29293	6302	29939	
23	7213	27438	6978	28047	6747	28669	6520	29303	6298	29950	7
	7209	27448	6974	28058	6743	28680	6516	29314	6294	29961	
24	7205	27458	6970	28068	6739	28690	6513	29325	6291	29972	6
	7201	27468	6966	28078	6735	28701	6509	29335	6287	29983	
25	7197	27478	6962	28089	6731	28711	6505	29346	6283	29994	5
	7193	27488	6958	28099	6728	28722	6502	29357	6280	30005	
26	7190	27498	6954	28109	6724	28732	6498	29367	6276	30015	4
	7186	27508	6951	28119	6720	28743	6494	29378	6272	30026	
27	7182	27518	6947	28130	6716	28753	6490	29389	6269	30037	3
	7178	27528	6943	28140	6712	28763	6487	29399	6265	30048	
28	7174	27539	6939	28150	6709	28774	6483	29410	6261	30059	2
	7170	27549	6935	28161	6705	28784	6479	29421	6258	30070	
29	7166	27559	6931	28171	6701	28795	6475	29432	6254	30081	1
	7162	27569	6927	28181	6697	28806	6472	29442	6251	30092	
30	7158	27579	6923	28191	6693	28816	6468	29453	6247	30103	0
	A	B	A	B	A	B	A	B	A	B	
′	122° 00′		121° 30′		121° 00′		120° 30′		120° 00′		′

WHEN LHA (E OR W) IS <u>GREATER</u> THAN 90°, TAKE "K" FROM <u>BOTTOM</u> OF TABLE

′	60° 00′ A	60° 00′ B	60° 30′ A	60° 30′ B	61° 00′ A	61° 00′ B	61° 30′ A	61° 30′ B	62° 00′ A	62° 00′ B	′
0	6247	30103	6030	30766	5818	31443	5610	32134	5406	32839	30
	6243	30114	6027	30777	5815	31454	5607	32145	5403	32851	
1	6240	30125	6023	30788	5811	31466	5603	32157	5400	32863	29
	6236	30136	6020	30800	5808	31477	5600	32169	5396	32875	
2	6232	30147	6016	30811	5804	31488	5596	32180	5393	32887	28
	6229	30158	6012	30822	5801	31500	5593	32192	5390	32898	
3	6225	30169	6009	30833	5797	31511	5590	32204	5386	32910	27
	6221	30180	6005	30844	5794	31523	5586	32215	5383	32922	
4	6218	30191	6002	30856	5790	31534	5583	32227	5380	32934	26
	6214	30202	5998	30867	5787	31546	5579	32239	5376	32946	
5	6210	30213	5995	30878	5783	31557	5575	32250	5373	32958	25
	6207	30224	5991	30889	5780	31569	5572	32262	5370	32970	
6	6203	30235	5987	30900	5776	31580	5569	32274	5366	32982	24
	6200	30245	5984	30912	5773	31591	5566	32285	5363	32994	
7	6196	30256	5980	30923	5769	31603	5562	32297	5360	33006	23
	6192	30267	5977	30934	5766	31614	5559	32309	5356	33018	
8	6189	30278	5973	30945	5762	31626	5555	32320	5353	33030	22
	6185	30289	5970	30956	5759	31637	5552	32332	5350	33042	
9	6181	30300	5966	30968	5755	31649	5549	32344	5346	33054	21
	6178	30311	5963	30979	5752	31660	5545	32355	5343	33065	
10	6174	30322	5959	30990	5748	31672	5542	32367	5340	33077	20
	6171	30334	5955	31001	5745	31683	5538	32379	5336	33089	
11	6167	30345	5952	31013	5741	31694	5535	32391	5333	33101	19
	6163	30355	5948	31024	5738	31706	5532	32402	5330	33113	
12	6160	30367	5945	31035	5734	31717	5528	32414	5326	33125	18
	6156	30378	5941	31046	5731	31729	5525	32426	5323	33137	
13	6152	30389	5938	31058	5727	31740	5521	32438	5320	33149	17
	6149	30400	5934	31069	5724	31752	5518	32449	5316	33161	
14	6145	30411	5931	31080	5720	31763	5515	32461	5313	33173	16
	6142	30422	5927	31091	5717	31775	5511	32473	5310	33185	
15	6138	30433	5924	31103	5714	31786	5508	32484	5306	33197	15
	6134	30444	5920	31114	5710	31798	5504	32496	5303	33209	
16	6131	30455	5917	31125	5707	31809	5501	32508	5300	33221	14
	6127	30466	5913	31137	5703	31821	5498	32520	5296	33233	
17	6124	30477	5909	31148	5700	31833	5494	32532	5293	33245	13
	6120	30488	5906	31159	5696	31844	5491	32543	5290	33257	
18	6116	30499	5902	31170	5693	31856	5487	32555	5286	33269	12
	6113	30510	5899	31182	5689	31867	5484	32567	5283	33281	
19	6109	30521	5895	31193	5686	31879	5481	32579	5280	33293	11
	6106	30532	5892	31204	5682	31890	5477	32590	5276	33306	
20	6102	30544	5888	31216	5679	31902	5474	32602	5273	33318	10
	6098	30555	5885	31227	5675	31913	5470	32614	5270	33330	
21	6095	30566	5881	31238	5672	31925	5467	32625	5266	33342	9
	6091	30577	5878	31250	5669	31936	5464	32638	5263	33354	
22	6088	30588	5874	31261	5665	31948	5460	32649	5260	33366	8
	6084	30599	5871	31272	5662	31960	5457	32661	5257	33378	
23	6080	30610	5867	31284	5658	31971	5454	32673	5253	33390	7
	6077	30621	5864	31295	5655	31983	5450	32685	5250	33402	
24	6073	30632	5860	31306	5651	31994	5447	32697	5247	33414	6
	6070	30643	5857	31318	5648	32006	5443	32709	5243	33426	
25	6066	30655	5853	31329	5644	32018	5440	32720	5240	33438	5
	6062	30666	5850	31340	5641	32029	5437	32732	5237	33450	
26	6059	30677	5846	31352	5638	32041	5433	32744	5233	33462	4
	6055	30688	5843	31363	5634	32052	5430	32756	5230	33475	
27	6052	30699	5839	31375	5631	32064	5427	32768	5227	33487	3
	6048	30710	5836	31386	5627	32076	5423	32780	5224	33499	
28	6045	30721	5832	31397	5624	32087	5420	32792	5220	33511	2
	6041	30733	5829	31409	5620	32099	5417	32803	5217	33523	
29	6037	30744	5825	31420	5617	32110	5413	32815	5214	33535	1
	6034	30755	5822	31431	5614	32122	5410	32827	5210	33547	
30	6030	30766	5818	31443	5610	32134	5406	32839	5207	33559	0
′	A	B	A	B	A	B	A	B	A	B	′
	119° 30′		119° 00′		118° 30′		118° 00′		117° 30′		

ALWAYS TAKE "Z" FROM BOTTOM OF TABLE, EXCEPT WHEN "K" IS SAME NAME AND GREATER THAN LATITUDE, IN WHICH CASE TAKE "Z" FROM TOP OF TABLE

′	62° 30′ A	B	63° 00′ A	B	63° 30′ A	B	64° 00′ A	B	64° 30′ A	B	′
0	5207	33559	5012	34295	4821	35047	4634	35816	4451	36602	30
	5204	33572	5009	34308	4818	35060	4631	35829	4448	36615	
1	5200	33584	5005	34320	4815	35073	4628	35842	4445	36628	29
	5197	33596	5002	34332	4811	35085	4625	35855	4442	36641	
2	5194	33608	4999	34345	4808	35098	4622	35868	4439	36655	28
	5191	33620	4996	34357	4805	35111	4619	35881	4436	36668	
3	5187	33632	4993	34370	4802	35123	4615	35894	4433	36681	27
	5184	33644	4989	34382	4799	35136	4612	35907	4430	36694	
4	5181	33657	4986	34395	4796	35149	4609	35920	4427	36708	26
	5178	33669	4983	34407	4793	35161	4606	35933	4424	36721	
5	5174	33681	4980	34420	4789	35174	4603	35946	4421	36734	25
	5171	33693	4977	34432	4786	35187	4600	35959	4418	36747	
6	5168	33705	4973	34444	4783	35200	4597	35972	4415	36761	24
	5164	33717	4970	34457	4780	35212	4594	35985	4412	36774	
7	5161	33730	4967	34469	4777	35225	4591	35998	4409	36787	23
	5158	33742	4964	34482	4774	35238	4588	36011	4406	36801	
8	5155	33754	4961	34494	4771	35251	4585	36024	4403	36814	22
	5151	33766	4957	34507	4767	35263	4582	36037	4400	36827	
9	5148	33779	4954	34519	4764	35276	4579	36050	4397	36841	21
	5145	33791	4951	34532	4761	35289	4576	36063	4394	36854	
10	5142	33803	4948	34544	4758	35302	4573	36076	4391	36867	20
	5138	33815	4945	34557	4755	35314	4569	36089	4388	36881	
11	5135	33827	4941	34569	4752	35327	4566	36102	4385	36894	19
	5132	33840	4938	34582	4749	35340	4563	36115	4382	36907	
12	5128	33852	4935	34594	4746	35353	4560	36128	4379	36921	18
	5125	33864	4932	34607	4742	35365	4557	36141	4376	36934	
13	5122	33876	4929	34619	4739	35378	4554	36154	4373	36948	17
	5119	33889	4925	34632	4736	35391	4551	36167	4370	36961	
14	5115	33901	4922	34644	4733	35404	4548	36180	4367	36974	16
	5112	33913	4919	34657	4730	35417	4545	36193	4364	36988	
15	5109	33925	4916	34669	4727	35429	4542	36206	4361	37001	15
	5106	33938	4913	34682	4724	35442	4539	36220	4358	37014	
16	5102	33950	4910	34694	4721	35455	4536	36233	4355	37028	14
	5099	33962	4906	34707	4718	35468	4533	36246	4352	37041	
17	5096	33974	4903	34719	4714	35481	4530	36259	4349	37055	13
	5093	33987	4900	34732	4711	35493	4527	36272	4346	37068	
18	5089	33999	4897	34744	4708	35506	4524	36285	4343	37081	12
	5086	34011	4894	34757	4705	35519	4521	36298	4340	37095	
19	5083	34024	4890	34770	4702	35532	4518	36311	4337	37108	11
	5080	34036	4887	34782	4699	35545	4515	36325	4334	37122	
20	5076	34048	4884	34795	4696	35558	4512	36338	4332	37135	10
	5073	34061	4881	34807	4693	35571	4509	36351	4329	37149	
21	5070	34073	4878	34820	4690	35583	4506	36364	4326	37162	9
	5067	34085	4875	34832	4686	35596	4503	36377	4323	37176	
22	5064	34097	4871	34845	4683	35609	4500	36390	4320	37189	8
	5060	34110	4868	34858	4680	35622	4497	36403	4317	37203	
23	5057	34122	4865	34870	4677	35635	4493	36417	4314	37216	7
	5054	34134	4862	34883	4674	35648	4490	36430	4311	37229	
24	5051	34147	4859	34896	4671	35661	4487	36443	4308	37243	6
	5047	34159	4856	34908	4668	35674	4484	36456	4305	37256	
25	5044	34172	4852	34921	4665	35686	4481	36469	4302	37270	5
	5041	34184	4849	34933	4662	35699	4478	36483	4299	37283	
26	5038	34196	4846	34946	4659	35712	4475	36496	4296	37297	4
	5034	34209	4843	34959	4656	35725	4472	36509	4293	37310	
27	5031	34221	4840	34971	4652	35738	4469	36522	4290	37324	3
	5028	34233	4837	34984	4649	35751	4466	36535	4287	37337	
28	5025	34246	4833	34997	4646	35764	4463	36549	4284	37351	2
	5022	34258	4830	35009	4643	35777	4460	36562	4281	37365	
29	5018	34270	4827	35022	4640	35790	4457	36575	4278	37378	1
	5015	34283	4824	35035	4637	35803	4454	36588	4275	37392	
30	5012	34295	4821	35047	4634	35816	4451	36602	4272	37405	0
	A	B	A	B	A	B	A	B	A	B	
′	117° 00′		116° 30′		116° 00′		115° 30′		115° 00′		′

WHEN LHA (E OR W) IS GREATER THAN 90°, TAKE "K" FROM BOTTOM OF TABLE

′	65° 00′		65° 30′		66° 00′		66° 30′		67° 00′		′
	A	B	A	B	A	B	A	B	A	B	
0	4272	37405	4098	38227	3927	39069	3760	39930	3597	40812	30
	4269	37419	4095	38241	3924	39083	3757	39945	3595	40827	
1	4266	37432	4092	38255	3921	39097	3755	39959	3592	40842	29
	4264	37446	4089	38269	3918	39111	3752	39974	3589	40857	
2	4261	37459	4086	38283	3916	39125	3749	39988	3587	40872	28
	4258	37473	4083	38297	3913	39140	3746	40003	3584	40887	
3	4255	37487	4080	38311	3910	39154	3744	40017	3581	40902	27
	4252	37500	4078	38324	3907	39168	3741	40032	3579	40916	
4	4249	37514	4075	38338	3904	39182	3738	40046	3576	40931	26
	4246	37527	4072	38352	3902	39197	3735	40061	3573	40946	
5	4243	37541	4069	38366	3899	39211	3733	40076	3571	40961	25
	4240	37554	4066	38380	3896	39225	3730	40090	3568	40976	
6	4237	37568	4063	38394	3893	39239	3727	40105	3565	40991	24
	4234	37582	4060	38408	3890	39254	3725	40119	3563	41006	
7	4231	37595	4057	38422	3888	39268	3722	40134	3560	41021	23
	4228	37609	4055	38436	3885	39282	3719	40149	3557	41036	
8	4225	37623	4052	38450	3882	39296	3716	40163	3555	41051	22
	4222	37636	4049	38464	3879	39311	3714	40178	3552	41066	
9	4220	37650	4046	38478	3876	39325	3711	40192	3549	41081	21
	4217	37663	4043	38492	3874	39339	3708	40207	3547	41096	
10	4214	37677	4040	38506	3871	39353	3705	40222	3544	41111	20
	4211	37691	4037	38520	3868	39368	3703	40236	3541	41126	
11	4208	37704	4035	38533	3865	39382	3700	40251	3539	41141	19
	4205	37718	4032	38547	3863	39396	3697	40266	3536	41156	
12	4202	37732	4029	38561	3860	39411	3695	40280	3533	41171	18
	4199	37745	4026	38575	3857	39425	3692	40295	3531	41186	
13	4196	37759	4023	38589	3854	39439	3689	40310	3528	41201	17
	4193	37773	4020	38603	3851	39454	3686	40324	3525	41216	
14	4190	37786	4017	38617	3849	39468	3684	40339	3523	41231	16
	4187	37800	4015	38631	3846	39482	3681	40354	3520	41246	
15	4185	37814	4012	38645	3843	39497	3678	40368	3517	41261	15
	4182	37828	4009	38660	3840	39511	3676	40383	3515	41276	
16	4179	37841	4006	38674	3838	39525	3673	40398	3512	41291	14
	4176	37855	4003	38688	3835	39540	3670	40413	3509	41307	
17	4173	37869	4000	38702	3832	39554	3667	40427	3507	41322	13
	4170	37882	3998	38716	3829	39569	3665	40442	3504	41337	
18	4167	37896	3995	38730	3826	39583	3662	40457	3502	41352	12
	4164	37910	3992	38744	3824	39597	3659	40471	3499	41367	
19	4161	37924	3989	38758	3821	39612	3657	40486	3496	41382	11
	4158	37937	3986	38772	3818	39626	3654	40501	3494	41397	
20	4155	37951	3983	38786	3815	39641	3651	40516	3491	41412	10
	4153	37965	3981	38800	3813	39655	3648	40530	3488	41427	
21	4150	37979	3978	38814	3810	39669	3646	40545	3486	41443	9
	4147	37992	3975	38828	3807	39684	3643	40560	3483	41458	
22	4144	38006	3972	38842	3804	39698	3640	40575	3480	41473	8
	4141	38020	3969	38856	3801	39713	3638	40590	3478	41488	
23	4138	38034	3966	38871	3799	39727	3635	40604	3475	41503	7
	4135	38048	3964	38885	3796	39742	3632	40619	3473	41518	
24	4132	38061	3961	38899	3793	39756	3630	40634	3470	41533	6
	4129	38075	3958	38913	3790	39771	3627	40649	3467	41549	
25	4127	38089	3955	38927	3788	39785	3624	40664	3465	41564	5
	4124	38103	3952	38941	3785	39799	3622	40678	3462	41579	
26	4121	38117	3949	38955	3782	39814	3619	40693	3459	41594	4
	4118	38130	3947	38969	3779	39828	3616	40708	3457	41609	
27	4115	38144	3944	38984	3777	39843	3613	40723	3454	41625	3
	4112	38158	3941	38998	3774	39857	3611	40738	3452	41640	
28	4109	38172	3938	39012	3771	39872	3608	40753	3449	41655	2
	4106	38186	3935	39026	3768	39886	3605	40768	3446	41670	
29	4103	38200	3933	39040	3766	39901	3603	40782	3444	41685	1
	4101	38213	3930	39054	3763	39915	3600	40797	3441	41701	
30	4098	38227	3927	39069	3760	39930	3597	40812	3438	41716	0
	A	B	A	B	A	B	A	B	A	B	
′	114° 30′		114° 00′		113° 30′		113° 00′		112° 30′		′

′	67° 30′		68° 00′		68° 30′		69° 00′		69° 30′		′
	A	B	A	B	A	B	A	B	A	B	
0	3438	41716	3283	42642	3132	43592	2985	44567	2841	45567	30
	3436	41731	3281	42658	3130	43608	2982	44583	2839	45584	
1	3433	41746	3278	42674	3127	43624	2980	44600	2836	45601	29
	3431	41762	3276	42689	3125	43641	2978	44616	2834	45618	
2	3428	41777	3273	42705	3122	43657	2975	44633	2832	45635	28
	3425	41792	3271	42721	3120	43673	2973	44649	2829	45652	
3	3423	41808	3268	42736	3117	43689	2970	44666	2827	45669	27
	3420	41823	3266	42752	3115	43705	2968	44682	2825	45686	
4	3418	41838	3263	42768	3112	43721	2965	44699	2822	45703	26
	3415	41853	3260	42783	3110	43737	2963	44715	2820	45720	
5	3412	41869	3258	42799	3107	43753	2961	44732	2818	45737	25
	3410	41884	3255	42815	3105	43769	2958	44748	2815	45754	
6	3407	41899	3253	42830	3102	43785	2956	44765	2813	45771	24
	3404	41915	3250	42846	3100	43801	2953	44782	2811	45788	
7	3402	41930	3248	42862	3097	43818	2951	44798	2808	45805	23
	3399	41945	3245	42878	3095	43834	2949	44815	2806	45822	
8	3397	41961	3243	42893	3092	43850	2946	44831	2804	45839	22
	3394	41976	3240	42909	3090	43866	2944	44848	2801	45856	
9	3391	41991	3237	42925	3088	43882	2941	44864	2799	45873	21
	3389	42007	3235	42941	3085	43898	2939	44881	2797	45890	
10	3386	42022	3233	42956	3083	43914	2936	44898	2794	45907	20
	3384	42038	3230	42972	3080	43931	2934	44914	2792	45924	
11	3381	42053	3227	42988	3078	43947	2932	44931	2789	45941	19
	3379	42068	3225	43004	3075	43963	2929	44947	2787	45958	
12	3376	42084	3222	43020	3073	43979	2927	44964	2785	45975	18
	3373	42099	3220	43035	3070	43995	2924	44981	2782	45992	
13	3371	42115	3217	43051	3068	44012	2922	44997	2780	46009	17
	3368	42130	3215	43067	3065	44028	2920	45014	2778	46026	
14	3366	42145	3212	43083	3063	44044	2917	45031	2775	46043	16
	3363	42161	3210	43099	3060	44060	2915	45047	2773	46061	
15	3360	42176	3207	43114	3058	44077	2913	45064	2771	46078	15
	3358	42192	3205	43130	3056	44093	2910	45081	2768	46095	
16	3355	42207	3202	43146	3053	44109	2908	45097	2766	46112	14
	3353	42223	3200	43162	3051	44125	2905	45114	2764	46129	
17	3350	42238	3197	43178	3048	44142	2903	45131	2761	46146	13
	3348	42254	3195	43194	3046	44158	2901	45147	2759	46163	
18	3345	42269	3192	43210	3043	44174	2898	45164	2757	46181	12
	3342	42285	3190	43225	3041	44190	2896	45181	2755	46198	
19	3340	42300	3187	43241	3038	44207	2893	45198	2752	46215	11
	3337	42316	3185	43257	3036	44223	2891	45214	2750	46232	
20	3335	42331	3182	43273	3033	44239	2889	45231	2748	46249	10
	3332	42347	3180	43289	3031	44256	2886	45248	2745	46266	
21	3329	42362	3177	43305	3029	44272	2884	45265	2743	46284	9
	3327	42378	3175	43321	3026	44288	2881	45281	2741	46301	
22	3324	42393	3172	43337	3024	44305	2879	45298	2738	46318	8
	3322	42409	3170	43353	3021	44321	2877	45315	2736	46335	
23	3319	42424	3167	43369	3019	44337	2874	45332	2734	46353	7
	3317	42440	3165	43385	3016	44354	2872	45348	2731	46370	
24	3314	42455	3162	43400	3014	44370	2870	45365	2729	46387	6
	3312	42471	3160	43416	3012	44386	2867	45382	2727	46404	
25	3309	42486	3157	43432	3009	44403	2865	45399	2724	46422	5
	3306	42502	3155	43448	3007	44419	2862	45416	2722	46439	
26	3304	42518	3152	43464	3004	44436	2860	45433	2720	46456	4
	3301	42533	3150	43480	3002	44452	2858	45449	2717	46473	
27	3299	42549	3147	43496	2999	44468	2855	45466	2715	46491	3
	3296	42564	3145	43512	2997	44485	2853	45483	2713	46508	
28	3294	42580	3142	43528	2994	44501	2851	45500	2711	46525	2
	3291	42596	3140	43544	2992	44518	2848	45517	2708	46543	
29	3289	42611	3137	43560	2990	44534	2846	45534	2706	46560	1
	3286	42627	3135	43576	2987	44551	2844	45551	2704	46577	
30	3283	42642	3132	43592	2985	44567	2841	45567	2701	46595	0
	A	B	A	B	A	B	A	B	A	B	
′	112° 00′		111° 30′		111° 00′		110° 30′		110° 00′		′

297

WHEN LHA (E OR W) IS **GREATER** THAN 90°, TAKE **"K"** FROM **BOTTOM** OF TABLE

′	70° 00′ A	70° 00′ B	70° 30′ A	70° 30′ B	71° 00′ A	71° 00′ B	71° 30′ A	71° 30′ B	72° 00′ A	72° 00′ B	′
0	2701	46595	2565	47650	2433	48736	2304	49852	2179	51002	30
	2699	46612	2563	47668	2431	48754	2302	49871	2177	51021	
1	2697	46630	2561	47686	2429	48772	2300	49890	2175	51041	29
	2694	46647	2559	47704	2427	48791	2298	49909	2173	51060	
2	2692	46664	2556	47722	2424	48809	2296	49928	2171	51080	28
	2690	46682	2554	47740	2422	48828	2294	49947	2169	51099	
3	2688	46699	2552	47758	2420	48846	2292	49966	2167	51119	27
	2685	46716	2550	47775	2418	48864	2290	49985	2165	51138	
4	2683	46734	2547	47793	2416	48883	2287	50004	2163	51158	26
	2681	46751	2545	47811	2413	48901	2285	50023	2161	51177	
5	2678	46769	2543	47829	2411	48920	2283	50042	2159	51197	25
	2676	46786	2541	47847	2409	48938	2281	50061	2157	51216	
6	2674	46804	2539	47865	2407	48957	2279	50080	2155	51236	24
	2672	46821	2536	47883	2405	48975	2277	50098	2153	51255	
7	2669	46839	2534	47901	2403	48993	2275	50117	2151	51275	23
	2667	46856	2532	47919	2400	49012	2273	50137	2149	51294	
8	2665	46873	2530	47937	2398	49030	2271	50156	2147	51314	22
	2662	46891	2528	47955	2396	49049	2269	50175	2145	51334	
9	2660	46908	2525	47973	2394	49067	2266	50194	2143	51353	21
	2658	46926	2523	47991	2392	49086	2264	50213	2141	51373	
10	2656	46943	2521	48009	2390	49104	2262	50232	2138	51392	20
	2653	46961	2519	48027	2387	49123	2260	50251	2136	51412	
11	2651	46978	2516	48045	2385	49141	2258	50270	2134	51432	19
	2649	46996	2514	48063	2383	49160	2256	50289	2132	51451	
12	2646	47014	2512	48081	2381	49179	2254	50308	2130	51471	18
	2644	47031	2510	48099	2379	49197	2252	50327	2128	51491	
13	2642	47049	2507	48117	2377	49216	2250	50346	2126	51510	17
	2640	47066	2505	48135	2375	49234	2248	50365	2124	51530	
14	2637	47084	2503	48153	2372	49253	2246	50385	2122	51550	16
	2635	47101	2501	48171	2370	49271	2243	50404	2120	51570	
15	2633	47119	2499	48189	2368	49290	2241	50423	2118	51589	15
	2631	47137	2496	48207	2366	49309	2239	50442	2116	51609	
16	2628	47154	2494	48226	2364	49327	2237	50461	2114	51629	14
	2626	47172	2492	48244	2362	49346	2235	50480	2112	51649	
17	2624	47189	2490	48262	2360	49365	2233	50499	2110	51668	13
	2622	47207	2488	48280	2358	49383	2231	50519	2108	51688	
18	2619	47225	2485	48298	2355	49402	2229	50538	2106	51708	12
	2617	47242	2483	48316	2353	49421	2227	50557	2104	51728	
19	2615	47260	2481	48334	2351	49439	2225	50576	2102	51747	11
	2613	47278	2479	48352	2349	49458	2223	50596	2100	51767	
20	2610	47295	2477	48371	2347	49477	2221	50615	2098	51787	10
	2608	47313	2474	48389	2345	49495	2218	50634	2096	51807	
21	2606	47331	2472	48407	2343	49514	2216	50653	2094	51827	9
	2604	47348	2470	48425	2340	49533	2214	50673	2092	51847	
22	2601	47366	2468	48443	2338	49551	2212	50692	2090	51867	8
	2599	47384	2466	48462	2336	49570	2210	50711	2088	51886	
23	2597	47402	2463	48480	2334	49589	2208	50730	2086	51906	7
	2594	47419	2461	48498	2332	49608	2206	50750	2084	51926	
24	2592	47437	2459	48516	2330	49626	2204	50769	2082	51946	6
	2590	47455	2457	48534	2328	49645	2202	50788	2080	51966	
25	2588	47472	2455	48553	2325	49664	2200	50808	2078	51986	5
	2585	47490	2453	48571	2323	49683	2198	50827	2076	52006	
26	2583	47508	2450	48589	2321	49702	2196	50846	2074	52026	4
	2581	47526	2448	48608	2319	49720	2194	50866	2072	52046	
27	2579	47544	2446	48626	2317	49739	2192	50885	2070	52066	3
	2576	47561	2444	48644	2315	49758	2190	50905	2068	52086	
28	2574	47579	2442	48662	2313	49777	2188	50924	2066	52106	2
	2572	47597	2439	48681	2311	49796	2185	50943	2064	52126	
29	2570	47615	2437	48699	2309	49815	2183	50963	2062	52146	1
	2568	47633	2435	48717	2306	49833	2181	50982	2060	52166	
30	2565	47650	2433	48736	2304	49852	2179	51002	2058	52186	
′	A	B	A	B	A	B	A	B	A	B	′
	109° 30′		109° 00′		108° 30′		108° 00′		107° 30′		

'	72° 30' A	B	73° 00' A	B	73° 30' A	B	74° 00' A	B	74° 30' A	B	'
0	2058	52186	1940	53406	1826	54666	1716	55966	1609	57310	30
	2056	52206	1938	53427	1824	54687	1714	55988	1607	57333	
1	2054	52226	1936	53448	1823	54708	1712	56010	1605	57356	29
	2052	52246	1935	53468	1821	54730	1710	56032	1604	57378	
2	2050	52266	1933	53489	1819	54751	1709	56054	1602	57401	28
	2048	52286	1931	53510	1817	54773	1707	56076	1600	57424	
3	2046	52306	1929	53531	1815	54794	1705	56099	1598	57447	27
	2044	52326	1927	53551	1813	54815	1703	56121	1597	57470	
4	2042	52346	1925	53572	1811	54837	1701	56143	1595	57493	26
	2040	52366	1923	53593	1809	54858	1700	56165	1593	57516	
5	2038	52387	1921	53614	1808	54880	1698	56187	1591	57538	25
	2036	52407	1919	53634	1806	54901	1696	56209	1590	57561	
6	2034	52427	1917	53655	1804	54922	1694	56231	1588	57584	24
	2032	52447	1915	53676	1802	54944	1692	56254	1586	57607	
7	2030	52467	1913	53697	1800	54965	1691	56276	1584	57630	23
	2028	52487	1911	53718	1798	54987	1689	56298	1583	57653	
8	2026	52508	1910	53738	1796	55008	1687	56320	1581	57676	22
	2024	52528	1908	53759	1795	55030	1685	56342	1579	57699	
9	2022	52548	1906	53780	1793	55051	1683	56365	1578	57722	21
	2020	52568	1904	53801	1791	55073	1682	56387	1576	57745	
10	2018	52588	1902	53822	1789	55095	1680	56409	1574	57768	20
	2016	52609	1900	53843	1787	55116	1678	56431	1572	57791	
11	2014	52629	1898	53864	1785	55138	1676	56454	1571	57814	19
	2012	52649	1896	53884	1783	55159	1674	56476	1569	57837	
12	2010	52670	1894	53905	1782	55181	1673	56498	1567	57860	18
	2009	52690	1892	53926	1780	55202	1671	56521	1565	57884	
13	2007	52710	1890	53947	1778	55224	1669	56543	1564	57907	17
	2005	52730	1889	53968	1776	55246	1667	56565	1562	57930	
14	2003	52751	1887	53989	1774	55267	1665	56588	1560	57953	16
	2001	52771	1885	54010	1772	55289	1664	56610	1559	57976	
15	1999	52791	1883	54031	1771	55311	1662	56632	1557	57999	15
	1997	52812	1881	54052	1769	55332	1660	56655	1555	58022	
16	1995	52832	1879	54073	1767	55354	1658	56677	1553	58046	14
	1993	52852	1877	54094	1765	55376	1657	56700	1552	58069	
17	1991	52873	1875	54115	1763	55397	1655	56722	1550	58092	13
	1989	52893	1873	54136	1761	55419	1653	56745	1548	58115	
18	1987	52914	1871	54157	1760	55441	1651	56767	1546	58138	12
	1985	52934	1870	54178	1758	55463	1650	56790	1545	58162	
19	1983	52954	1868	54199	1756	55484	1648	56812	1543	58185	11
	1981	52975	1866	54220	1754	55506	1646	56835	1541	58208	
20	1979	52995	1864	54242	1752	55528	1644	56857	1540	58232	10
	1977	53016	1862	54263	1750	55550	1642	56880	1538	58255	
21	1975	53036	1860	54284	1749	55572	1641	56902	1536	58278	9
	1973	53057	1858	54305	1747	55593	1639	56925	1534	58302	
22	1971	53077	1856	54326	1745	55615	1637	56947	1533	58325	8
	1969	53098	1854	54347	1743	55637	1635	56970	1531	58348	
23	1967	53118	1853	54368	1741	55659	1634	56992	1529	58372	7
	1966	53139	1851	54390	1739	55681	1632	57015	1528	58395	
24	1964	53159	1849	54411	1738	55703	1630	57038	1526	58418	6
	1962	53180	1847	54432	1736	55725	1628	57060	1524	58442	
25	1960	53200	1845	54453	1734	55746	1627	57083	1523	58465	5
	1958	53221	1843	54474	1732	55768	1625	57106	1521	58489	
26	1956	53241	1841	54496	1730	55790	1623	57128	1519	58512	4
	1954	53262	1839	54517	1728	55812	1621	57151	1517	58536	
27	1952	53283	1837	54538	1727	55834	1619	57174	1516	58559	3
	1950	53303	1836	54559	1725	55856	1618	57196	1514	58583	
28	1948	53324	1834	54581	1723	55878	1616	57219	1512	58606	2
	1946	53344	1832	54602	1721	55900	1614	57242	1511	58630	
29	1944	53365	1830	54623	1719	55922	1612	57265	1509	58653	1
	1942	53386	1828	54644	1718	55944	1611	57287	1507	58677	
30	1940	53406	1826	54666	1716	55966	1609	57310	1506	58700	0
'	A	B	A	B	A	B	A	B	A	B	'
	107° 00'		106° 30'		106° 00'		105° 30'		105° 00'		

WHEN LHA (E OR W) IS GREATER THAN 90°, TAKE "K" FROM BOTTOM OF TABLE

′	75° 00′ A	75° 00′ B	75° 30′ A	75° 30′ B	76° 00′ A	76° 00′ B	76° 30′ A	76° 30′ B	77° 00′ A	77° 00′ B	′
0	1506	58700	1406	60140	1310	61632	1217	63181	1128	64791	30
	1504	58724	1404	60164	1308	61658	1215	63208	1126	64819	
1	1502	58748	1403	60189	1306	61683	1214	63234	1125	64846	29
	1500	58771	1401	60213	1305	61709	1212	63260	1123	64873	
2	1499	58795	1399	60238	1303	61734	1211	63287	1122	64901	28
	1497	58818	1398	60262	1301	61759	1209	63313	1120	64928	
3	1495	58842	1396	60287	1300	61785	1208	63340	1119	64956	27
	1494	58866	1394	60311	1299	61810	1206	63366	1117	64983	
4	1492	58889	1393	60336	1297	61836	1205	63392	1116	65011	26
	1490	58913	1391	60360	1295	61861	1203	63419	1114	65038	
5	1489	58937	1390	60385	1294	61887	1202	63445	1113	65066	25
	1487	58960	1388	60410	1292	61912	1200	63472	1112	65093	
6	1485	58984	1386	60434	1291	61938	1199	63498	1110	65121	24
	1484	59008	1385	60459	1289	61963	1197	63525	1109	65148	
7	1482	59032	1383	60483	1288	61989	1196	63551	1107	65176	23
	1480	59055	1381	60508	1286	62014	1194	63578	1106	65204	
8	1479	59079	1380	60533	1284	62040	1193	63605	1104	65231	22
	1477	59103	1378	60557	1283	62065	1191	63631	1103	65259	
9	1475	59127	1377	60582	1281	62091	1190	63658	1101	65287	21
	1474	59151	1375	60607	1280	62117	1188	63684	1100	65314	
10	1472	59175	1373	60631	1278	62142	1187	63711	1099	65342	20
	1470	59198	1372	60656	1277	62168	1185	63738	1097	65370	
11	1469	59222	1370	60681	1275	62194	1184	63764	1096	65398	19
	1467	59246	1368	60706	1274	62219	1182	63791	1094	65425	
12	1465	59270	1367	60730	1272	62245	1181	63818	1093	65453	18
	1464	59294	1365	60755	1270	62271	1179	63845	1091	65481	
13	1462	59318	1364	60780	1269	62296	1178	63871	1090	65509	17
	1460	59342	1362	60805	1267	62322	1176	63898	1089	65537	
14	1459	59366	1360	60830	1266	62348	1175	63925	1087	65564	16
	1457	59390	1359	60855	1264	62374	1173	63952	1086	65592	
15	1455	59414	1357	60879	1263	62400	1172	63978	1084	65620	15
	1454	59438	1356	60904	1261	62425	1170	64005	1083	65648	
16	1452	59462	1354	60929	1260	62451	1169	64032	1081	65676	14
	1450	59486	1352	60954	1258	62477	1167	64059	1080	65704	
17	1449	59510	1351	60979	1257	62503	1166	64086	1079	65732	13
	1447	59534	1349	61004	1255	62529	1164	64113	1077	65760	
18	1445	59558	1348	61029	1253	62555	1163	64140	1076	65788	12
	1444	59582	1346	61054	1252	62581	1161	64167	1074	65816	
19	1442	59606	1344	61079	1250	62607	1160	64194	1073	65844	11
	1440	59630	1343	61104	1249	62633	1158	64221	1071	65872	
20	1439	59654	1341	61129	1247	62659	1157	64248	1070	65900	10
	1437	59679	1340	61154	1246	62685	1155	64275	1069	65928	
21	1435	59703	1338	61179	1244	62711	1154	64302	1067	65957	9
	1434	59727	1336	61204	1243	62737	1152	64329	1066	65985	
22	1432	59751	1335	61229	1241	62763	1151	64356	1064	66013	8
	1430	59775	1333	61254	1240	62789	1150	64383	1063	66041	
23	1429	59800	1332	61279	1238	62815	1148	64410	1061	66069	7
	1427	59824	1330	61304	1237	62841	1147	64437	1060	66098	
24	1425	59848	1329	61330	1235	62867	1145	64464	1059	66126	6
	1424	59872	1327	61355	1234	62893	1144	64491	1057	66154	
25	1422	59896	1325	61380	1232	62919	1142	64518	1056	66182	5
	1421	59921	1324	61405	1230	62945	1141	64546	1054	66211	
26	1419	59945	1322	61430	1229	62971	1139	64573	1053	66239	4
	1417	59969	1321	61456	1227	62998	1138	64600	1052	66267	
27	1416	59994	1319	61481	1226	63024	1136	64627	1050	66296	3
	1414	60018	1317	61506	1224	63050	1135	64655	1049	66324	
28	1412	60042	1316	61531	1223	63076	1133	64682	1047	66352	2
	1411	60067	1314	61556	1221	63103	1132	64709	1046	66381	
29	1409	60091	1313	61582	1220	63129	1130	64736	1045	66409	1
	1407	60116	1311	61607	1218	63155	1129	64764	1043	66438	
30	1406	60140	1310	61632	1217	63181	1128	64791	1042	66466	0
	A	B	A	B	A	B	A	B	A	B	
′	104° 30′		104° 00′		103° 30′		103° 00′		102° 30′		′

′	77° 30′ A	B	78° 00′ A	B	78° 30′ A	B	79° 00′ A	B	79° 30′ A	B	′
0	1042	66466	960	68212	881	70034	805	71940	733	73937	30
	1040	66495	958	68242	879	70065	804	71973	732	73971	
1	1039	66523	957	68272	878	70097	803	72005	731	74005	29
	1038	66552	955	68301	877	70128	802	72038	730	74039	
2	1036	66580	954	68331	876	70159	800	72070	729	74073	28
	1035	66609	953	68361	874	70190	799	72103	728	74107	
3	1033	66638	951	68391	873	70221	798	72136	726	74142	27
	1032	66666	950	68421	872	70252	797	72168	725	74176	
4	1031	66695	949	68450	870	70284	796	72201	724	74210	26
	1029	66724	947	68480	869	70315	794	72234	723	74245	
5	1028	66752	946	68510	868	70346	793	72266	722	74279	25
	1026	66781	945	68540	867	70377	792	72299	721	74313	
6	1025	66810	943	68570	865	70409	791	72332	719	74348	24
	1024	66838	942	68600	864	70440	790	72365	718	74382	
7	1022	66867	941	68630	863	70471	788	72397	717	74417	23
	1021	66896	939	68660	862	70503	787	72430	716	74451	
8	1020	66925	938	68690	860	70534	786	72463	715	74486	22
	1018	66953	937	68720	859	70566	785	72496	714	74520	
9	1017	66982	935	68750	858	70597	783	72529	712	74555	21
	1015	67011	934	68781	856	70629	782	72562	711	74589	
10	1014	67040	933	68811	855	70660	781	72595	710	74624	20
	1013	67069	932	68841	854	70692	780	72628	709	74659	
11	1011	67098	930	68871	853	70723	779	72661	708	74693	19
	1010	67127	929	68901	851	70755	777	72694	707	74728	
12	1008	67156	928	68931	850	70786	776	72727	706	74763	18
	1007	67185	926	68962	849	70818	775	72760	704	74797	
13	1006	67214	925	68992	848	70850	774	72794	703	74832	17
	1004	67243	924	69022	846	70881	772	72827	702	74867	
14	1003	67272	922	69053	845	70913	771	72860	701	74902	16
	1002	67301	921	69083	844	70945	770	72893	700	74937	
15	1000	67330	920	69113	843	70976	769	72926	699	74972	15
	999	67359	918	69144	841	71008	768	72960	698	75007	
16	997	67388	917	69174	840	71040	767	72993	696	75042	14
	996	67417	916	69204	839	71072	765	73026	695	75077	
17	995	67447	914	69235	838	71104	764	73060	694	75112	13
	993	67476	913	69265	836	71135	763	73093	693	75147	
18	992	67505	912	69296	835	71167	762	73127	692	75182	12
	991	67534	910	69326	834	71199	761	73160	691	75217	
19	989	67563	909	69357	833	71231	759	73193	690	75252	11
	988	67593	908	69387	831	71263	758	73227	688	75287	
20	987	67622	907	69418	830	71295	757	73260	687	75322	10
	985	67651	905	69449	829	71327	756	73294	686	75358	
21	984	67681	904	69479	828	71359	755	73328	685	75393	9
	982	67710	903	69510	826	71391	753	73361	684	75428	
22	981	67739	901	69541	825	71423	752	73395	683	75464	8
	980	67769	900	69571	824	71455	751	73429	682	75499	
23	978	67798	899	69602	823	71488	750	73462	680	75534	7
	977	67828	897	69633	821	71520	749	73496	679	75570	
24	976	67857	896	69664	820	71552	747	73530	678	75605	6
	974	67886	895	69694	819	71584	746	73563	677	75641	
25	973	67916	894	69725	818	71616	745	73597	676	75676	5
	972	67945	892	69756	816	71649	744	73631	675	75712	
26	970	67975	891	69787	815	71681	743	73665	674	75747	4
	969	68005	890	69818	814	71713	742	73699	673	75783	
27	968	68034	888	69849	813	71746	740	73733	672	75819	3
	966	68064	887	69879	811	71778	739	73767	670	75854	
28	965	68093	886	69910	810	71810	738	73801	669	75890	2
	964	68123	885	69941	809	71843	737	73835	668	75926	
29	962	68153	883	69972	808	71875	736	73869	667	75961	1
	961	68182	882	70003	807	71908	735	73903	666	75997	
30	960	68212	881	70034	805	71940	733	73937	665	76033	0
	A	B	A	B	A	B	A	B	A	B	
′	102° 00′		101° 30′		101° 00′		100° 30′		100° 00′		′

WHEN LHA (E OR W) IS GREATER THAN 90°, TAKE "K" FROM BOTTOM OF TABLE

′	80° 00′ A	B	80° 30′ A	B	81° 00′ A	B	81° 30′ A	B	82° 00′ A	B	′
0	665	76033	600	78239	538	80567	480	83030	425	85644	30
	664	76069	599	78277	537	80607	479	83072	424	85689	
1	663	76105	598	78315	536	80647	478	83114	423	85734	29
	661	76141	597	78352	535	80687	477	83157	422	85779	
2	660	76176	595	78390	534	80727	476	83199	421	85825	28
	659	76212	594	78428	533	80767	475	83242	420	85870	
3	658	76248	593	78466	532	80807	474	83284	419	85915	27
	657	76284	592	78504	531	80847	473	83327	418	85960	
4	656	76320	591	78542	530	80887	472	83369	418	86006	26
	655	76357	590	78580	529	80927	471	83412	417	86051	
5	654	76393	589	78618	528	80967	470	83455	416	86096	25
	653	76429	588	78656	527	81008	469	83497	415	86142	
6	652	76465	587	78694	526	81048	468	83540	414	86187	24
	650	76501	586	78733	525	81088	467	83583	413	86233	
7	649	76537	585	78771	524	81129	467	83626	412	86278	23
	648	76574	584	78809	523	81169	466	83668	411	86324	
8	647	76610	583	78847	522	81210	465	83711	411	86370	22
	646	76646	582	78886	521	81250	464	83754	410	86415	
9	645	76683	581	78924	520	81291	463	83797	409	86461	21
	644	76719	580	78962	519	81331	462	83840	408	86507	
10	643	76756	579	79001	518	81372	461	83884	407	86553	20
	642	76792	578	79039	517	81413	460	83927	406	86599	
11	641	76828	577	79078	516	81453	459	83970	405	86645	19
	639	76865	576	79116	515	81494	458	84013	405	86691	
12	638	76902	575	79155	514	81535	457	84056	404	86737	18
	637	76938	574	79193	513	81576	456	84100	403	86783	
13	636	76975	573	79232	512	81617	455	84143	402	86829	17
	635	77011	571	79271	511	81657	454	84186	401	86876	
14	634	77048	570	79309	510	81698	454	84230	400	86922	16
	633	77085	569	79348	509	81739	453	84273	399	86968	
15	632	77122	568	79387	508	81780	452	84317	399	87015	15
	631	77158	567	79426	507	81821	451	84361	398	87061	
16	630	77195	566	79465	506	81863	450	84404	397	87107	14
	629	77232	565	79503	505	81904	449	84448	396	87154	
17	627	77269	564	79542	504	81945	448	84492	395	87201	13
	626	77306	563	79581	504	81986	447	84535	394	87247	
18	625	77343	562	79620	503	82027	446	84579	393	87294	12
	624	77380	561	79659	502	82069	445	84623	392	87341	
19	623	77417	560	79698	501	82110	444	84667	392	87387	11
	622	77454	559	79737	500	82151	444	84711	391	87434	
20	621	77491	558	79777	499	82193	443	84755	390	87481	10
	620	77528	557	79816	498	82234	442	84799	389	87528	
21	619	77565	556	79855	497	82276	441	84843	388	87575	9
	618	77602	555	79894	496	82317	440	84887	387	87622	
22	617	77639	554	79933	495	82359	439	84931	387	87669	8
	616	77677	553	79973	494	82400	438	84976	386	87716	
23	615	77714	552	80012	493	82442	437	85020	385	87764	7
	614	77751	551	80051	492	82484	436	85064	384	87811	
24	612	77788	550	80091	491	82526	435	85109	383	87858	6
	611	77826	549	80130	490	82567	434	85153	382	87906	
25	610	77863	548	80170	489	82609	434	85197	381	87953	5
	609	77901	547	80209	488	82651	433	85242	381	88001	
26	608	77938	546	80249	487	82693	432	85286	380	88048	4
	607	77976	545	80288	486	82735	431	85331	379	88096	
27	606	78013	544	80328	485	82777	430	85376	378	88143	3
	605	78051	543	80368	484	82819	429	85420	377	88191	
28	604	78088	542	80407	483	82861	428	85465	376	88239	2
	603	78126	541	80447	482	82903	427	85510	376	88286	
29	602	78164	540	80487	482	82945	426	85555	375	88334	1
	601	78201	539	80527	481	82987	426	85599	374	88382	
30	600	78239	538	80567	480	83030	425	85644	373	88430	0
	A	B	A	B	A	B	A	B	A	B	
	99° 30′		99° 00′		98° 30′		98° 00′		97° 30′		′

′	82° 30′		83° 00′		83° 30′		84° 00′		84° 30′		′
	A	B	A	B	A	B	A	B	A	B	
0	373	88430	325	91411	280	94614	238. 6	98076	200. 4	101843	30
	372	88478	324	91462	279	94670	237. 9	98137	199. 8	101908	
1	371	88526	323	91514	279	94725	237. 2	98197	199. 2	101974	29
	371	88574	323	91565	278	94781	236. 6	98257	198. 6	102040	
2	370	88623	322	91617	277	94836	235. 9	98318	198. 0	102106	28
	369	88671	321	91668	276	94892	235. 3	98378	197. 4	102172	
3	368	88719	320	91720	276	94948	234. 6	98439	196. 8	102238	27
	367	88767	319	91772	275	95004	233. 9	98499	196. 2	102304	
4	366	88816	319	91824	274	95060	233. 3	98560	195. 6	102371	26
	366	88864	318	91876	274	95116	232. 6	98621	195. 0	102437	
5	365	88913	317	91928	273	95172	232. 0	98682	194. 4	102504	25
	364	88961	316	91980	272	95228	231. 3	98743	193. 8	102570	
6	363	89010	316	92032	271	95285	230. 7	98804	193. 2	102637	24
	362	89059	315	92085	271	95341	230. 0	98865	192. 6	102704	
7	362	89107	314	92137	270	95397	229. 4	98926	192. 0	102771	23
	361	89156	313	92189	269	95454	228. 7	98988	191. 4	102838	
8	360	89205	313	92242	269	95510	228. 1	99049	190. 8	102905	22
	359	89254	312	92294	268	95567	227. 4	99111	190. 2	102973	
9	358	89303	311	92347	267	95624	226. 8	99172	189. 6	103040	21
	357	89352	310	92399	267	95681	226. 1	99234	189. 0	103107	
10	357	89401	310	92452	266	95737	225. 5	99296	188. 4	103175	20
	356	89450	309	92505	265	95795	224. 8	99357	187. 8	103243	
11	355	89499	308	92558	264	95851	224. 2	99419	187. 2	103311	19
	354	89548	307	92610	264	95909	223. 5	99482	186. 7	103379	
12	353	89597	307	92663	263	95966	222. 9	99544	186. 1	103447	18
	353	89647	306	92716	262	96023	222. 3	99606	185. 5	103515	
13	352	89696	305	92769	262	96080	221. 6	99668	184. 9	103583	17
	351	89746	304	92823	261	96138	221. 0	99731	184. 3	103651	
14	350	89795	304	92876	260	96195	220. 3	99793	183. 7	103720	16
	349	89845	303	92929	260	96253	219. 7	99856	183. 2	103788	
15	349	89894	302	92982	259	96310	219. 1	99918	182. 6	103857	15
	348	89944	301	93036	258	96368	218. 4	99981	182. 0	103926	
16	347	89994	301	93089	257	96426	217. 8	100044	181. 4	103995	14
	346	90044	300	93143	257	96484	217. 2	100107	180. 8	104064	
17	345	90093	299	93196	256	96542	216. 5	100170	180. 3	104133	13
	345	90143	298	93250	255	96600	215. 9	100233	179. 7	104202	
18	344	90193	298	93304	255	96658	215. 3	100296	179. 1	104272	12
	343	90243	297	93358	254	96716	214. 6	100360	178. 5	104341	
19	342	90293	296	93411	253	96774	214. 0	100423	178. 0	104411	11
	341	90344	295	93465	253	96833	213. 4	100487	177. 4	104480	
20	341	90394	295	93519	252	96891	212. 8	100550	176. 8	104550	10
	340	90444	294	93573	251	96950	212. 1	100614	176. 2	104620	
21	339	90494	293	93628	251	97008	211. 5	100678	175. 7	104690	9
	338	90545	292	93682	250	97067	210. 9	100742	175. 1	104760	
22	337	90595	292	93736	249	97126	210. 3	100806	174. 5	104830	8
	337	90646	291	93790	249	97184	209. 6	100870	174. 0	104901	
23	336	90696	290	93845	248	97243	209. 0	100934	173. 4	104971	7
	335	90747	289	93899	247	97302	208. 4	100998	172. 8	105042	
24	334	90798	289	93954	247	97361	207. 8	101063	172. 3	105113	6
	333	90848	288	94009	246	97420	207. 1	101127	171. 7	105183	
25	333	90899	287	94063	245	97480	206. 5	101192	171. 1	105254	5
	332	90950	287	94118	245	97539	205. 9	101256	170. 6	105325	
26	331	91001	286	94173	244	97598	205. 3	101321	170. 0	105397	4
	330	91052	285	94228	243	97658	204. 7	101386	169. 5	105468	
27	330	91103	284	94283	243	97717	204. 1	101451	168. 9	105539	3
	329	91154	284	94338	242	97777	203. 5	101516	168. 4	105611	
28	328	91205	283	94393	241	97837	202. 8	101581	167. 8	105683	2
	327	91257	282	94448	241	97897	202. 2	101646	167. 2	105754	
29	326	91308	281	94503	240	97957	201. 6	101712	166. 7	105826	1
	326	91359	281	94559	239	98017	201. 0	101777	166. 0	105898	
30	325	91411	280	94614	239	98076	200. 4	101843	165. 6	105970	0
	A	B	A	B	A	B	A	B	A	B	
	97° 00′		96° 30′		96° 00′		95° 30′		95° 00′		′

WHEN LHA (E OR W) IS <u>GREATER</u> THAN 90°, TAKE "K" FROM <u>BOTTOM</u> OF TABLE

′	85° 00′		85° 30′		86° 00′		86° 30′		87° 00′		′
	A	B	A	B	A	B	A	B	A	B	
0	165. 6	105970	134. 1	110536	105. 9	115641	81. 1	121432	59. 6	128120	30
	165. 0	106043	133. 6	110616	105. 5	115732	80. 7	121536	59. 2	128241	
1	164. 5	106115	133. 1	110696	105. 0	115823	80. 3	121639	58. 9	128362	29
	163. 9	106187	132. 6	110777	104. 6	115913	79. 9	121743	58. 6	128483	
2	163. 4	106260	132. 1	110858	104. 2	116004	79. 5	121848	58. 2	128605	28
	162. 8	106333	131. 6	110939	103. 7	116096	79. 2	121952	57. 9	128727	
3	162. 3	106406	131. 1	111020	103. 3	116187	78. 8	122057	57. 6	128849	27
	161. 7	106479	130. 6	111101	102. 9	116278	78. 4	122161	57. 3	128972	
4	161. 2	106552	130. 1	111183	102. 4	116370	78. 0	122267	56. 9	129095	26
	160. 6	106625	129. 6	111264	102. 0	116462	77. 6	122372	56. 6	129218	
5	160. 1	106698	129. 2	111346	101. 6	116554	77. 3	122478	56. 3	129342	25
	159. 6	106772	128. 7	111428	101. 1	116647	76. 9	122584	56. 0	129466	
6	159. 0	106846	128. 2	111510	100. 7	116739	76. 5	122690	55. 7	129591	24
	158. 5	106919	127. 7	111592	100. 3	116832	76. 1	122796	55. 3	129716	
7	157. 9	106993	127. 2	111674	99. 8	116925	75. 8	122903	55. 0	129841	23
	157. 4	107067	126. 7	111757	99. 4	117018	75. 4	123010	54. 7	129967	
8	156. 9	107141	126. 2	111839	99. 0	117112	75. 0	123117	54. 4	130093	22
	156. 3	107216	125. 8	111922	98. 5	117205	74. 6	123225	54. 1	130219	
9	155. 8	107290	125. 3	112005	98. 1	117299	74. 3	123332	53. 7	130346	21
	155. 2	107364	124. 8	112088	97. 7	117393	73. 9	123441	53. 4	130473	
10	154. 7	107439	124. 3	112171	97. 3	117487	73. 5	123549	53. 1	130600	20
	154. 2	107514	123. 8	112255	96. 8	117581	73. 2	123657	52. 8	130728	
11	153. 6	107589	123. 4	112338	96. 4	117676	72. 8	123766	52. 5	130856	19
	153. 1	107664	122. 9	112422	96. 0	117771	72. 4	123875	52. 2	130985	
12	152. 6	107739	122. 4	112506	95. 6	117866	72. 1	123985	51. 9	131114	18
	152. 1	107814	121. 9	112590	95. 2	117961	71. 7	124095	51. 6	131243	
13	151. 5	107890	121. 5	112674	94. 7	118056	71. 3	124204	51. 3	131373	17
	151. 0	107965	121. 0	112759	94. 3	118152	71. 0	124315	51. 0	131503	
14	150. 5	108041	120. 5	112843	93. 9	118248	70. 6	124425	50. 7	131633	16
	149. 9	108117	120. 1	112928	93. 5	118344	70. 3	124536	50. 3	131764	
15	149. 4	108193	119. 6	113013	93. 1	118440	69. 9	124647	50. 0	131896	15
	148. 9	108269	119. 1	113098	92. 7	118537	69. 5	124759	49. 7	132027	
16	148. 4	108345	118. 7	113183	92. 3	118633	69. 2	124870	49. 4	132159	14
	147. 8	108421	118. 2	113269	91. 8	118730	68. 8	124982	49. 1	132292	
17	147. 3	108498	117. 7	113354	91. 4	118827	68. 5	125094	48. 8	132425	13
	146. 8	108574	117. 3	113440	91. 0	118925	68. 1	125207	48. 5	132558	
18	146. 3	108651	116. 8	113526	90. 6	119022	67. 8	125320	48. 2	132692	12
	145. 8	108728	116. 3	113612	90. 2	119120	67. 4	125433	47. 9	132826	
19	145. 2	108805	115. 9	113699	89. 8	119218	67. 1	125546	47. 6	132961	11
	144. 7	108882	115. 4	113785	89. 4	119316	66. 7	125660	47. 3	133096	
20	144. 2	108960	114. 9	113872	89. 0	119415	66. 4	125774	47. 1	133231	10
	143. 7	109037	114. 5	113958	88. 6	119513	66. 0	125888	46. 8	133367	
21	143. 2	109115	114. 0	114045	88. 2	119612	65. 7	126003	46. 5	133503	9
	142. 7	109192	113. 6	114133	87. 8	119711	65. 3	126118	46. 2	133640	
22	142. 2	109270	113. 1	114220	87. 4	119811	65. 0	126233	45. 9	133777	8
	141. 6	109348	112. 7	114307	87. 0	119910	64. 6	126349	45. 6	133914	
23	141. 1	109426	112. 2	114395	86. 6	120010	64. 3	126465	45. 3	134052	7
	140. 6	109505	111. 7	114483	86. 2	120110	63. 9	126581	45. 0	134191	
24	140. 1	109583	111. 3	114571	85. 8	120211	63. 6	126697	44. 7	134330	6
	139. 6	109662	110. 8	114659	85. 4	120311	63. 3	126814	44. 4	134469	
25	139. 1	109740	110. 4	114747	85. 0	120412	62. 9	126931	44. 2	134609	5
	138. 6	109819	109. 9	114836	84. 6	120513	62. 6	127049	43. 9	134749	
26	138. 1	109898	109. 5	114925	84. 2	120614	62. 2	127166	43. 6	134890	4
	137. 6	109978	109. 0	115014	83. 8	120715	61. 9	127284	43. 3	135031	
27	137. 1	110057	108. 6	115103	83. 4	120817	61. 6	127403	43. 0	135173	3
	136. 6	110136	108. 1	115192	83. 0	120919	61. 2	127521	42. 7	135315	
28	136. 1	110216	107. 7	115282	82. 6	121021	60. 9	127640	42. 5	135457	2
	135. 6	110296	107. 3	115371	82. 2	121124	60. 6	127760	42. 2	135600	
29	135. 1	110375	106. 8	115461	81. 9	121226	60. 2	127880	41. 9	135744	1
	134. 6	110455	106. 4	115551	81. 5	121329	59. 9	128000	41. 6	135888	
30	134. 1	110536	105. 9	115641	81. 1	121432	59. 6	128120	41. 4	136032	0
	A	B	A	B	A	B	A	B	A	B	
′	94° 30′		94° 00′		93° 30′		93° 00′		92° 30′		′

′	87° 30′		88° 00′		88° 30′		89° 00′		89° 30′		′
	A	B	A	B	A	B	A	B	A	B	
0	41. 4	136032	26. 5	145718	14. 9	158208	6. 6	175814	1. 7	205916	30
	41. 1	136177	26. 2	145899	14. 7	158450	6. 5	176178	1. 6	206646	
1	40. 8	136322	26. 0	146081	14. 6	158693	6. 4	176544	1. 5	207388	29
	40. 5	136468	25. 8	146264	14. 4	158938	6. 3	176914	1. 5	208143	
2	40. 3	136615	25. 6	146448	14. 2	159184	6. 2	177287	1. 4	208912	28
	40. 0	136761	25. 4	146632	14. 1	159431	6. 1	177663	1. 4	209695	
3	39. 7	136909	25. 2	146817	13. 9	159680	6. 0	178042	1. 3	210491	27
	39. 4	137057	24. 9	147003	13. 7	159930	5. 9	178424	1. 3	211303	
4	39. 2	137205	24. 7	147190	13. 6	160182	5. 8	178810	1. 2	212130	26
	38. 9	137354	24. 5	147377	13. 4	160435	5. 7	179200	1. 2	212974	
5	38. 6	137503	24. 3	147566	13. 3	160690	5. 6	179593	1. 1	213834	25
	38. 4	137653	24. 1	147755	13. 1	160946	5. 5	179990	1. 1	214711	
6	38. 1	137804	23. 9	147945	13. 0	161204	5. 4	180390	1. 1	215607	24
	37. 8	137955	23. 7	148135	12. 8	161463	5. 3	180794	1. 0	216521	
7	37. 6	138106	23. 5	148327	12. 7	161724	5. 2	181201	1. 0	217455	23
	37. 3	138258	23. 3	148520	12. 5	161986	5. 1	181613	0. 9	218409	
8	37. 1	138411	23. 1	148713	12. 4	162250	5. 0	182029	0. 9	219385	22
	36. 8	138564	22. 8	148907	12. 2	162516	4. 9	182448	0. 9	220384	
9	36. 5	138718	22. 6	149103	12. 1	162783	4. 8	182872	0. 8	221406	21
	36. 3	138872	22. 4	149299	11. 9	163052	4. 7	183300	0. 8	222452	
10	36. 0	139027	22. 2	149495	11. 8	163322	4. 6	183732	0. 7	223525	20
	35. 8	139182	22. 0	149693	11. 6	163594	4. 5	184168	0. 7	224624	
11	35. 5	139338	21. 8	149892	11. 5	163868	4. 4	184609	0. 7	225752	19
	35. 3	139494	21. 6	150092	11. 3	164144	4. 3	185055	0. 6	226910	
12	35. 0	139651	21. 4	150292	11. 2	164422	4. 2	185505	0. 6	228100	18
	34. 7	139809	21. 2	150494	11. 0	164701	4. 1	185959	0. 6	229324	
13	34. 5	139967	21. 0	150696	10. 9	164982	4. 1	186419	0. 5	230583	17
	34. 2	140125	20. 8	150899	10. 8	165265	4. 0	186883	0. 5	231879	
14	34. 0	140285	20. 6	151104	10. 6	165550	3. 9	187353	0. 5	233215	16
	33. 7	140445	20. 5	151309	10. 5	165836	3. 8	187827	0. 4	234594	
15	33. 5	140605	20. 3	151515	10. 3	166125	3. 7	188307	0. 4	236018	15
	33. 2	140766	20. 1	151722	10. 2	166415	3. 6	188793	0. 4	237491	
16	33. 0	140928	19. 9	151931	10. 1	166708	3. 6	189283	0. 4	239015	14
	32. 8	141090	19. 7	152140	9. 9	167002	3. 5	189780	0. 3	240594	
17	32. 5	141253	19. 5	152350	9. 8	167298	3. 4	190282	0. 3	242233	13
	32. 3	141417	19. 3	152561	9. 7	167597	3. 3	190790	0. 3	243936	
18	32. 0	141581	19. 1	152774	9. 5	167897	3. 2	191303	0. 3	245709	12
	31. 8	141745	18. 9	152987	9. 4	168200	3. 2	191824	0. 2	247558	
19	31. 5	141911	18. 7	153201	9. 3	168505	3. 1	192350	0. 2	249488	11
	31. 3	142077	18. 6	153417	9. 1	168811	3. 0	192883	0. 2	251508	
20	31. 1	142243	18. 4	153633	9. 0	169121	2. 9	193422	0. 2	253627	10
	30. 8	142411	18. 2	153851	8. 9	169432	2. 9	193969	0. 2	255855	
21	30. 6	142579	18. 0	154070	8. 7	169745	2. 8	194522	0. 1	258203	9
	30. 4	142747	17. 8	154290	8. 6	170061	2. 7	195082	0. 1	260685	
22	30. 1	142916	17. 6	154511	8. 5	170379	2. 7	195650	0. 1	263318	8
	29. 9	143086	17. 5	154733	8. 4	170700	2. 6	196225	0. 1	266121	
23	29. 6	143257	17. 3	154956	8. 2	171023	2. 5	196808	0. 1	269118	7
	29. 4	143428	17. 1	155180	8. 1	171348	2. 4	197399	0. 1	272336	
24	29. 2	143600	16. 9	155406	8. 0	171676	2. 4	197998	0. 1	275812	6
	28. 9	143773	16. 8	155633	7. 9	172006	2. 3	198605	0. 1	279591	
25	28. 7	143946	16. 6	155861	7. 8	172339	2. 3	199221	0. 0	283730	5
	28. 5	144120	16. 4	156090	7. 6	172674	2. 2	199846	0. 0	288306	
26	28. 3	144295	16. 2	156320	7. 5	173012	2. 1	200480	0. 0	293421	4
	28. 0	144470	16. 1	156552	7. 4	173352	2. 1	201124	0. 0	299221	
27	27. 8	144646	15. 9	156784	7. 3	173696	2. 0	201777	0. 0	305915	3
	27. 6	144823	15. 7	157019	7. 2	174042	1. 9	202440	0. 0	313833	
28	27. 4	145000	15. 6	157254	7. 1	174391	1. 9	203113	0. 0	323524	2
	27. 1	145179	15. 4	157490	6. 9	174742	1. 8	203797	0. 0	336018	
29	26. 9	145358	15. 2	157728	6. 8	175097	1. 8	204492	0. 0	353627	1
	26. 7	145538	15. 1	157967	6. 7	175454	1. 7	205198	0. 0	383730	
30	26. 5	145718	14. 9	158208	6. 6	175814	1. 7	205916	0. 0	--------	0
	A	B	A	B	A	B	A	B	A	B	
′	92° 00′		91° 30′		91° 00′		90° 30′		90° 00′		′

1•Reference Sources

Governmental sources of navigation publications and charts are listed below. Prices are not generally quoted because of their tendency to follow inflationary trends and the latest agency catalog should therefore be consulted. It will usually be found more convenient to purchase from a local authorized sales agent, however orders may be made direct to the agency if desired.

UNITED STATES

Distribution Division C44, National Ocean Survey (formerly the Coast and Geodetic Survey), Washington, D.C. 20235:

Charts of the coasts of the United States and possessions:

Harbor charts, scale 1:50,000 and larger.
Coast charts, scales from 1:50,000 to 1:100,000
General charts, scales 1:101,000 to 1:600,000
Sailing charts, scales smaller than 1:600,000
Intracoastal waterway charts, scale 1:40,000
Small craft charts

Coast Pilots containing essential information which cannot be conveniently presented on charts of coastal areas and inland waterways:

No. 1 Eastport to Cape Cod
No. 2 Cape Cod to Sandy Hook
No. 3 Sandy Hook to Cape Henry
No. 4 Cape Henry to Key West
No. 5 Gulf of Mexico, Puerto Rico, U.S. Virgin Islands
No. 6 (not issued)
No. 7 California, Oregon, Washington, Hawaii
No. 8 Dixon Entrance to Cape Spencer
No. 9 Cape Spencer to Beaufort Sea

Tide Tables (annual). Predictions of the times and heights of high and low water at principal harbors, and the differences for numerous other places:

East Coast, North and South America
West Coast, North and South America
Europe and West Coast of Africa
Central and Western Pacific and Indian Oceans

Tidal Current Tables (annual). Daily predictions:
Atlantic Coast of North America
Pacific Coast of North America and Asia

Tidal Current Charts depict the direction and velocity of tidal current each hour of the tidal cycle in selected waterways, and are applicable to any year. The Narragansett Bay and New York Harbor charts are used with *Tide Tables,* the others with *Tidal Current Tables*:
Boston Harbor
Narragansett Bay to Nantucket Sound
Narragansett Bay
Long Island Sound and Block Island Sound
New York Harbor
Delaware Bay and River
Upper Chesapeake Bay
Charleston (S.C.) Harbor
San Francisco Bay
Puget Sound, Northern Part
Puget Sound, Southern Part

National Ocean Survey, Lake Survey Section, 630 Federal Building, Detroit, Michigan 48226 issues charts for the Great Lakes and connecting waters, including the New York State barge canal system, Lake Champlain, the St. Lawrence River to Cornwall, Canada, and the Minnesota-Ontario border lakes.

U.S. Naval Oceanographic Office, Washington, D.C. 20390:

Charts of waters outside the geographic limits of the United States and possessions (certain areas classified and not available to the public). Reproductions of foreign charts are not for sale and should be ordered from the appropriate foreign agency or its authorized sales agent. USNO also publishes special charts including *Great Circle* (gnomonic), *Pilot Charts, Loran* and *Omega Charts* and many others.

Sailing Directions (Pilots) for approximately sixty overseas areas, containing detailed information not shown on charts.

List of Lights, covering principal coasts outside of the United States and possessions, in six volumes.

Plotting Sheets in four series, of which #3000 is especially suited to yachtsman's purposes.

H.O. Publications:

9   *American Practical Navigator.* Popularly known as *Bowditch,* this is the standard reference work for navigational theory and practice. Presupposes a familiarity with mathematics not possessed by all sailors and its 1500 pages cover many subjects of little interest to the cruising yachtsman; nevertheless *Bowditch* is a valuable addition to a ship's library. The student wishing to pursue navigation history and theory in depth will find it of great interest. The tables, which may be purchased separately as *H.O. 9 Tables,* are frequently useful when navigating at sea.

103   *International Code of Signals,* Vol. I (visual).

117A   *Radio Navigational Aids,* Atlantic and Mediterranean.

117B   *Radio Navigational Aids,* Pacific and Indian Oceans.

211   *Dead Reckoning and Altitude Tables.* Out of print; reproduced herein as Appendix H.

214   *Tables of Computed Altitude and Azimuth.* Nine volumes, each covering 10° of latitude (see also British six volume equivalent).

229   *Sight Reduction Tables for Marine Navigation.* Six volumes, each covering 15° of latitude.

249   *Sight Reduction Tables for Air Navigation.* Vol. I, altitude and azimuth of selected stars. Vol. II, altitude and azimuth for all celestial bodies with declinations

from 0° to 29° for use in latitudes from 0° to 39°. Vol. III, declinations 0° to 29°, latitudes 40° to 89°.

Notive to Mariners, a weekly periodical in two parts giving changes of aids to navigation and corrections to charts, sailing directions, light lists, etc. See Coast Guard listing for *Local Notices to Mariners.*

> *Part I.* Atlantic and Mediterranean
> *Part II.* Pacific and Indian Oceans
> 2102-D *Star Finder and Identifier.* No longer available for public purchase. Obtainable through marine specialty retail stores as the Sillcocks-Miller 2102 Starfinder.

Note: "H.O." symbolizes the old Navy Hydrographic Office, now the Oceanographic Office. Publications, however, continue to be designated by the H.O. prefix.

Superintendent of Documents, U.S. Government Printing Office, Washington, D.C. 20402 is the distributing agent for the following publications, all of which may also be purchased at authorized sales agencies for H.O. publications and N.O. charts:

The Nautical Almanac, published annually by the U.S. Naval Observatory and the *Air Almanac,* published every four months (January, May, September) by the same agency. Both almanacs are available well in advance of the publication date and are a joint effort with H. M. Nautical Almanac Office.

Light Lists prepared by the U.S. Coast Guard and containing all aids to navigation maintained in the United States and possessions:

> I *Atlantic Coast,* St. Croix River, Maine, to Little River, S.C.
> II *Atlantic and Gulf Coasts,* Little River, S.C. to Rio Grande River, Texas
> III *Pacific Coast and Pacific Islands*
> IV *Great Lakes*
> V *Mississippi River System*

The Superintendent of Documents is also a sales agent for the H.O. publications of the U.S. Navy Oceanographic Office.

United States Coast Guard District Headquarters provide *Local Notice to Mariners,* covering changes to navigation within the district and other changes of general interest. Other Coast Guard publications available from the district include:

C.G. 169 *Rules of the Road,* International and Inland
C.G. 172 *Rules of the Road,* Great Lakes
C.G. 193 *Aids to Marine Navigation of the United States*

There is no charge for *Local Notice* or the C.G. series. Observe that the Coast Guard's *Light Lists* are distributed by the Superintendent of Documents (above) and not available from Coast Guard offices.

CANADA

Canadian nautical charts, *Light Lists, Sailing Directions (Pilots), Radio Aids, Rules of the Road, Notices to Mariners,* and related material are available from one single source: Hydrographic Chart Distribution Office, Department of Energy, Mines, and Resources, 615 Booth Street, Ottawa, Ontario, Canada. Some publications are bilingual. Sales agents abound in all Canadian provinces and in the border states of the U.S. east and west coasts and Great Lakes. Persons planning to cruise Canadian waters are well advised to obtain the complete catalogue (75¢) of Canadian Hydrographic Service charts and publications.

GREAT BRITAIN

Her Majesty's Stationery Office, The Government Bookstore, 49 High Holborn, London WC1, England (mail to P.O. Box 569, London SE1) is the distribution agency, in concert with its many sales agencies throughout the U.K., for:

Nautical Almanac, published annually in cooperation with the U.S. Naval Observatory, and the *Air Almanac,* published every four months (January, May, September) and also a joint venture.

Admiralty Manual of Navigation, four superbly written and illustrated volumes. While not as comprehensive in scope as *Bowditch* (q.v.) the subjects omitted are, in general, those of little interest to the passage-making yachtsman. Theory and practice of navigation, as explained in these volumes, provide an ideal textbook for the serious student. Volume I covers coastal navigation (piloting), Volume II celestial navigation and meteorology, Volume III advanced subjects and theory. Volume IV is classified and not available to the public.

Admiralty List of Radio Signals:
  Vol. I *Communications*
  Vol. II *Direction Finding Stations and Radiobeacons*
  Vol. V *Radio Time Signals, Standard Frequency Services, Standard Times, Radio Navigational Warnings, Position Fixing Systems.*

Admiralty List of Lights, Fog Signals and Visual Time Signals. Known as the "Lights List" and published in twelve volumes covering the world.

Admiralty Sailing Directions (Pilots) cover the world in seventy-five volumes.

Ocean Passages of the World contains information and cautions concerning routes, winds, and currents.

The Hydrographer of the Navy, Ministry of Defence, Taunton, Somerset, England, is the publisher of charts and navigational tables for position finding, tides, and currents. These publications are not available through H.M. Stationery Office but are sold by the same authorized dealers who handle charts, almanacs, and related navigation material. Admiralty catalog NP131 (18 shillings) lists all Admiralty charts and publications. Selected publications of use to cruising yachtsmen include:

H.D. 486 *Tables of Computed Altitude and Azimuth.* These six volumes (each covering 15° of latitude) are virtually identical with the U.S. Navy's H.O. 214 which presents the same data, plus star identification tables, in nine volumes (10° latitude brackets).

H.D. 605 *Sight Reduction Tables for Marine Navigation.* Six volumes, each covering 15° of latitude, identical with the U.S. *H.O. 229.*

A.P. 3270 *Sight Reduction Tables for Air Navigation.* Three volumes identical with U.S. *H.O. 249,* which see for description.

H.D. 505 *Admiralty Tide Tables,* published in three volumes of which Volume I covers the British Isles and provides the official predictions for the whole of that area. Volumes II and III are compilations of the predictions of other countries.

Notice to Mariners, weekly corrections to charts, sailing directions, aids to navigation, etc.

The official government agencies are not geared to speedy handling of civilian orders from overseas and it is suggested that, among the many authorized sales agents specializing in rapid and efficient handling of foreign yachtsmen's requirements, two in particular have large American clientele:

Messrs J. D. Potter, Ltd., 145 Minories, London E.C.3 (Cable ADCHARTS LONDON EC3, Phone 01–481–1369) maintain complete stocks of every Admiralty chart and all other Hydrographic publications.

Capt. O. M. Watts, Ltd. 49 Albemarle Street, London W1 (phone 01–493–4633) is conveniently situated in the block between Brown's Hotel and Piccadilly and carries complete Admiralty charts, tide tables, and navigation instruments. Captain Watts is the editor of *Reed's Nautical Almanac,* a 1200 page compendium of much valuable data on radio aids, tides, currents, and visual aids to navigation, as well as much astronomical data; coverage is not only of the U.K. but also includes the west coast of Europe and the Baltic and Mediterranean areas.

Americans planning to cruise British waters will find the British Information Service, 835 Third Avenue, New York, N.Y. 10022 (phone 212/752–8400) helpful in providing the names of sales agents in the U.S. who handle the charts and publications described above.

J • Anglo-American Equivalents

The nomenclature in this book is based on standard American practice, which differs slightly from that of other English language countries. In most instances the differences are slight, and easily understood; however certain names may require clarification as shown below:

	American	British
Altitude:	Sextant altitude (hs)	same
	Apparent altitude (ha)	Rectified altitude
	Observed altitude (ho)	same
	Computed altitude (Hc)	True altitude
Position:	Assumed position	Chosen position
Tables:	H.O. 211	no equivalent
	H.O. 214	H.D. 486
	H.O. 229	A.P. 3270
	H.O. 249	H.D. 605

Index